D0874896

FAILURE TO FLOURISH

Failure to Flourish

HOW LAW UNDERMINES FAMILY RELATIONSHIPS

Clare Huntington

OXFORD
UNIVERSITY PRESS

OXFORD
UNIVERSITY PRESS

Oxford University Press is a department of the University of Oxford. It furthers the University's objective of excellence in research, scholarship, and education by publishing worldwide.

Oxford   New York
Auckland   Cape Town   Dar es Salaam   Hong Kong   Karachi   Kuala Lumpur   Madrid
Melbourne   Mexico City   Nairobi   New Delhi   Shanghai   Taipei   Toronto

With offices in
Argentina   Austria   Brazil   Chile   Czech Republic   France   Greece   Guatemala   Hungary
Italy   Japan   Poland   Portugal   Singapore   South Korea   Switzerland   Thailand   Turkey
Ukraine   Vietnam

Oxford is a registered trademark of Oxford University Press in the UK and certain other countries.

Published in the United States of America by
Oxford University Press
198 Madison Avenue, New York, NY 10016

© Oxford University Press 2014

All rights reserved. No part of this publication may be reproduced, stored in a retrieval system, or transmitted, in any form or by any means, without the prior permission in writing of Oxford University Press, or as expressly permitted by law, by license, or under terms agreed with the appropriate reproduction rights organization. Inquiries concerning reproduction outside the scope of the above should be sent to the Rights Department, Oxford University Press, at the address above.

You must not circulate this work in any other form
and you must impose this same condition on any acquirer.

Library of Congress Cataloging-in-Publication Data

Huntington, Clare.
    Failure to flourish : how law undermines family relationships / Clare Huntington.
    pages cm
    Includes bibliographical references and index.
    ISBN 978-0-19-538576-2 (hardback : alk. paper)
1. Domestic relations—Social aspects—United States. I. Title.
    KF505.H86 2013
    346.7301'5—dc23
                                                                                2013003368

9 8 7 6 5 4
Printed in the United States of America on acid-free paper

Note to Readers
This publication is designed to provide accurate and authoritative information in regard to the subject matter covered. It is based upon sources believed to be accurate and reliable and is intended to be current as of the time it was written. It is sold with the understanding that the publisher is not engaged in rendering legal, accounting, or other professional services. If legal advice or other expert assistance is required, the services of a competent professional person should be sought. Also, to confirm that the information has not been affected or changed by recent developments, traditional legal research techniques should be used, including checking primary sources where appropriate.

*(Based on the Declaration of Principles jointly adopted by a Committee of the
American Bar Association and a Committee of Publishers and Associations.)*

You may order this or any other Oxford University Press publication
by visiting the Oxford University Press website at www.oup.com.

For Nestor, Zoe, and Sam

Contents

Acknowledgments ix
Introduction xi

PART ONE | POSITIVE RELATIONSHIPS AND NEGATIVE FAMILY LAW

1. The Place of Relationships 5

2. Families in Transition and Families in Crisis 27

3. The State's Role in Relationships 55

4. Negative Family Law 81

PART TWO | FLOURISHING FAMILY LAW

5. A New Vision for Resolving Family Disputes 113

6. Implementing the New Vision 123

7. A New Vision for Structuring Family Relationships 145

8. Implementing the New Vision, Part Two 165

9. The Limits of Flourishing Family Law 203

Conclusion 223

NOTES 225
INDEX 309

Acknowledgments

WRITING IS NOT a solitary endeavor, and I am deeply grateful to many colleagues, family members, and friends for their key insights and interventions. Beginning with my colleagues, I especially thank Jamie Abrams, Erez Aloni, and Jill Hasday for reading the entire book and offering detailed and constructive comments. Numerous other colleagues provided invaluable feedback at multiple stages, including Kathryn Abrams, Kerry Abrams, Cynthia Bowman, Naomi Cahn, June Carbone, Maxine Eichner, Robert Emery, Cynthia Godsoe, Leigh Goodmark, Maya Grosz, Jonathan Haidt, Meredith Johnson Harbach, Margaret Johnson, Alicia Kelly, Suzanne Kim, Laurie Kohn, Sarah Krakoff, Robin Lenhardt, Solangel Maldonado, Terry Maroney, Hiroshi Motomura, Angela Onwuachi-Willig, Elizabeth Scott, Barbara Stark, Phil Weiser, and Benjamin Zipursky. I thank participants at several workshops and conferences where I presented drafts of this book: the Center on Applied Feminism at the University of Baltimore Law School, Emerging Family Law Scholars and Teachers, Feminist Legal Theory Collaborative Research Network, International Society of Family Law, Law and Society Annual Meeting, and New York Area Family Law Scholars. I am also grateful to Chris Collins, formerly of Oxford University Press, who saw the book before I knew there was one, and to Barbara Kancelbaum, who suggested the perfect title. Many students helped with research over the past several years, and I am thankful to each one: Georgia Barker, Patricia Bates, Samantha Bloodworth, Jamie Clouser, Jennifer Head, Meredith Lammers, Rebecca Marlin, Lauren Michaeli, Kristin Oketani, Jennifer Parker, Lauren Ristau, Tanya Rolo, and

ix

Zaneta Wykowska. Finally, Alison Shea is an extraordinary librarian, and I thank her for tracking down countless obscure sources and facts. I developed the ideas in this book in numerous articles published in several journals, including *Duke Law Journal, Emory Law Journal, Family Court Review, Michigan Law Review, Notre Dame Law Review, UCLA Law Review*, and *Virginia Journal of Law and Public Policy*.

On the family front, I am fortunate to have one sister-in-law, Catherine Davidson, who is a brilliant writer and another sister-in-law, Anna Budayr, who is a brilliant psychiatrist. Both read and commented on the manuscript, and the book is hugely improved thanks to their gentle but probing reactions and comments. My husband, Nestor Davidson, law professor and editor extraordinaire, provided exceptional advice at every stage.

Although this book is about families, I know firsthand that lifelong friends are irreplaceable. I am particularly thankful to Amy Houston, David Huntington, and Staci Haines for decades of support and friendship and to Carole Symer, who showed me myself. I also thank James Steinman-Gordon for an inspirational marriage speech and his generosity in sharing it.

Finally, I want to acknowledge my own, multiple families. The family that created me—my late father, Sam, whose spirit animates me every day; my immensely engaged and supportive brother, Henry; and my mother, Jennifer, who is exactly the mother I need at this point in my life and is an unparalleled third parent to my own children. The family I married into—the accepting and emotive Davidsons. I love you as my own. And the family I helped create—Zoe, a poet whose perception and insights astound me daily; Sam, who combines a fierce will with deep sensitivity and laughter; and, of course, Nestor, whom I could not love any more, and yet every day I do.

Introduction

WALK DOWN THE self-help aisle in any local bookstore, and you will see a wealth of titles about improving relationships. There's ready advice about finding loving partners, raising responsible children, salvaging foundering relationships, and ending marriages with as little acrimony as possible. Typically, these books imply that creating strong relationships or leaving them gracefully is something we do purely as individuals.

But relationships do not exist in a vacuum. Neighborhoods matter. Raising a child in a community with safe streets, adequate playgrounds, and good schools means a parent's job is that much easier. Families matter. The relationships we grow up with as children influence our experience in school and the kinds of relationships we envision for ourselves as adults. And the workplace matters. Whether a job pays enough to support a family and whether an employer makes it possible to meet family responsibilities affect relationships at home. In all these ways, context matters.

Beneath neighborhoods, families, and workplaces, however, there is an even deeper, more pervasive influence on relationships: the law. The law's effect may be intuitive when we think of the legal rules governing divorce, paternity, child abuse, and other kinds of family conflicts—what this book calls "dispute-resolution family law." In this context, the impact of the law is readily apparent. A custody order specifying how often a parent can see a child clearly affects that relationship. A determination by a court that a child must be placed in foster care does so even more.

But there is another kind of law—what this book calls "structural family law"—that has just as much, if not more, influence on all of our most intimate relationships. Structural family law decides who is a family in the first place, with some groupings, such as same-sex couples in a majority of states, losing out. Structural family law also determines what family members owe one another, such as a parent's duty to support a child financially, and who will make important decisions for children—parents or the various institutions of the government.

Sweeping even more broadly, structural family law influences the context for relationships. Zoning laws specifying the layout of a community influence access to safe play spaces and interaction among neighbors. Employment-discrimination laws that make it possible for women and people of color to work and develop successful careers influence a family's income. And criminal laws that emphasize punishment over rehabilitation mean that many children grow up without fathers in their daily lives. In these and so many other ways, the law profoundly shapes families and family life, even if its presence is not immediately detectable.

The core argument of this book is that this broad system of family law—both in resolving familial disputes and in setting the structural framework for family life—fails to nurture the strong, stable, positive relationships that are the key to individual and societal flourishing. Acting in its dispute-resolution mode, the law intervenes in a heavy-handed and adversarial fashion, often exacerbating family conflicts by pitting one family member against another in a zero-sum, win-lose battle. When a parent abuses a child, for example, the government often removes the child from the home and puts the matter in the hands of a court, with each party represented by a lawyer. The ensuing proceedings, which are filled with acrimony and reproach, do little to heal the relationship between the parent and the child and often intensify the problems that led to the breach in the first place. The same can be said of the legal system governing conflicts over divorce, child custody, adoptions, and parentage, with the law relying on traditional adversarial methods for resolving disagreements that are emotional and fraught.

This approach to family disputes ignores the reality that even as legal relationships change—from spouse to former spouse, from parent to nonparent—familial connections typically endure. Divorced spouses continue to co-parent, many adopted children maintain relationships with their biological parents, and approximately half of all children placed in foster care will return to their biological families.[1] Maintaining good relations in all these contexts is so much harder in the wake of a pitched legal battle. The ex-spouses who are fighting in court today must attend a parent-teacher conference tomorrow, and their oppositional stance will inevitably carry over from one setting to the other.

As a structural matter, the pervasive regulation is ill-conceived, doing far too little to strengthen relationships to avoid familial conflicts in the first place. Instead of bolstering relationships long before marriages break down, teenagers become pregnant, or parents get to the end of their rope, the legal system regulates families with insufficient attention to family well-being. The law is everywhere in family life, but this ubiquitous presence fails to strengthen family relationships.

To replace this cycle of inattention to well-being before crisis and overreaction after, this book argues that the entire structure of family law must be changed to an orientation that seeks to foster strong, stable, positive relationships from the beginning and then approaches conflict with an eye to repairing relationships, knowing they will continue long after the legal battles are over. This would be a truly flourishing family law.

THE ARGUMENT, IN A NUTSHELL

Understanding how far wrong our family-law system has gone and what we need to do to heal it will take us from ancient Greece to cutting-edge psychological research and from the chaotic corridors of local family courts to a quiet revolution under way in how services are provided to families in need. Part one of this book begins by introducing a World War II nutritionist, ancient philosophers, and modern neuroscientists to underscore what we all sense intuitively, which is that strong, stable, positive relationships are essential to both individual and societal well-being. This understanding draws on a recent shift in the field of psychology, from studying not only human dysfunction but also human flourishing. The emerging field of positive psychology examines the elements of a well-lived, satisfying life. A repeated finding in positive psychology and related work is that close interpersonal relationships are significantly correlated with individual well-being in addition to desirable outcomes on a societal level, from greater academic achievement to thriving communities.

The book then describes the extraordinary challenges facing families that impede the development of relationships, including unemployment, poverty, teen parenting, domestic violence, and high rates of divorce and incarceration. Although these challenges may sound familiar, what is often unappreciated is the place of the law in both creating some of these problems and failing to respond effectively. The central problem is that the law largely ignores family well-being until a family falls apart and then intervenes in a manner that often makes things worse—an approach this book calls "negative family law."

Part two sets forth a new vision for family law, arguing that it must be reoriented to nurture strong, stable, positive relationships. The primary focus is on children, because there is so much to be gained—on an individual level and a societal level—from strengthening families raising children. Thus, much of this book concerns the relationship between caregivers and children. But as the book repeatedly shows, the quality of the relationship between parents has a profound effect on children, particularly for children born to unmarried parents. In the world of modern families, we can separate marriage and parenthood but not relationships and parenthood. When parents stay together, it is much easier for both parents to be involved in a child's life. When romantic relationships end, it is still possible to co-parent and for the nonresidential parent to maintain a connection with the child, but this typically requires that the parents develop a working relationship around their shared child. It is thus essential to strengthen relationships between parents, as romantic partners or as co-parents.

The new vision recognizes that family conflicts are inevitable. Families break apart, sometimes voluntarily, sometimes involuntarily, for good reasons and for bad reasons. Divorce has its place in family life. Adoptions ensure that children are raised by adults who are able to care for them. And some children should be removed from their parents' care because of abuse or neglect. But we need to change the way family law addresses these conflicts and alterations in legal status, because these relationships will almost certainly continue long after the judge and the lawyers go home. This means that dispute-resolution family law must restructure families with an eye to the future. This requires developing a dispute-resolution system that can address conflict in ways that preserve and repair relationships. This will allow former family members to relate to each other and work together when necessary, as with co-parenting following a divorce. This interest in restructuring families and repairing relationships, however, must be balanced against the need to ensure that family members are safe in their homes, as violence remains a regular part of too many lives. In some contexts, there are good reasons to avoid ongoing contact, and the law must also be attentive to this reality.

This approach to dispute-resolution family law—restructuring families with an eye to the future, preserving and repairing relationships, and keeping family members safe—creates a framework for understanding what the government should be doing in structural family law: proactively nurturing strong, stable, positive relationships to avoid these conflicts as much as possible. The first step is to acknowledge that families and the government are mutually dependent. Families need the government in myriad ways, from establishing clear rules about parentage to ensuring basic opportunities, such as education. And the government needs families. An excellent example of this interdependency is early childhood development. Society benefits when children stay in school and become productive adults, but this requires a solid foundation in the first years of life. It is parents and other caregivers who are with children during these crucial formative years, and thus, simply put, the government needs families to do the essential work of nurturing very young children.

To foster strong, stable, positive relationships does not mean calling for a cradle-to-grave welfare state. Rather, it requires a reorientation of the ubiquitous role that the legal system *already* plays in relationships. To foster *strong* relationships, structural family law should grant legal recognition to a broader range of families, rather than recognizing only traditional nuclear families. To foster *stable* relationships, structural family law should encourage long-term commitment between parents—commitment to each other or at least commitment to the shared work of raising children. To foster *positive* relationships, structural family law should make subtle but crucial changes to the context in which families live. To take one example, zoning laws can be changed to build communities where there are enough opportunities for children to play, families can interact easily, and parents and children can get to work and to school relatively easily. This physical environment would increase family interaction and build social ties between families and the larger community. Finally, to put it all together and foster strong, stable, positive relationships, structural family law should help parents with their critical child-development work by providing support during key periods of stress and transition. The moment of family formation is particularly important, so helping teens avoid pregnancy and teaching basic parenting skills to young, at-risk, first-time parents during the first years of a child's life are crucial.

Cultivating strong, stable, positive relationships does not require a traditional structure for every family, but the dramatic changes under way in American families make it all the more critical to think about how the law can fortify a wide range of families. More than 41 percent of children are born to unmarried parents,[2] more than a quarter of all children live with only one parent,[3] a significant number of children live in households with adults in a same-sex relationship,[4] and children are increasingly conceived through donated sperm and eggs.[5] The model of a married mother and father living with their biological children is on the wane, and the challenge for family law is to strengthen the many different kinds of families living in America today.

Although this book does have a view about relationships, it does not seek to reinforce the primacy of the traditional family. There is a lot of debate these days about family form, from the fast-moving battle over marriage equality to the ongoing concern about families headed by single mothers, to name just two points of contention. Focusing on whether the law should give legal legitimacy to one kind of relationship and not another misses the point that children and adults need strong, stable, positive relationships in order to flourish.

Family form is relevant only to the extent that it nurtures or hinders these kinds of relationships. Marching an unstable couple down to city hall and issuing a marriage license is not going to ensure that the two stay together and become good parents. It is true that there is strong evidence that children raised by two married parents have better outcomes, as measured by a variety of metrics, than children raised in other family structures. And there is increasing evidence that family form is one causal factor in these outcomes. But it is also true that poverty and other factors go a long way in explaining the differential, a reality that is too often lost in debates about family form. The government must address the entire range of factors—including family structure *and* poverty—that influence child outcomes. This book argues that the law should encourage a long-term commitment between parents, but this is far more complicated than simply saying the government should promote marriage.

One thing this book does not do is focus on strong, stable, positive relationships outside the family. For many people, especially adults, relationships with friends, coworkers, and others are just as important, if not more so, as relationships with family members. But for children, particularly very young children, relationships within the family (broadly defined) are the most influential, and these are the relationships that have a lasting impact on individual and societal well-being. For this reason, the book focuses primarily on the family relationships that affect and involve children.

EXISTING, NARROW REFORMS

A few narrow reforms embody several of these principles. Some legislatures, judges, attorneys, academics, and individuals have tried to move family law in a more positive direction, and many of these efforts have been successful. Rather than a winner-takes-all approach to child custody, for example, the law now allows joint custody between parents, recognizing the important role both parents play in a child's life and the reality that family relationships continue after legal restructuring. Procedurally, there have been developments such as the widespread use of mediation in the field of divorce. And some lawyers already adopt a more conciliatory, cooperative approach to family conflicts.

These efforts, however, are haphazard, unconnected, and sometimes actively challenged. There is no overarching theory of family law that would help unite these developments and encourage more complete change. Even in areas where there has been significant reform, such as the field of divorce, there is still considerable room for improvement. Despite the availability of joint custody, for example, many committed fathers end up without meaningful relationships with their children. Much work remains to be done, and having a clear vision for what family law is trying to achieve is an essential first step.

More fundamentally, reforms that are emerging have largely been in the system of dispute-resolution family law. Structural family law continues to adopt a reactive approach to family well-being, doing far too little to strengthen families to avoid conflict. The vision articulated in this book—that family law in all of its aspects should nurture strong, stable, positive relationships—is a way of uniting these disparate developments, bringing them under one theoretical umbrella and fostering more systematic and systemic reform for families, and ultimately society, to flourish.

ANTICIPATING RESISTANCE

Of course, there are limits to what the law can achieve, and there are political challenges in rethinking family law. A dominant theme in politics, today and throughout our history, is a deep-felt need to limit the government's reach, especially into the family. What this understandable instinct for nonintervention fails to recognize, however, is that the law is already, and inevitably, in our lives, forming and shaping families. It is simply present in a largely unproductive way. Rather than pretend that legal regulation of families is minimal, it is far more useful to reflect honestly and holistically on the role of the law and reconsider what the law can do to help build strong, stable, positive relationships. Further, strengthening families before a crisis and intervening afterward in a manner that addresses conflict more constructively will foster greater self-determination for families. Anyone who has been through a contested divorce can tell horror stories about the devastating loss of control that accompanies court involvement. And the child-welfare system, where children are often removed from their homes and placed in foster care, can be a bewildering, if not outright terrifying, experience of direct legal control of a family.

Particularly in a time of fiscal constraints, another concern may be that the reforms suggested in this book will simply be too expensive. To be sure, some programs will require up-front investments. But special education, the child-welfare system, and the criminal-justice system are all expensive back-end programs that exist, at least in part, because we are doing too little to help families provide children with the strong, stable, positive relationships they need. The only question is whether we pay now or pay later, and overwhelming evidence shows that targeted prevention programs that work with families when children are very young are far more cost-effective than back-end programs that pick up the pieces farther down the road.

In short, it is easy to argue that the government should stay out of family life and that there is no money to strengthen families, but the reality is that the government is already present in our lives, and we are already paying for the costs associated with poorly functioning families. The question is whether we want the government's presence to be positive and cost-effective, not whether we want the government involved at all.

These are rational arguments, however, and debates about government involvement in the family are rarely dispassionate exchanges about the costs and benefits of various measures. Instead, these issues raise strong emotions and tap into deep belief systems about the world and the proper place of government in our lives. Thus, the concluding chapter focuses on the political valence of the reforms proposed in this book, showing how it is possible to garner support across red/blue political lines, but that doing so will require a conscious effort to frame the problems and solutions in "purple" terms.

JUDGING FAMILIES AND THE DANGERS OF STATE-SPONSORED CHANGE

To talk of families is inevitably to talk of race, class, and sexual orientation. This book treads cautiously when drawing conclusions about families that function well and families that do not. Families across the income spectrum and with a variety of family forms face challenges, and this book identifies and discusses these issues. But the book also focuses on the challenges facing unmarried, low-income families. This is not because these parents love their children any less than financially stable, married parents do. Rather, it simply acknowledges the many challenges facing families with limited financial resources and complex family structures.

I am well aware that it is sensitive for an outsider to draw conclusions and make judgments about nondominant families. In 1965, Daniel Patrick Moynihan, then the assistant secretary of Labor, completed a government report titled *The Negro Family: The Case for National Action*, which came to be known as the Moynihan Report.[6] The Moynihan Report argued that efforts such as the Civil Rights Act of 1964 were insufficient to assure African Americans of full participation in society.[7] Instead, the Moynihan Report identified the heart of the problem as "the deterioration of the Negro family," which centered around a "tangle of pathology . . . capable of perpetuating itself without assistance from the white world."[8] Although the report placed the blame squarely on "three centuries of exploitation,"[9] unsurprisingly, the report's reductionism and paternalism about families drew a strong negative reaction from civil-rights leaders, the press, academics, and the African American community.[10]

One legacy of the report has been a reluctance to talk about problems in families, particularly low-income families of color. This book takes its cue from the work of sociologist William Julius Wilson, who distinguishes structural challenges from cultural challenges facing nondominant families. As Wilson argues, there are structural challenges—such as institutionalized discrimination, dangerous neighborhoods, low-quality schools, and a lack of economic opportunities—that make it harder for some families to raise their children.[11] But there are also cultural challenges, such as a devaluation of men making a long-term commitment to the mothers of their children, resulting in single-parent homes and paternal disengagement.[12] Addressing cultural issues is far more delicate, but any meaningful discussion must acknowledge both kinds of challenges, as this book does.

An additional reason to tread cautiously is that although this book argues for governmental support of families, the history of state involvement in family life is too often a history of discrimination against nondominant families—families in poverty, single parents, people of color, same-sex couples, immigrant families, the disabled, and others marginalized by a legal system predicated on a two-parent, married, opposite-sex, white, suburban, middle-class paradigm of the family. Government-sponsored "improvement" programs often have a paternalistic stance and make negative judgments about families that do not fall into this supposed heartland.

Accordingly, this book addresses relationships that go beyond the traditional nuclear family of a married mother and father living with their biological or adopted children. The book focuses on the pressing need to find a more positive approach to other types of families, too, particularly those with strong emotional ties but often without legal recognition, such as same-sex partners, multiple adults with ties to the same child, donor families, other-mothers, and so on. As this book elaborates, flourishing comes in many stripes, and family law can support flourishing in diverse family forms, not just in traditional, nuclear families. A core lesson from the book, then, is that the law can be more ecumenical about family form while still nurturing the strong, stable, positive relationships that foster individual and societal well-being.

* * *

In sum, despite the essential role that families play in society, too often families do not have the resources—economic, social, emotional, or otherwise—for the task. The broad system of family law is a significant part of the problem when families fail, but it can also be part of the solution. Engaging on both a practical and theoretical level, this book offers concrete reforms to family law that would encourage flourishing families while simultaneously seeking to change the way we think about families and family law. The approach envisioned in this book would transform not only family law but society itself.

PART ONE
Positive Relationships and Negative Family Law

THIS BOOK BEGINS with a lot of talk about relationships, which may seem better suited for the therapist's couch than a book about the law. Where are the imposing courtrooms? The lawyers in suits? The heavy statute books? They're coming. Before getting to the law and its place in our most intimate relationships, it is worth considering why relationships matter so much. Chapter 1 thus begins by exploring the clear and overwhelming evidence that strong, stable, positive relationships—especially during childhood—are the linchpin for both individual and societal well-being. This is perhaps intuitively obvious, but from the foundations of our philosophical tradition to neuroscience charting a startling inner landscape, this proposition finds remarkably consistent support.

The problem facing society, however, is that too often families are unable to provide children with the kinds of relationships that are essential for healthy development and in turn create engaged, productive citizens. Chapter 2 describes the substantial challenges facing families today—from domestic violence and divorce to poverty and unemployment—which make it much harder for parents to form and maintain strong, stable, positive relationships with each other and with their children. This chapter also explores the seismic demographic changes in families, particularly the decline in marriage rates and the accompanying rise of single-parent and cohabiting households, which often complicate a family's ability to nurture children. This is not to say that every child needs two, married parents and certainly not that a child needs two, opposite-sex, married parents. Rather, it is to highlight the complexity of families today and the challenges facing policymakers.

These formative family relationships—both positive and negative—do not take place in a vacuum. Instead, the law shapes relationships in ways that may not be apparent at first glance. People in intimate relationships make numerous decisions, such as whether to get married, whether to rear children, and how to share financial and family responsibilities. Similarly, the parent-child relationship involves myriad decisions, from momentous choices about education and religion to prosaic decisions about eating and play. These may seem like individual choices that partners and parents make on their own, but, as chapter 3 demonstrates, in reality, the law influences families from the very beginning to the very end. From determining which groupings of individuals are "a family," and thus deserving of the rights and responsibilities the law accords families, to influencing behavior through subsidies, indirect regulation, and social norms, the law permeates family life.

This pervasive regulation, however, does little to nurture strong, stable, positive relationships. Despite the law's influence over nearly every aspect of family life, there is in our culture a persistent (albeit mistaken) belief that families do and should operate autonomously, independently of the government. The central problem with this myth of family autonomy is that it reinforces an ideology of nonresponsibility for the government, leading to policies that fail to strengthen families before crisis. When crises do occur, the government takes a more active role but often in a way that makes things worse. And to the extent that the government lets families operate with relative autonomy, it often does so unevenly, deferring to the decisions of some families while directly intervening and second-guessing the choices of others. This difference in treatment generally turns on race and class lines, with the government far more ready to intervene in the lives of low-income, nonwhite families. All of this adds up to "negative family law" and is the central topic of chapter 4.

This talk of dysfunction may seem depressing, but it is essential groundwork for the hard but necessary work of reframing our legal system's approach to relationships, an optimistic undertaking that is the heart of part two of the book. It is possible to nurture the strong, stable, positive relationships that are the cornerstone of flourishing, but first we need to know how we are failing to do so.

A quick note on a key term: Beginning in chapter 1, this book uses the shorthand "the state"—rather than "the law" or "the government"—to refer to actions taken by public institutions. Legal academics use this term regularly, but its meaning can be uncertain in other circles. What is meant by "the state" in this book is the American system of government, with its multiple layers and institutions and diverse actors. As any middle-schooler can describe, ours is a federal system, with one national government regulating concurrently with state and local governments. States and the federal government have their own executive, legislative, and judicial branches, largely exercising different kinds of authority. This "state" is messy in numerous and interesting ways. Structurally, the different layers of government can work at cross purposes. Internally, the different branches of government can act in opposition to one another. And politically, both legal and extralegal constraints hinder action. To use a shorthand for such a complex institution is not to imply that the state is somehow monolithic or acts with one voice and one purpose. Rather, it is simply a useful way to capture the many ways in which family law, acting through this complicated state, fails to help families.

1

The Place of Relationships

⌒—————————————————————————————

DURING WORLD WAR II, the English government wanted to know how much food its citizens needed to survive—or, more to the point, how little they needed. The government turned to Elsie Widdowson, a nutrition expert.[1] Widdowson's experience helping answer this question shaped research she conducted after the war ended. Interested in the effect of additional calories on children's growth, Widdowson followed one hundred children in two German orphanages.[2]

The children in both homes were subsisting on the same meager rations, but Widdowson noted in the first six months of observation—before she had done anything to change the rations—that the children in the two homes had different growth rates. Surprisingly, the growth rate of the children in the first home was what would be predicted for relatively well-fed children, not children living on very little food. The children in the second home had lower-than-normal growth rates, or what would be expected for children with access to very limited nutrition. After the initial observation period, Widdowson gave the children in the first home additional food—orange juice, bread, and jam. (This decision was made at random, before the initial growth rates were known.) She anticipated that these additional calories would mean that these children would grow even more and the children in the other home would continue to lag farther behind.

Instead, the opposite happened. The growth of the children with the additional calories slowed down, and the growth of the children without the additional calories accelerated dramatically. What was going on? Widdowson knew she had to look for another factor—what researchers call an "intervening variable." She found it in the nature of the two matrons running the homes. When both homes were receiving the same slender rations but had different growth rates, the children with the stronger growth rate, in the first home, were supervised by a matron who was warm and bright and showed much love for the children. By contrast, in the home with the slower growth rate, the matron was a cold and capricious disciplinarian, often berating the children for no reason, particularly at mealtimes. This observation alone might have been enough to draw at least initial conclusions about the effect of relationships on child well-being, but there was an additional wrinkle that confirmed the insight that relationships matter tremendously.

Completely by coincidence, at the time the additional food was given to the children in the first home, the abusive matron was transferred there and began her tyrannical rule in the new setting. In her place at the second home, a new matron with a sunny, warm disposition took over. Now under the supervision of a warm matron but receiving no additional calories, these children began to thrive, and their growth surpassed that of the children in the first home, who had the better initial growth rates and were receiving the additional calories but were now living with the wrathful matron. Widdowson determined that the quality of the emotional care was the decisive factor. Quoting a proverb, Widdowson concluded, " 'Better is a dinner of herbs where love is than a stalled ox and hatred therewith.' "[3]

For all of its visceral power, this insight—that relationships play a key role in human flourishing—is not new. From ancient philosophers to modern psychologists, there is widespread agreement that strong, stable, positive relationships are essential for human growth and well-being. But we have a great array of tools now to understand *why* relationships matter, what matters *in* relationships, and what matters *for* relationships. We can think of this as the effect, the content, and the context of relationships, and each plays a distinct but critical role in understanding what law should do in approaching families.

EFFECT: WHY RELATIONSHIPS MATTER

It may be intuitive that strong, stable, positive relationships matter in life, but understanding why the state should actively nurture these kinds of relationships first requires a more precise understanding of why they matter—for both individuals and society.

Relationships and individual well-being

A good place to begin any discussion about individual well-being is the relatively new field of positive psychology. In 1998, Martin Seligman, a psychology professor at the University of Pennsylvania, used his term as the president of the American Psychological Association to call for a new orientation for psychology.[4]

Collaborating with other leading psychologists, such as Mihaly Csikszentmihalyi and Ed Diener, Seligman argued that psychology was overly focused on disease and dysfunction to the exclusion of understanding healthy functioning.[5] He believed that although we can learn much from understanding pathology, there are equally important insights to be found in the study of human flourishing.

The resulting field of positive psychology is too often portrayed as the glib study of "happiness,"[6] but it is a rigorously scientific field that brings the familiar methods of psychology—control groups, large sample sizes, and so on—to bear upon questions of well-being. The animating proposition of the field is that it is possible to measure, understand, and build upon the conditions that lead to human flourishing.[7] This greater understanding can then be used to help cultivate the conditions that encourage flourishing.

A repeated finding in positive psychology—and from researchers who do not self-identify as scholars of positive psychology but who focus nonetheless on the beneficial impact of relationships—is that close interpersonal relationships are highly correlated with individual well-being.[8] (Positive psychologists sometimes use different terms to describe this insight, such as "life satisfaction," "subjective well-being," "happiness," and "flourishing," but the basic idea is the same.) The following discussion explores the impact of relationships in five contexts: child development, adult well-being, health, healing, and the acquisition of social capital.

First, relationships affect child development. Relationships affect nearly every aspect of child development but are particularly important for brain development. During early childhood, the brain lays down neural pathways that become the foundation for future brain development, with brain cells—neurons—forming circuits. The neural circuits that are used repeatedly grow stronger, but those that are not used regularly die off through a process called pruning. Neural circuits become the basis for the development of language, emotions, logic, memory, motor skills, and behavioral control. With repeated use, the circuits become more efficient, connecting different areas of the brain more rapidly and thus affecting a person's ability to think well and regulate emotions. If the foundation is strong, it is easier to build upon in later years, but if the foundation is weak, it is much harder for the brain to develop the higher-level skills that rely on efficient connections between different areas of the brain.[9]

Genetics and the pre- and postnatal environment both affect brain development,[10] but a child's relationships are the other key factor. A critical mechanism for making and strengthening neural connections is what some neuroscientists call "serve-and-return" interaction between an attentive, responsive caregiver and a child. The child initiates interaction through babbling, movements, and facial expressions, and the adult responds with sounds and gestures. Through this serve and return, neural connections between different areas of the brain are established and rein-forced. As neuroscientist Daniel Siegel explains, "where you are focusing attention stimulates the firing of certain neurons. And when neurons fire, they increase their synaptic connectivity to one another."[11] In other words, "relational experience drives neural firing, and neural firing drives neural wiring."[12] These neural connections forged through interactions with a caregiver become the basis for future communi-cation and social skills.[13]

To appreciate the role of families in brain development, it is important to under-stand that much critical brain development occurs before a child enters formal schooling at age five.[14] Different capacities develop during "sensitive periods," with the basic neural circuitry for vision and hearing developing shortly before and soon after birth and the circuits used for language and speech production peaking before age one.[15] The higher-level circuits used for cognitive functions develop throughout the first several years of life.[16] For example, the so-called executive functions—the brain's ability to hold information in the short term, ignore distractions, and switch gears between contexts and priorities (or, to use slightly more formal terminology, "working memory," "inhibitory control," and "cognitive flexibility")—are developed from birth through late adolescence, but with a particularly important period occur-ring from ages three to five.[17]

These sensitive periods are a time of particular vulnerability for neural circuits. A relationship with an attentive, responsive caregiver during sensitive periods is vital for proper development. Conversely, significantly adverse relationships during the sensitive periods can have lasting impacts on the circuitry as the circuits develop in response to the adverse conditions. This can be demonstrated with the concept of toxic stress. Learning how to cope with stress is an important part of child develop-ment. For example, the temporary disappearance of a caregiver or a minor injury may trigger a child's stress-response system, with an increased heart rate and height-ened levels of stress hormones. When a caregiver promptly comforts the child, the response system is quickly deactivated, and the child develops a sense of mastery over stressful events.[18] Neuroscientists refer to this as positive stress.[19]

But prolonged, severe, or frequent stress stemming from abuse, neglect, extreme poverty, and maternal clinical depression creates "toxic stress,"[20] which has a serious adverse impact on brain development. When there is no caring adult able to relieve this stress or when the caregiver is the source of the stress, as in the case of abuse and neglect, the child's stress response remains activated. This constant activation overloads the developing brain and impedes the construction of neural pathways. In extreme cases, toxic stress can lead to the development of a smaller brain. In cases of moderate toxic stress, the brain can change such that it develops a hair trigger for stress, activating the stress response system in reaction to events that others might not perceive as difficult or threatening.[21] These changes can influence how individuals respond to adversity throughout life.[22]

This lasting effect is because the neural circuits involved in the transmission of stress signals are particularly flexible during early childhood, meaning that the effect of toxic stress leaves a lasting impression on the creation of these circuits, affecting how easily the stress response is turned on and off.[23] This, in turn, creates a greater vulnerability to physical illnesses, such as diabetes, stroke, and cardiovascular disease, and mental illnesses, such as depression and anxiety disorders.[24] Further, the heightened level of cortisol, the hormone triggered by stress, has consequences for the development of the areas of the brain dedicated to memory and learning, weakening the neural connections to these parts of the brain.[25] A child's relationship with a caregiver affects the production of cortisol, with a responsive caregiver helping to prevent its production, even in a child temperamentally predisposed to be anxious. By contrast, when a caregiver is depressed, abusive, or neglectful, a child's cortisol levels increase, both during stress and even after the stressful period ends.[26] Compromised circuits are harder, although not impossible, to repair later in life.[27]

The effect of toxic stress is particularly strong during sensitive periods when neural circuits are forming and maturing.[28] During these periods, the genetic plan and brain architecture can be significantly modified. By contrast, once a circuit has matured, environment and experiences affect the genetic plan and architecture to a much lesser degree.[29]

To appreciate the effect of toxic stress on serve-and-return interactions, and to underscore the role of relationships, consider maternal depression (meaning clinical depression, not the "baby blues" that many women experience after giving birth). Instead of engaged serve-and-return interactions, a clinically depressed mother typically is either hostile and aggressive toward her children or withdrawn and disengaged.[30] Both parenting styles negatively affect the serve-and-return interaction that is crucial for brain development, either because the mother's serve is unappealing to the child or because the mother does not return a serve from the child.[31] When this pattern continues for a prolonged period, the child's brain architecture can be affected, with long-term consequences for the child.[32] Indeed, brain scans conducted through an electroencephalogram (EEG) reveal that children with depressed mothers show brain activity similar to that of depressed adults. This result was found both with infants and toddlers.[33]

Maternal depression is particularly worrisome because it is widespread. One in eleven infants will experience a mother going through a major depression before the child turns age one.[34] Maternal depression is also correlated with poverty. Of mothers with nine-month-old infants, 25 percent of the women living below the poverty level were severely depressed; the rate is also quite high—11 percent—for women who are not poor (women with income levels more than 200 percent of the poverty level).[35] Further, maternal depression often occurs alongside other adverse conditions: depressed mothers are more likely to be young, have had stressful childhoods, and be socially isolated;[36] they are also more likely to be victims of domestic violence, have poor health, and struggle with substance abuse.[37] This raises complex questions about cause and effect, but the correlation—and impact on neural development—is clear.

Second, relationships affect adult well-being. If relationships are essential for children, they also are critically important for adults. As Seligman says, "Other people are the best antidote to the downs of life and the single most reliable up."[38] When studying life satisfaction,[39] positive psychologists have found that the most consistent feature of people who rank in the top tenth percentile of happiness is that they have strong personal relationships.[40] A study by Seligman and Diener of 222 undergraduate students, for example, categorized the participants as "very happy," "average," and "very unhappy" based on self-reports and peer reports.[41] After following the participants for a semester, the authors found that the very happy people were highly social and had strong relationships with family, friends, and romantic partners. By contrast, the relationships of the very unhappy people were significantly worse than average. Several possible factors that might influence satisfaction—level of exercise, degree of religiosity, or experience with objectively positive events—were not determinative; instead, the primary difference between the groups was in the quantity and quality of their relationships.[42]

This description does not tell us, however, whether people are happier because of their relationships or whether happy people are more likely to create and maintain strong relationships. One way to get at this causal question is to look at studies of adults in long-term, committed relationships. There is overwhelming evidence that married people in an ongoing relationship[43] have greater life satisfaction than single people. (I will turn to cohabiting couples below.) As compared with singles, married couples have lower levels of depression and higher subjective well-being, they experience less violence in their lives and are more likely to have well-adjusted children, they are likely to earn more money and have less financial stress, and they experience less chronic disease and are likely to live longer.[44]

One tricky question about this "marriage benefit" concerns causation: does marriage make a person happier, wealthier, and healthier, or are happy, wealthy, and healthy individuals more likely to get married? It appears that the cause and effect run in both directions. There is some evidence that people who have high life satisfaction as singles are more likely to get married, remain married, and express satisfaction about their marriages,[45] but there is also evidence that marriage plays at least some causal role in producing the better outcomes.

Consider one study that attempted to tease out this important causation question. Two researchers examined survey data generated over seventeen years by participants in the German Socio-Economic Panel.[46] Participants answered numerous questions, including life satisfaction as rated on a scale from one to ten. As with many other studies, the researchers found that married people had the highest level of life satisfaction.[47] In economic terms, the life-satisfaction bump from marriage was equivalent to having 2.5 times the mean household income.[48] Looking at the causation question and holding other variables—such as income, place of residence, and citizenship status—constant, the authors found strong support for the conclusion that happy people tend to get married.[49] The happier singles were more likely to get married and stay married than the unhappier singles.[50]

What is notable about this study, however, is that it also examined the variation of happiness levels within the same person by looking at the self-reports of life satisfaction over the period of the study. In this way, it was possible to determine the effect of marriage within the same individual. The authors found that even though happily married individuals may begin with high life satisfaction, they become even more satisfied after marriage.[51]

In another study seeking answers to the causation question, researchers compared identical twins and the general population. By examining identical twins raised together, the researchers could control for genetic and social differences that might influence outcomes. Depression, for example, is strongly correlated with marriage, particularly for men, with married men experiencing less depression than single men.[52] These differing rates of depression, however, could be caused by a combination of genetic or social differences between married and unmarried men, rather than marriage itself. By looking only at a population of married and unmarried identical twins, the researchers found that the difference in depression rates could not be explained by genetic or childhood differences, and instead, marriage was likely the influential factor.[53]

The benefits of marriage are not necessarily limited to those couples who are legally married. Although most studies find a benefit to marriage over cohabitation,[54] a recent study suggests that cohabiting couples—especially those who stay together—experience many of the same benefits from their union as married couples.[55] Chapter 2 discusses the differences between cohabitation and marriage in greater detail, particularly as it relates to the well-being of children. The point here is simply that there is abundant evidence that long-term, committed relationships are enormously important for adults.

Third, relationships affect health. In the context of children, consider the Adverse Childhood Experiences (ACE) Study and its findings on the long-term health effects of childhood relationships.[56] The participants in this study reported their childhood exposure to seven different categories of abuse and trauma: psychological abuse, physical abuse, sexual abuse, domestic violence, substance abuse, living with someone mentally ill or suicidal, and living with an ex-prisoner.[57] A significant correlation was found between childhood exposure to these stressors and future adult health problems such as heart disease, lung disease, cancer, obesity, depression, alcoholism, and drug abuse.[58] Part of the explanation is that adverse childhood experiences can lead to behaviors such as smoking, drug or alcohol abuse, and overeating because individuals engage in these behaviors as a short-term coping mechanism for intense stress and abuse, and the behaviors then become chronic.[59]

But negative health behaviors are not the whole picture. Researchers have found that even after controlling for age, sex, race, and education and traditional risk factors such as smoking, physical inactivity, body mass index, diabetes, and hypertension, participants with a very high ACE score had a 310-percent increase in their risk of ischemic heart disease, the most common cause of death in the United States, over those who had no history of an ACE.[60] There is not a complete explanation for this nonbehavioral link, but evidence suggests that adverse childhood experiences can lead to long-lasting negative chemical changes in the body that then affect adult health.[61]

Turning to adults, negative relationships also have a detrimental effect on health. Studies have shown that domestic violence, for example, has health effects that persist over time, with individuals who have experienced a high level of domestic violence over their adult lifetimes consistently reporting poorer health status, even long after the exposure to violence has passed.[62] A person who has a prolonged experience with high levels of domestic violence has a similar health status to that of a chronically ill, economically disadvantaged person.[63] Many of the health problems, such as chest pains, abdominal pains, and acid reflux, are not directly associated with the specific violence.[64]

Fourth, relationships can be a source of healing. Just as relationships can be a source of harm, they can also be a source of healing. Consider a thirty-year study of 698 infants on the Hawaiian island of Kauai.[65] The study followed the children from before birth through age thirty-two. One-third of the children were classified as high-risk because of exposure to perinatal stress and other factors such as poverty, low parental education, an alcoholic or mentally ill parent, or divorce.[66] Despite these life circumstances, a third of the children in the high-risk category developed into competent, caring adults. The researchers found that the distinguishing factor for the children with better outcomes was that they had emotional support from extended family, neighbors, teachers, or church groups, and they had at least one close friend.[67]

Similarly, relationships can help young people caught up in the juvenile-justice system. A long-standing approach to juvenile delinquency has been to put teens in boot camps, marked by a military-style environment, a regimented schedule, hard labor, and physical training.[68] Or some teens are sent to "scared straight" programs, where juvenile offenders and at-risk youths observe prison life and have first-hand interaction with inmates.[69] Neither approach, however, reduces recidivism rates.[70] By contrast, programs that focus on relationship development and try to cultivate prosocial behaviors in teens and improve the emotional connections between the family and a teen have helped reduce recidivism.[71] For example, when juvenile offenders with histories of violent and aggressive behavior are enrolled in a program providing multisystemic therapy—with therapists delivering in-home treatment for both parents and youths, including a focus on coping skills—these offenders have a 30-percent lower recidivism rate than teens in regular juvenile case processing.[72]

In a final example, relationships can help heal childhood trauma, including severe abuse and neglect. Bruce Perry is a child psychiatrist who has spent his career working with children who have been abused, neglected, or traumatized by horrific events. In his riveting coauthored book about childhood trauma, Perry describes the deep neurological impact of childhood trauma on child development, especially during the early years.[73] But he also shows how children can heal from even the most unthinkable childhoods—being left alone as an infant for most of the day for the first eighteen months of life; being raised in a cage from ages one to six; witnessing the rape and murder of a mother at age three and then being left alone with the corpse for eleven hours, and so on. Over his many decades working with children, Perry developed a number of protocols designed to help heal trauma and in particular get brain development back on track, but the essence of his approach is to ensure that the child has healthy, loving, stable relationships. Speaking colloquially, Perry says that "the research on the most effective treatments to help child trauma victims might be accurately summed up this way: what works best is anything that increases the quality and number of relationships in the child's life."[74]

Fifth, relationships create social capital. Social capital is the idea that social networks—ties with friends, neighbors, faith groups, civic groups, and so on—have value. Just as we talk about education creating human capital, social networks create social capital. This social capital benefits individuals by providing information, reciprocity, trust, and a sense of belonging. A young teen walks a sick neighbor's dog; after the neighbor recovers, she brings over dinner for the teen's family, knowing the single mother works late. A middle-school parent tells another parent about a good orthodontist. A book group meets and (maybe) talks about the book, but the members also talk about their families and jobs, sharing successes and disappointments. A neighborhood group hosts a block party and collects signatures to present to city hall requesting the installation of a speed bump. And so on.

Social commentators and social scientists have long touted the value of social capital, from Jane Jacobs's *The Death and Life of Great American Cities*, criticizing urban-renewal projects because they replaced functioning, vibrant neighborhoods with impersonal towers that did little to foster connections between residents,[75] to Robert Putnam's *Bowling Alone*, documenting the demise of social networks in the United States.[76] As these and others note, social networks are important for people in all income groups. On the individual level, when a person benefits directly from the help of friends and neighbors, that person is likely to return the favor, thus helping all the people within the network.[77] On the collective level, when individuals come together to address a common problem, everyone benefits. Putnam gives the example of a neighborhood watch; an individual family is interested in protecting their home, but the group effort reduces crime in the neighborhood for everyone, even those who are not a part of the watch.[78] Service clubs such as Rotary or the Kiwanis, alumni associations, and religious associations such as churches and synagogues often have a public mission, which benefits those outside the club, but also provides the benefits of friendships, networking opportunities, and community to individual members.[79]

Social networks can be critically important for low-income families. When anthropologist Carol Stack spent three years living in and studying relationships in a small unnamed Midwestern city in the 1960s, she produced an enduring, and still apt, description of the social ties that bind low-income families. Stack described how the daily trading of goods and services between friends, families, and neighbors was a necessity of the community, because income, either from jobs or from welfare, was insufficient to meet the needs of most families. Stack became close friends with a woman her age, Ruby Sparks, who described how even in desperate times in each household, the trading culture meant that the needs of others were still a priority. In Sparks's words, "Sometimes I don't have a damn dime in my pocket, not a crying penny to get a box of paper diapers, milk, a loaf of bread. But you have to have help from everybody and anybody, so don't turn no one down when they come round for help."[80]

Stack found that this swapping of goods, services, and child care between families reinforced strong social networks and often symbolized trust between close friends. Sparks explained to Stack how friends could be called upon to lend anything and knew they would be repaid: "If a friend has on a new dress that I want, she might tell me to wait till she wear it first and then she'll give it to me, or she might say, well take it on."[81] In a community where new dresses were hard to come by, such a favor signaled deep trust between two women and mutual benefit, as the borrower understood the obligation to return the favor. A common service that performed a similar bonding function between friends was watching each other's children. Children of friends within the community would stay at Stack's home for days, and her son would similarly stay at their homes.[82] Temporarily exchanging children was a sign of deep trust, and families who did so developed strong ties and established a broader sense of responsibility for childrearing within the community. As numerous commentators have noted since, Stack's description remains as accurate today as it was then.[83]

By their very definition, social networks—and the social capital they create—turn on relationships. Social capital is about who we know and what we are inclined to do based on these ties. Without relationships, there is no social capital.

Relationships and societal well-being

Chapters 7 and 9 explore this topic in detail, but to get a sense of the connection between relationships and the well-being of society, consider the health-care implications for children with very high ACE scores. Or think about the impact on academic achievement when children grow up without the all-important serve-and-return interactions from an attentive caregiver. Or contemplate the broad impact of domestic violence, which causes tremendous physical, psychological, and economic harm to the victims and is also a social and economic problem for society. To expand on this last example, the Centers for Disease Control estimate that each year there are 550,000 instances of intimate-partner violence (rape, physical assault, and stalking) toward women ages eighteen and older that require medical attention.[84] These injuries translate into a loss of nearly 8 million days of work, or the equivalent of 32,000 full-time jobs.[85] The Centers for Disease Control calculate that this violence costs at least $5.8 billion dollars annually—including $4.1 billion in direct medical costs (including mental health services) and $900 million in productivity losses.[86] These figures do not include the many medical costs when domestic violence is not formally cited as the cause for the medical treatment or the other economic costs of domestic violence, such as women's shelters.[87] There is no doubt that we are all affected—economically and socially—by other people's relationships.

CONTENT: WHAT MATTERS IN RELATIONSHIPS

As the above description demonstrates, relationships can have a positive or negative impact on the individual and society. For relationships with a beneficial effect, there are three particularly important attributes: that the relationship is strong, stable, and positive. As each attribute leads to particular reform proposals for family law, it is worth exploring them in some level of detail.

Strong and stable relationships

Between parents and children. Any book about the importance of relationships would be incomplete without mentioning Harry Harlow and his monkeys. Working in his lab at the University of Wisconsin in the 1950s, Harlow, a psychologist, was interested in the influence of biological instincts on human behavior.[88] Harlow decided it would be easier to breed the rhesus monkeys he needed for his experiments than to import them from Asia.[89] To ensure that the monkeys were physically healthy, he separated the baby monkeys from their mothers shortly after birth and raised each in its own cage.[90] But when Harlow later brought these monkeys into contact with other monkeys, the monkeys could not get along. They had no social skills.[91] Harlow and his graduate students noticed that the monkeys raised alone would hold soft diapers that lined the bottom of the cage. The monkeys would cling to these diapers when they were afraid and even bring a diaper with them when moved to a new cage.[92]

Curious about this behavior, Harlow designed an experiment to test the reigning behavioral and psychoanalytic theory that mother-child relationships were based on the provision of sustenance. Harlow raised another round of infant monkeys, this time in cages with two substitute "mothers"—a cylinder made of wire and a cylinder covered in soft terry cloth. One group of monkeys received milk from the wire mother, and another group received milk from the soft terry-cloth mother. Both groups of infant monkeys strongly preferred the soft mother substitute, regardless of the source of food. The baby monkeys that received food from the wire mother would cling to the terry-cloth mother fifteen hours a day and to the wire mother for only an hour or two.[93] Later, the monkeys that received food from the wire mother would turn to the cloth mother for comfort if presented with a stressful situation.[94] This is not to suggest that the terry-cloth mother was an adequate substitute for the real thing. The monkeys raised with the fake mothers grew into adolescents with little interest in recreation or procreation and later became abusive parents.[95] The study does demonstrate, however, that there is more to a parent-child relationship than the provision of food.

The clinical evidence of this need for nurturance is reflected in what is called attachment theory, first articulated by psychiatrist and psychoanalyst John Bowlby and later developed by others such as Mary Ainsworth.[96] Attachment theory contends that an infant will seek proximity to a caregiver, protest when separated from this caregiver, and seek out this caregiver when in danger or need.[97] Bowlby argued that natural selection favored attachment behavior because proximity to a mother meant the child was more likely to be protected and thus more likely to survive.[98] As with Harlow, Bowlby's theory was a sharp split from earlier beliefs that a child's tie with a caregiver stemmed from the provision of food.[99] In attachment theory, the caregiver often is, but need not be, the person who provides the child with sustenance.

Bowlby demonstrated that children will attach to almost any consistent caregiver, even an abusive one or a cold, emotionless stand-in, as with Harlow's monkeys, but the quality of the attachment turns on the quality of the caregiving.[100] Although the child's temperament and genetic predisposition both likely affect attachment patterns, parental caregiving is a dominant factor in determining a child's attachment.[101]

The four basic styles of attachment are secure, anxious, avoidant, and disorganized.[102] If the primary caregiver consistently responds to a child's needs for comfort and reassurance, the child will develop a *secure* attachment to the caregiver. By contrast, if the primary caregiver is unpredictable and inconsistent, the model of attachment may be *anxious*, with the child constantly worried about the caregiver's presence and attention. And if the caregiver is reluctant and rejecting, the child may develop an *avoidant* attachment style, rejecting the caregiver. The final attachment pattern—*disorganized*—occurs when a child does not use any of the other three strategies for relating to attachment figures. It is most common when the caregiver is frightened or frightening precisely when the child looks to the caregiver for reassurance.

The attachment relationship between child and caregiver has ramifications for the child's development. A secure attachment with a caregiver both alleviates stress and, when there is no immediate stress, facilitates engagement with the larger world. When children have a "secure base," for example, they confidently explore their surroundings, knowing that they can come back to the caregiver for comfort and familiarity at any time.[103] Securely attached children learn to regulate their own emotions and solve problems because they feel effective, and they learn that negative emotions can be tolerated and managed. They can test reality because they are able to evaluate their own behaviors and other people's reactions. As a result, they develop good problem-solving skills, emotional balance, and positive expectations for relationships, meaning they can find and absorb positive emotional support.[104]

Attachment patterns also lay the groundwork for an adult's future patterns of relating, because the child's experience of relating to the caregiver becomes the internal working model for relationships and is carried forward into adulthood. Adults who have internalized a secure model of attachment are comfortable with emotional intimacy and can turn to their partners for support. Adults who have internalized an anxious model of attachment repeatedly seek intimacy and reassurance and worry about being abandoned. Adults who have internalized an avoidant model of attachment have difficulty forming close relationships and do not like to trust or be dependent on others. And the disorganized attachment style in a child is predictive of later difficulties, such as anxiety disorders and serious antisocial-behavior problems.[105]

Recent neuroscience research confirms the importance of attachment. As research-ers have demonstrated, there likely is no one attachment circuit in the brain; instead, attachment is made up of various social and emotional processes.[106] Psychologist James Coan has noted that "because so many neural structures are involved one way or another in attachment behavior, it is possible to think of the entire human brain as a neural attachment system."[107] Coan posits a social baseline model in which the brain's primary means of regulating emotions is through relationships. The pre-frontal cortex is heavily involved in the self-regulation of emotion, but because an infant's prefrontal cortex is underdeveloped, the caregiver acts as a sort of stand-in for the infant's prefrontal cortex, helping the infant regulate emotions.[108] To under-stand his or her own emotions, the infant follows the nonverbal communication of a caregiver, including a caregiver's facial expression, vocal variation, gestures, and eye contact.[109] The caregiver thus reflects and shapes the infant's emotional experience.

Neuroscientist Daniel Siegel explains the relevance of what he calls "resonance circuits." These circuits are a combination of the prefrontal areas of the brain and "mirror neurons," which allow a person to determine the intention of another per-son. When an individual sees another person in a state of distress, the resonance circuits create a similar state within the watcher, who then experiences the other's emotion on a number of levels. This emotional attunement is the main building block for social interactions and social intelligence later in life. These resonance cir-cuits thus help a person connect with another person and are the neurological key to healthy attachment. Through attuned interaction between a securely attached child and a caregiver, the child develops these resonance circuits.[110]

In sum, attachment theory explains the importance of strong and stable relation-ships, particularly for very young children. Developing a secure attachment with a caregiver requires repeated, ongoing contact between the child and the caregiver. When a caregiver is inconsistently available or disappears entirely, this can affect a child's attachment. This is particularly true for very young children. Consider the extreme case of a caregiver who dies during a period of critical growth for the child, say at age nine months. This experience can change the child's brain development in a way that affects the child's ability to regulate emotions in the future.[111] A similar loss for a nine-year-old child may result in temporary disorganization and regres-sion, but for the infant, the loss may have a lasting effect on brain functioning.[112] This does not mean that a parent must be a constant presence in a child's life, every moment of every day. Rather, what is important is that a parent or other caregiver is a steady, reliable presence.

Between adults. Bowlby disliked the word "dependency" because it seemed too age-specific and gave the sense that it was something to be outgrown.[113] He believed that secure attachment is also important for adult relationships and that all humans need others, regardless of their age.[114] In Bowlby's words, attachment is "a fundamental form of behaviour with its own internal motivation distinct from feeding and sex, and of no less importance for survival."[115] Bowlby argued that attachment is easily observed with young children but that it is also present, albeit in different forms, throughout the life cycle and thus can be understood as a fundamental part of human nature.[116]

Much as children seek out their attachment figures when they feel frightened, adults, too, seek the attachment figures in their current lives (typically, romantic partners or close friends) when they feel threatened, either by real or imagined events and circumstances.[117] If the attachment figure is regularly available and responsive, the stress associated with the threat is mitigated, and the relationship is deepened. If the attachment figure is neither regularly available nor responsive, however, then the distress is compounded, and the person either becomes hypervigilant about maintaining contact with the attachment figure or distances himself or herself from the attachment figure to avoid more pain.[118]

Here, too, recent neuroscience research confirms these insights. Neurologically speaking, adults in attachment relationships become a part of each other's emotional-regulation strategy.[119] The existence and quality of a relationship help an adult withstand difficulties by decreasing the need to be vigilant and self-regulate emotion,[120] because although a person can regulate negative emotions alone, it is easier to do so in a relationship.[121] An illustration of this phenomenon is a study of the brains of married women. While administering a mild shock, the researchers took brain scans of each woman when she was alone, holding a stranger's hand, and holding her husband's hand. The highest degree of threat-related brain activation occurred when the women were alone, with somewhat less activity while holding a stranger's hand and considerably less activity when holding a husband's hand. In a later iteration of the study, the researchers compared the threat activity with the self-reported quality of the marriage. The lowest level of threat activation occurred for married women who were in the highest-quality relationships, with more brain activity for women in somewhat lower-quality marital relationships.[122] This neurological intermingling is one reason divorce (and, of course, death) is so devastating: a former spouse's internal regulation system literally no longer functions as it did because part of it is missing.[123]

Even the simple act of talking to a partner can make a world of difference. UCLA researchers who closely examined the lives of thirty-two middle-class, dual-income families in the Los Angeles area found that although the parents' lives were highly demanding, if the wife could talk with her husband at the end of the day, her stress level (measured by the amount of cortisol in saliva samples taken by the researchers) quickly decreased.[124]

More broadly, a secure attachment between two adults is associated with greater interdependence, satisfaction, trust, commitment, caregiving, and support and less jealousy, whereas an insecure attachment is associated with lower relationship satisfaction.[125] Not surprisingly, adults with secure attachments tend to stay married for longer periods of time.[126]

The security that comes from a good attachment relationship also helps facilitate other positive traits, such as resilience, hope, optimism, the capacity to love and forgive, kindness, and so on.[127] Looking at forgiveness, securely attached adults are more likely to forgive their romantic partners than are those with anxious or avoidant attachment patterns.[128] Adults with avoidant attachment are less likely to forgive and more likely to seek revenge or withdraw.[129] And both anxious and avoidant attachments are correlated with domestic violence.[130]

Positive relationships

As the discussion of secure attachment makes clear, for relationships to have beneficial effects, it is not enough that a relationship be strong and stable. It must also be positive. This does not mean that every exchange between parents and children or intimate adults is loving and responsive, but it does mean that the relationship is not abusive and that the parent or partner is responsive to the needs of the other person much of the time. As English psychoanalyst Donald Winnicott argued long ago, a child simply needs a "good enough" mother, not a perfect mother.[131] The "good enough" mother, being a mere human being, is unable to adapt completely and perfectly to her child's every need. Rather than being a detriment, however, her failure to be completely attentive teaches the child to manage the realities of the real world. According to Winnicott, the mother's lack of perfection is a benefit, not a flaw.[132] In this way, a "positive" relationship between a parent and a child simply means that the parent must be reasonably attentive to the needs of the child.

Turning to adult relationships, there are several aspects of a positive relationship. Psychologists believe that self-disclosure, for example, is the building block of intimacy, with each disclosure further connecting the two individuals, to the extent that disclosure is met with validation, understanding, and care.[133] Emotional disclosures are particularly salient in developing intimacy.[134] Intimacy is built upon the idea of "minding" the relationship—the idea that individuals engage in a mutual and ongoing process of acting, thinking, and feeling for each other.[135] There are five parts to minding: (1) behavior aimed at knowing the other better, such as self-disclosure and active listening; (2) attributing the other's behavior in a way that understands that person to be caring, loving, and thoughtful; (3) accepting and respecting what is learned in the self-disclosure process; (4) engaging in reciprocal behavior, thoughts, and feelings; and (5) continually engaging in the first four behaviors.[136]

Positive relationships are not always warm and fuzzy. Instead, a positive relationship is one that handles conflict well. Couples with positive relationships tend to defuse conflict by accommodating each other, meaning that they do not threaten to leave the other person or simply neglect the problem but instead try to solve the problem by either talking it through or waiting for a good moment to do so. This shift to putting the relationship first, instead of indulging in a desire to fight, is called a "transformation of motivation."[137] This accommodation, however, must be mutual, with each party considering the needs of the other and the relationship.

Being able to handle conflict is essential because it is inevitable. A widespread human experience is that individuals experience love, inevitably transgress against those they love, feel guilt about the transgression, and then seek to repair the damage.[138] Individuals experience this cycle repeatedly throughout their lifetimes, with transgressions ranging from the minor, such as parents raising their voices to their children, to the more egregious, such as an individual undermining a marriage. In healthy parent-child and adult relationships, a person is able to acknowledge the transgression and then seeks to repair the damage.

This cycle of intimacy, and particularly the drive to repair relationships, is a widely shared human experience, reflected throughout Western culture. (The focus here is on Western culture because it is the foundation for the American legal system, but the reparative drive is also present in other cultures.[139] The veneration of repair—albeit in different forms and with different terms—is found in nearly all major world religions, for example.[140]) Classical literature gives us both the compulsion of Antigone to honor her brother with a proper burial, and thus repair the damage done to him by Creon, and Psyche's efforts to amend her betrayal of Eros. Shakespeare's work is permeated with themes of rupture and repair, with *King Lear* as a stark but by no means solitary example. The theme of cyclical emotions and the importance of repair also echoes throughout popular culture. Think of almost any romantic comedy (or buddy movie, for that matter): after the meet-cute, the pair inevitably finds conflict, which is then resolved with a reconciliation. Indeed, like synchronicity, once perceived, examples of the drive to repair abound, and scholars across a range of disciplines have studied the phenomenon.[141]

The reparative drive does not always reign supreme, however, nor is it inevitable or uncomplicated. As any casual student of human nature and history can attest, the reparative drive is often mediated by other, more destructive impulses. Some studies show, for example, that the immediate reaction to a transgression in an intimate relationship is often to seek retaliation.[142] Sustained rupture, as much as repair, is a possibility in familial relationships, and it, too, echoes throughout culture. As Tolstoy's *Anna Karenina* makes clear, not all stories end happily, and the protagonist may end up on the tracks instead of at the altar. But one need not take the Pollyanna-ish position that humans are innately good and that the reparative drive always prevails to recognize that after an expression of anger or a transgression, humans do often seek to repair the damage inflicted.

In sum, a positive relationship means the parties are mindful of each other and the relationship, and even after inevitable conflict, they seek to repair the damage to the relationship. It is thus not enough that a relationship is strong and stable—indeed, many child and adult victims are strongly attached to their abusers—the relationship must also be positive.

CONTEXT: WHAT MATTERS FOR RELATIONSHIPS

If strong, stable, positive relationships are closely correlated with individual and societal well-being, the next question is what influences relationships. Looking just at the family, there is an entire body of literature typically referred to as "family-systems theory." The idea is that to understand any one person within the family, it is necessary to understand the family system and its dynamics, because each member influences the other members. In a family-systems approach, when a psychologist works with one family member, say a child, the psychologist considers the behavior of the child—positive and negative—not as an individual phenomenon but rather as the result of interactions among all family members.[143] Mental-health professionals will sometimes use genograms to understand the family context. Far more complex and nuanced than a family tree, a genogram can include emotional and social relationships, disorders that run in the family such as alcoholism and depression, and causes of death such as suicide or accidental death. Understanding the larger family context is essential for understanding the person nominally in treatment.

Moving beyond family members, there are significant external influences on relationships, including culture, social networks, religion, and the physical structure of a community. To appreciate the power of context, consider just one of these influences: the physical context for family life and the effect of this on the quality of relationships.

As described above regarding the importance of social capital, families need support from others, and for many people, this support comes from strong local ties, developed over time by reciprocity and trust. These relationships provide critical caregiving support, especially in communities with fewer resources, and give a sense of belonging, which in turn promotes personal health, happiness, and self-esteem.[144]

A neighborhood's design can greatly affect the development of social networks. An essential component is physical proximity. A classic study of the Dyckman Houses, a public-housing project in Manhattan intended for middle-income families, showed that even though individuals tend to befriend people who are similar to them in terms of race, age, and sex, physical proximity is a separate factor that strongly influences friendships.[145] When the residents identified their "best" friends, 88 percent of these friends were living in the same building, nearly 50 percent on the very same floor.[146] When friendships cut across age and race lines, the friendships were typically between residents on the same floor.[147]

Beyond proximity, certain design elements in a neighborhood make a tremendous difference. Residents are less likely to develop ties in an overly crowded or noisy area, for example.[148] By contrast, when properties are laid out in a way that requires residents to share common paths, they are more likely to develop ties based on the frequent, informal contact.[149] Similarly, for people to be drawn to common areas where they will have these frequent, face-to-face, informal contacts, the common area must be visually appealing. The simple addition of trees and grass has been shown to encourage the use of common areas and increase the development of social ties. One study comparing two housing centers in inner-city Chicago that had nearly identical populations, architecture, and economics found that in the development with greener common areas, residents reported more neighborhood ties, more social activities, and a greater sense of safety and adjustment.[150]

Although the conventional wisdom is that vegetation provides cover for criminal activity, human environmental researchers Frances Kuo and William Sullivan discovered in an extensive study of ninety-eight Chicago public-housing units that there was an inverse relationship between reported crime and vegetation levels surrounding building structures. This relationship held even after Kuo and Sullivan controlled for the number of apartments in the dwellings, the vacancy rate, and building height.[151] The researchers speculated that because more vegetation led to increased use of common areas, the presence of additional people raised the level of informal surveillance.[152] This creates a virtuous cycle because when people feel safe, they are more likely to spend time in common areas, increasing ties with one another, which then encourages the residents to spend even more time in the common area, benefitting the residents and lowering the localized crime rate.

The design of single-family homes also affects the creation and maintenance of social ties. When developers add front porches, for example, these facilitate daily interactions with neighbors and passersby, encouraging residents to come together and form stronger communities.[153] A study of eight neighborhoods in Portland, Oregon, found that residents in neighborhoods with continuous sidewalks and front porches had greater interaction, reciprocity, and trust than neighborhoods without these features.[154] The researchers believed that these physical features created "soft edges" where neighbors could interact with one another.[155]

These social interactions influence family relationships. Return again to the idea of social capital. When neighbors interact with one another, they are more likely to develop social capital—they can share information, establish reciprocity, build trust, and give one another a sense of belonging. This social capital makes a parent's job easier, because a parent who has social support is better able to attend to the needs of a child—in other words, the parent is better able to establish a strong, stable, positive relationship with the child.

Similarly, as many working parents can attest, their happiness and their family's well-being are directly tied to the size of the triangle created by home, workplace, and the child's school or day-care center. The bigger the triangle, the less time there is for family life.[156] Additionally, how a parent travels the sides of this triangle has an enormous impact on happiness and well-being. If a parent commutes by car along congested streets, rather than on a quiet bus or train or perhaps even a bike or walking route, this will affect the parent's daily experience and, by extension, the ability to parent well (or well enough). How does the parent feel when he or she walks in the door? Harried? Exhausted? Frustrated? Or tired from a day's work but somewhat rejuvenated from the easy walk home from work, with a quick stop off at the after-school program, knowing that the child spent the afternoon engaging in physical play with classmates at a local playground?

In short, context matters. Families do not thrive on their own. Instead, individual relationships are embedded within a social context, and this context can have a tremendous influence on the nature of the relationship.

CONCLUSION

Modern psychologists and neuroscientists may be proving as a scientific matter that strong, stable, positive relationships are essential to well-being, but this is hardly a new insight. Aristotle argued that meaningful relationships should be the focus of life.[157] He spoke in terms of eudaimonia—meaning happiness or flourishing—which he contrasted to hedonism, or maximizing pleasure and minimizing pain.[158] For Aristotle, the pursuit of pleasure was for "ordinary or vulgar people."[159] He was also dismissive of the pursuit of honor, because it is "too superficial" and "seems to depend more upon the people who pay it than upon the person to whom it is paid."[160] By contrast, Aristotle named eudaimonia as the ultimate goal of life.[161] In Aristotle's conception of eudaimonia, relationships are essential. He believed that through our relationships with others, we are able to see what is virtuous and pursue a virtuous life.[162] He often spoke in terms of "friendship"—for him, this term included parents and children, romantic relationships, and spouses—[163] and believed that friendship is "indispensable to life," because "nobody would choose to live without friends."[164]

We can understand this as a fundamental "need to belong."[165] This motivation drives people to develop and maintain significant, ongoing relationships with a small number of people and also to resist the end of these relationships.[166] These relationships may be with friends, colleagues, and fellow community members, but for many people and particularly for children, the place to find these relationships is in the family. The problem, however, is that families increasingly are unable to provide strong, stable, positive relationships, as the next chapter describes.

2

Families in Transition and Families in Crisis

⌒﹏﹏﹏﹏﹏﹏﹏﹏﹏﹏﹏﹏﹏﹏﹏﹏﹏﹏﹏﹏﹏﹏﹏﹏﹏﹏﹏﹏﹏﹏﹏﹏﹏

IF FAMILIES ARE where we typically find our most influential relationships, how are families doing? Are parents providing the strong, stable, positive relationships that children need for healthy development? Are adults engaging in the satisfying relationships that are correlated with health and well-being? The answer is mixed. As chapter 1 showed, families can cultivate human flourishing, or they can be the source of much harm. Too many families today are struggling with numerous challenges—from poverty and social isolation, to crushing commutes and work schedules that leave little time for family interaction. These circumstances make it difficult to provide the relationships that encourage flourishing.

The challenges facing families are entwined with another reality of American family life: the traditional model of two, opposite-sex, married parents raising their biological or adopted children is undergoing fundamental changes, particularly in some communities. Whether this transformation makes it harder for families to provide the relationships children need to flourish, however, is a complex question, raising difficult issues of causation and social values. Some of the changes this chapter describes, particularly the increasing number of same-sex parents, do not affect family functioning. Others transformations in the family, however, particularly the rise in single-parent and cohabiting families, are more worthy of concern given the strong correlation between child outcomes and family structure.

Without idealizing the past, and remembering that the traditional family can present its own problems, this chapter first explores the transformation of American families. The goal is to determine which changes undermine the ability of families to provide the relationships crucial to flourishing and which transformations may be either neutral or positive. The chapter then describes the specific challenges that make it harder for families to provide the strong, stable, positive relationships that individuals, especially children, need to flourish.

FAMILIES IN TRANSITION

A great deal of activity typically associated with "the family," particularly long-term coupling and raising children, now occurs outside of marriage. The traditional family—married, opposite-sex parents raising biological or adopted children together—accounts for only 20 percent of all households in the United States,[1] as compared with 44 percent of all households in 1960.[2] This decline is explained by a number of related changes in family behavior. Fewer couples marry, more couples divorce, cohabitation is widespread, large numbers of children are born outside marriage, and same-sex couples are raising children in increasing numbers.

A sea change in family form

Fewer adults are getting married, especially in some socioeconomic groups. In 1960, the national marriage rate was 72 percent. In 2010, it was down to 51 percent.[3] (The marriage rate is the number of adults older than eighteen who are currently married.) In the past, marriage rates tended not to differ depending on socioeconomic status—marriage rates were relatively high across all income groups—but that has changed.[4] In 2010, the marriage rate for individuals with at least a college degree was 64 percent, but for those with a high school diploma or less, the marriage rate was only 47 percent.[5] Marriage rates also differ by race. The marriage rate for non-Latino whites has declined from 74 percent in 1960 to 55 percent in 2010; but the decline for African Americans is even more steep, from 61 percent in 1960 to 31 percent.[6] The marriage rate for Latinos is in between, at 48 percent (down from 72 percent in 1960).[7] In light of the strong correlation between income and marriage and between income and race, it is not surprising that African Americans as a group have a lower marriage rate. But once income is separated out, the marriage rate for African Americans looks quite different. Among African Americans earning less than $12,000 a year, for example, only 22 percent are married,[8] but among African Americans earning more than $70,000 a year, 59 percent are married.[9]

As marriage rates have declined, cohabitation rates have risen. In 1960, approximately 439,000 unmarried couples lived together, as compared with more than 7.5 million today.[10] For many couples, cohabitation is simply a change in the pathway to marriage. Instead of dating and then getting married, couples date, move in together, and then get married.[11] Couples with higher levels of education are more likely to follow this pathway, marrying not long after living together.[12] For other couples—particularly low-income African Americans and Latinos—cohabitation does not lead to marriage.[13] It is an end unto itself. These cohabiting relationships are relatively brief, with more than half ending within five years.[14]

Given the trends in marriage and cohabitation, it is unsurprising that children increasingly are born to unmarried parents. In 1960, approximately 5 percent of all children were born to unmarried parents (what demographers call the "nonmarital birth rate"), and in 1980, 18 percent of children were born to unmarried parents.[15] In 2010, 41 percent of all children were born to unmarried parents.[16] In some communities, the rate of nonmarital births is even higher: Nearly 72 percent of all African American children and 53 percent of Latino children were born to unmarried parents in 2010.[17]

One way to understand the difference between marital and nonmarital families is that there are two different paths to family life. Broadly speaking, middle- and upper-income individuals finish high school and often college, begin a career, find a partner, get married, and then have a child. By contrast, lower-income individuals typically get involved with another person and have a child together. Rather than a commitment preceding the child, the child precedes the commitment. Unsurprisingly, this latter route means a less stable home for the child, because the relationship between the unmarried adults is less likely to last.

But this is not to say that marriages always endure. It is remarkably difficult to obtain reliable statistics on divorce, because, unlike marriage, states vary in their reporting of statistical data to the National Center for Health Statistics, with six states, including California, not reporting divorce data at all.[18] Further, divorce statistics often use different measures, leading to different divorce rates.[19] We do know, however, that the divorce rate varies significantly depending on socioeconomic factors and age at marriage. The divorce rate is lowest, for example, among couples with at least a college degree[20] and who marry after age 25.[21] Additionally, it is clear that the divorce rate peaked in 1979 and has been declining ever since, although it is still higher than it was in 1960.[22]

Putting these trends together, it is unsurprising that single-parent homes are increasingly common, especially in some communities. When a child is born to unmarried parents, the child is likely born into a single-parent household or will soon live in one. Only 50 percent of unmarried parents are living together at the time of the birth.[23] And even if the parents are cohabiting when the child is born, that relationship is likely to end relatively soon. Thus, 27 percent of the children in the United States live in homes with only one parent.[24] This number is up sharply from 1965, when only 10 percent of all children lived with a single parent.[25] Single-parent homes are strongly correlated with income and race. African Americans are only

13 percent of the overall population but nearly 24 percent of all single parents.[26] Latinos account for 17 percent of the population but 19 percent of the single parents.[27] Whites are 63 percent of the population but 53 percent of the single parents.[28] And Asians are 5 percent of the total population but only 3 percent of the single-parent population.[29] Similarly, single-mother homes tend to be low-income, with approximately 27 percent of single-mother families living below the poverty line[30] and 68 percent living below 200 percent of the poverty line.[31]

Children do not necessarily spend their entire childhoods in single-parent homes. Rather, families are increasingly fluid. Sociologist Andrew Cherlin calls this the "marriage-go-round," where couples have a child, sometimes within a marriage and sometimes not, split up, then the mother finds a new partner, has another child with this new partner, then that relationship ends, and so on.[32] The technical term for this is "multipartner fertility," but the marriage-go-round is a more evocative image, if not completely accurate, because many couples do not actually marry. One of Cherlin's most telling statistics is that regardless of whether their parents are married or cohabiting, 40 percent of children in the United States will experience a family breakup by the time they are fifteen years old.[33] As Cherlin describes, almost half of the children who see their parents break up are living with a new adult within three years.[34] And one in twelve children experience three or more partners in their mothers' lives by age fifteen.[35] Researchers refer to such families as "complex families" rather than single-parent families, because children are often living with two adults, but both adults are not the parents to all the children in the home.

This fluidity—or complexity—is found in both married and unmarried families, but it is more common in unmarried families. Within the first three years of life, for example, only 12 percent of children with married parents experience their parents' separation, as compared with 40 percent of children with cohabiting parents.[36] This translates into a greater chance that the child will live with a single parent: 78 percent of children born to cohabiting parents will spend at least part of their childhood in a single-parent family.[37] The rate is lower, although still significant (35 percent), for children born to married parents.[38]

Another way the landscape has changed for families is the increasing recognition of relationships between adults of the same sex. There is no reason to think that more people are gay, lesbian, or bisexual today than in the past, but it is now more acceptable in many, although by no means all, communities for same-sex couples to be public about their relationships. There is also greater legal recognition of these relationships, with a growing number of states allowing same-sex couples either to marry or to form civil unions or domestic partnerships[39] and the federal government recognizing same-sex marriages under federal law.[40]

Increasingly, same-sex couples are raising children in significant numbers. A report from the Census Bureau found 115,000 same-sex-couple households with children, although this may be a significant undercount.[41] People of color in same-sex relationships are more likely to raise children than white people in same-sex relationships. For example, 16 percent of whites in same-sex couples are raising children, as compared with 40 percent of African Americans, 28 percent of Latinos, and 24 percent of Native Americans/Alaska Natives.[42]

A final change to families today is that children increasingly are conceived through donated sperm and eggs, sometimes with the help of a gestational surrogate.[43] When choosing to create a family through assisted reproductive technology, couples often want the child to be genetically related to at least one parent and any potential siblings.[44] Frequently, couples also attempt to replicate the genetic makeup of the non-biological parent by selecting a donor based on characteristics such as hair color, eye color, personality, education, and even SAT scores.[45] Similarly, a gay couple may use eggs from the same donor to fertilize with each man's sperm so that their children have a biological connection.[46] A lesbian couple may use one woman's egg that is then fertilized and implanted in the other woman's uterus.[47]

Donor-conceived families are increasingly open about the process. Parents are more likely than in the past to tell their children that they are donor-conceived, and the Internet has made it easier to track down donors and other genetic relatives.[48] These searches sometimes result in "kin networks," with donor-conceived children maintaining varying degrees of contact with other children conceived with the same genetic material and with the donors themselves.[49] These new relationships develop outside of the law's traditional definition of family and can be quite challenging to navigate.[50]

Cause for concern?

These transitions are fascinating on many levels, but the question for this book is whether the changes make it harder for families to provide the strong, stable, positive relationships children need to flourish. The first step is to look at outcomes for children living in different family structures.

Children of single or cohabiting parents. There is overwhelming evidence that children raised by single or cohabiting parents have worse outcomes than children raised by married, biological parents. Sociologist Sara McLanahan has been studying single-parent homes for more than three decades and has found that when comparing children growing up in these homes with children growing up with two married parents, there are notably different outcomes, even after controlling for income, parental education, and similar factors. Children raised in single-parent homes score lower on measures of academic achievement[51] and measures of academic self-concept, a scale that gauges a student's self-assessment of academic performance and potential.[52] They do not stay in school as long,[53] are more likely to show negative behaviors such as aggressiveness,[54] are more likely to use illegal substances and have contact with the police,[55] are more likely to have sex at an early age and begin bearing children at an early age,[56] have worse physical and mental-health outcomes as adults,[57] and earn less in the labor market as adults.[58] Numerous researchers have made similar findings.[59] Finally, children living in homes with a single parent and a live-in partner had the highest levels of child abuse and neglect, experiencing ten times more abuse and eight times more neglect than children of married parents.[60]

Even in families where the children are raised by two cohabiting, biological parents rather than two married, biological parents, the differences still persist. Data from forty thousand nationally representative households reveal that the children living with cohabiting parents have worse outcomes than the children living with married parents, as measured by a child's performance in school and behavioral problems.[61] In other words, the difference in outcomes is between children living with married, biological parents on the one hand and other family structures on the other.[62]

In the typical family, it does not seem to help when a single mother marries or cohabits with a man who is not the father of the child. In these cohabiting or married stepparent households, the outcomes for children remain roughly the same as for children with single parents or children living with cohabiting, biological parents.[63] And in some instances, the outcomes are even worse. For example, one study found that girls growing up in a stepparent family had a 16-percent chance of becoming teen parents as compared with only a 6-percent chance for girls growing up with two, married parents and an 11-percent chance for girls growing up in a single-mother, divorced home.[64]

Children of divorced parents. Turning to children of divorced parents, the evidence is mixed about the long-term impact of divorce on children. Not all parents get along well, and sometimes ending a marriage is the right decision for any number of reasons. Studies have shown, for example, that among children living in a household with a high-conflict marriage, those whose parents stay together have more behavioral problems than those whose parents end such marriages.[65] Separating from a conflicted and stressful two-parent household to a more peaceful divorced, single-parent household can be advantageous for both children and parents.[66]

In looking at the effects of divorce on children more generally, the picture is complicated. Several factors influence outcomes, including the circumstances of the divorce and the parents' ability to provide children with the relationships they need following the divorce.[67] Mavis Hetherington, a leading divorce researcher, has found, based on a study of more than fourteen hundred families over three decades, that children of divorce tend to have initial adjustment problems but generally improve within two years, and by six years, the vast majority are functioning in the normal range.[68] She did find that these children, as compared with children from nondivorced families, are more likely to face issues such as teen pregnancy, truancy, and substance abuse,[69] but these effects are often mediated by high-quality parenting.[70]

One reason for the popular belief that divorce is always bad for children is that policymakers have often relied on the work of one researcher, Judith Wallerstein, who followed a group of children from divorced families through the 1980s and 1990s into their adulthood. Among other negative findings, Wallerstein reported that these children often had great difficulty with adult relationships because they lacked a model template for a successful partnership.[71] Another leading divorce researcher, Paul Amato, has tried to reconcile Wallerstein's work with her critics, arguing that her data were overstated because of the lack of a comparison group but that her general finding is sound—that children of divorce are at a higher risk for emotional problems and problems with their own marriages down the road.[72] Hetherington's work is consistent with this view, finding children at greater risk for behavioral issues, particularly if they do not have the support of a parent following the divorce.

Setting aside the question of whether a "normal" divorce negatively affects children, it is clear that there are problems for children when the divorce is deeply acrimonious. High-conflict divorces—which are characterized by ongoing legal battles, an inability of the parents to coordinate childrearing practices after the divorce, hostile family environments, and children witnessing overt verbal and physical aggression[73]—put children at a greater risk for developing psychological and behavioral problems.[74] When comparing children who experienced high-conflict divorce with children whose parents minimized conflict during divorce, researchers have found that the former had worse outcomes.[75] The children of high-conflict divorce struggled with painful feelings of anger, grief, and distress, and were uncertain and self-conscious about their own intimate relationships.[76] They also had lower self-esteem and lower life satisfaction[77] and were more likely to experience behavioral and discipline problems in school.[78]

Psychologists have elaborated a theory—emotional security theory—for the idea that children seek a sense of security within the family and that their response to marital conflict comes from a desire to maintain this security. When faced with destructive marital conflict, children deploy a number of behavioral tactics to try to end the conflict and regain a sense of emotional security within the family. These tactics—such as distracting the parents by beginning a conflict with a sibling, withdrawing emotionally, and acting out—may be effective in the short term, which reinforces the importance of these tactics to the child, but they create much larger problems in the long term. Destructive marital conflict also has cognitive implications, with children developing negative perceptions and internal representations about family relationships. Together, these behavioral, emotional, and cognitive responses to high-conflict divorces lead to problems with child development, including relationships with peers and performance in school.[79]

The other main problem associated with divorce is that it often means that a child will lose contact with one parent—almost always the father. Studies suggest that fathers with joint custody tend to see their children more often,[80] but many divorced fathers have little or no regular contact with their children. Fewer than one in three fathers communicate weekly with their children after a divorce, and of those who do communicate regularly, only 40 percent are actively involved in their children's lives and take on a parenting role by setting limits and so on.[81] This means that only a small minority of fathers following a divorce continue as active parental figures.

There are several possible causes for the existence of this postdivorce paternal disengagement. One possibility is that the brief and often unsatisfying nature of the contact following the divorce can lead fathers to take the paradoxical step of avoiding the contact altogether.[82] This is particularly true for fathers who were heavily involved in their children's lives before the divorce. The dramatic change in parental involvement can be so painful that the fathers abandon any sort of relationship.[83] Additionally, because fathers are not violating a social norm by disengaging—as opposed to the social norm that exists against withdrawing financial support—there is little social pressure on fathers to remain engaged with their children.[84]

Children of same-sex parents. Unlike children raised by cohabiting and single parents, there is little reason to be concerned about children raised by same-sex couples. Studies have overwhelmingly found that these children have no worse outcomes than children raised by two opposite-sex parents. A comprehensive review of twenty-one studies of the effect of parent sexual orientation on child development reported no significant differences between children of same-sex parents and those of opposite-sex parents on measures of self-esteem, anxiety, depression, behavioral problems, performance in social settings, use of psychological counseling, hyperactivity, unsociability, and so on.[85] A study of adolescents found that being raised by same-sex parents had no bearing on adolescent self-esteem, depressive symptoms, anxiety, academic achievement, trouble in school, feelings of connectedness, care from adults and peers, neighborhood integration, or parental warmth.[86] And one longitudinal study found that children with lesbian parents had significantly higher levels of academic and social performance than children of heterosexual parents.[87]

Questions of causation

As the above description shows, there is ample evidence that, with the exception of families headed by same-sex couples, children raised by two married, biological parents have better outcomes than children raised in other family structures. But this does not tell us the *cause* of the better outcomes. Is it the family structure—married versus other forms—or factors that tend to accompany family structure, such as income level, family stability, parental resources, age of parents, and level of education? Unmarried parents in the United States are likely to be young, have low incomes, and have limited education.[88] So, is the problem having a *single* parent or having a *low-income, young, less educated* parent?

The answer matters because it tells us where the state should be focusing its efforts: increasing the marriage rate, discouraging divorce, fighting poverty, instituting parenting programs, or reducing teen pregnancies, and so on. If, for example, it is poverty and not single-parenthood that causes the worse outcomes for children, then policymakers should focus their efforts on ameliorating poverty, not trying to reduce the number of single-parent homes. By contrast, if single-parenthood causes worse outcomes regardless of income level, then policymakers should address family structure. Of course, the answer is never straightforward, and, as shown below, it is a mix of factors, but trying to tease apart the causes of poor outcomes for children is essential to developing effective policies.

Beginning with divorce, the short-term negative outcomes are partly explained by the experiences that often follow a divorce, including a loss of income that precipitates multiple moves (sometimes to a poorer neighborhood with worse schools), parental depression, lack of social supports, less time under the supervision of adults and more time in the company of peers, "parentification" (where the parent relies on a child for emotional support or help with basic caretaking and household tasks), and, crucially, loss of contact with a noncustodial parent.[89] The primary factor mediating the effect of divorce, especially for younger children, is the quality of parenting, notably whether the parent is responsive, warm, communicative, and authoritative.[90] In other words, if both parents continue to provide strong, stable, positive relationships with the child, this helps mediate some of the largely unavoidable consequences of divorce, such as a loss of the economies of scale in running a household.

A more difficult, and politically contentious, causation issue concerns single and cohabiting parents. Determining whether family form is part of the cause of the worse outcomes is complicated, because although there are some never-married college graduates with considerable economic and social resources who are raising children alone, there are far fewer of these families and almost no research tracking the outcomes of their children.[91] This means the non-marriage-based families that researchers study are qualitatively different from the marriage-based families. One way to think about the data is to remember that family form now turns largely on socioeconomic factors. Educated, relatively well-off adults are far more likely to get married, stay married, and have children within marriage than adults with lower levels of education and income.[92] By contrast, unmarried parents are likely to be young, have low income, and have limited education. This overlap between income, parental education, and family form makes it more difficult to study the cause and effect of family form alone.

To put this in the language of scientific research, researchers are struggling with the issue of selection bias, which means the real-world dynamics that affect who is in each group being studied. Choosing study participants using a randomized method ("random selection") and then assigning study participants to different study conditions at random ("random assignment") are foundational building blocks of scientific study. When testing the effect of exercise on health, for example, researchers will try to draw a random selection of study participants and then will assign those participants at random either to the group that is supposed to exercise or to the group that is not. Researchers make these assignments without considering the separate characteristics of the participants. If the researchers did not abide by the principle of random selection and instead studied only housebound octogenarians, then the results of the study might not be relevant to the general population. Similarly, if the researchers did not abide by the principle of random assignment and instead put all the relatively healthy people in the group assigned to exercise, then the findings of the study would not tell us much about the impact of exercise on overall health for the general population. Finally, if researchers let the study participants choose whether they wanted to be in the exercising or the nonexercising group, the healthier, already-exercising participants likely would choose to continue exercising, and the couch potatoes would stay on the couch. This selection bias would mean that the results of the study would tell the researchers only about the effect of exercise on already-healthy people.

In studies of family structure, researchers can follow the principle of random selection, but it is not possible to honor the principle of random assignment. For practical and ethical reasons, researchers cannot simply assign a family to a particular family structure—married, cohabiting, and single parents. Moreover, selection bias affects who is in each group. People with different characteristics likely are drawn into different family structures. Poverty, for example, might influence a woman's ability to get married because there might be few good marriage prospects in her social circle. But this means that the unmarried family is also low-income.

As a result of this overlap between family form and other characteristics that can have an independent influence on child outcomes, it is difficult to isolate family form as a causal factor. Researchers try to do so by comparing, for example, low-income single parents and low-income married parents. Consider the study of the forty thousand families, where the researchers compared outcomes for children living with two married, biological parents and children living with two cohabiting, biological parents and found worse outcomes for the latter. Once the researchers controlled for poverty and parental resources, the differences between the groups were far less pronounced, explaining some, although not all, of the negative outcomes.[93] This kind of analysis helps tease apart the multiple factors that affect outcomes. It also suggests that family structure is at least a contributing factor to the worse outcomes.[94]

The problem persists, however, because there may be other, nonobservable characteristics that also affect both family structure and outcomes. A person with strong interpersonal skills might choose to get married and stay married, and this kind of person might also be a more effective parent. This separate characteristic would drive the family structure and the child outcome, but it is very difficult for an outside researcher to identify this characteristic. Researchers try to account for this selection bias in a number of different ways, but there is no easy way around the problem.[95]

Sara McLanahan and social worker and economist Irwin Garfinkel are helping to lead a team of researchers who are trying to answer the causal questions surrounding family structure and child outcomes. The ongoing Fragile Families and Child Well-Being Study is following nearly five thousand children born between 1998 and 2000 to married and unmarried parents, and the data are generating important insights.[96] In determining the effect of family structure on children, however, the Fragile Families Study faces the same problem as other researchers: the single and cohabiting parents in the study are different in several important respects from the married parents. As compared with the married parents, the unmarried[97] parents at the time of the birth are predominantly African American and Latino, are younger, are more likely to have children by multiple partners, lack high school diplomas at twice the rate of the married parents, have higher rates of depression, show higher rates of drug use (among the unmarried fathers but not the unmarried mothers), have much higher rates of incarceration (among the unmarried fathers), and generate lower earnings.[98] As would be expected given some of these differences between the married and unmarried parents, thus far, the children of the unmarried parents in the Fragile Families Study are showing worse outcomes than the children of the married parents, as measured by tests of cognition, behavior, physical health, and mental health.[99]

In an attempt to disaggregate the various factors that might influence child outcomes, the researchers are tracking parental income, parental time, the mental health of the parents, the relationship between the parents, the quality of the parenting, and the involvement of the fathers. The researchers are also looking at the stability of the family unit—whether the family structure stays constant over time—which might be its own separate variable affecting outcomes. Finally, researchers are trying to account for selection bias.[100] Given the importance of the issue and the policy questions that hang in the balance, it is worth exploring these possible causal factors in detail, showing how various factors can affect child outcomes.[101]

Parental income. Single mothers typically earn low wages and do not receive child support. Recall that 27 percent of single-mother households live in poverty and 68 percent have incomes below 200 percent of the poverty threshold. Single fathers, a group that is relatively small but increasing, have lower levels of poverty, at 13 percent,[102] although this is still above the national poverty rate for families, which is 10 percent.[103] Cohabiting families have two adults to make money, but they typically have lower incomes than married parents and are less likely to share that income with each other than are married families.

A lower income can affect child outcomes in a variety of ways. Looking at educational outcomes, for example, a lack of financial resources makes it difficult for parents to invest in children's cognitive development through after-school programs, summer camps, and so on—experiences that have become routine for children from more economically stable families.[104] In the 1970s, parent spending on enrichment activities was already pronounced, with families in the top quintile of income spending $2,700 more per year (adjusted for inflation) than families in the bottom quintile. But by 2006, the gap had almost tripled to $7,500.[105] The "summer slide"—the well-documented loss in academic skills during summer vacation—is particularly pronounced for low-income children, because they typically do not spend their summers engaged in non-school-based, intellectually stimulating activities.[106]

Parental income also affects the quality of the schools that children attend, which in turn can affect educational outcomes. Given local attendance rules, which typically require children to attend a school within the district, children from low-income families tend to be concentrated in the same schools or in the same school district. In the 2010–2011 school year, 20 percent of students nationwide attended schools where at least 75 percent of the students were eligible for free or reduced-cost lunch.[107]

And the differences between schools can be staggering. The majority of funding for schools comes from state and local governments, with local governments providing funds largely from property taxes. In some states, as much as 65 percent of funds come from local property taxes.[108] This means that families who can afford to live in wealthier districts enjoy the benefits of well-funded schools. Take two suburban schools in the Chicago area, for example, both serving largely white populations. Taft Elementary School is in Lockport, a suburb thirty miles southwest of Chicago with a population of twenty thousand people. Residents of the town enjoy above-median incomes, but it is far from wealthy. About an hour's drive away is Rondout Elementary School, in Lake Forest, a wealthy northern suburb of Chicago. A student at Taft has no access to arts, language, or technology classes, while a student at Rondout can take Spanish in every grade, will likely receive a laptop computer, and has access to extensive art, band, drama, and dance offerings.[109] Taft spends a total of $9,833 per student each year, while Rondout spends more than $25,189.[110] The average class size at Taft is twenty-six students, compared with only sixteen at Rondout.[111] Families unable to buy or rent a home in a well-funded school district are left with few good educational options.

Parental income is associated with other kinds of related investments in children. Sociologist Annette Lareau has explored precisely how the advantage of being raised by economically stable parents is passed on to their children. She conducted an in-depth study of the parenting styles of twelve families—middle-class, working-class, and low-income.[112] She found that the middle-class parents engaged in what she called "concerted cultivation," focusing intensively on a child's development through music lessons, athletic teams, cultural outings, and so on. Through these activities, the parents passed on skills the children needed to succeed both in school and later in the workplace. For example, children were taught to relate to adults as equals, to look adults in the eye when speaking, and to perform well in a variety of settings.[113] By contrast, the working-class and poor parents in the study took a more laissez-faire approach to child development, allowing their children ample time to play with other children and entertain themselves, in what Lareau calls the "accomplishment of natural growth" attitude toward parenting.[114]

Lareau found that both parenting styles were effective in establishing a close bond between parents and children and that the working-class and poor children were "slower-paced, less-pressured, and less-structured than their middle- and upper-middle class counterparts."[115] But the children of middle-class parents did better in school and were being prepared for the workplace, in large part, she argues, because of the training they received from their parents.[116]

Another study showed the difference in language acquisition depending on parental income. Following forty-two families of varying income levels for two and a half years, researchers extrapolated that the children of professional parents in the study heard approximately 30 million words spoken to them by the time the children reached age three.[117] The children of very low-income parents (defined as those receiving welfare) heard approximately 10 million words.[118] Further, the content of the words differed depending on income level. The children of the professional parents heard many more encouragements than discouragements, at a ratio of more than six to one.[119] By contrast, the children of the low-income parents heard more than two discouragements for every one encouragement.[120] Finally, the professional parents spoke to their children about a variety of topics, including abstract concepts, whereas the children of low-income parents heard only basic instructions about what to do in the immediate context.[121]

Given these differences in parental investment and school quality, it is not surprising that children in low-income families have worse educational outcomes.[122] The question is whether lower income explains *all* of the difference between children from married families and children from single and cohabiting families.

Parental time. In addition to lower incomes, single parents typically have less time to spend with their children because they cannot share the burden of caring for a family with another parent. Although cohabiting couples theoretically have more time, when the man in the couple is not the biological parent, he typically invests less time in the child.[123] Imagine, for example, the challenges facing a single mother working two low-paying service jobs, each requiring a long commute. It is exceedingly difficult for this mother to give her child what researchers call "developmental time"—reading to the child, visiting the library, and engaging in other activities that develop social and cognitive skills. Instead of reading to a child after dinner, the single mother must do the dishes and laundry and get the household ready for the next day. In 1975, there was little difference in the amount of developmental time college-educated and non-college-educated parents spent with their children, but this once-nonexistent gap has now grown to nearly fifty minutes a day.[124] This time gap is most pronounced in children's early years, precisely when it is most valuable to their development.[125] Moreover, many low-income families live in communities with few resources, so going to the library is not as easy as it sounds. As explained in chapter 1, interactions between parents and very young children lay the foundation for child development, but children in single-parent and cohabiting homes often have less of this crucial attention.

Parental mental health. Both single and cohabiting mothers have higher rates of depression than married mothers.[126] More generally, having children by more than one partner (multipartner fertility), which is more common in unmarried families, is strongly linked with depression, for both mothers and fathers.[127] Whether multipartner fertility causes depression or depression causes multipartner fertility is unclear,[128] but the effect on children is unmistakable. As described in chapter 1, clinical depression clearly interferes with parenting and, in turn, child development. Paternal depression, for example, is correlated with a lower frequency of father engagement, higher levels of father aggravation and stress, less co-parenting supportiveness, and lower father-mother relationship quality.[129]

Quality of parenting. The quality of parenting, particularly a parent's warmth and responsiveness, is directly related to the development of young children. For older children, parenting quality also matters—parents influence children's safety, nutrition, engagement in school, television use, and so on. Single and cohabiting parents are more likely than married parents to use harsh parenting strategies and are less likely to breastfeed, engage in literacy activities with their children, and have household routines such as a consistent bedtime, all of which are associated with positive health and development outcomes.[130]

Relationship between the parents. The quality of the relationship between the parents has an effect on children. Single and cohabiting parents tend to have more relationship conflict and less cooperation in parenting than married parents. This conflict can be a source of stress for parents, which then affects parenting quality. Additionally, as described above, this conflict can directly affect children, contributing to emotional and behavioral issues.[131]

Another way in which parental conflict directly affects children is that in families where the mother and father live apart, the father's access to the children—and thus his ability to have a relationship with them—turns in large part on his relationship with the mother. Consider the findings of a multiyear, in-depth study of 110 low-income, unmarried fathers in Camden and Philadelphia, conducted by sociologist Kathryn Edin and public-policy scholar Timothy Nelson. Edin and Nelson found that the men they interviewed did not become fathers as the result of a conscious decision to find a suitable partner and raise children together. As the men described it, they would start seeing a woman, and soon after the relationship reached some minimum level of stability, the couple would stop using birth control regularly.[132] The ensuing pregnancies were neither planned nor avoided.[133]

Contrary to stereotype, the men in their study typically greeted the news of impending fatherhood with enthusiasm and looked forward to the birth of the child. And during the pregnancy and the early days of the child's life, the relationship was relatively smooth. But soon after the baby arrived, problems started. The couple did not know each other well. They had not chosen each other after a long search for a compatible mate. And both parents were struggling with the stresses of poverty. Not surprisingly, the relationship between the parents typically unraveled.[134]

What happened after the adult relationship broke down is what matters for children. Once the romantic relationship ended, the fathers' connection to their children was much more tenuous. Part of the problem was that the men were facing their own challenges—substance abuse, criminal behavior, and so on—but another central barrier was the relationship between the mother and the father. When the parents did not get along, the fathers were much less likely to see their children. Additionally, mothers would keep the children away from the fathers to keep the mothers' lives simpler, because by then, a mother was often seeing another man, who would become jealous of the father.[135]

Involvement of the father. The strongest predictor of whether a father will make financial and social investments in his children is whether he lives with them.[136] But children born to unmarried parents often do not live with their father. In the Fragile Families Study, for example, only 35 percent of the unmarried fathers were living with their children at age five.[137] As would be expected, this typically means less contact with fathers. For the children born to unmarried parents who were not living with their fathers, nearly half had not seen their fathers in the previous month.[138]

There are also differences between divorced fathers and unmarried fathers. Following the end of a cohabiting relationship, fathers typically see their children less often and are less involved in the lives of their children than fathers who were married and then divorced.[139] Additionally, never-married fathers are less likely to pay child support than previously married fathers.[140] There are important nuances in these data, however, such as the finding among the Fragile Families participants that, contrary to stereotype, African American fathers who do not live with their children are more likely to be involved with their children than Latino or white fathers; they are also more likely to maintain better co-parenting relationships with the mothers of their children.[141]

* * *

It should be clear from this brief review that numerous related factors influence child outcomes, and a few of these factors are driven by family structure. The time crunch facing single parents, for example, means that a single parent does not have as much time to invest in a child. But many of the factors are simply correlated with family structure, particularly income. No one denies that these factors, separately and together, contribute to poor child outcomes. The question, then, is whether these correlated factors *entirely* explain the different outcomes for children born to married parents and children born into other family structures or whether family structure is an additional causal factor. Again, this matters because it tells us whether the state should try to encourage marriage or some other form of long-term commitment between parents or whether the state should focus solely on other factors, such as those listed above.

Using the Fragile Families data generated thus far, the researchers are concluding that family structure is an independent causal factor. Running different analyses, the researchers have controlled for the observable characteristics that might influence child outcomes. They found that the worse outcomes for children born to the unmarried parents persisted, although were less marked, after controlling for income, parental time, parental mental health, and so on.[142] Looking at the worse behavioral outcomes for children in single-parent homes, for example, only half of the effect could be attributed to higher levels of stress and poorer parenting quality.[143]

The assessment of the two principal investigators, McLanahan and Garfinkel, is that the factors that are associated with nonmarital childbearing—lower income, lower levels of education, and so on—certainly contribute to the poor outcomes for children, but these factors alone cannot fully explain the worse outcomes for the children.[144] They argue that nonmarital childbearing is part of a new approach to family life, in which women have high hopes for finding a reliable partner down the road but do not see the absence of one today as a reason to delay having a child.[145] McLanahan and Garfinkel believe that this attitude toward bearing children—that finding a long-term partner need not precede motherhood—leads to higher levels of relationship instability and multipartner fertility, factors that themselves contribute to the worse outcomes for children. Consider each in turn.

Stability of the family unit. In the Fragile Families Study, by the time the child was five, more than half of the unmarried mothers were living with or dating new partners, 18 percent had two new partners, and 10 percent had three or more new partners.[146] The unmarried fathers had similar levels of new partners. This instability can contribute to negative outcomes for mothers and children. A transition in partners is associated with a decrease in the mother's physical and mental health, especially when there is more than one transition.[147] After switching partners, mothers experience greater stress, are more likely to use harsh parenting strategies, and are less likely to engage in literacy activities with their children.[148] Transitions in partners also mean that a child is less likely to see a biological father. When a mother takes on a new partner, the biological father decreases his involvement with his child, although if she leaves the new partner, the biological father's involvement increases.[149] Additionally, because stepparents tend not to invest as much in their stepchildren, a stepfather is not necessarily making up for the absent biological father.[150]

Multipartner fertility. One of the most significant findings of the Fragile Families Study is that the unmarried parents are much more likely to have children by multiple partners. This family "complexity" is associated with a host of problems, which can contribute to negative outcomes. When a father has a child from a prior relationship, this can be a source of stress for the new relationship, making it more likely that the relationship will end and that co-parenting afterward will be more difficult.[151] Mothers are resentful of the time the fathers spend with children in other households because it takes away from the children in the current households. Compounding the problem, when mothers take on new partners, their families and friends are less willing to help the mothers, especially financially.[152] Further, when a mother has an additional child by the new partner, the existing child is more likely to have behavioral problems, a phenomenon that is associated only with half-siblings, not full siblings.[153]

McLanahan and Garfinkel believe that both of these factors—instability and family complexity—are contributing causal factors to the worse outcomes. Family instability increases stress in the home and makes it harder for both mothers and fathers to invest in their children. Similarly, multipartner fertility means that parents have conflicting loyalties and that it is harder to manage the family. In other words, the fact that the parties are not married at birth—or, more precisely, that the parents are not choosing to have a child together after deciding that they have found long-term partners—contributes to the worse outcomes. The absence of a reliable, long-term partner means that the relationship is less likely to last, more partners are likely to come into the family, and the parents will have a harder time investing in their children.[154] As described in detail above, this is exactly what Edin and Nelson found in their ethnographic study of low-income, unmarried fathers.

In sum, there is growing evidence that family structure affects a family's ability to provide children with strong, stable, positive relationships. This is not to blame families or to understate the contribution of other factors, particularly poverty. Rather, it is simply to show that the instability and complexity of nonmarried families are additional factors that make it harder for parents in these families to provide children with the relationships they need.

FAMILIES IN CRISIS

In addition to the transitions in family form, there are other specific challenges facing American families—including violence, substance abuse, incarceration, and social isolation—that make it harder for parents to provide children, and adults to provide each other, with strong, stable, positive relationships. It is worth detailing several of the most persistent and widespread challenges to give a sense of just how difficult family life today can be.

Violence in the home. In 1995, the federal government commissioned a telephone survey of a nationally representative sample of eight thousand women and eight thousand men.[155] The survey found that 22 percent of women and 8 percent of men had been victims of a physical assault by an intimate partner at some point in their lives.[156] Sexual violence was also relatively common in adult relationships: 8 percent of the women surveyed reported that they had been raped by an intimate partner in their lifetime.[157] As with other categories of violent crimes, the rate of domestic violence is decreasing, but it is still a widespread problem.[158] In 2010, for example, there were approximately 907,000 nonfatal instances of victimization between intimate partners, including rape, sexual assault, robbery, aggravated assault, and simple assault,[159] and 1,095 women were killed by an intimate partner.[160]

Turning to violence against children, in 2011, the child-welfare system (described in greater detail in chapters 3 and 4) documented 676,569 victims of child abuse.[161] Eighteen percent of the cases were physical abuse involving at least a moderate injury.[162] About three-quarters of the cases involved neglect, which is strongly correlated with poverty.[163] Not all of these children end up in foster care, but in 2011, there were 400,540 children in the custody of the state.[164]

Children of color are disproportionately represented in the child-welfare system. The racial breakdown of children in foster care in 2011 was 41 percent white, 27 percent African American, 21 percent Latino, and 2 percent Native American.[165] By contrast, the overall population in the United States is 63 percent white, 13 percent African American, 17 percent Latino, and 1 percent Native American.[166] There is a heated debate about whether this disparity is a result of racial bias or the correlation in the United States between poverty and race,[167] but there is no question that the disparity exists or that the vast majority of children in the system come from low-income families.

Only 9 percent of the documented cases in the child-welfare system involved sexual abuse,[168] but this statistic far undercounts the actual rate of child sexual abuse. The true rate is exceedingly difficult to ascertain with any certainty,[169] but there is considerable evidence that child sexual abuse is endemic, with as many as 31 percent of girls and 16 percent of boys being sexually abused by the age of eighteen.[170] In nearly all the cases, the perpetrator is known to the family,[171] and for 30 percent of the girls who are abused, the perpetrator *is* a family member.[172]

Even when they are not the direct victims of violence, children are often witnesses. A comprehensive national survey sponsored by the U.S. Department of Justice found that one in four children witness family violence during childhood, and one in nine were exposed to family violence in the year preceding the survey; the vast majority of children saw, not just heard, the violence.[173]

Substance abuse. Twelve percent of children live in a house where at least one parent is dependent on or abuses alcohol or drugs,[174] with alcohol by far the most common substance abused.[175] Fathers appear to abuse drugs and alcohol at higher rates than mothers, with approximately 5.4 million children exposed to paternal substance abuse as compared with 3.4 million children exposed to maternal substance abuse.[176] Government reports undercut the stereotype that African Americans are more likely to use illegal drugs than whites. Whites report higher rates of illegal use in their lifetime (53.5 percent) compared with both African Americans (47.7 percent) and Latinos (38.2 percent).[177]

Poverty and unemployment. Fifteen percent of the U.S. population lives below the poverty line,[178] including 16.4 million children, which amounts to 22 percent of all children, or more than one in five children, living in poverty.[179] Insufficient food— what policymakers call "food insecurity," not having enough food to eat on a regular basis to sustain active, healthy living—is widespread, with 15 percent of all households with children experiencing food insecurity in 2011.[180] As of this writing, the

Department of Labor measured unemployment at 7.0 percent.[181] The U-6 unemployment rate—a broader measure used by the Department of Labor that includes frustrated workers who have quit looking for work, along with part-time workers who are unable to obtain full employment—is considerably higher, at 13.2 percent, or more than one in seven adults.[182] In an average month of 2012, there were an estimated 6.2 million children living with an unemployed parent.[183] Poverty typically translates into a family living in a community with few resources, from poor schools to little access to healthy food and safe areas for children to play. To give just one data point, consider that half of the children in the United States do not have access to a park or community center.[184] They live in "play deserts."[185]

A changing economy that disadvantages the middle class. The American workplace is changing. Various forces have contributed to the loss of middle-class jobs, including technology (with data processing now done by computers instead of low-skilled clerical workers), globalization, and the growing manufacturing power of the developing world, most notably India and China.[186] Manufacturing jobs with decent wages are in decline and projected to erode even further.[187] The result is a marketplace that needs workers with analytical skills and higher education on the one hand and workers for low-paying service jobs on the other.[188]

This market polarization has resulted in a strong contraction of the middle class.[189] The job market for an individual with only a high school diploma or less has radically shifted, especially for men. Instead of having relatively stable manufacturing jobs, individuals without college degrees are far more likely to work in the service sector, doing low-skilled work in retail, health care, educational settings, and food service.[190]

At the same time, educational attainment—again, especially for men—has not kept pace with the demand for college-educated workers.[191] The rate of college completion for white men ages twenty-five to thirty-four, for example, has increased from 20 percent in 1970 to 26 percent in 2008,[192] but this lags behind college gains among white women in the same age group. The college-completion rate for these women jumped from 12 percent in 1970 to 34 percent in 2008.[193] The four-year-college graduation rate is even starker for African American men in this age group, at 16 percent in 2008; the graduation rate for African American women was 22 percent in 2008.[194]

This means that an increasing number of men do not have the skills demanded by the marketplace and are left with only low-paying service jobs. It is exceedingly hard for a parent to help support a family on the wages from these kinds of jobs. A checkout cashier at Target earning $8.11 an hour will make $16,224 over the course of the year,[195] a home health aide earning $9.70 an hour will make $20,170 in a year,[196] a fast-food worker earning $8.72 an hour will make $18,130 in a year,[197] and a teacher's assistant typically earns about $23,220 a year.[198]

Overall, earnings for workers without a college education have gone down for the past thirty years, with men experiencing the greatest decline.[199] The lost wages and increasing unemployment experienced by men have caused some to label the most recent economic downturn the "Mancession."[200] Women have not experienced the same job loss, including women with lower levels of educational attainment, partly because of the growth in so-called pink-collar jobs—low-skill, service-based jobs that women have traditionally done, such as home health aides.[201] These changes led urban-studies theorist Richard Florida to characterize men as "the victim[s] of deep structural change in the economy."[202]

Incarceration. The United States is quick to resort to prison as a response to crime. As compared with other developed countries that also have high rates of reported crime, the United States incarcerates a far greater proportion of its population—730 out of every 100,000 people are incarcerated as compared with 152 in England and Wales and 74 in Sweden.[203] This high incarceration rate is not spread evenly among demographic groups. In 2010, for every 100,000 people, 4,347 African American men, 1,775 Latino men, and 678 white men were incarcerated.[204] Despite being approximately 13 percent of the total population and despite their lower rates of illegal drug use (as described above), African Americans account for 32 percent of all drug arrests[205] and 45 percent of those imprisoned for drug crimes[206] because of racial disparities in enforcement, prosecution, and sentencing.[207] One statistic brings the reality of these racial disparities home: every day, nearly one out of every three African American men between the ages of twenty and twenty-nine are in prison, on parole, or on probation.[208]

Women also are sent to prison,[209] and, as with men, women of color experience disproportionate incarceration rates. In 2010, for example, 133 African American women were incarcerated for every 100,000 people, as compared with 47 white women for every 100,000.[210]

This high incarceration rate for men and women means that many parents are in prison: 744,200 fathers and 65,600 mothers to 1.7 million minor children.[211] Twenty-two percent of the children of state inmates and 16 percent of the federal inmates are younger than five.[212] The imprisonment of parents has a disproportionate impact on children of color because of the higher incarceration rates for African Americans and Latinos, with African American children seven and a half times as likely as white children to have at least one parent in prison and Latino children two and a half times as likely.[213]

Teen pregnancy. Teen births have declined significantly—from a high of 644,708 births in 1970[214] to 367,752 births in 2010[215]—but the rate is still higher than most other industrialized countries. And teen births present a major challenge to family life, a challenge that is felt more deeply by families of color, with African American and Latino teens giving birth at more than twice the rate of white teens.[216] Part of the problem is that giving birth as a teenager derails education. Only 50 percent of teenagers who give birth go on to graduate from high school, compared with 90 percent of women who do not give birth as teens.[217] With these low rates of educational attainment, finding employment and making a living become significantly more difficult for teenage parents, and they have considerably lower earnings and economic productivity than women who delay childbearing.[218] Over their first fifteen years of parenthood, teen mothers earn an average of less than $6,500 annually, and their access to a spouse's income is less than $12,000 annually, leading teen mothers to depend on public assistance for a third of those years.[219]

The children of teen mothers also face dismal prospects. Fourteen percent of the girls become teen mothers and 20 percent of the children have chronic health conditions.[220] They are also more likely to be incarcerated, drop out of high school, be placed in foster care, and be unemployed.[221]

Social isolation. Many (although by no means all) of the preceding challenges are strongly associated with income, but moderate- and upper-income families also face numerous challenges. Even setting aside domestic violence, substance abuse, and child sexual abuse—all of which occur across class lines—families with adequate means also struggle to provide their children with strong, stable, positive relationships. Having put off childbearing to pursue careers, many older couples face fertility issues and struggle with having children at all. Families with adequate means also have a difficult time balancing the demands of work and home and are increasingly living isolated lives, without the support of nearby extended family or community or faith groups.

With the emergence of the dual-earner household, married-couple-with-children families are spending more hours at work than in 1965.[222] At the same time, they are devoting more hours to focused child care. They are managing this feat by cutting back on housework and child-free leisure time. This does not come without stress. As many as 60 percent of married, dual-earner parents report feeling that they are operating under a substantial time deficit.[223]

This time crunch is exacerbated by increasingly longer commutes. In 2011, 36 percent of commuters had to travel at least thirty minutes in each direction.[224] Americans who live outside of a major city and who work in the city have the longest commutes.[225] Eighteen percent of people who work in New York City and 27 percent of people who work in Washington, D.C., commute an hour or more.[226]

Long commutes make it that much harder to spend time on family and personal relationships, and researchers theorize that long commutes are closely associated with social isolation. As political scientist Robert Putnam describes the phenomenon, "There's a simple rule of thumb: Every ten minutes of commuting results in ten percent fewer social connections. Commuting is connected to social isolation, which causes unhappiness."[227]

Additionally, moving homes is strongly associated with a loss of social capital. The United States is a highly mobile society, with people moving longer distances and more often than citizens of other developed countries.[228] Between 2008 and 2009, more than 37 million Americans moved, or slightly more than 12 percent of the population.[229] These moves ranged from within the same county to across state lines.[230]

Chapter 4 returns to this theme, showing how development patterns—particularly the emphasis on suburban and exurban single-family homes—exacerbate the social isolation of families.

Unequal division of labor between married mothers and fathers. Another challenge facing moderate- and upper-income families is the unequal division of paid and unpaid labor between married, opposite-sex parents. Becoming a parent is a time of economic vulnerability, particularly for women who are married to men, because married, opposite-sex couples tend to divide paid and unpaid labor unevenly. Before having children, a husband and a wife generally work about the same amount, but once a married, opposite-sex couple has children, one parent typically invests in the family—working part-time, taking a less demanding job, or ceasing to work altogether—while the other parent invests in a career.[231] This division follows gender lines. Although a majority of mothers remain in the workforce,[232] they shoulder a much greater share of the family responsibilities.[233] Even in couples where both spouses are employed full-time, the wife does considerably more housework and caregiving than her husband, and she typically spends fewer hours in the workplace.[234]

A study of the graduates of the class of 1990 from the University of Virginia Law School illustrates this traditional gender dynamic. In the study, there was a direct correlation between the number of children a woman had and her workforce participation. Ninety-five percent of the women with no children were working full-time, but zero percent of the women with four children were working full-time. In between, there was a predictable decrease, with 70, 66, and 22 percent working full-time with one, two, and three children, respectively. The vast majority of women not working full-time said they were doing so "in order to care for children."[235] For men, however, there was no correlation between parenthood and workforce involvement. The men worked full-time if they had no children, and they worked full-time if they had four children.[236]

This unequal division of labor for married, opposite-sex couples is not necessarily an economic problem for intact families, but it can quickly become one if the couple splits up. Journalist Ann Crittenden has examined the economic cost of divorce, explaining that when a couple divorces, there is almost never enough money to maintain two households at the same standard of living as the marital household and that child support does not come close to closing the gap.[237] The parent who invested in the family is economically disadvantaged, unless she has readily market-able skills and is able to integrate quickly back into the workforce or turn a part-time job into a full-time job—a challenge for many parents. Given the low rate of savings for most Americans, the main asset an individual has is her earning capacity, but that capacity is often severely compromised by becoming a primary caregiver. Thus, even when the primary caregiver gets a larger share of the marital assets, she is still more likely to have less money after the divorce.[238] And lifetime spousal support is a thing of the past, with most women not receiving any payments and those who do receiv-ing money only for a few years while they get themselves back into the paid-labor force.[239]

Same-sex couples tend to structure their family lives somewhat differently.[240] Although most have a general split of breadwinning and caregiving roles, they do not divide the responsibilities as starkly as opposite-sex couples, even if one partner makes significantly more money than the other.[241] One study, for example, com-pared traditional heterosexual families and lesbian families. The lesbian couples were more likely to share the responsibilities of paid work and unpaid work than were the heterosexual couples.[242] One of the differences was that the division-of-labor patterns for the lesbian couples turned on ideological variables; when the partners held egalitarian views, they divided the unpaid family labor more evenly.[243] (Like same-sex couples, cohabiting opposite-sex couples tend to have a more equal split between paid and unpaid work than married opposite-sex couples.[244]) Of course, one question that will have to be answered over time is whether the introduction of marriage equality will lead to family patterns more similar to those of married opposite-sex couples. It is possible that the more even split of paid and unpaid work is a rational response to the absence of protections for a partner who invests in the family, including marital assets, child support, and spousal support.

Regardless of sexual orientation and marital status, the loss of earning potential that occurs when one partner invests in the family rather than a career poses consid-erable economic risks for that person down the road, should the relationship end.

Effects on families

All of these challenges, separately and in combination, make it harder for family members to provide each other with strong, stable, positive relationships. Violence between intimate partners and between parents and children is antithetical to posi-tive relationships. Substance abuse interferes with intimacy and parenting. Poverty and unemployment mean that parents struggle to provide children with basic neces-sities and can be consumed by economic stress, which distracts from parenting.

Incarceration directly interferes with an individual's ability to be an involved parent or partner. Teens typically lack the social, emotional, and financial resources to be effective parents. And modern life, with demanding jobs, long commutes, and multiple moves, means that families struggle to find time to be with one another and build the social networks that support families.

To spell out the connection more clearly, consider some details in the context of incarceration, which affects relationships in numerous ways. Most obviously, the incarceration of a father means that the child will not see him on a regular basis. Most incarcerated fathers—78 percent—have some kind of contact with their children while in prison, but the frequency and type of contact vary tremendously.[245] Fifty percent of fathers in state prison and 63 percent of fathers in federal prison have telephone contact with their children at least once a month, but only 18 percent of fathers in state prison and 19 percent of fathers in federal prison have personal visits with their children once a month or more.[246] Many fathers—59 percent of fathers in state prison and 45 percent of fathers in federal prison—do not see their children at all while they are in prison.[247] When children do see their fathers in prison, they must often travel long distances. A majority of parents are held more than one hundred miles from their last place of residence.[248]

Incarceration has a substantial social, emotional, and financial impact on the families it affects, as legal scholar Donald Braman has demonstrated. Consider one family Braman studied: Kenny, an African American single father from Washington, D.C. One night while Kenny walked home from a convenience store, a man physically assaulted him on the street. Kenny stabbed the man and ran away. The knife had gone through the man's heart and killed him. Kenny was identified by a witness and arrested for murder.[249] The responsibility of caring for Kenny's two sons, his daughter, and his grandchild fell on his sixty-two-year-old mother, Edwina. Kenny's absence deeply affected his sons' behavior. They were angry with Kenny for not being around and were openly hostile toward him. Kenny and Edwina particularly worried about the toll that the stigma of Kenny's incarceration was taking on the boys. Not only were they acting out and neglecting schoolwork, but they had also withdrawn from their friends.[250] As Edwina put it, "The boys, no, they don't speak to no one about it. My family wears it more as a badge of shame. It's not like we're proud, so we just keep it to ourselves."[251]

Prior to his incarceration, Kenny held a full-time job, cared for his children, helped pay the mortgage, made repairs around the house, and contributed to his niece's college tuition.[252] Within a month of Kenny's incarceration, his family was feeling the financial strain of his absence, and by six months, the effects of his arrest were extensive.[253] Edwina was forced to delay her retirement and take on a second mortgage to make ends meet.[254] For families like Kenny's, incarceration means a cumulative effect on a family's financial situation, felt across generations.[255] Imprisoning parents drains the resources of the extended family and reduces the ability of the family to save and pass on wealth to children and grandchildren.[256] Kenny is not alone: 54 percent of incarcerated fathers were the primary source of support for their children prior to their arrests.[257]

When a mother goes to prison, the impact on the family is also devastating. The woman is often the sole parent of the children or the primary caregiver: more than 40 percent of mothers in state prison were single mothers prior to incarceration.[258] As a result, children are commonly cared for by their grandparents (45 percent) or other relatives (23 percent).[259] Another 11 percent of children end up in foster care.[260]

Consider a different example of the effect of multiple challenges: social isolation can wreak havoc on a family's relationships. Although mobility means that workers can move to areas of the country with better, higher-paying jobs,[261] legal scholar Naomi Schoenbaum argues that long-distance moves have underappreciated costs.[262] These moves make it harder for families to build and sustain support networks, with each move resulting in a loss of connections to social, religious, and familial groups. As chapter 1 demonstrated, social networks help families function, providing critical caregiving support and a sense of belonging,[263] but long-distance moves uproot families from these support networks and relationships based on proximity, such as day cares and schools.[264] Although new technology helps families stay connected to old networks, Facebook, Skype, and e-mail cannot provide babysitting and other critical supports. Families that move away from their support networks often increase their reliance on one another. A weakened social network thus creates a feedback loop, where family members look only to one another rather than others, further weakening the network.[265] Parenting is challenging enough with a strong support network; it is much harder when a parent is struggling alone without family and friends to help share the burdens and provide crucial emotional support.

In short, family life today can be exceptionally difficult.

PUTTING THE TRANSITIONS AND CHALLENGES IN CONTEXT

Fundamental changes in the American family are undeniable, but it is also important to resist nostalgia. As historian and sociologist Stephanie Coontz has argued, the idealization of the traditional family based on the iconic and revered 1950s is misplaced. That era was an entirely new phenomenon made possible largely because of unprecedented, broad economic gains.[266] Wages increased more in the 1950s than in the previous fifty years, making family formation easier and more stable.[267] Further, the government actively supported families with housing benefits and educational loans, particularly for returning veterans from World War II, and also created jobs with major public-works projects.[268]

These economic gains and the governmental support allowed nuclear families to flourish, but this was a historical aberration. Before the 1950s, a nuclear family in which children and women were set apart from the paid-labor force was far from the norm. Earlier in the century, child labor was widespread, with children as young as six and seven often working twelve-hour mill shifts. The Great Depression saw an increase in multiple-family homes and three-generation households. The 1950s, far from being a return to tradition, marked the first time economic growth was expansive enough to allow nuclear families to become prevalent.[269] As Coontz states, before the 1950s, the "emphasis on producing a whole world of satisfaction, amusement, and inventiveness within the nuclear family had no precedents."[270]

Moreover, despite the prosperity of some families in the 1950s, the gains were not universal, and poverty rates reached 25 percent, far higher than today and even more devastating given the absence of supports such as food stamps and housing subsidies.[271] African Americans, in particular, did not benefit from the economic gains of the 1950s. The poverty rate for two-parent African American families was more than 50 percent, and African Americans faced extensive, systemic discrimination.[272]

Further, many women were forced out of their war-era jobs and did not become housewives by choice. Women who did not find complete fulfillment through family life were often pathologized and diagnosed with psychological disorders.[273] Domestic violence was not considered a real crime and was widely underreported; the same was true for child sexual abuse.[274] Surveys revealed high levels of marriage dissatisfaction, and 25 to 33 percent of marriages from the 1950s ended in divorce.[275] Finally, teen pregnancy was widespread and much more common than today: 97 births for every 1,000 girls,[276] as compared with 34 births for every 1,000 girls in 2010.[277] The only difference is that back then, a teen pregnancy often meant a teen marriage. As Coontz puts it, "young people were not taught how to 'say no'—they were simply handed wedding rings."[278]

This more mixed view of the family's place in recent history is not to argue that the tremendous challenges facing families today are unimportant. Nor does it mean that the seismic shifts in family form are imagined. Rather, it is simply to caution against waxing nostalgic about some imagined past.

CONCLUSION

Members of every generation may feel that they are facing unprecedented change and challenge. Families have always been the place where society's upheavals are reflected, but there is no question that the state of the American family is precarious.

Families across the income spectrum are struggling with specific challenges that make it exceedingly difficult for them to provide the strong, stable, positive relationships necessary for human flourishing. The state of the American family is not good.

In particular, without demonizing nonmarital families, and recognizing that broad statistics mask individual differences, there is increasing evidence that family form plays a causal role in child outcomes. We must think anew about how to address the numerous challenges facing families and how to nurture the strong, stable, positive relationships that are essential to child development and healthy adult relationships across a variety of family forms. Before doing so, however, it is important to understand the role that the law plays in both strengthening and undermining relationships. This is the topic of chapter 3.

3

The State's Role in Relationships

IMAGINE THE MORNING routine in three different families. In the first, a single mother wakes up in her apartment, where she is raising her three children. She goes to the kitchen and notices a stack of papers containing her food-stamps debit card and the lottery form for a local charter school. She prepares her children for school, lamenting for the thousandth time that their local school has such poor teachers that her children learn little over the course of the year. She sends the two older children out the door without food, knowing they will receive a subsidized breakfast and lunch at school. She walks her youngest child to a local Head Start program, dropping him off for his three hours of preschool. With the children gone, she takes the bus to the office of her welfare caseworker, where she receives a list of dead-end job prospects. She is obligated to pursue these prospects because trying to find a job is a condition of receiving state support.[1] She is already working off the books, helping to care for a neighbor's child, but the additional money from the government is keeping her family afloat. That said, she knows that she has only five years of support during her adult lifetime and that the clock is ticking. She also knows that she must be careful not to get pregnant again, because she will not receive additional support for any child conceived while she is receiving welfare.[2]

In the second family, a father wakes up in his urban apartment, thinking about the day ahead for him, his husband, and their young child. Although the two fathers refer to each other as "my husband" and have a marriage certificate from a state that allows same-sex couples to marry, they now live in a state that does not recognize their relationship. Additionally, under state law, only the biological father is treated as the child's legal parent. Unless the couple goes through the costly and time-consuming process of having the nonbiological father adopt the child, he cannot fill out his child's medical forms or sign his child out from preschool if the child is ill. He is a legal stranger to the child, although in the eyes of the child, he is simply "Daddy." The waking father is also worrying about the expense of health insurance. He earns the higher salary and has health insurance through work, but his employer's plan does not cover domestic partners, leading the couple to pool their earnings to pay for the health insurance of the lower earner. They also know that if one of them became incapacitated, the other could make medical decisions as a "close friend" but would be able to exercise this privilege only after any adult child, parent, sibling, or relative declined to do so.[3] The two fathers end the morning at the kitchen table going over their expenses to ensure that any money one has spent on their joint expenses is not treated as a taxable gift to the other person. Although the federal government now recognizes their relationship, because the state where they currently live does not, they must file separate state tax returns, a considerable expense in preparation fees over the years.[4] Later at their workplaces, the two men do not speak of their relationship with colleagues, out of fear that their bosses might not prove tolerant. No federal law exists that protects gay individuals from employment discrimination, and they live in one of twenty-nine states, at this writing, where it is legal to discriminate on the basis of sexual orientation.

In the third family, two school-age children wake up in their single-family, suburban home. Their father prepares their breakfast while their mother gets ready for work. The married couple leaves the house in two cars. The mother drops the children off at their nearby school and then drives to work. The father drives directly to work, although this takes forty-five minutes and must be done in a car because there is no public transportation available. When dropping the children off at school, the mother signs a form for the school to administer antibiotics to one of the children, who is recovering from strep throat. Later that morning, the father has to leave work and return to the school to pick up the other child, who is now running a fever and complaining of a sore throat. The father brings the child home for the remainder of the day and telecommutes.

Three American mornings. Three examples of a pervasive state. When the single mother looks at her food-stamps debit card, she is reminded that government regulations will allow her to buy a raw chicken and cook it at home but not to buy an already-roasted chicken because of the exception for "hot foods."[5] In thinking about her children's school, she knows she cannot afford private or parochial school, but the state's decision to allow charter schools in her district means she may have some control over their education. The hot breakfasts and lunches subsidized by the state mean that her children will have two meals a day. The meals are not particularly healthy, but there is little she can do about this. Unhealthy food is better than no food. And although she is glad to have a Head Start program for her youngest child, the program is not the same as child care, because it runs for only half the day.[6] When she does find a job, she will have to find real child care. And the law in her state prohibiting welfare payments for any child born while she is already receiving assistance makes her especially worried about pregnancy.

For the urban fathers, the state plays a particularly strong—and pernicious—role, because at the individual state level, the two men and their child are not a family at all. Instead, they are treated as a single father and his child living with a friend. In addition to the insult to their dignity and the extra hurdles for the nonbiological father in securing parental rights, the absence of legal recognition costs the couple considerably more money to function as a family than it would if their state—like the federal government and a growing number of other states—extended legal status, and all the accompanying benefits, to same-sex couples.[7]

The middle-class family with married, opposite-sex parents may appear to operate free from state influence, but even here, the state is omnipresent. To begin, federal and state antidiscrimination laws ensure that the mother has equal access to employment and will not be discriminated against simply because she is a woman. Through these laws, the state is enabling women to work as a practical matter and also influencing public opinion on the question of whether women *should* work outside the home. Similarly, federal laws protected both parents' jobs when the children were born, providing job security while they took unpaid leave. This time at home with each newborn helped set the stage for the father to be an active, confident parent, capable of responding to his children's needs.

Despite this job protection, however, most men at the father's workplace do not leave work early to care for a sick child. The father felt that he had to keep up appearances all afternoon, sending e-mails and making phone calls, to let others know that he was not really "off." He is supportive of his wife's career, but he knows that most workplaces frown on men taking time away from work on a regular basis to care for children. Most men simply don't do it, apart from the odd school play or family vacation.[8] This may seem like a matter purely of social preferences, but the law sways these preferences in myriad ways, as described below.

The state does not directly micromanage this family's life. If the parents want to buy a ready-roasted chicken with the additional money available to them because of the dependent deductions they claim on their income tax, no one is going to stop them. But the state's influence is widespread nonetheless. The local zoning laws in their town, for example, did not require the developer to build sidewalks in their neighborhood.[9] Having no sidewalk means the children cannot safely walk to school; instead, the parents must drive them. Similarly, the state did not invest in high-speed public transportation, so the parents drive to work, the father a particularly long distance. The state *did* invest in public education, which means that the parents do not have to pay directly for their children's education. Instead, this cost is shared among taxpayers. Similarly, the town where this family lives emphasizes the importance of neighborhood schools, so most children attend the local school and thus know one another and play together after school, bringing neighbors closer together. In the neighboring town, where children may attend any school in the district, the neighborhood children do not know one another as well, and by extension, neither do the parents.

The state's presence in the life of this traditional family can also be seen in a much broader sense. The state has determined that this grouping of individuals is a legal family and thus deserving of legal rights. Under state law, it is significant that the father married the children's mother before the children were born and is on the children's birth certificates. If he had not taken one of these actions, he might not be considered a legal father (despite his biological tie to the children) and therefore could not assert parental rights. And these parental rights are important. The form that the mother signed at school ensured that the school would not dispense medicine without parental permission and thus usurp the parent's privileged role as medical decision-maker. When the father came to pick up the sick child, the school allowed him to take the child because he is the legal father.

As these three mornings demonstrate, the state is present in the lives of all families, albeit in different ways and with varying degrees of scrutiny and invasiveness. The goal of this chapter is to develop a clearer sense of exactly how—and how thoroughly—the state influences family relationships. This is an essential predicate for chapter 4, which argues that this pervasive state regulation is largely negative, both failing to foster and at times actively undermining strong, stable, positive relationships within families.

A PERVASIVE STATE

If you took a family law course in law school, you would study the legal rules governing marriage, divorce, adoption, and surrogacy. You likely would not, however, learn about zoning ordinances, tax policies, or the laws governing workplace discrimination. Those subjects are taught in other courses. As the anecdotes above illustrate, however, state regulation of family life is deep and broad, covering all these subjects and many more. Properly understood, family law is the many ways the state influences families. Defining family law this way is not simply a conceptual marker—or a play for more turf in the legal academy—but rather is essential if we want to think more creatively about how the state can nurture strong, stable, positive relationships.

Direct regulation

Without the state, there is no family, legally speaking. There may be groups of individuals with emotional and economic ties, but there is no family until the state calls it such. As the following description makes clear, the state controls the entry and exit from the legal status of family, and many tangible and intangible benefits hang in the balance.

Beginning with marriage, the state determines who can and cannot get married. In the vast majority of states, a same-sex couple cannot get legally married, even though their relationship may be the functional and emotional equivalent of a marriage between an opposite-sex couple. Similarly, the state decides when a couple can end their marriage. This is much easier than in the past, because every state now allows a couple to get a "no-fault" divorce, meaning that one party simply has to file for the divorce and the court will grant it. But to end the legal marriage, the couple still needs state authorization. As a foundational legal matter, then, a marriage does not exist without the state's blessing.

This control over the contours of the legal family also extends to parent-child relationships. A common understanding is that a child's biological parents are the legal parents, but this is not always the case. Setting aside for the moment the complicated question of gestational surrogates and egg and sperm donors, a man who is the biological father of a child he conceived naturally with the mother is not always considered the legal father. If the mother is married to another man, there is often a legal presumption that the husband, and not the biological father, is the legal father.[10] Or if the woman is unmarried and the father is not on the birth certificate and takes no steps to establish a relationship with the child, he is not necessarily considered the legal father of the child, able to exercise parental rights over the child.[11]

Just as the state decides when a parent-child relationship begins, it also decides when it ends. Legal rules determine when and how a parent can relinquish a child for adoption. Legal rules also specify when the state can initiate an action to terminate parental rights, typically following severe child abuse or neglect. In this way, the state can end a parent-child relationship, both with the parent's permission and without it.

The question of who is a legal parent is increasingly difficult with the rise of assisted reproductive technologies and alternative family forms. For example, when one woman donates her egg, a second woman gestates the embryo, and a third woman is the intended mother, it is not always clear which woman is the legal mother, and courts have reached different conclusions.[12] Or, as in one of the anecdotes above, when two men are jointly raising a child, the nonbiological parent may not be a legal parent, depending on the state where they live. Family law is still struggling to answer these questions, and there are a variety of answers depending on the jurisdiction, but the point here is that it is the *state* deciding who wins the coveted label of "family," and it is the state making very pointed judgments in setting the terms of recognition.

The state does not just decide who is a legal spouse or a legal parent. The state also places tremendous weight on this designation. Legal marriage, for example, is a powerful institution that comes with a host of tangible benefits and obligations. When a person says "I do," the state says "Welcome to a new world." The legal rights and benefits under both federal and state law that accompany marriage are far too numerous to list but include inheritance rights, Social Security survivor benefits, preferential treatment under immigration law, family leave if a spouse gets sick, the right to make medical decisions as the next of kin, testimonial privileges in court, health insurance under a spouse's plan, the ability to transfer property within the marriage and pool resources without adverse tax consequences, access to marital assets if the marriage ends (discussed below), and much more.

Although individual states have different rules, the dominant approach is to make a sharp distinction between married and cohabiting couples, with the latter receiving fewer of the rights and owing fewer of the obligations.[13] To play out one of the examples above, if one person in a married couple dies without a will, the default rules governing inheritance ensure that the surviving spouse is entitled to inherit at least some of the deceased spouse's property. But if the couple only lived together and was not legally married, then, absent a will, the surviving partner is not automatically entitled to inherit.

There are also legal obligations that accompany marriage, such as the duty of spouses to support each other financially during the marriage and to divide shared assets if the marriage dissolves. And some "benefits" can be liabilities. Consider the increased tax liability that can accompany marriage. Without getting into the details of the tax code, the basic idea is that when one spouse earns most of the family's income, the married couple can file a joint tax return, typically putting the couple in a lower tax bracket because the income is shared between two people. For a dual-earner, middle-income couple, however, the joint tax return results in the so-called marriage penalty, because the combined income pushes the couple into a higher tax bracket.

The bottom line is that the state treats married couples very differently from cohabitants, for better and for worse. Both the benefits and the obligations can be understood as incentives to invest in the relationship and as protections for those who do invest.[14]

State recognition of an adult romantic relationship also brings significant intangible benefits. The idea that the relationship matters to others, and is privileged by the state, confers tremendous dignity on the relationship. This is partly because of the mutually reinforcing nature of state-sanctioned marriage and the social understanding of marriage. As legal scholar Elizabeth Scott has put it, there are centuries of traditions and norms inherent in marriage that enhance its meaning to something far greater than a state-condoned status. The norms of loyalty, sexual faithfulness, emotional and financial sharing, and commitment are deeply entrenched with our understanding of marriage.[15] And there is a deep emotional resonance to marriage in modern society, even if marriage is idealized. As Andrew Sullivan wrote about his own marriage to his longtime partner and the marriage-equality movement more generally, marriage is the embodiment of the "highest form" of love, but "To feel you will never know that, never feel that, is to experience a deep psychic wound that takes years to recover from. It is to become psychologically homeless.[16]

Turning to the rights and obligations that flow from legal parenthood, the law places legal parents in the most privileged position vis-à-vis children, and many of these rights are rooted in the Constitution and thus are highly protected. The most fundamental protection is that children cannot be taken away from a legal parent without showing that the parent is unfit. This means that in, say, a custody battle between two legal parents, each will have an equal claim to the child, and the presumption is strongly in favor of some form of continued contact between the child and both parents. Beyond mere physical contact with a child, the Constitution also protects a parent's right to make important decisions for the child, including schooling, medical treatment, and religious training. Parents also have significant responsibilities, such as the obligation to provide financial support, even if the parent does not live with the child.

Finally, legal recognition of marriage and of parenthood are related. Historically, family law favored marital relationships and thus penalized "illegitimate" children born to either extramarital or nonmarital partners. Today the legal stigma associated with birth outside marriage is largely gone,[17] but marriage continues to shadow parental rights, which are more tenuous outside marriage. The two caveats to a father's rights, noted above, are significant. Many states have a presumption that a child born within a marriage is the legal child of the married couple, even if this may not be true as a biological fact. And an unwed father not on a birth certificate often has to establish an initial relationship with the child to fully protect parental rights; the father cannot rely on the biological connection alone.

Another form of direct regulation is the child-welfare system, which is designed to protect children believed to be abused or neglected by their families and to strengthen families where children are at imminent risk for abuse and neglect.[18] If the state believes the child can remain safely at home with additional supports, then the state will offer preventive services, such as family or individual counseling, substance-abuse treatment, domestic-violence intervention, parenting classes, and so on. The goal of these services is to help the family and avoid the placement of the child in foster care. But if the state determines that the child cannot remain safely in the home or if the preventive services are not effective, the state places the child in foster care, either with a relative or an unrelated family or in an institutional setting. The state typically has a duty to reunite the children with their families, but when this is not possible, the state can move to terminate parental rights and place the child for adoption.

When the violence in the home is between adults, the state also has the authority to intervene. In many jurisdictions, if the police respond to a call and determine with reasonable certainty that a domestic-violence crime has been committed, the officers are required to make an arrest, regardless of what the victim may want.[19] Once the arrest is made, many prosecutors' offices have a "no-drop" policy and will charge and prosecute the offender even if the victim refuses to cooperate and does not want the perpetrator charged.[20] In some jurisdictions, the prosecutor also must request a temporary order of protection from the criminal court, which prohibits the defendant from making any contact with the victim, including third-party contact, and excludes the defendant from the victim's home, school, business, and place of employment.[21] A defendant who contacts the victim or returns to the home can be arrested and prosecuted for violating the order, even if it is the victim who invites the defendant into the home.[22] The temporary order can be made permanent as part of the conditions for a plea deal or with the dismissal of the case, prohibiting any contact by the partners.[23] The state also allows victims to take many of these steps themselves by providing means for obtaining a civil order of protection against a partner.[24] Typically, a civil protection order prohibits the offender from having any contact with the victim and requires the offender to vacate the shared home, even if the offender is the sole owner of the property.[25] The criminal and the civil protections apply to both cohabiting couples and married couples.[26]

All of these examples of direct regulation illustrate the reach of the state into family life. By deciding who is a legal family and what flows from this designation, the state sets legal families apart from other groupings, who typically have little or no protection for their relationships. If an adult is not a parent to a child, he or she is a legal stranger, with no rights or responsibilities. Similarly, couples who cohabit instead of marrying get very few of the legal protections available to married couples when their relationships end. (As noted above, however, domestic-violence protections do apply to cohabiting couples.) There is no question that direct regulation has a tremendous impact on family relationships. Whether this impact encourages or discourages strong, stable, positive relationships is the subject of chapter 4.

Indirect regulation

In addition to the extensive reach of direct regulation, the state also influences families indirectly through incentives and subsidies, "choice architecture," myriad laws and policies seemingly unrelated to the family, and by shaping social norms. Through all these means, the state's influence is felt in nearly every corner of family life. Acting indirectly, the state regulations embody a certain view of what families should do.

Incentives and subsidies. The state creates incentives and provides subsidies that profoundly shape familial behavior. Subsidized child-care programs, for example, influence family behavior by encouraging parents to work and place their children in the care of others. When these are also early-childhood programs, such as Head Start, the subsidies teach parents what children need to begin on the path to academic success, influencing parents' behavior at home. In a randomized study of Head Start, for example, researchers found that after enrollment in the program, the parents whose children were assigned to attend Head Start were more likely to read to their children and take them to cultural-enrichment activities than the parents whose children were in the control group.[27]

State decisions about where to locate subsidized housing also deeply affect families. When the state concentrates public housing in already-poor neighborhoods, it virtually ensures poor outcomes for the children growing up there. There are numerous reasons for this, but consider just three: The schools likely will be of far lower quality and receive much less funding than schools in moderate- and upper-income neighborhoods. Concerned about an unsafe neighborhood, many parents will require children to stay inside, which means that those children will watch more TV and will be less physically active and have less opportunity for enriching physical play and exploration. And a family's access to healthy food will be severely limited, because poorer neighborhoods have far fewer grocery stores and more convenience stores, both of which are correlated with low fruit and vegetable consumption by children.[28] By contrast, when the state places subsidized housing in an area with strong schools, greater economic integration, and more resources such as playgrounds and supermarkets, it will be easier for parents to be confident in the schools, allow their children to play outside, and purchase healthier food.

State subsidies also influence the behavior of middle- and upper-income families. With the introduction of 529 college-savings plans, which allow parents to save money for higher education and not pay taxes on the growth of these savings, the state changes economic behavior and also encourages parents to save for college.[29] The mortgage-interest deduction encourages families to buy rather than rent homes.

And on a deeper level, the state's scheme of funding public education largely through property taxes affects families' decisions about where to live and means that middle- and upper-income families choose enclaves with similarly resourced families.

Choice architecture. The state influences families by setting default rules and describing, framing, or presenting choices in a manner that affects decisions. Sometimes referred to as choice architecture,[30] this important state role can profoundly sway families, although the effect is often unseen. The default rules for the distribution of property at divorce are an example of choice architecture at work in family law. In most states,[31] the default rule is one of equitable property distribution. Assets accumulated during the marriage belong to both parties. It does not matter who paid for the asset. (There are exceptions, but the basic rule is one of sharing.) Individuals can contract around these rules through prenuptial and postnuptial agreements, but most couples do not sign such agreements. Instead, the default rule is applied.

Through this default rule, the state is telling parties that marriage is a shared economic enterprise. And they act accordingly. Most married couples treat the family as one economic unit, pooling income and making joint decisions about financial matters without regard to who earned the money.[32] Further, economic sharing allows married couples to divide paid labor and care work. As chapter 2 described, in the typical opposite-sex, married family with children, one person invests time and energy in a career and the other person invests time and energy in the family, either by leaving the paid-labor force or, more often, by taking a less demanding, and less remunerative, career path. The default rule of sharing assets upon divorce encourages this specialization by ensuring that the individual who invested in the family has a claim to the marital assets even though that person may not have earned the money that purchased the assets.

Seemingly unrelated laws and policies. Many areas of law and policy may not appear to affect relationships, but in practice they have a tremendous impact. As legal scholar Katherine Silbaugh has argued, zoning laws, urban planning, and housing design play an unappreciated role in affecting work-family balance.[33] She contends that the prevalence of government-imposed, single-use zoning, which has traditionally separated residential, commercial, and industrial development, has a negative effect on family relationships. In well-planned, dense, urban neighborhoods, residents can preserve valuable family time by accessing everything they need within a short walk.[34] By contrast, suburban residents are geographically separated from possible employers, increasing commute times and straining the work-family balance.[35] As lower-paid service-sector jobs follow residents out into the suburbs, low-income workers have difficult "reverse commutes."[36] These work-home spatial arrangements can force parents to take a half-day off of work to handle simple tasks such as bringing a child to the dentist.[37]

Rather than being the result of market demands, this inferior setup is the direct result of government policies such as the Federal Housing Administration preferring these arrangements for loan guarantees,[38] the home-mortgage interest deduction, which encourages larger suburban homes,[39] and large road and utility subsidies, which encourage inefficient sprawl.[40]

Even seemingly smaller decisions made by the state—for example, whether to require a developer to install sidewalks in a new housing or commercial development—affect family life. As illustrated in the anecdotes above, a family living in a development without sidewalks will think twice about allowing children to walk to school or to a friend's house. This, in turn, affects the parents' lives, requiring parents to do more driving. It also affects the formation of friendships among children and the social connections among neighbors. As chapter 2 explained, the physical layout of a neighborhood can foster or inhibit the growth of these social ties.

Legal scholar Elizabeth Emens has taken this argument even further, contending that because the state controls the infrastructure of daily life, it inevitably influences romantic relationships.[41] As she argues, state regulation of public spaces, schools, workplaces, and neighborhoods affects who we meet and come to know over time. As an example, Emens explains that the state often separates individuals who are disabled by sending them to different schools.[42] This separation means that abled and disabled people have less interaction and therefore are less likely to form romantic relationships. Even without separate schooling, the lack of accessibility for disabled individuals in public transportation, restaurants, housing, and shops makes it difficult to engage in an intimate relationship. Although the Americans with Disabilities Act has made public spaces more accessible, it does not reach private homes and thus means that members of an abled-disabled couple may have a hard time visiting each other.[43] This is not to argue that the state should mandate that all homes be built with, say, a wheelchair ramp but rather simply to highlight the extent of the state reach into our seemingly personal lives.

Social norms. There are many "rules" that we follow, even without the threat of legal sanction, such as wearing a suit to a business meeting or not talking about bodily functions at the dinner table, and the state plays an indirect role here, too. In the family context, an intricate web of these rules, or social norms, often eclipses the significance of direct legal regulation. As any parent can attest, norms of proper parenting abound. There is no law requiring women to breastfeed their newborns, for example, but in some communities, strong breastfeeding norms mean that a woman using a bottle faces a social sanction. In her book about motherhood, Ayelet Waldman recounts a hilarious but telling anecdote about feeding her infant son from a bottle while standing in line in a Berkeley bakery. An older woman leans over and says, "You know, breast really is best." Rather than telling the woman to mind her own business, Waldman feels compelled to launch into a long explanation about how the milk in the bottle is expressed breast milk because her son had been having difficulty breastfeeding.[44]

Parenting norms are regularly enforced by fellow family members, teachers, religious-community members, neighbors, and even strangers, as the Waldman anecdote illustrates. Ask any parent for a story of a complete stranger weighing in on some manner of parenting—telling a pregnant woman in the check-out line that she should not be buying junk food or informing a parent in the park that a child's helmet is not on properly. Children can be norm enforcers, too, such as when they tell a parent what is acceptable to wear at school or when they respond to advertising that targets them, thus enforcing certain consumerist norms. Parenting norms are also far-reaching, creating expectations that parents will, depending on the community, baptize or circumcise a child (or follow a similar religious ritual for a young child), dress a child in gender-specific clothing, teach a child not to use swear words, volunteer in a child's school, value homework, provide a religious education, and so on.

These norms change over time, of course. In the 1920s and 1930s, mothers were discouraged from picking up crying infants and rocking them.[45] Experts feared this would inculcate bad habits, breed self-indulgence, and make the child dependent on attention.[46] Today, theories of attachment parenting encourage parents to hold their children as much as possible.[47] Similarly, norms about corporal punishment have changed, at least in some communities. In the first edition of his iconic advice book published in 1961, Benjamin Spock told parents that a "slap on the hand or the behind works like a charm for" some parents and children.[48] By contrast, the most recent edition, published in 2012, is far more equivocal, noting that "most parents in the United States say that they believe in spanking,"[49] but "[m]ost scientific studies don't find that spanking, in itself, is either particularly harmful or particularly beneficial."[50]

It may appear that the state has little sway over these social norms, but in reality, the law plays an active role in creating and perpetuating the norms.[51] To give one example of state influence over social norms in the family context, consider the regulation of abortion. States cannot directly prohibit all abortions, so instead, some states try to cultivate a social norm that stigmatizes abortions. One way to do so is by passing laws that seek to impose or evoke the emotions of motherhood in all pregnant women.[52] An Arkansas law, for example, requires an abortion provider to inform the patient about the pain the "unborn child" may experience during the abortion and to let the patient know whether an analgesic or anesthetic would lessen or eliminate this pain.[53]

This law and similar laws do not directly regulate abortion[54] but instead operate to shape social norms around reproductive choice. The desired norm is that women are mothers, and mothers love their children and would never harm them. A woman who violates this norm should feel guilty for rejecting motherhood and, by extension, her womanhood.

The work of legal scholar Carol Sanger illuminates how the state contributes to a social norm that stigmatizes abortion. Sanger has argued that statutes seemingly unrelated to abortion, such as infant-safe-haven laws, play a particular role in the "culture of life."[55] Safe-haven laws, passed in quick succession in numerous states with virtually no opposition,[56] allow a mother to leave her newborn child anonymously in a designated spot, such as a hospital or a fire station, without fear of prosecution, thereby making the child a ward of the state and effectively placing the child for adoption.[57] The laws were passed partially in response to a few high-profile cases of young women killing or abandoning their newborns.[58]

These laws may be unobjectionable on their face, but their deeper meaning relates to pro-life social-norm entrepreneurship, as such laws seek to change the emotional resonance of the abortion decision. The thought of a newborn in a dumpster is horrific, and it is precisely this image that the safe-haven laws seek to imprint on citizens and on individual women considering whether to have an abortion. The horror and revulsion at a woman who would throw out her child can be superimposed onto a woman who would throw out her child a different way—by having an abortion.[59]

Infant-safe-haven and fetal-pain-notification laws likely have little practical effect on a woman's decision to have an abortion. The idea that a woman would not have an abortion because she knows she can keep her pregnancy secret, give birth in private, and then drop off the newborn at a designated spot is ludicrous. Similarly, the woman who learns about potential fetal pain has already decided to have the abortion. Some women may choose not to abort a fetus as a result of the pain information, but the more pervasive effect of these laws is subtle and far-reaching. The laws contribute to the creation of a social norm that a fetus is a human being, that pregnant women are mothers who must conform to maternal norms, and that having an abortion is a shameful act.

A prescriptive vision for the family

Another aspect of state regulation is that the state is not neutral about family choices. Instead, state regulation embodies a prescriptive vision for the family, which is to say that the state interacts with families with some sense, intentional or not, of what might be considered ideal and tries to direct families in the state's preferred direction.

Historical laws concerning "illegitimate" children, for example, determined which intimate relationships would receive state favor (marital) and which would not (extramarital or nonmarital) based on very strong moral views about the supposed sanctity of marriage. As societal attitudes about illegitimacy changed, so, too, did the legal consequences of being born to unmarried parents. With a few narrow exceptions, the law no longer distinguishes between marital and nonmarital children, but the law continues to embody particular views on what is right for families.

Take any set of laws, and the state's ideals are discernible. Welfare laws that exclude children born while a parent is receiving aid reflect the ideal that parents should be able to care for their own children financially, and if they cannot, the state will try to control procreation.[60] The mortgage-interest deduction embodies the judgment that families do best in a home owned by the adults.[61] And immigration laws that recognize certain family ties but not others and then rank those ties in order of importance (spouses before adult children, adult children before adult siblings, and so on) indicate which relationships matter the most in the eyes of the state.[62]

These multiple ideals of what constitutes an acceptable or valuable relationship, in turn, marginalize those who fall on the wrong side of those strictures. It is no coincidence that the movement for marriage equality has consciously sought to portray gays and lesbians as ball-throwing dads and soccer moms. Advocates know that it is easier to fit same-sex couples into a familiar mold than to create a new idea of family.

* * *

All of this is family law. Chapter 4 breaks family law down into the two categories established in the introduction—dispute-resolution family law (essentially the court system and its alternatives) and structural family law (everything else)—but for now, the point is simply that family law, as a whole, encompasses the multitude of ways the state influences families and family life. This is not to argue that every single state action is family law. Taken to its extreme, this broader definition of family law could sweep in virtually every piece of the tax code that either increases or decrease a family's net income or every criminal conviction that sends a parent to prison. Rather, the aim of this broader definition is simply to show that the traditional definition of family law—the rules governing marriage and divorce, for example—is far too limited. The state influences family relationships in myriad ways. This broader understanding of how the state does influence families is essential for rethinking how the state *should* influence families.

THE RHETORIC OF FAMILY AUTONOMY

One of the most fascinating paradoxes of family law is that despite the breadth and depth of state regulation, a bedrock principle of family law is that families are autonomous, operating apart from the law. Family autonomy is the belief that a clear line divides the family from the state and that legal rights form a protective barrier against state intervention. This could not be farther from the truth, but it is a persistent belief nonetheless. As chapter 4 demonstrates, the continued belief in family autonomy presents a significant barrier to reforming family law, so it is important to explore this myth in some detail.

The creation myth

The modern foundation for family autonomy is a pair of Supreme Court cases from the 1920s. Picture the backdrop: World War I was raging in Europe, and the United States had just joined the fight. American patriotism was running high, with citizens across the country forming civic associations to support the war. The German-American community in the United States—a large and cohesive group that retained many of its own traditions, including speaking German, at least in some settings—became a target for anti-German sentiment and fears about domestic espionage. This wave of hostility focused particularly on the use of the German language. In a claim that will sound familiar from today's immigration debates, there was a widespread belief that speaking German meant that the immigrants, especially young people, would not properly absorb American values and would remain loyal to Germany, not the United States.[63]

Toward the end of the war and in the immediate aftermath, twenty-three states enacted statutes restricting the teaching of foreign languages, especially German.[64] In Nebraska, anti-German sentiment ran particularly high. As in many other states, during the war, Nebraska had formed a State Council of Defense to help with the war effort.[65] Although the State Council performed many useful activities, it was also a means for harassing the German-American community by investigating the loyalty of the community, particularly the Lutheran clergy and its parochial schools.[66] These efforts continued even after the war ended. At the recommendation of the State Council, in 1919, the Nebraska legislature enacted a statute prohibiting the teaching of any language except English in elementary school.[67]

In response to the law, parochial schools offered classes in the German language outside of normal hours.[68] In Hamilton County, Nebraska, which was known for its anti-German sentiment, the parochial schools run by the Evangelical Lutheran Zion's Church extended the recess period by thirty minutes and offered German instruction during that time.[69] The pastor of the congregation later testified that the sole purpose of the German class was to ensure that the children could participate in religious activities at home and at church.[70] In May 1920, the county attorney and the county school superintendent came to the school and saw the teacher, Robert Meyer, teaching the students in German during the recess period. On a second occasion, when Meyer was teaching a ten-year-old boy to read the Bible, the county attorney charged Meyer with violating the Nebraska statute.[71]

The resulting conviction, along with challenges to similar statutes in other states, made its way up to the U.S. Supreme Court. In the 1923 decision of *Meyer v. Nebraska*, the Court found that the statute violated the Fourteenth Amendment's prohibition on the deprivation of life, liberty, or property without due process of law. The Court decided that although the state had a clear interest in the education of its citizens and could lawfully require that children attend school, Meyer had a right, grounded in the liberty interest protected by the Due Process Clause, to pursue his occupation, and the parents had a similar liberty interest in engaging him "to instruct their children."[72] Elaborating on the idea of liberty at issue, the Court said:

> Without doubt, [liberty] denotes not merely freedom from bodily restraint but also the right of the individual to contract, to engage in any of the common occupations of life, to acquire useful knowledge, to marry, establish a home and bring up children, to worship God according to the dictates of his own conscience, and generally to enjoy those privileges long recognized at common law as essential to the orderly pursuit of happiness by free men.[73]

Thus, although the actions of the teacher were at issue in the criminal prosecution, the Supreme Court also recognized a constitutional right on behalf of the parents.

In this same postwar, nativist era, citizens in Oregon were engaged in a movement to ban parochial schools, particularly Catholic schools, altogether. The supporters of this movement believed that only public schools would promote "Americanism."[74] Met by cheers of agreement, State Senator Charles Hall had delivered a message across Oregon: "The public school is one of the fundamental factors in our system of government. I favor compulsory attendance in the primary grades. Teach pure Americanism to all pupils at an early age. Continue to strengthen and build up this typical American Institution."[75] In response, the Oregon legislature enacted a statute in November 1922 requiring all children to attend public school through the eighth grade.[76] The Society of Sisters of the Holy Names of Jesus and Mary, the largest providers of Catholic education in Oregon, teamed up with Hill Military Academy, a nonsectarian private school, to fight the new law.[77]

In a decision handed down in 1925, called *Pierce v. Society of Sisters*, the Supreme Court decided that the state could not require children to attend public school. The Court stated:

> The fundamental theory of liberty upon which all governments in this Union repose excludes any general power of the State to standardize its children....

The child is not the mere creature of the State; those who nurture him and direct his destiny have the right, coupled with the high duty, to recognize and prepare him for additional obligations.[78]

Again, although the case concerned the action of the schools, the Supreme Court also recognized the interest of the parents, concluding that the statute "unreasonably interferes with the liberty of parents and guardians to direct the upbringing and education of children under their control."[79]

These two decisions,[80] still good law today, laid the groundwork for the principle that the Constitution protects families from overreaching by the state and the deeply ingrained belief that families stand apart from the state.

A descriptive inaccuracy

At first blush, these cases seem to form a bulwark for families against the state, but in practice, this freedom is highly circumscribed. The decision in *Pierce* says that parents can choose which kind of school their child attends, but direct state regulation mandates that young children attend *some* school, even if it is at home. And indirect state regulation influences parents' decisions about education in multiple ways. The state, for example, determines the funding scheme for public education, which affects the quality of the schools available to children. The state also decides whether charter schools are allowed, thus increasing or decreasing a parent's options. In areas where children can attend any school in the district, the state typically does not provide school buses for every school, making the "choice" illusory for some families. And the state generally does not allow parents to take a tax deduction for the cost of private, K–12 education, increasing the appeal of public schools.[81]

Similarly, parents can make important medical decisions for their children but only up to a point. A parent cannot withhold medically necessary treatment if doing so would pose an imminent danger to the child or the community, even if the decision not to treat the child is based on religious beliefs.[82] Simple decisions, such as whether to put a child's pants on before his or her shirt or vice versa, are not influenced by the state, but the state does determine whether a child wears clothes at all and whether those clothes are adequate and appropriate. If a parent sends a young child to school in subzero weather without a jacket or adequate footwear, this may make school officials suspicious of parental neglect. As mandatory reporters of child abuse and neglect, the school will be obliged to call the local department of social services if they have a reasonable suspicion that the child is being maltreated.[83]

Even more fundamentally, the state determines which individuals get to make these decisions for a child. In a hypothetical world where children are raised only by their biological mother and father, this may not seem like much state influence. But in a complex modern world, where a number of different individuals might qualify for the role of legal parent, the state has tremendous control over families by deciding who is a legal parent and who is not.

Finally, families are not independent of the state because the state supports all families in myriad ways, from the provision of public education to food stamps and unemployment programs. It may seem that this state support is more directed at low-income families, but this is not true. One reason the notion of family autonomy persists is that some types of state support are so familiar—such as public education—that they are taken for granted and not easily understood as the state taking a role in familial life. This state role is simply background noise. By contrast, a new form of state support—such as the health-care program passed during the first Obama administration—*is* perceived as an aid to families because it changes the status quo and thus is foreground noise. This kind of salience differential makes it much harder to see the ubiquitous state. In other words, the state is involved in our lives to such an extent that it has become invisible, and only new initiatives draw fire for state interference.

Another reason people persist in believing that their families stand apart from the state is that the program design of some forms of state support—typically those for middle- and upper-income families—obscures the state role. Political scientist Suzanne Mettler has explored this phenomenon. Through the Cornell Survey Research Institute, Mettler polled fourteen hundred Americans in 2008, asking them if they had "ever used a government social program." Fifty-seven percent of the respondents said no. When the respondents were then asked whether they had personally used any of twenty-one listed programs, including unemployment insurance, Social Security, student loans, and the home-mortgage-interest deduction, 92 percent had, in fact, used at least one such program.[84] The average respondent had used four programs.[85]

As might be expected, a person's political views correlated with his or her acknowledgment of using government support programs,[86] but the design of the government programs was also important. Mettler found that when individuals do not have to interact intensively or frequently with the state to receive a benefit, they are less likely to acknowledge or understand that they are receiving a governmental benefit.[87] Mettler calls this the "submerged state"—programs that run through the tax code, such as tax exemptions for employer-provided retirement and health-care benefits, and tax deductions for items such as interest payments on a home mortgage.[88] The beneficiaries of these kinds of government programs do not see the presence of the state in their lives.

In short, the kind of constitutional family autonomy supposedly enshrined in *Meyer* and *Pierce* hides the reality of pervasive state influence. The rhetoric of family autonomy in the cases is simply not an accurate description of the state's treatment of families.

This is not to say that family autonomy is meaningless. Perhaps most important, family autonomy means that the state cannot simply remove a child from a parent's custody because the state believes another parent would provide a better environment for the child. The state can remove a child from the home only if it can demonstrate that the child is at risk of imminent harm or has actually been abused or neglected. Further, the doctrine of family autonomy provides some measure of self-determination for families. The state cannot control every aspect of a child's life, and instead, parents do get to decide, broadly speaking, which values to inculcate in a child. This protection of a diversity of decision-making among families prevents the state from imposing a uniform view of parenting on all families and helps safeguard cultural and moral diversity in matters of childrearing. This antitotalitarian function for the family is reflected in the *Pierce* decision.

An uneven application

Another important aspect of the myth of family autonomy is that to the extent that the state does allow families to make some decisions, historically and still today, there is less state deference to low-income and nondominant families, such as recent immigrants and families of color. It would take volumes to document all the ways state regulation of families has been used as an instrument of the powerful against the powerless, but a few brief examples will demonstrate that the state is more willing to intervene overtly in the lives of some families than others.

Slavery is, of course, the quintessential example of the state's failure to respect family autonomy. Numerous accounts of slavery have demonstrated how the law forbade slaves to marry and how owners could, and very often did, separate family members through the sale of parents or children.[89] But even after the end of slavery, the state continued to use the law to break up African American families. Legal scholar Katherine Franke, for example, has written about the regulation of newly freed slaves during Reconstruction. She has shown that many of the family practices that the freed slaves engaged in—including serial relationships and divorcing only informally, not through the courts—led to criminal prosecutions by the state for adultery, bigamy, and fornication.[90] After African American men were convicted of these offenses, the prisoners were leased out to white farmers, essentially recreating and perpetuating the forced-labor regime that had just been abolished.[91] The end of slavery was hardly the beginning of a new era of family autonomy for African Americans.

The various iterations of welfare programs during the twentieth century also demonstrate how the state treats lower-income families differently, pathologizing their need for state support while pretending that middle- and upper-income families are not also reliant on the state. The precursor of today's welfare law was the Aid to Dependent Children, created through the Social Security Act of 1935, and was motivated by conflicting interests.[92] Policymakers recognized the need to support at least some poor mothers (the laws were aimed at white widows) and their children, but lawmakers were also concerned about the behaviors and habits of these women. State laws thus excluded certain children from welfare eligibility if their mothers strayed from the state-approved lifestyle.[93] A number of states enacted "suitable home" laws that declared illegitimate children ineligible for welfare.[94] Sexual behavior was the most common gauge of a suitable home, giving the state license to regulate domestic behavior.[95] States enacted surveillance laws, establishing investigative units to find women whose behaviors were immoral or unacceptable.[96] This surveillance ranged from agents keeping recipients' homes under observation to investigators randomly entering and searching a beneficiary's home.[97] States later replaced this form of regulation with another: family-cap laws, which deny support payments for children born or conceived while the mother receives state assistance.[98]

The current version of welfare—the Temporary Assistance to Needy Families (TANF) program—continues this tradition of scrutinizing the family life of welfare recipients. In addition to permitting states to adopt family-cap provisions,[99] TANF allows states to impose "individual responsibility plans," which condition the receipt of benefits on a parent ensuring that a child attends school regularly, immunizes children, and attends parenting classes.[100] Contrast this, and other, intrusions on family life with the virtually nonexistent scrutiny of families receiving Social Security survivor benefits. Following the death of a qualifying person, family members (typically a spouse, an ex-spouse, and children) can receive Social Security benefits. Recipients need not show that they are caring adequately for their children and instead receive the payments simply by virtue of their relationship to the insured.[101] This is true of other federal programs typically used by middle- and upper-income families, such as the tax deductions for dependents.[102] These deductions are not contingent on parents using the money for the benefit of children. It is simply presumed that families will do so.

Finally, consider North Carolina's experience with sterilization. From 1929 to 1975, North Carolina sterilized approximately seventy-six hundred people.[103] Thirty-two other states had similar eugenics programs, but North Carolina's stands out because of the large numbers and the design of the program. Most state programs targeted institutionalized patients, such as the mentally ill and the physically disabled,[104] but in North Carolina, social workers often coerced young teens to consent to sterilization by threatening to cut off the family's welfare.[105] Under the guise of "preventive medicine," low-income youth, especially girls and those with low IQ test scores or the undereducated, were sterilized.[106] Many girls were sterilized after giving birth in the hospital, even if the pregnancy was the result of rape or incest.[107] Racial minorities made up 40 percent of the sterilized victims nationwide.[108]

But rather than continue this whistle-stop tour of the many ways the state has protected entrenched interests at the cost of marginalized families, the fairly straightforward point that relates to the larger theme of this book is that state regulation of vulnerable families often comes in the guise of state improvement programs. The state may recognize that it is overriding the ideal of family autonomy, but it justifies its actions in the name of the betterment of the family. A historical example, with its modern counterpart, illustrates this point well. The "child-saving" movement, from roughly 1880 to 1910, saw upper-middle-class white men and women seeking to "save" children by bringing child abuse to the forefront of social and political debate. Their focus, however, was solely on low-income and marginal families.[109] The founders of Societies for the Prevention of Cruelty to Children (SPCCs) were private organizations that later operated with considerable state authority. Although there were clearly cases of horrific abuse (one such case was the impetus for these efforts), more typically, the child savers judged the immigrant homes using white, upper-class norms.[110] The child savers, for example, were horrified by the immigrants' use of garlic in cooking and their habit of drinking wine with dinner, and they decided that these were adequate bases for removing children.[111] Appalled by what they perceived as the deviant lifestyles of immigrant families, the child savers sought to "improve" these families by insisting that children be quiet and clean, dress well, and eat "good" food, not traditional immigrant cuisine.[112]

Some SPCCs, such as the Massachusetts Society, allowed children to remain in the care and custody of their parents but only under extensive supervision.[113] Others—the New York Society, for example—responded by forcefully removing children from the "corrupted" environments, particularly when the children were performing on the streets, which the society considered child labor.[114] The children were then placed in institutions, where they were kept out of the public eye, and parents were held criminally liable.[115] Their reach was extensive: in the last two decades of the nineteenth century, the New York Society won 49,330 convictions against parents and removed 90,078 children from their homes.[116]

Although arguably well-intentioned, the zeal of the child savers was limited to the lives of marginal families. They were not concerned with the multiple ways children in all families were treated poorly. An ongoing criticism of the modern child-welfare system is that it continues to embody this child-saving approach to low-income families. As chapter 4 explores in greater detail, the child-welfare system is largely an ill-conceived, late-in-the-day response to poverty. Rather than responding to child maltreatment in all families—such as the sexual abuse that occurs across all classes— the child-welfare system focuses predominantly on poverty-related neglect among low-income families of color. The state intervention is done in the name of protecting children, but it comes at a very high cost to the well-being of both children and parents, and it is deeply intrusive, second-guessing and micromanaging nearly every aspect of family life. Chapter 9 returns to this problem of well-intentioned state efforts, exploring how it sounds a strong note of caution for the proposals in this book.

* * *

In sum, the ideological construct of family autonomy is overdeterminate, misstating the actual relationship between the state and families. It is possible to believe family autonomy exists, because some state involvement is not perceived as such. This is not to undervalue some measure of deference to families or to understate the importance of a strict rule limiting the removal of children from parental custody. But a broad conception of family autonomy oversimplifies the complex relationship between families and the state, leading to a misunderstanding of the actual relationship. It also opens the door to the political argument that the state *can* stay out of family life.

RESISTANCE TO ACKNOWLEDGING AN OMNIPRESENT STATE

The notion of a pervasive state is an unsettling and unwelcome one for many, and there is considerable resistance from different political and cultural perspectives to acknowledging both the extent and the inevitability of state regulation. Beginning with libertarian arguments, the premise underlying a call for limited government is the belief that it is possible to disentangle the state from families. Charles Murray, for example, believes the state should play only a minimal role in family life. In his most recent iteration of this argument, he contends that socioeconomic inequality among whites in the United States—particularly between the top 20 percent and the bottom 30 percent—can be attributed to a difference in values.[117] To Murray, the top quintile lives according to what he describes as the four "founding virtues" of America: marriage, industriousness, honesty, and religiosity.[118] The bottom 30 percent, by contrast, do not live according to these values, which has led to a loss of social capital for this group and a concomitant loss of the life satisfaction that comes from not living in civic, engaged communities.[119] Murray contends that the lower life satisfaction stems from the bottom 30 percent abdicating responsibility for their lives. He says, "Knowing that we have responsibility for the consequences of our actions is a major part of what makes life worth living."[120]

The solution, according to Murray, is libertarianism. When the government tries to help the bottom 30 percent, he argues, it only robs them of responsibility for their lives.[121] He cites raising children as an example: "if you're a low-income parent who finds it easier to let the apparatus of an advanced welfare state take over," this diminishes "the deep satisfactions that go with raising children."[122] He believes that families and communities are strong only because they know that it is up to them to "get things done" but that when government takes over for these institutions, both families and communities disintegrate.[123] For this reason, Murray argues that the welfare state can be justified only to prevent starvation or death from exposure.[124] Murray's approach is consistent with a strong belief in family autonomy. Underlying his argument is the idea that families *can* be independent of the state.

The problem with this libertarian argument is that it fails to account for the inevitable role of the state in family life. Organized government—which is a reality in this modern age—necessarily affects families, in all the ways elaborated above.[125] In terms of more direct intervention in family life, legal scholar Frances Olsen has argued that opponents of state intervention would still expect the state to reinforce parental authority over children. If a child ran away, for example, they would expect the police to return the child home. Similarly, opponents of state intervention would expect the state to protect the family from interference by third parties, such as a doctor who would perform nonemergency surgery without parental consent or a neighbor who would take a child on vacation without parental permission.[126] Claims for nonintervention are better understood as an objection to the content of state regulation, rather than to its existence.[127]

The libertarian claim, then, is really a call for a radically scaled-back government. But how far does this argument extend? Should we dismantle the public-education system, for example? Or does the concern really center on programs that benefit low-income families because these programs, according to their critics, create an unhealthy dependency on the government?

Let's focus on this latter argument, because it also animates another group: conservatives. They, too, use family autonomy as the lodestar for policy prescriptions, although the conservative concern is less with the state per se. Conservatives generally believe in "limited government," but their focus is more on the *kind* of state role, believing that some programs remove the incentive for low-income families to better their own lot.

The bootstrap solution to poverty is an overly familiar, if also effective, trope. Many of the leading Republican candidates for the 2012 presidential nomination, for example, cast the solution to struggling families in personal, rather than structural, terms.[128] One debate during the primaries posed the following question: "Given the crisis situation among a group of historically disadvantaged Americans, do you feel the time has come to take special steps to deal with poverty afflicting one race?" Rick Santorum answered by explaining, "A study done in 2009 determined that if Americans do three things, they can avoid poverty. Three things: work, graduate from high school, and get married before you have children. Those three things result in only 2% of people ending up in poverty."[129]

The problem with the argument that individuals are best served by a tough-love approach is that it fails to account for the substantial governmental support received by those at the top of the economic ladder, including Medicare, public education, and the home-mortgage-interest deduction. As described above, Suzanne Mettler's work shows that virtually all Americans benefit from specific state support programs but that the programs benefitting middle- and upper-income families are submerged and thus are easy to ignore. As Mettler has shown, the submerged state operates under the public radar, funneling money and resources away from lower- and middle-income families and directing it to upper-income families.[130] The programs are not perceived as part of the welfare state, and most recipients are not aware that they are receiving government assistance of any kind.[131]

Mettler provides the example of the government-backed private student loans that primarily benefit middle- and upper-income families.[132] Instead of a direct subsidy to students, the submerged program enables students to borrow from the private lender of their choice, but this program costs the government billions of dollars each year in guarantees, interest-rate reductions, and deferred payments.[133] Most students view their loans as "private," believing that they financed their education without any assistance, despite serious government investment delivered via the submerged state.[134] And conservatives support this government spending. The 2012 Republican Platform stated, "The federal government should not be in the business of originating student loans; however, it should serve as an insurance guarantor for the private sector as they offer loans to students."[135]

The failure to see the government's role in their own lives makes it easier to argue against support for low-income families. In Mettler's survey, respondents who received support through the "submerged state" were less likely to agree with the statement that the "government has provided me opportunities to improve my standard of living" than respondents who used programs that required them to interact frequently or intensively with a public official, such as food stamps and subsidized-housing programs.[136]

Moreover, the conservative concern about dependency is uneven and does not extend to subsidies that benefit important constituencies. The Freedom to Farm Act of 1996 provides farmers with direct government payments in addition to market prices.[137] The Food, Energy, and Conservation Act of 2008 continues agricultural subsidies for corporate farmers.[138] The Taylor Grazing Act permits private ranchers to graze their livestock on public lands.[139] And federal energy subsidies provide tax relief for oil and gas exploration and development.[140] Generally speaking, conservatives are not worried about these subsidies creating an unhealthy dependency. It seems, then, that the argument against dependency is not about the existence of state support or even the form of state support but rather the identity of the beneficiaries.

In sum, libertarian and conservative arguments about family autonomy are based on an inaccurate view of the actual relationship between families and the state. The erroneous perception that some families operate without state support makes it easier to pathologize those families whose dependencies are more visible.

It is not only libertarians and conservatives who are concerned with state regulation. Many liberals, too, want less state regulation or less of a certain kind of state regulation. These commentators acknowledge that the state is omnipresent and do not think families are autonomous, but they take issue with the content and manner of some existing regulation. Their concern is particularly with a state-prescribed view of family life, which elevates some choices while denigrating others. Katherine Franke, for example, has sounded a cautionary note about the marriage-equality movement. Although she strongly supports equal rights for LGBT individuals, Franke is concerned that the push for marriage equality limits sexual liberties. Franke believes that the option of marriage should be open to same-sex couples, but she contends that the emphasis on marriage, with all of its legal and social implications, limits the recognition of nonmarital relationships.[141] Instead of so quickly moving same-sex couples into the heavily regulated category of marriage, Franke believes advocates should capitalize and expand on the right to sexuality outside marriage, which was recognized in the Supreme Court's decision in *Lawrence v. Texas*.[142] And legal scholar Martha Fineman critiques the state's focus on the sexual relationship between adults, arguing that it obscures the need to support caregivers. Fineman believes that the state should construct the family around what is most important to society—caretaking—rather than marriage, which does not have an impact on the collective whole.[143]

I am sympathetic to these concerns about the state overly focusing on adult relationships, but as this chapter has established, even if the state wanted to regulate adult relationships less than parent-child relationships, this would be difficult to do. Certainly, there could be less direct regulation—no civil marriage, for example—but the state cannot stop all indirect regulation. Zoning laws will continue to influence where and how groupings of individuals live. Antidiscrimination laws will continue to influence the workplace and a person's ability to support a family. Funding patterns for public education will continue to influence where adults, even those without children, live, because property values and property taxes reflect the quality of the local schools. And so on.

The goal is to figure out how best to redirect this pervasive state so that it encourages strong, stable, positive relationships within the family. As the second part of this book argues, there are greater societal justifications for focusing on children and the parent-child relationship, but ensuring that children have strong, stable, positive relationships with their parents necessarily involves the relationships between a child's parents. Whether liberals want to admit it or not, the relationship between adults affects children, as chapter 2 explained in detail. This does not mean that the state needs to promote marriage as the solution—and certainly not the *sole* solution—to struggling families. There are numerous ways to foster strong, stable, positive relationships within families. But we cannot ignore relationships between adults. They are part of the equation for family flourishing.

CONCLUSION

Rather than pretending that families are a refuge from the outside world and that the arm of the state does not reach into the home, it is essential to recognize that the state is an active force in the lives of all American families. A realistic, historically grounded view of the state's influence on family life elicits caution, but current arguments that would try to eliminate the state's role altogether are simply unrealistic. The continued belief in a robust ideal of family autonomy is more than self-delusion; it is deeply problematic, because it limits a sense of how the state can encourage strong, stable, positive relationships within families. By recognizing, rather than denying, the breadth and depth of state regulation, it is possible to engage in a more productive debate about the form and content of that regulation. The goal is not to disentangle the state from family life but rather to reorient the role the state already plays. The problem, as chapter 4 explains, is that the state role in regulating families fails to nurture strong, stable, positive relationships, to the great detriment of both families and society.

4

Negative Family Law

VERNICE HILL GREW up in Brooklyn with eleven siblings and half-siblings and not nearly enough money to go around.[1] When she was eight years old, her parents separated, and by age fifteen, Hill was pregnant. She dropped out of ninth grade and tried to take care of her daughter, but, as she says, "I started life at too young an age. I was a child taking care of a child."[2] After Hill's mother kicked the teen and her baby out of their shared apartment, Hill moved in and out of different homes and homeless shelters. She subsequently had five more children, by two different men. By her own account, Hill drank heavily and sometimes hit the children with her hand or a belt, but, according to her, she "didn't abuse them."[3]

On numerous occasions, the child-welfare system removed some or all of the children, putting them in foster care for relatively brief periods.[4] But then, one day in May 2005, when her oldest child had already moved out of the home and one of the younger children was still in foster care, Hill left the four other children, ages three, six, thirteen, and fifteen, alone while she went to visit a neighbor. The older boys were supposed to look after the younger girls while they napped, but instead, they left the apartment, with Hill's keys locked inside. Returning drunk from the neighbor's apartment, Hill called 911 for help opening the door. When the police and firefighters arrived, they found the girls inside, hungry and alone in a filthy apartment infested with roaches and spiders. All four children were removed from the home, and this time, they did not return quickly.

Instead, the case fell into the black hole of family court. The children were split up and put in two different homes. The two older boys had trouble with their foster family and were moved into a residential treatment facility. The two younger girls also had trouble with their first foster family, and they were moved to a new family. By 2006, Hill was able to regain custody of the two boys and the other son who was in care, but the two girls remained in their foster home, where they had become settled. Their foster parents gave them love, attention, and a middle-class lifestyle, with a trip to Disney World and new toys and clothes.

According to a court decision, the agency did almost nothing to reunite Hill and the girls. The agency offered neither services for Hill nor family therapy for the girls and their mother. Instead, the agency made it exceedingly difficult for Hill to visit the girls. Although the agency claimed that Hill could not be trusted with the girls, it returned the three boys to her care. By 2008, the foster-care agency ended all visits between Hill and the girls, decided that the girls should live permanently with the foster family, and filed a petition in court to terminate Hill's parental rights. The trial took three years because of the tremendous caseload straining the Bronx Family Court. When the judge finally issued an opinion in 2011, the court was highly critical of the agency and refused to terminate Hill's parental rights. In response, the agency brought a new petition, this time claiming that Hill had abandoned the girls and failed to visit them, even though it was the agency that had stopped facilitating these visits in 2008. A new trial began in 2013 and at the time this book was going to press, it was ongoing.

This story represents so much of what is wrong with family law today. Returning to the frame established in the introduction, family law is both the system for addressing particular conflicts in families, *dispute-resolution family law*, and the multiple ways in which the state sets the terms for family life, such as determining who is a family in the first place, shaping family behavior through subsidies and incentives, and setting the context for relationships through rules governing workplace access, incarceration, and neighborhood design, *structural family law*.

Beginning with dispute-resolution family law, this system was not designed for mothers, fathers, parents, and children to resolve their most intimate disputes in a way that maintains strong, stable, positive relationships. Instead, dispute-resolution family law is based on the same adversarial system that was developed to address commercial disputes and the like. When this adversarial approach is overlaid on families, it does not begin to address the real problems facing families and instead creates a win-lose dynamic that pits one family member against the other. For Vernice Hill's family, this means that either the girls return home to her care or remain with their foster parents, to whom they have become understandably attached after years of living together. Whatever the outcome of the court case, no one will win.

The real tragedy of this impossible situation is that it probably could have been avoided if the state, through structural family law, had tried to foster strong, stable, positive relationships much earlier in the day. Rather than combat her family's poverty in a meaningful way, help Vernice Hill avoid a teen pregnancy, or give her the tools to be a more effective parent, the state waited for her family to fall apart. Only then did the state begin its overt efforts to "help."

As this story illustrates, the central problem with structural family law is that despite pervasive regulation, the state takes a reactive approach to family well-being, failing to nurture strong, stable, positive relationships within the family at the time of creation and during key periods of transition. Instead of helping families early on, much state regulation is ill-timed, ill-conceived, or inadequate. This reactive approach virtually ensures poor outcomes for parents and children alike. It also makes it more likely that families will end up in the court system.

The systemic failings of both dispute-resolution family law and structural family law create what this book calls *negative family law*. We know from chapter 1 that strong, stable, positive relationships within the family are essential to flourishing. We know from chapter 2 that many adults are struggling to provide these kinds of relationships to each other and to their children. And we know from chapter 3 that the state has a tremendous influence over a family's ability to provide these relationships. This chapter brings these three points together and shows that the state is partly to blame for the poor family outcomes. As elaborated below, the real problem with pervasive state regulation is not its existence but rather *how* the state regulates families: the state fails to nurture strong, stable, positive relationships to help families avoid conflict, and then, when conflict does occur, the state fails to resolve family disputes in a way that would maintain strong, stable, positive relationships.

DISPUTE-RESOLUTION FAMILY LAW: RUPTURE WITHOUT REPAIR

Minor ruptures are a part of everyday life. Parents miss cues from children, resulting in momentary misattunements, and romantic partners experience misunderstandings and moments of irritation and frustration. These ruptures are not necessarily a problem and can actually play an important role in strengthening relationships. Studies of mothers and children, for example, have found that a mother is correctly attuned to her infant's emotions only about 30 percent of the time.[5] This initial misattunement is not a lasting problem, because the mother often corrects her reaction to the infant based on the infant's response.[6] This temporary misattunement followed by a correction is essential to healthy child development, because it helps the infant build a sense of mastery, develop coping mechanisms, and experience despair changing into positive emotions.[7] It is only the repeated failure to repair these minor ruptures that creates developmental problems for the child.[8]

Unfortunately, major ruptures—from child abuse and domestic violence to illicit affairs and other betrayals—also mark the lives of many families, and these conflicts often end up in the court system. The problem with dispute-resolution family law is that it imposes on family disputes the existing legal system designed to resolve other kinds of conflicts. This one-size-fits-all approach does not account for three essential differences between family disputes and other legal cases. First, family conflicts typically involve intense emotions. Second, the parties will almost certainly continue to relate to one another long after the court action ends. And third, the parties need help repairing their relationships so that the future contact among family members—and particularly parents and children—can be strong, stable, and positive. When the current legal system is used for family conflicts, it both freezes the relationship at the moment of breakdown and fuels the conflict with the adversarial process, doing nothing to help repair relationships. This chapter describes a few interesting reforms, but too many of these are underdeveloped or not widely adopted.

Three hallmarks of family-law cases

Intense emotions. The people involved in family disputes often know one another on the deepest personal level and are likely to have, as nearly all people do, complicated, emotional relationships with particular histories. Parties include spouses and other romantic partners, biological and adoptive parents, children, extended family members, birth parents, donors of eggs and sperm, gestational surrogates, and prospective parents. Their disputes typically involve intense, usually negative, emotions. Divorce, for example, is generally understood to be one of the greatest emotional upheavals in a lifetime.[9] The emotional process typically is not linear but rather cyclical, with emotions moving back and forth between love, anger, and sadness.[10]

In the child-welfare context, the emotions accompanying abuse and neglect for the child victims are complex and include fear, anger, anxiety, guilt, sadness, and bewilderment.[11] The emotional response is necessarily complex, and even though a child will almost certainly experience relief when away from the abuse or neglect, being removed from the home, even temporarily, can be deeply traumatizing.[12] For parents who abuse or neglect their children, the emotions are similarly complex. Parents often experience guilt over the abuse, along with anger, denial, and fear of losing a child permanently.[13]

Likewise, adoption can evoke complex and conflicting emotions—joy, guilt, loss, fear, anxiety, and denial—for birth parents, adoptive parents, and adopted children, both at the time of adoption and later.[14] A biological parent whose parental rights are terminated by a court, for example, may well feel tremendous loss, grief, and regret; and parents who voluntarily relinquish a child may feel ambivalent about the decision. An adoptive parent is often on an emotional roller coaster, worried about the finality of the decision. And adopted children can experience a range of emotions toward their birth and adoptive parents. This is not to perpetuate the narrative that parents who voluntarily relinquish their children are bad parents, inflicting a primal wound on their children,[15] but rather to acknowledge that the emotions surrounding adoption are complex and, of course, will vary with the individual.[16]

These emotional issues underlying family-law disputes can lead family members to engage in a range of self- and relationship-destructive behaviors, which, in turn, often affect the legal proceedings. The consequences of this are discussed below.

Ongoing relationships. Even after significant shifts in legal status—a marriage dissolved, parental rights terminated, legal parentage changed from a birth parent to an adoptive parent—the relationship between former family members typically endures. This is unlike many other areas of the law, such as criminal law, where the state is prosecuting an individual, or much tort law, where a stranger is suing another stranger or a corporation. By contrast with these legal disputes, a divorcing couple with children will continue to communicate with each other for years to come. Long after the lawyers have moved on to another case, the couple will still be talking to each other to coordinate holiday plans, decide whether a child needs tutoring, or deal with a medical emergency. In the child-welfare system, approximately half of the children in foster care return home to their parents. Those who do not return home are often adopted by a relative and so will continue to see their parents.[17] Looking at adoptions outside the child-welfare system, statistics belie the dominant image of an infant placed in the home of a nonrelative: 41 percent of domestic adoptions are by relatives, and in 71 percent of these adoptions, the child had lived at some point with his or her birth family.[18] Even when an infant is placed with a nonrelative, adopted children may remain in touch with their birth parents if their adoptions were "open," or they may reconnect with their birth parents at some later point in their lives.[19]

To elaborate on one example, it is easy to assume that a young person who has been abused or neglected and has spent years in the foster-care system will cease feeling close to his or her biological family. But a study of foster youth who "age out" of the foster-care system—young people who are never adopted but also are not returned to the custody of their biological families—documented the strong ties these young people maintain with family members, including their parents. Seventeen percent of such foster youths returned to live with their parents after being released from foster care, and two-thirds of these young people, even if they did not live with their parents again, reported feeling "somewhat close or very close" to their biological mothers.[20]

Changing a legal status may be the right decision for a family. Some marriages should end. Finalizing an adoption gives both the adoptive parents and the child peace of mind. And terminating the parental rights of some children is the right answer. But these changes do not mean that the relationships are over. Far from it.

The need to repair relationships. This ongoing contact means that it is critical to repair relationships. As chapter 2 described, American families are increasingly fluid. To reiterate just one of the statistics, regardless of whether their parents are married or cohabiting, 40 percent of children in the United States will experience a family breakup by the time they are fifteen years old.[21] Although the romantic relationship between the two parents may be over, the children still need strong, stable, positive relationships with both parents. For this to happen, the parents will need to get along well enough to facilitate these relationships and function as co-parents. In the child-welfare context, for the children who eventually return home, it is essential to repair their relationships with their parents. Even when children do not return home, as explained above, they often still maintain contact with their parents, and their parents remain an important influence in their lives. Here, too, repair is needed. And in the adoption context, although the issues are complex and vary with each case, it is important to pay attention to a child's relationships with both birth and adoptive parents.

In some family-law cases—particularly those involving domestic violence—a complete break is essential for the safety and well-being of the parties. Too often, however, dispute-resolution family law takes this complete-rupture approach and imposes it on all cases, rather than recognizing that in many cases, relationships will and should continue even after a change in legal status.

A mismatch between the existing legal system and family disputes

Despite these important differences between family disputes and most other kinds of legal actions, the substance, process, and practice of family law is built on the same adversarial system that we use for parties with no emotional connection and who need not interact following the legal action. There are important values at the heart of the Anglo-American legal system, including finality, uniformity, judicial efficiency, and an adversarial process,[22] but as they play out in family law, too often these values undermine the ability of family members to maintain or create strong, stable, positive relationships after the dispute is over.

One way to think about the problems with the current approach is that it is at odds with the cycle of intimacy described in chapter 1. As that chapter explained, a widely shared human experience is that individuals experience love, inevitably transgress against those they love, feel guilt about the transgression, and then seek to repair the damage. This cycle of emotions, and in particular the drive to repair a relationship, is an important and fundamental dynamic in human relations. Traditional dispute-resolution family law, however, works against this cycle of intimacy.

Substance. With a few limited exceptions described below, the substance of family law embodies the broader legal system's win-lose, binary approach to conflict. A couple is either married or divorced. In the child-welfare system, a parent must regain custody of the children or face termination of parental rights. In the adoption context, after giving birth, a biological parent either places the child for adoption, thus losing all parental rights, or retains custody of the child with parental rights completely intact. Gestational surrogates and donors of eggs or sperm are either granted parental rights or not. And legal parenthood more generally is an all-or-nothing proposition. An individual is either a legal parent with full rights and responsibilities or a legal stranger to the child, with no rights and responsibilities.

Additionally, when it comes to legal parenthood, family law's "rule of two" recognizes only two legal parents for each child. In blended families, for example, stepparents are not considered legal parents, even though they may act as parents in the common understanding of the word, caring for children, sharing the expenses of raising children, and so on. If the marriage ends, a stepparent has no legal right to see the stepchild and no accompanying legal responsibility to pay child support. The only way around this is for the stepparent to adopt the child through what are often called "stepparent adoptions," where the legal rights of one of the existing parents are terminated and the stepparent becomes the adoptive parent. This maintains the two-parent requirement. There are some exceptions to this limited approach to legal parenthood, such as the increasing recognition that grandparents have a special interest in their children, possibly entitled to legal protection,[23] and open adoption, discussed below, but by and large, family law is reluctant to enlarge the pie of legal parenthood.

More broadly, family law's win-lose, binary substance leaves little room to recognize and protect ties outside the traditional family. Although families come in many stripes, the prototype of a married mother and father together raising their children remains family law's "family." The majority of states do not allow partners of the same sex to marry. Adoption law insists on severing all legal bonds between birth parents and the adopted child. And cohabitants receive little legal protection.

A final example of the win-lose approach is the continued use of marital fault in at least some aspects of divorce law. Before the 1970s, family law required a party seeking a divorce to show that the other party had committed fault, such as adultery or cruelty.[24] Every state now offers some form of no-fault divorce,[25] but more than half the states still consider marital fault relevant to an award of spousal support.[26] This kind of rule, which tends to recognize only one wrongdoer and one innocent, is too simplistic and one-sided. It fails to capture the reality of most marriages, where there is inevitably a dynamic that feeds transgressions. But even more important, it gives the couple a reason to bring the worst aspects of the marriage into the legal dispute.

Process. In the divorce context, some alternatives are developing, and mediation is increasingly common, but the litigation-based adversarial system is still an important force, with the parties well aware that if they cannot decide important issues, the court will do so for them. Child-welfare cases are largely decided in courtroom proceedings, and other kinds of family disputes, say between an adoptive parent and a biological parent, are addressed through the court system.[27]

The adversarial process valorizes clean lines, assigning parental rights and child custody to one person over another, dividing marital assets between the parties, and otherwise bringing legal relationships to what the legal system perceives to be closure. Parents often share custody of a child, but the sense that the person with more time with the child has won persists. And although marital assets are generally divided in a way the court considers to be "equitable," parties often experience a sense of victory or defeat in this context and certainly fight that way.[28]

Practice. Too often, family-law attorneys reinforce the oppositionalism that this substance and process generate. Rather than helping a client find common ground with the family member, family-law practitioners are criticized for fueling their clients' winner-take-all mentality. One study found that family-law practitioners are far more likely to engage in relationship-destroying, adversarial behavior than lawyers in any other type of practice.[29] The study found that family law, as compared with other practice areas, had the highest percentage of "unethically adversarial" attorneys, described as those who do not listen to their clients' needs, are uncooperative and rigid, and inflict unnecessary harm on the opposing side.[30]

The example of child custody

It will help explain the shortcomings of dispute-resolution family law by looking more closely at a particular area, such as child custody. An enduring source of conflict in divorcing families is the battle between parents over who will have the right to make important decisions about their children's lives (typically called "legal custody") and with whom the child will live (typically called "physical custody"). Increasingly, divorcing couples share these responsibilities through joint custody,[31] especially joint legal custody, but for many couples, disputes over the Solomonic task of dividing the child remain a particularly painful and contentious aspect of the divorce. Each state has its own custody regime, but the central idea animating all of these systems is that custody is determined based on the "best interests" of the child. State custody laws suffer from four central problems that arise from the basic adversarial legalism that frames these disputes.

First, custody disputes pit one parent against the other, increasing acrimony and conflict. If both parents agree about legal and physical custody from the beginning of the divorce or if they reach an agreement through mediation, then courts will generally adopt that agreement, so long as it is in the child's best interests.[32] But if the parents do not agree, then the court must decide what is in the child's best interests. In these disputes, whether resolved by a court, through mediation, or by the parties somewhere along the way,[33] the basic framework places the parents in competition with each other, each one arguing that "it is in the child's best interests to live with *me*." Even if it is left unsaid—and often it is not—the implication is "I am a better parent than my soon-to-be ex." Custody battles thus fuel the hurt, pain, and anger that many divorcing spouses already have for each other, providing a new, high-stakes battlefield on which to fight an old war.

Second, court-driven decisions do not lay the groundwork for future co-parenting. After a decision is reached, the parents—who have spent several months, if not years, locked in legal combat with each other—are now expected to turn on a dime and co-parent their children together. As divorce lawyers sometimes quip, "marriage is for now, but divorce is forever." Custody disputes make it much harder to cooperate in the "forever," because these disputes undermine the goal of spouses establishing a working relationship. This is a particular problem for children, because the fighting between the parents often leads one parent to disengage from the family.

Third, custody decisions are notoriously difficult for outsiders to make, and there is considerable doubt about the competence of the courts to make good decisions for families.[34] Courts inevitably have to rely on contested testimony from the parents and third parties, who bring their own biases and agendas to these emotionally fraught contests. Often it is not even judges who are making the decisions based on their own determinations. Instead, in many cases, the court will assign a third party, often but not always a mental-health professional, to prepare a custody evaluation. This position goes by different names depending on the state—such as child-custody evaluator, custody investigator, forensic evaluator, parental-responsibilities evaluator, and child and family investigator—but their tremendous power is consistent. Courts often simply adopt the recommendation. This person may have spent more time with the parents and children than the judge, often meeting separately with each parent, visiting the homes, speaking with teachers and others who know the family, and sometimes ordering extensive psychological testing for the parents. But it is still a third party making relatively snap judgments about the fate of a family.

It is easy to think that mental-health professionals are better positioned to make these sorts of assessments, but this is not necessarily true. The evidence needed to make a custody decision is exceedingly difficult to obtain, because so much of it occurs behind closed doors.[35] Mental-health professionals have no lie-detection skills or particular expertise in culling reliable information out of an often emotionally volatile situation, with contesting parents determined to make positive, and often misleading, impressions.[36] Despite the limitations of the observational data they are working with, mental-health professionals often make extended inferences about the ultimate issue of custody.[37] Their reliance on psychological tests carries the veneer of scientific objectivity but delivers very little of proven probative value.[38]

Finally, custody decisions made by anyone other than the parents are intrusive, with outsiders, rather than the parents, determining what is best for the child. There is no such system for an intact family. If married parents cannot agree about, say, whether a child should go to parochial school or the local public school, a court does not become involved. Parents must work it out on their own. But when a couple is getting divorced and the parents cannot agree about what is best for their child, the state makes the decision for them. Divorcing parents thus face a far more intrusive state than nondivorcing parents. Moreover, the distinction is not simply between intact and divorcing couples but rather between intact couples and amicably divorcing couples on the one hand and acrimonious divorcing parents on the other.

To understand this difference, picture three different couples, each trying to decide whether one of the spouses should move out of the state to pursue a job opportunity and, if the parent does move, where the child should live:

Couple 1: Alice and Barbara are married and cannot reach a decision. They almost wish a court would decide for them, but no court will listen to their dispute, because courts lack the authority (technically, "subject-matter jurisdiction") to decide the issue.

Couple 2: Clarice and Devon are getting divorced and are struggling with the same decision. After much debate, they come up with a workable solution: their child will stay with the in-state parent during the school year and spend long vacations with the out-of-state parent. They present the court with a settlement agreement laying out this solution. Absent some egregious circumstance, the court will approve the decision and will not second-guess it.

Couple 3: Eva and Franco also are divorcing, but the couple vehemently disagrees about what to do in this situation and cannot reach a compromise on their own. The court steps in and makes the decision for them.

It does not make sense to have a different regime for the third set of parents, simply because they cannot agree *and* are getting divorced. If the principle was that the state should step in to protect children from quarrelsome parents, then we would have a very different family-law system. The state would intervene for both couple 1 and couple 3. Instead, the rule is one of deference for intact couples and divorcing-but-agreeable couples and paternalism for divorcing-but-quarrelsome couples.

In short, family law's system for resolving child custody is a paradigmatic example of the failings of dispute-resolution family law, but it is not the only area where the law undermines relationships. It is simply one example among many.

The consequences

In all these ways, dispute-resolution family law pits one family member against the other, taking the complex and ongoing relationships it regulates and reducing disputants into narrow categories. The current orientation takes the norms that prevail in the most arm's-length, impersonal legal disputes and imposes these norms on the most intimate and emotional of conflicts.

This adversarial approach reinforces, and sometimes creates, acrimony between family members, especially in the context of divorce and child welfare, and thus is poorly calibrated to the reality of ongoing relationships. Whatever breach the members of the family have suffered, subjecting that breach to the pressures of the adversarial system is likely to heighten the emotions surrounding the breach. There is little recognition in the legal system that "winning" a family-law dispute may further weaken a fragile relationship with an ex-spouse, who will now be a co-parent and with whom the litigant must work out myriad issues. Divorce and other family-law actions simply cannot be viewed through the same lens as, say, criminal law and tort law, where the parties have no ongoing relationship after the case is closed.

The legal system's approach to resolving familial disputes, moreover, thwarts any instinct that people may have for reconciliation and compromise. It is no wonder that in these win-lose contexts, family members are frequently unable to move beyond whatever rupturing event led them to become entangled in the legal system. Caught up in anger, disappointment, hurt, and any number of other strong emotions that accompany family disputes, it is hard enough for family members to heal ruptures. But any tendency to do so is driven away by the current approach to family disputes. Some practitioners try to help disputants reach amicable solutions, but in a fundamentally adversarial system, there are substantial constraints on the practice. Family law thus does violence to the cycle of relationships by forestalling the tendency to repair relationships.

Finally, the harm that the rupture orientation inflicts is felt not just by clients but also by family-law attorneys and judges. There are numerous symptoms of this disaffection, including the increased risk of physical violence to family-law attorneys and the reluctance of many judges to hear family-related cases.[39] In a survey conducted by the American Bar Association, nearly 60 percent of family-law attorneys reported violence or threats of violence, usually by opposing clients but sometimes by their own clients.[40]

In sum, dispute-resolution family law actively thwarts the constructive human tendency to feel guilt and seek reparation. By adopting a win-lose, binary approach to conflict, family law freezes familial relationships at the moment of rupture. But because former family members so often continue to relate to one another, stopping at the moment of rupture hinders the ability of individuals to heal their rifts and engage in the repair work necessary for future relating. A regulatory system that governs intimate, emotionally fraught relationships should fundamentally differ from a regulatory system that governs other kinds of interactions, yet family law largely does not. Strong, stable, positive relationships never seemed so far away.

STRUCTURAL FAMILY LAW: A REACTIVE APPROACH
TO FAMILY WELL-BEING

Not only does family law fail to resolve conflicts constructively, but it also fails to prevent these conflicts in the first instance. Instead of structuring family life to foster strong, stable, positive relationships, the state takes a largely reactive stance toward family well-being, expecting families to build these relationships on their own. This can be a Herculean, if not Sisyphean, task.

One of the reasons the state takes this reactive approach is the dominant (if also erroneous) understanding of the family-state relationship: that families stand apart from the state. The doctrine of family autonomy conceives of little proactive role for the state in strengthening families. Consider the fundamental example of paid parental leave. The United States is the only country besides Papua New Guinea, Swaziland, and Liberia that does not guarantee new mothers some form of paid leave.[41] In the United States, the federal Family and Medical Leave Act requires employers to allow workers to take up to twelve weeks to care for a new child or an ailing family member, but not all employers and employees are covered and, more important, the leave is *unpaid*.[42] Given what we know about the importance of parent-child interactions in the very early stages of life and the central role that attachment plays in children's well-being, having a parent spend time with a newborn is a vital first step in creating a strong, stable, positive relationship between the parent and the child. But for many families, particularly low- and moderate-income families, it simply is not possible to take unpaid time off from work to care for a newborn child. Three more examples will help flesh out this picture of a reactive state, which does too little to nurture strong, stable, positive relationships within the family.

The example of the child-welfare system

Consider another story about the child-welfare system, this time from the child's perspective. As a young child, Meloney lived alone with her mother, who worked at a nearby airport.[43] They had a close relationship until Meloney was in elementary school and her mother married a new man and gave birth to four children. Meloney's stepfather was a drug addict, full of rage and abusive to Meloney and her mother. He left the four younger children alone, but Meloney was the focus of his anger. Eventually, Meloney's mother escaped with all the children. They briefly lived on the streets, then moved to a domestic-violence shelter and finally into a house in a different state. Things seemed to be turning around.

But then Meloney's stepfather tracked them down. He persuaded Meloney's mother to let him move into their new home, and not long after, drug dealers took over the house as payment for the stepfather's drug debts. When she was ten years old, life became a nightmare for Meloney, as her stepfather allowed these men to sexually abuse her in exchange for drugs. One day, the police raided the home, and the children were removed and placed in a group home. Meloney's three brothers were relocated three times before being adopted together, and her younger, autistic sister was adopted by a foster family who took in children with special needs. At the age of twelve, Meloney was placed in the home of an elderly couple, the Taylors.

At this point, Meloney fell apart emotionally. She desperately wanted to be reunited with her mother and siblings, and she attempted suicide several times. She was suffering from the constant verbal harassment and emotional abuse of her foster mother. Mrs. Taylor would not let Meloney leave the house or interact with peers, and when Meloney was diagnosed with endometriosis at the age of fourteen, Mrs. Taylor berated her and refused to let her be treated. She never hesitated to remind Meloney that she was "only a foster child" and not "one of her own" and accused her of having a relationship with her foster father. Meloney's only release was school, where she excelled and felt safe. In her senior year of high school, Meloney begged her social worker to let her move into the home of a friend from school. In her friend's home, Meloney had a year of stability before she went to college, a difficult transition to independence. She stayed focused and graduated, but she is still working through deep issues of distrust of others and feelings of unworthiness left from her traumatic experiences at home and in foster care.

The central problem with the child-welfare system is that it suffers from a fundamental misorientation. Rather than trying to prevent abuse or neglect long before it occurs, the prevailing approach to family well-being is to wait for a crisis and then intervene in a heavy-handed manner. This means that what the state calls "preventive services"—counseling, substance abuse treatment, and so on—are offered only after the family has come to the attention of the authorities and is deemed to be at risk of abuse and neglect. Often, this is too little, too late. It also means that drastic responses, such as removing children from the home and placing them in foster care, are often necessary, or at least perceived as necessary, because the family has fallen apart to such a great degree.

This approach is supposedly about respecting parental rights, but in practice, it offers little protection for parents. The constitutionally protected right to the care and custody of a child means little to a mother who is struggling with multiple issues related to poverty. The right does ensure that the state has to meet a heightened standard of harm before it removes a child, but it does not mean that the state must make any effort to help her before she is at real risk for losing her child.

Instead of a system that truly protects children, the child-welfare system is a late-in-the-day mechanism for dealing with the effects of poverty. A widespread misconception about the child-welfare system is that the state intervenes in a family only when a parent severely abuses or neglects a child, as in the case of Meloney. In reality, it is estimated that only 10 percent of all cases in the child-welfare system warrant criminal charges.[44] By contrast, the majority of cases are poverty-related neglect, which typically involves substance abuse, inadequate housing, or inappropriate child-care arrangements,[45] as reflected in the story about Vernice Hill. Although these issues can be serious and may well present a substantial threat to the well-being of a child, the child-welfare system, with its extreme sanction of removing children and placing them in foster care, is not the right tool for addressing poverty. And in cases of severe abuse, as with Meloney, state intervention may be needed to remove the child from a dangerous situation, but this intervention comes with its own costs.

Regardless of the reason for removal, children who are placed in foster care often languish there for months and even years, moving from one home to another. Many foster parents offer excellent, loving care, but it is not the same as a child's own family. Even if eventually reunified with a parent, children who were once in foster care typically suffer significant economic, educational, and psychological hardship. One study found the rate of post-traumatic stress disorder (PTSD) among adults previously placed in foster care to be roughly twice as high as the incidence among war veterans.[46] In addition to PTSD, former foster-care children suffer from depression, social phobia, panic syndrome, and anxiety disorders.[47] It is difficult to tell whether the poor outcomes are attributable to the prior abuse and neglect or the foster-care placement, but it is likely some combination of the two.

The reactive approach extends to the next generation. Many parents of children in foster care today were once in foster care themselves.[48] But the system does not address this cyclical nature of abuse and neglect, investing too little, for example, in mental-health programs that would help victims heal their own trauma and prevent the cycle from repeating.

The reactive approach also means that the state loses an opportunity to work with parents cooperatively. By the time the state intervenes, there is a fundamentally adversarial relationship between the state and families. With the impending threat of removing children from the home, parents are understandably suspicious of state involvement. And the state is wary of parents, because the state is intervening at a stage when the functioning of the parents is likely at a nadir. At this late point, the state's posture is intrusive and judgmental. This adversarial relationship hinders cooperation and highlights the power imbalance between the state and families.

Further, the "help" the state offers at this late stage is largely ineffective. While children are in foster care, the state is supposed to work to reunite families, but it often provides "treatment" that consists of little more than boilerplate plans, with parents required to attend parenting classes and substance-abuse treatment programs. The state allocates scant resources for such treatment, virtually ensuring that parents will not succeed. And this "help" does not come cheap. The direct cost to federal, state, and local governments is more than $29 billion a year.[49] Factoring in the indirect costs of physical and mental-health problems, juvenile delinquency, adult criminality, special education needs, and lost productivity makes the price even higher, with one estimate reaching $100 billion.[50]

In short, instead of proactively nurturing strong, stable, positive relationships to prevent abuse and neglect, the state steps in only after a parent-child relationship has broken down. This reactive approach means that by the time the state intervenes, the abuse or neglect has already occurred, or the family has broken down to such a degree that abuse or neglect is imminent. It is important to keep children safe, but state intervention comes with a high economic and social cost. Moreover, removing a child can cause lasting damage to the parent-child relationship, as children often blame parents for the upheaval,[51] making it harder to repair that relationship if the child is returned home, as approximately half of all children are.[52]

The example of child care

As chapter 2 described, numerous challenges make it harder for parents in low-income families to provide their children with strong, stable, positive relationships. And yet the state does very little to help parents out of poverty, even when the means would seem to be unobjectionable politically. Child-care subsidies are an excellent example. Child care makes it possible for parents to work and is a good

investment in child development.[53] Quality child care for young children has a sustained effect on a child's ability to learn and on overall well-being.[54] School-age children also benefit from quality after-school care, showing better work habits and peer
relationships, stronger social skills, and better overall adjustment than children not
in after-school care.[55]

The problem is that quality child care is expensive. It is cheaper for a family to
pay the annual tuition at a public college in twenty-six states than it is for a family to pay for child care for a four-year-old child.[56] Federal, state, and local governments dedicate some money for subsidizing child care but not nearly enough. Only
one in seven children eligible for federally subsidized child care actually receives a
subsidy.[57] Although preschool programs often do not provide nearly enough coverage for working parents, they are a start. And yet the state allocates meager funds
for these programs as well. Only half of all eligible four year olds receive Head Start
services, and only three percent of eligible three year olds participate in Early Head
Start programs.[58] Affordable after-school care is also a problem. Eleven percent of
children ages nine to eleven and 36 percent of children ages twelve to fourteen are
unsupervised in the period after school.[59]

This inadequate funding at the federal, state, and local levels is a recurring problem. Consider one of the main sources of federal funding for child care, the Child
Care and Development Block Grant. This block grant has never come close to providing sufficient funds, even during economic boom times,[60] but the shortfall is particularly noticeable in economic downturns. The budget allocation of $5.1 billion in
2013, for example, was nearly the same as in 2006, despite the much greater number
of families in need of subsidies following the economic recession.[61] To put this number in perspective, consider that the United States spent more than $168 billion on
the wars in Iraq and Afghanistan in 2011 alone.[62]

Additionally, child-care subsidies, like other programs with short-term costs and
long-term benefits, are often the first to be cut from strained budgets. State spending on pre-K programs dropped $30 million in fiscal year 2010 and an additional
$60 million in fiscal year 2011, affecting twenty-six states.[63] In New York City,
137,225 children used to receive city-subsidized child care and after-school programs,
but budget cuts have led to more than forty thousand children losing access to these
services since 2009.[64]

The inability to secure subsidized child care makes it harder for parents to provide
children with strong, stable, positive relationships. A parent who does not work will
fall even deeper into poverty, and this economic stress will likely affect the parent's
ability to relate to the child. Distracted by mounting bills and no way out, the parent
may become depressed or perhaps begin a relationship with someone who helps out
financially but is also physically abusive. Alternatively, a parent may work but leave

the child in substandard care, perhaps with an inattentive neighbor or a low-quality provider. This parent may ultimately lose his or her job when the child care proves unreliable and the parent misses too many days of work. Meanwhile, the child is suffering from inadequate care during the key developmental years. Either way, economic strain places an enormous burden on family relationships.

Child care is a specific example of a much larger phenomenon: the failure to support low- and moderate-income families. Looking at single-mother households, other developed countries also have relatively high numbers of children living with single mothers—21 percent of all children in the United Kingdom live with a single mother, and in Sweden 19 percent do[65]—but these countries do much more to support these households, so that fewer children are growing up in low-income conditions. Counting only the wages that mothers earn from their market labor and defining poverty as less than half the median income, the majority of children in single-mother households in all three countries would be poor: 80 percent in the United Kingdom, up to 60 percent in Sweden, and 66 percent in the United States.[66] But the *actual* poverty rate for children in single-mother households in these three countries varies greatly. Thirty-nine percent of children in single-mother households in the United Kingdom are poor, and only 6 percent of children in single-mother households in Sweden are poor, as compared with 51 percent of children in single-mother households in the United States.[67]

So what accounts for the difference? A large part of the answer is social spending. Both Sweden and the United Kingdom spend much more money on supporting low-income families. Counting cash and in-kind supports such as food stamps and housing allowances, one study found that the United States spent roughly 3 percent of the Gross Domestic Product in 1999 on these kinds of supports, as compared with the United Kingdom, which spent more than 6 percent of its GDP, and Sweden, which spent 12 percent.[68] Some of the specific supports include a child allowance to help cover the costs of raising children and Sweden's child-support payment system, which makes up the difference when absent fathers do not fully pay.[69]

Another big difference between the United States and Sweden is market earnings for single mothers. The employment rate for low-income single mothers in the United States is 65 percent, but this work does not help them raise their children out of poverty, because single mothers tend to work in low-paying service jobs in the private sector, with few, if any, benefits.[70] By contrast, in Sweden, approximately 75 percent of low-income single mothers are employed, but these jobs tend to be in the government or social-service sector, which pay higher wages and come with benefits.[71]

All of this adds up to an environment where it is much harder for single mothers, who are working long hours and still not making ends meet, to provide children with strong, stable, positive relationships. This is not to criticize single mothers in the United States but rather to highlight the daunting task of trying to raise a child with very little money and almost no support from the state. Raising children is not easy for anyone, even two parents with substantial economic and social resources. But for a single parent in the United States, who is likely to be young, with limited education and multiple partners, it is significantly more challenging. If the single mother had a job with decent wages that provided benefits such as sick leave, and if she also had access to guaranteed child support and a child allowance, then it would be somewhat easier to provide her children with strong, stable, positive relationships. But if, as is the case in the United States, a single mother has none of this and instead works long hours for little pay and no benefits and also does not have crucial assistance, then providing her children with strong, stable, positive relationships is much harder.

The example of suburban sprawl

Suburban sprawl is a final example of state regulation not working to build strong, stable, positive relationships within the family. As chapter 1 explained, the physical context for family life has a tremendous impact on the quality of family relationships, affecting whether a parent has time to spend with a child and whether the family is able to establish social connections within the community, providing the family with critical support.

The dominant pattern of development—the explosion of suburban and exurban communities in the latter half of the twentieth century—does not foster strong ties within the family and the community. Government policies that encourage suburban sprawl, particularly the subsidizing of roads and highways, are responsible for this kind of development.[72] Additionally, much of the problem stems from zoning codes that mandate single-use areas and limit density to single-family homes. This kind of development, which separates homes and schools from workplaces, means that parents will have long commutes, making it harder to balance work and family.[73] More time in the car getting to and from work inevitably means less time at home to cook dinner, help with homework, or read a book to a child. It also means less time to socialize with neighbors or join community organizations. This, in turn, decreases a family's social embedment in a community, making it harder for the family to build up a social network that would support the family. The lack of time to socialize with neighbors is exacerbated by the absence of sidewalks, which would provide an opportunity for casual interaction. Having no sidewalks also makes it harder for children to play with one another, which would further embed a family in a community.

Single-family zoning also makes it harder for extended families to live together. Partly in response to the recent recession but also reflecting changing values and the demands on families, homes increasingly include aging parents and the so-called boomerang generation, young adults who have finished college but are living at home again.[74] More than 51 million families now live in multigenerational homes, a significant shift from the post–World War II era.[75] And 29 percent of adults ages twenty-five to thirty-four live with their parents, as compared with only 11 percent in 1980 (the low for multigenerational families).[76] Multigenerational living can help families. Nearly half of the young adults living with their parents pay rent, and almost all help in some way with the cost of running the house.[77] Similarly, bringing an aging parent into the house may be challenging but can also mitigate at least some of the stress of caring for the parent.

The problem is that to house these multiple generations, families often want different spaces, with separate cooking facilities or even a separate building, located next to the main house, but single-family zoning rules make this difficult. Developers have to contend with zoning boards that are unwilling to approve variances that would allow the construction of homes that meet the needs of multigenerational families.[78]

Car-oriented cities can also increase the social isolation of families. In Florida, for example, a study found that the state has the four most dangerous cities in America for pedestrians.[79] Although a greater number of deaths occur in pedestrian cities such as New York, the small percentage of people who walk in cities such as Orlando are at greater risk of death, with a fatality rate of 3.0 per 100,000—as compared with a national average of 1.6 per 100,000.[80] The study found that the most dangerous places to walk are those without the proper infrastructure to ensure safety and that more than half of the fatal pedestrian crashes happen on high-capacity, high-speed arterial roads.[81] This danger of walking encourages people to drive everywhere, decreasing family interaction and the development of social connections.

Families do not necessarily want to live in sprawling suburbia, but they move to these areas for a combination of reasons, including better schools, lower housing costs, and access to parks and green spaces. And yet these amenities come at a serious cost to family interaction.

Finally, although not directly related to family interaction, the physical design of a region affects a family's opportunities. In regions of the country with highly concentrated areas of poverty—where entire communities are segregated from good schools and work opportunities—there is much less economic mobility than in regions with less concentrated poverty.[82] Atlanta, for example, is one of the most income-segregated regions and has one of the worst track records for lifting families out of poverty as compared with other similar cities.[83] By contrast, cities with more economically integrated communities—which does not happen by accident but instead is the product of conscious urban planning—provide their residents with greater opportunities to rise out of poverty.[84]

These examples of urban and suburban development are somewhat different from the other examples of a reactive state described above. In those contexts, the state is ostensibly trying to help families, but its efforts are vastly inadequate or poorly conceived. The Family and Medical Leave Act is intended to nurture attachment between parents and children, but the failure to ensure paid leave means that only economically stable families benefit. Similarly, the Child Care and Development Block Grant recognizes the important of subsidized child care, but it is so radically underfunded that it does not begin to meet the vast need for subsidized care.

By contrast, in the context of suburban sprawl and other zoning and land-use regulations, the problem is that the state often is pursuing other objectives largely without considering the impact on families. The state may be trying to provide housing at a lower cost and so does not require developers to install parks or sidewalks, but these shortcuts have a real impact on family functioning. Or the state may well have a vision for family life—that families do best in large, single-family homes—but this vision undercuts what we know about the importance of relationships.

In all these ways and many more, the state does little to nurture strong, stable, positive relationships with families. Sometimes the state acts too late, sometimes it acts inadequately, and sometimes it acts without considering the effect on families.

Family autonomy as an ideology of nonresponsibility

The principle of family autonomy underlies this reactive approach to families. As chapter 3 demonstrated, family autonomy is a myth. All families rely on and are regulated by the state. But the *rhetoric* of family autonomy, coupled with the hidden nature of much state regulation, reinforces an ideology of nonresponsibility. The well-being of a family is seen as a purely private matter, not a state responsibility.

This continued belief in family autonomy is rooted in the Constitution's embrace of negative liberty. Rather than guaranteeing what the government must do, the Constitution (or, more precisely, its Bill of Rights) is largely a set of rules about what the government may *not* do. The government cannot limit freedom of speech. The government cannot treat similarly situated people differently. The government cannot deprive a person of life, liberty, or property without following certain processes. But nowhere in the Constitution does it say that the government must ensure that all its citizens have adequate housing, education, or the means to survive. Instead, state efforts to support families are purely voluntary, making them all the more vulnerable to shifting political winds and strained budgets.

This constitutional ideal of negative government translates into social policies that venerate independence. Instead of worrying that the state is doing too little to support families, the constitutional structure worries about the state doing too much, reaching into family life. Again, the idea that the state could stay out of family life even if it wanted to is a myth. The state is a pervasive, inevitable presence in the lives of all families. But the belief that some families stand apart from the state encourages the state to take a reactive approach to family well-being.

Part of the problem is that in the United States, there is a widespread belief that state support is somehow antithetical to democracy. British social theorist T. H. Marshall contended that citizenship rights could be divided into three categories: civil, political, and social.[85] He defined civil rights as "composed of the rights necessary for individual freedom," political rights as "the right to participate in the exercise of political power," and social rights as "the whole range from the right to a modicum of economic welfare and security to the right to share to the full in the social heritage and to live the life of a civilized being according to the standards prevailing in the society."[86] Historically, if an individual obtained social rights by receiving support from the state, that person suffered a de jure forfeiture of political rights and a de facto forfeiture of civil rights.[87]

By contrast, Marshall believed that if the state protected social rights, a person would be better able to exercise his or her civil and political rights. As he said, "the components of a civilized and cultured life, formerly the monopoly of the few, were brought progressively within reach of the many.... These aspirations have in part been met by incorporating social rights in the status of citizenship and thus creating a universal right to real income which is not proportionate to the market value of the claimant."[88] Marshall pointed to the virtues of state cash benefits, where the "aim was to ensure that all citizens should attain at least to the prescribed minimum [in order to obtain] a general enrichment of the concrete substance of civilized life."[89]

Marshall's argument for state support, however, is not the basis for U.S. domestic policy. The United States does not explicitly condition the exercise of civil or political rights on the receipt of state support, but the idea that recipients of state aid are somehow lesser citizens is still implicit in so much of the debate surrounding social-welfare programs. Philosophers Will Kymlicka and Wayne Norman summarize this view:

> Whereas Marshall had argued that social rights enable the disadvantaged to enter the mainstream of society and effectively exercise their civil and political rights, the New Right argues that the welfare state has promoted passivity among the poor, without actually improving their life chances, and created a culture of dependency. Far from being the solution, the welfare state has itself perpetuated the problem by reducing citizens to passive dependents who are under bureaucratic tutelage.[90]

This view has largely taken hold in the United States and continues to drive social policies such as those described above. It bears repeating that this antagonistic attitude toward state support does not extend to the myriad programs that benefit middle- and upper-income families. Chapter 9 returns to the political valence of state programs.

STRUCTURAL FAMILY LAW: ACTIVE UNDERMINING

In some instances, structural family law actively undermines relationships. This is particularly true for families headed by same-sex couples and low-income families. Beginning with same-sex couples, gays and lesbians are increasingly choosing to have children. Data from the U.S. Census Bureau indicate that of the approximately 415,000 same-sex unmarried-partner households, nearly 14 percent of gay male households and more than 26 percent of lesbian households included children.[91] The federal government and a growing number of states provide some level of protection for same-sex relationships, but a majority of states still do not.

On a tangible level, the lack of legal recognition leads to a host of practical problems that make it more difficult for same-sex couples to provide each other and their children with strong, stable, positive relationships. Imagine a couple, Juanita and Deborah, who live together in a state that does not recognize their relationship. Deborah is the biological mother of the two children they are raising together, and Juanita is the primary breadwinner. As explained in chapter 3, when a married couple bears a child, the state typically recognizes both adults as the legal parents, even if there is no biological basis for this, as when an opposite-sex couple uses a sperm donor. The husband is presumed to be the father and does not have to go through adoption proceedings. But when same-sex couples live in a state that does not recognize their relationship, they do not get the benefit of this same rule. Instead, the parent who is not the biological or adoptive parent must go through the time-consuming and costly process of adopting the child using what are called second-parent adoptions, available in some, but by no means all, states.[92] Many parents cannot afford to do a second-parent adoption or, thinking that the relationship will last, do not see the necessity.

This lack of legal recognition means that the relationship between Juanita and the children is particularly vulnerable. Assuming that Deborah and Juanita have not done a second-parent adoption, then Juanita is not the legal parent of the children. If she and Deborah break up, there is no guarantee that Juanita will be able to continue parenting, or even see, the children. The lack of legal recognition also makes the family more economically vulnerable. If Juanita died without a will, for example, the default inheritance rules would mean that Deborah and the children would not inherit Juanita's property. In the eyes of the law, they would simply be family friends, not family. The list of tangible problems facing same-sex couples in states without legal recognition goes on and on.

On an intangible level, the failure to recognize same-sex relationships imposes a psychic and dignitary harm that can also undermine relationships. It tells the couple and their children that the relationship is not worthy of state recognition and protection. This harm is also felt when the state provides some form of relationship recognition, such as civil unions and domestic partnerships, but still withholds access to marriage. For this reason, marriage-equality advocates have fought for access to the term "marriage" and the underlying tangible benefits.

California is a case in point. Under California law, a same-sex couple can register for a domestic partnership and enjoy virtually all the benefits and obligations that a married couple enjoys. With a few largely inconsequential exceptions, such as the ability to have a sealed marriage not publicly recorded, the California domestic-partnership law grants same-sex couples the same rights and obligations as opposite-sex couples *except* for the right to use the word "marriage." This denial led to a decision in May 2008 by the California Supreme Court that struck down the domestic-partnership law on state constitutional grounds.[93] In response, a coalition of conservative advocacy groups, including Focus on the Family and the Family Research Council,[94] gathered enough signatures to bring the issue to a statewide vote in November 2008. The infamous Proposition 8 successfully amended the California constitution to define marriage as only between one man and one woman.[95] In subsequent litigation over the federal constitutionality of Proposition 8, the U.S. Supreme Court ultimately declined to rule on the question,[96] but a lower appellate court found it significant that California would not use the word "marriage" to dignify same-sex relationships. As the court put it, the California law case concerns

> the extraordinary significance of the official designation of "marriage." That designation is important because "marriage" is the name that society gives to the relationship that matters most between two adults. A rose by any other name may smell as sweet, but to the couple desiring to enter into a committed lifelong relationship, a marriage by the name of "registered domestic partnership" does not.[97]

As this court recognized, when the state establishes a hierarchy of committed relationships, giving only some the coveted moniker of "marriage," there is an implicit message that those on the bottom of the hierarchy are less important than those on the top.

Turning to low-income families, there are numerous ways in which structural family law undermines families and family stability. Consider child-support laws, which impose obligations on nonresidential parents (almost always fathers) without regard for their ability to repay. For low-income parents, these obligations are a source of much frustration and tension, undermining their ability to co-parent a child. As an examination of the Fragile Families data set has shown, fathers who do not marry or live with the mothers of their children tend to be disadvantaged in numerous ways. They have lower levels of education and are more likely to have been incarcerated than the other fathers in the study.[98] Not surprisingly, their levels of income are low, and their prospects for future earnings are poor.[99] Given their education levels and rates of incarceration, these fathers have a limited ability to take on jobs that would allow them to pay child support in meaningful amounts.

And yet child-support laws create unrealistic obligations, failing to take account of these fathers' very low or nonexistent earnings. When fathers are in prison, for example, many states continue to impose child-support obligations, meaning that men leave prison terms only to face extraordinarily high debts and very few options for lawful work.[100] The average increase in child-support debts during a prison term is $5,000.[101] In light of a very strict enforcement scheme required under federal law, fathers who are behind in their payments—as these men surely are—face serious penalties, including incarceration. Moreover, some of the penalties for nonpayment of child support, such as the suspension of a driver's license, make it even harder for men to earn money. This creates a vicious cycle, where fathers who are behind in their child-support payments face sanctions that virtually ensure that they will fall even farther behind.

As chapter 2 explained, a nonresidential father's ability to maintain a relationship with his children turns in large part on his relationship with the mother of the children. When the two parents get along, the father sees his children. When the two parents fight, the mother often keeps the father away. Child-support policies create friction between mothers and fathers, making an already-difficult situation worse. Part of the problem is the "assignment" rules under the federal welfare program, Temporary Assistance to Needy Families (TANF). To receive TANF funds, a mother must cooperate with the state in establishing paternity[102] and then assign to the state her right to receive child support.[103] This means, in effect, that the state is the beneficiary of the child-support obligation, and instead of owing the mother money, the father owes the state money. Fathers understandably resent this policy, and it ends up creating tension between the father and the mother, because the father associates the family with his predicament, often leading him to withdraw emotionally and physically.[104]

Many policies also create an incentive for low-income couples not to marry or live together. In the past, governmental assistance programs were explicitly limited to single mothers.[105] In addition to being unmarried, a woman also had to live alone, with no cohabiting partner.[106] Even though assistance programs no longer have these explicit requirements, the effect is often the same: penalizing recipients for being married or living with a partner.

Consider two of the most important assistance programs for low-income families: the Earned Income Tax Credit (EITC) and the Supplemental Nutrition Assistance Program (SNAP, commonly known as food stamps). Administered through the tax code, the EITC is a tax credit that individuals apply for when they would ordinarily file to pay their taxes. In 2012, 27 million individuals and families received $62 billion in tax credits.[107] Through a formula that accounts for the number of children in the home and the income of the worker, a family can receive a lump-sum tax credit (in effect, a payment) of several thousand dollars.[108] The tax credit increases with additional earnings by the worker, up to a plateau, and then decreases as the worker earns more money. The problem, however, is that the program contains a so-called marriage penalty, because if the worker is married, then the earnings of both spouses are counted in the calculation. By contrast, if the worker is single, then only the earnings of the filer are counted. In 2013, the income limits for a family with three children were $46,227 for a single filer but only marginally more—$51,567—for a married couple.[109]

Like the EITC, food stamps are an enormously important part of the safety net for low-income families. In 2012, more than 46 million people in the United States received benefits.[110] Also like the EITC, food stamps are means-tested. When a family applies for assistance, the state looks at the income of the entire household. Married spouses are automatically considered part of the household,[111] but the definition of household also includes "[a] group of individuals who live together and customarily purchase food and prepare meals together for home consumption."[112] Thus, to the extent that unmarried parents want to live together and raise children jointly, the income of both parents counts toward the eligibility requirement. This is not only a marriage penalty but also a cohabitation penalty.

It is difficult to prove as an empirical matter that rules like this influence the decision to marry or live together.[113] Despite anecdotal evidence to the contrary,[114] studies have not found an impact.[115] Moreover, eligibility rules that consider pooled income have the important goal of identifying which families need assistance most.[116] Nonetheless, there is a legitimate concern that program structures that create a disincentive to marry or live together have some impact on family behavior or, at the very least, send a mixed message about the importance of two adults jointly raising a child. There are countless other examples of the state actively undermining strong, stable, positive relationships within the family. The state may be omnipresent, but this presence is often to the detriment of family relationships.

NARROW REFORMS

Not all state regulation is negative. As a foundational matter, legal recognition of family ties is a means for strengthening family relationships. This recognition, for example, protects the parent-child relationship from interference by third parties. The highly influential books by Joseph Goldstein (a law professor), Anna Freud (a child analyst), and Albert Solnit (a child psychiatrist), beginning with *Beyond the Best Interests of the Child*, introduced the idea that the law should respect a child's psychological relationship with a caregiver,[117] and the law generally tries to do so.[118] Similarly, laws that allow couples of mixed nationality to live together in the United States help these families live together. And intestacy rules provide some measure of economic protection. As Part two of this book elaborates, the state should continue this legal privileging of relationships between adults and especially between parents and children. But even in this context, family law is still negative, because the legal recognition is both too narrow, excluding some families, especially same-sex couples, and too outdated, failing to keep up with the change in family form, particularly the move from marriage to cohabitation. Part two returns to these themes.

In the context of dispute-resolution family law, there have been some narrow reforms to the substance, process, and practice in the last several decades, particularly in the field of divorce.[119] The trend toward awarding joint custody,[120] for example, rather than complete custody to one parent and only visitation rights to the other,[121] recognizes the ongoing tie between a child and both parents and the possibility that former spouses can co-parent after a divorce.[122] No-fault divorce is an acknowledgment that relationships do not always persist and that couples can choose, amicably, to end their marriages.[123] The widespread use of mediation in divorce proceedings is an attempt to move away from the adversarial process.[124] And family-law practitioners are experimenting with new forms of practice, most notably in the growing field of collaborative law.[125]

These and other promising developments are discussed in greater detail in chapter 6, but the problem is that these narrow reforms remain incomplete and at times actively challenged, in part because they lack an overarching framework. To give a sense of the work that remains to be done, consider a study that found that very few parents actually engage in co-parenting following a divorce, despite the growing availability of joint custody, the widespread use of mediation, and so on. In this study, researchers using data from the National Survey of Families and Households looked at how cooperative parenting and conflict over childrearing affected the relationship between nonresident fathers and their children.[126] The researchers found that where the two parents worked together and were both involved in the life of the child—in other words, they were engaged in cooperative co-parenting—the nonresident fathers had greater contact with their children, which in turn allowed for higher relationship quality and responsive fathering.[127] This cooperative co-parenting, however, was far from the norm. Many mothers and fathers in the study communicated very little about their children, and 66 percent of the mothers said the father had no influence over childrearing decisions.[128] Only 6 percent of mothers reported the father as having a great deal of influence in childrearing.[129]

No-fault divorce allows a couple to end their relationship without proving that one party was the victim and the other the wrongdoer, but fighting over the grounds for divorce has now shifted to fighting over children and property. These issues provide fertile ground for emotionally charged conflict that tends to mire the couple in the dysfunction that caused the litigation in the first place. And adversarial behavior in at least some contexts is waxing, not waning. For example, judges and lawyers report that high-conflict custody cases—cases that are rightly described as "combat"—are on the rise, with an increase in the number of allegations of sexual and physical abuse and claims of custody being made for financial gain.[130]

Similarly, mediation is important, but it is no panacea for the problems associated with divorce. Consider the research of psychologist Robert Emery, who has studied the long-term consequences of mediated divorces and litigated divorces. In a study he conducted, cases were randomly either assigned to court-ordered mediation or allowed to proceed along the litigation track. Most cases settled, regardless of which track they were on. And the parties in the two groups reached relatively similar agreements. The real difference came later. Twelve years after the cases ended, the families who had gone through mediation reported far closer contact between the noncustodial parent (almost always the father) and the children. For example, 30 percent of the noncustodial parents who had gone through mediation saw their children at least weekly, compared with only 9 percent of noncustodial parents in the litigation group.[131] Similarly, the parents who went through mediation reported lower levels of co-parenting conflict and acrimony.[132]

This is a strong argument in favor of mediation in divorce, evidence that mediation, as compared with litigation, increases paternal engagement and parental cooperation. But the study also underscores the persistence of the problem. Even the mediation participants did not have strong outcomes—only 30 percent of the fathers saw their children on a weekly basis. This is obviously better than the 9 percent of fathers in the litigation group who saw their children that often, but it shows that simply using more mediation will not ensure that fathers continue to be involved in their children's lives following divorce.

Finally, it is hard to shift the legal profession. To give just one example of the resistance to change, the Ethics Committee of the Colorado Bar Association in

2007 declared the practice of collaborative law unethical.[133] The American Bar Association quickly responded with an opinion of its own, sanctioning the use of collaborative law,[134] but the Colorado response reflects a general discomfort with placing the family-law attorney in a different role.

These reforms, then, are best understood as islands in a sea of dysfunction.[135] The resistance to and limited effectiveness of the reforms are evidence that a more complete move away from negative family law is needed. The goal of this book is to provide a framework that will guide—on both the theoretical and the practical level—family law from negativity to flourishing.

CONCLUSION

With a few exceptions, family law is fundamentally negative. Rather than strengthening families long before a crisis, structural family law does little to foster the strong, stable, positive relationships that would help avert a crisis. Then, when crises do arise, dispute-resolution family law freezes relationships at the moment of breakdown, solidifying relationships at a time of conflict and then fueling that conflict with the adversarial process. A system that focuses on the black-and-white contrast between winners and losers elides the rich, multihued ecosystem of family relationships. Family law cannot solve all the problems in a relationship, but it does hold great potential either to exacerbate or to alleviate emotional harm. Too often it just makes things worse.

To highlight the negative orientation of family law is not to argue that family law should always try to repair relationships. Family law must continue to be alert to the real dangers that exist in families, including violence, abuse, neglect, and sexual assault. The problem with today's family law, however, is that it takes these dangers as the motivating paradigm for all laws and policies, focusing myopically on rupture without accounting for the importance of repair.

It does not have to be this way. The remainder of this book shows how we can move away from negative family law toward a family law that nurtures strong, stable, positive relationships, encouraging not just flourishing families but also a flourishing society.

PART TWO
Flourishing Family Law

FAMILY LAW IS in need of a basic reorientation. Instead of doing little to strengthen families and then intervening in a manner that often makes things worse, family law should strive to foster strong, stable, positive relationships from the beginning. As the previous chapters demonstrated, these kinds of relationships are essential for both individual and societal flourishing, and yet negative family law undermines family relationships at nearly every turn. Creating a flourishing family law that would foster strong, stable, positive relationships will mean changing both the way the state resolves the inevitable conflicts that mark family life and the broader structural relationship between families and the state.

Beginning with the dispute-resolution system, family law should allow parties to change their legal relationships through, say, a divorce or an adoption. But the law must recognize that even as a legal status may change—from spouse to ex-spouse or from parent to nonparent—former family members will likely remain in contact, through co-parenting, an open adoption, or other social ties. This reality of ongoing contact means that in altering legal relationships, family law should seek to preserve and repair emotional relationships, preparing the former family members for the contact that will almost certainly continue after the legal proceedings end.

This approach would not abolish divorce or leave children in the homes of abusive parents. Some relationships do end, and some relationships should end. But family law should concern itself more with the *manner* of transition, paving the way for smoother relationships following the legal conflict. Throughout this process, family law should balance the possibility of repair with the necessity of keeping family members safe, remaining attentive to violence in the home, an ever-present problem that cannot be ignored or minimized. Together, then, dispute-resolution family law should work toward three goals: restructuring families with an eye to the future, opening the door to repairing relationships, and keeping family members safe.

To avoid conflict in the first place, the state should proactively nurture strong, stable, positive relationships within families. To do so, structural family law should be built on four cornerstones. To foster strong relationships, structural family law should recognize a broader range of families. To create stable relationships, structural family law should encourage a long-term commitment between parents. To cultivate positive relationships, structural family law should enable greater family interaction and increase families' social embedment. Finally, to put it all together, structural family law should support parents in their critical child-development work. This need not entail a cradle-to-grave welfare state but rather the provision of supports during key periods of stress and transition. A structural family law built on these four cornerstones would both help families avoid conflicts and ensure the well-being of individuals and society.

This new approach to structural family law is deeply relevant to the policy questions that commentators tend to think of in abstract terms, such as whether the state should be concerned about dependency and whether family structure matters to child outcomes. The approach developed here allows us to look at these policy questions in concrete terms, with a clear understanding that the state is trying to foster strong, stable, positive relationships to avoid future breakdowns. As chapters 7 and 8 illustrate, for example, the state should invest in efforts that promote attachment between parents and children, and these chapters explain what happens if it does not. We can pay now or we can pay later, but paying now is more cost-effective and leads to better outcomes for individuals and society.

This part of the book focuses primarily on children, partly because no book can be comprehensive, and using children provides an example to work through the new model of flourishing family law. This focus on children is not intended to denigrate or downplay the other very real dependency needs in families, including those of disabled adults and the elderly. Indeed, much of what this part discusses also applies in these contexts. But the more fundamental reason for focusing on children is that there are so many children who do not have strong, stable, positive relationships in their lives, and this has such enormous negative implications for society, that the case for reforming family law is particularly strong in this context.

By contrast, the state interest in relationships between able adults is largely instrumental. We know from chapter 1 that strong, stable, positive relationships between adults likely contribute to their well-being, but the state interest in cultivating these kinds of relationships for the sake of the adults is less compelling than the state interest in cultivating these kinds of relationships for the sake of children. This is true for two reasons. First, the interest of adults in self-determination and ordering their own relationships is greater than the state interest in the nature of the relationship. Second, in an age of limited resources, the state should focus on the well-being of children because of the enormous stakes in child development. Even with this focus on children, this part of the book makes clear that the well-being of adults raising children is intimately tied to the well-being of those children. Strong, stable, positive relationships between adults benefit children.

This part first sets forth this new vision for flourishing family law and then provides concrete examples of how to implement the vision. It concludes with a chapter on the limitations of flourishing family law, identifying the inherent constraints on what the law can achieve and acknowledging that the political reality of modern America creates substantial headwinds for efforts to reform something as significant—and fraught—as the role of the state in family life. Even with these limitations, however, state regulation that works to strengthen families ex ante and intervenes post hoc with an eye toward repairing relationships would help reorient family law away from its reactive approach to relationships. It would help both individual well-being and societal flourishing—a worthwhile aim if ever there was one.

5

A New Vision for Resolving Family Disputes

IMAGINE A FAIRLY typical couple and their experience getting a divorce. Rick and Carol had been married for ten years. Although they had hoped to have children, they were unable to conceive for many years. Their relationship was rocky during those years, but when Carol finally became pregnant, they hoped that having a child would bring them closer together. Unfortunately, it did not. Unable to get along well in the best of times, they found that the stress of raising a child only exacerbated the problems in their marriage. By the time their daughter, Julie, was three, they had separated, and a year later, they began divorce proceedings. If their relationship was shaky before, now it was awful.

Rick and Carol spent the next two years fighting in court. They fought about who should get the house. They fought about how much Rick should pay Carol in spousal support. But mostly, they fought about Julie. And this is where it really got ugly. They fought through their lawyers, in front of the judge, and in front of the mediator. But they also fought in front of—and, at times, through—Julie.

The events of one October afternoon are particularly seared in her young memory. As their temporary custody agreement provided, Carol was supposed to meet Rick in the parking lot of a local supermarket to pick up Julie after a weekend with Rick. Because she had to manage other commitments, Carol decided to get Julie early, so she went directly to Rick's house, an hour ahead of time. Rick was angry that Carol was taking away an hour of his time with his daughter, and he let her know it. Fed up, Carol grabbed Julie and tried to walk out the door. Rick blocked the door, still yelling, so Carol took Julie into the hall bathroom. From there, she and Rick yelled at each other, repeatedly. Julie's cries could be heard through the yelling, but neither of them was paying attention. Using her cell phone, Carol called 911 from the bathroom. When the police arrived, Julie was still crying, and Carol and Rick were still yelling. Although the officers did not arrest either parent—there was no evidence of physical violence—the incident became the central feature of yet more rounds of litigation and acrimony. Julie, certainly, will never forget it.

Even after Carol and Rick worked through all the financial issues and a permanent custody order was in place, they still fought about Julie. Through a parenting coordinator assigned to their case to help them resolve the ongoing conflicts, they made unreasonable demands of each other, both remaining fully convinced of their own views. When Carol wanted to take Julie out of first grade for a few days to visit an ailing grandparent, Rick insisted that Julie not miss any school time. When Rick asked for a few additional hours one Sunday so he could take Julie to the circus, Carol would not hear of it, claiming that Rick was interfering with her legal right to spend time with Julie. And on and on.

As chapter 4 explained, in this and countless other families, the legal system does not even begin to resolve the conflicts. It only makes them worse, giving family members a new venue to vent their anger and frustration and new forces to fight for them. When Rick and Carol had to disclose their assets, their lawyers fought about whether each had been entirely forthcoming. When they could not agree on a custody arrangement, the court asked a custody evaluator to assess their relationships with Julie. After the evaluator filed her report, Carol and Rick claimed it unfairly represented them and their relationship with Julie. When the judge ordered them to mediation, they fought there, neither side trusting the other to make real compromises. And even after the custody order was finalized, they each tried to change it over the following years. Throughout this process, the two lawyers were proxies for Carol and Rick, regularly sending each other nasty e-mails threatening to derail settlement agreements and making unreasonable demands that immediately put the other party on the defensive. And the other professionals—the judge, the mediator, the custody evaluator, the parenting coordinator—also could not, and did not, help Carol and Rick move beyond the fighting.

THE BASIC ARGUMENT

There are many families like Carol, Rick, and Julie. We can all think of someone who *seems* like the perfect parent or the always-loving, supportive spouse, but in reality conflict, pain, and anger are part of family life. When these inevitable emotional ruptures lead to a legal rupture—a divorce, an adoption, or a case of child abuse and neglect—relationships are still likely to continue. This means that the couple who broke apart because of repeated affairs is going to meet again at a school conference or a birthday party. The child who is adopted by a stepfather will see his biological father, at least on occasion. And the teenager removed from her home because of parental neglect may well return to that home.

As chapter 4 explained, the problem with family law is that it approaches family conflicts through an all-or- nothing, adversarial lens that only reinforces the ruptures and does little to prepare the family for the future relating that will almost certainly occur. This undermines the strong, stable, positive relationships we all need to flourish.

Recognizing that conflict is inevitable but that relationships will continue leads to three goals for dispute-resolution family law. First, in changing the status of family members—from spouses to exes, from parent to nonparent, and so on—the law must restructure the family with an eye to the future. The end of the legal proceeding is only the beginning of a new phase in a family's life. This leads to the second goal. When resolving conflicts and altering legal status, family law must open the door to preserving and repairing relationships. Family ruptures are unavoidable, but it is possible to heal the underlying relationships more often than we tend to assume. The legal decision—granting a divorce, finalizing an adoption, terminating parental rights—can be a chance for the relationship to continue on new terms. This can only happen if the parties are able to heal the rifts that led to the legal proceeding in the first place. Finally, throughout this restructuring and repairing, family law must remain vigilant about abuse and violence within families. There are tensions among these goals—it can be hard to tell when repairing a relationship might be putting a family member in harm's way, for example—but there is a fruitful tension in thinking about all three goals together, as demonstrated below.

Repairing relationships does not mean that ex-spouses must become best friends, that children will be returned to abusive parents, or that adoptive parents will now raise their children alongside biological parents. Rather, the idea is to resolve conflicts in a way that ensures that children maintain the strong, stable, positive relationships they need. When a divorce proceeding involves so much acrimony that a father withdraws from his child's life afterward, the child loses out. When a child is placed in an unknown foster home and the state pursues formalistic legal proceedings that do little to help the biological parents address the issues leading to the neglect, the child loses out. And when a court terminates parental rights to a teenage daughter without recognizing that the teenager has few other adults in her life, the child loses out. Restructuring families with an eye to the future, preserving and repairing relationships when possible, and keeping family members safe will go a long way toward fostering and maintaining strong, stable, positive relationships. Some reforms already in place are consonant with this vision, but, as explained in chapter 4, these reforms are too scattered and lack an overarching theory to unite them.

THREE GOALS

Restructuring families with an eye to the future and opening the door to repair

As described in chapter 1, many relationships follow an emotional cycle that begins with love and inevitably involves some kind of transgression, which then leads to guilt about the transgression and ultimately the urge to repair the damage. Rather than reflecting only love and transgression, as negative family law does, the law should embrace the full cycle of intimacy as its framework. This would mean that even when the legal system is facilitating the resolution of conflicts—with divorce, termination of parental rights, or adoption—it would also allow for the possibility of the relationship continuing in some new and perhaps unfamiliar way.

Consider each phase of the cycle of intimacy, beginning with the transgression. Although negative family law recognizes transgressions, it may not do so sufficiently. We should not return to the days when a divorce could be obtained only by showing that one party was at fault, but no-fault divorce can be more wishful thinking than reality. One study of divorce lawyers and their clients found that

> divorce clients consider marriage and marital conduct a highly moralized domain where judgments of right and wrong still seem both necessary and appropriate. Marriage is more than an economic union. The meaning of marriage remains tied to ideas of loyalty, commitment, and personal responsibility. As a result, lawyers and clients in divorce cases engage in conversations involving a reconstruction of the past in which descriptions of the behavior of the parties within the marriage play a large part.[1]

Legal scholar Barbara Bennett Woodhouse has argued that it is difficult to avoid judgments about fault, because constructing a narrative around events is central to human experience, and everyone involved in the family-law system—legislators, judges, and especially the litigants themselves—uses fault in the stories they tell about the reasons for the divorce.[2] No-fault divorce provides no room to acknowledge these feelings.

To respond appropriately to the transgression phase of the cycle of intimacy, dispute-resolution family law must not gloss over harms or negative feelings but instead must acknowledge them fully. In other words, the new vision for dispute-resolution family law should be not a conflict-muting process but rather a process for first recognizing and only then resolving conflict. In this way, family law would not simply be a dry rendering of legal status but would take seriously the emotional harm that led to the legal proceeding.

In recognizing the negative emotions and pain that led to some legal conflict, however, it is important not to prolong those emotions. As psychologist Robert Emery has explained, divorcing spouses often use anger to remain connected with each other and to protect themselves from more painful emotions, such as grief over the loss of the relationship.[3] And, he argues, family law abets this defense mechanism by giving the divorcing spouses a means for fighting.[4] Instead of allowing families to remain mired in negative feelings, it is important to view negative emotions as a tool that helps open the door to the emotion of guilt.

Guilt is a tricky idea. Although it has strong negative connotations, guilt can be a productive emotion, fueling the reparative drive.[5] Unlike empathy, which is a "bystander emotion" experienced by someone who is not responsible for hurting another, guilt is the recognition that the person feeling it played a role in hurting another.[6] It thus becomes a signal to that person that a relationship is threatened and some action should be taken.[7]

In the context of adult relationships, the point is not to identify a wrongdoer and a victim, expecting one person to make amends to the other. Instead, the aim is to acknowledge mutual responsibility for wrongdoing, at least in some instances. As chapter 9 explores in greater detail, there are some cases, particularly those involving domestic violence, where emphasizing mutual responsibility could reinforce the victim's tendency toward self-blame and the perpetrator's tendency to deny responsibility. But in cases that do not involve domestic violence or other forms of abuse, it may be useful for all adult family members to consider how they contributed to the rupture.

In parent-child relationships, the idea of guilt is recognizing that the vast majority of parents intend well by their children, even if they do not always act accordingly. In the typical child-abuse or neglect case, for example, the idea is to help the parent see the harm he or she has inflicted and then work with that parent to make amends. There are some horrific parents who inflict unimaginable abuse on their children, but these cases should be handled by the criminal-justice system, where the central purpose is to identify and punish wrongdoers. In such cases, family law plays only a secondary role, changing the legal status as might be needed, such as terminating a parent's rights to a child. In the more usual case, the idea of emotional guilt (not legal guilt) can play an important role in healing the parent-child relationship.

The final phase is the heart of the new approach. As chapter 1 explored, the capacity to repair damage, with the drive to do so, is a widely shared human experience. Precisely how, in practical terms, family law can incorporate this reparative drive is the subject of chapter 6, but it is worth highlighting here that this does not mean encouraging only a stylized reparation, which would do little to change the family dynamic. For example, some states still require courts to attempt to reconcile a couple filing for divorce.[8] This type of law is a superficial attempt to "repair" the relationship. By the time one person in the couple has initiated divorce proceedings, the time for reconciliation is typically over. The real focus for the repair should be on the future relationship of the couple as co-parents.

Negative family law could be understood as a type of repair. Facilitating a divorce and conceiving of no ongoing relationship between the parties, for example, might be an attempt to repair the damage of an unhappy marriage and free a person to enter into a new, more functional relationship. Similarly, adoption laws could be seen as an attempt to repair the damage to a child by an original family or, in the case of voluntary adoptions, to allow a mother to relinquish the child to a home that she hopes will be better for the child and permit the mother to continue with her life.

But this cramped vision of repair ignores the reality of ongoing emotional ties. True reparation means attending to the relationships that will persist after the legal action ends. Divorcing spouses with no children may be best left to go their separate ways, if they so choose. But divorcing spouses with children will continue to relate to each other whether they want to or not. At a minimum, this means settling finances, putting a clear child-support order in place, and determining a workable custody and parenting plan. But far more important, reparation means helping the ex-spouses understand that theirs will continue to be a joint enterprise, built on a shared love for the children, rather than a shared love for each other.

In the adoption context, repairing relationships means helping the parties understand that a child, particularly an older child, will likely have emotional ties to both the birth family and the adoptive family. For some adoptees and birth parents, an adoption can lead to a sense of loss.[9] But allowing a child to maintain contact with a birth parent means that the adoption is not an all-or-nothing proposition, for the adoptee or for the birth parent. Instead, the law would recognize the multiple ties a child has with different adults, in both birth and adoptive families. This is particularly important when a child is, as so many are, adopted by an extended-family member or a stepparent. In this context, the child is likely to see the birth parent anyway, and maintaining a relationship with the biological parent may help the child feel more connected to the various parts of his or her life, assuming that is appropriate in the particular context.

Finally, in the child-welfare context, repairing the relationship between the parent and the child means recognizing that a child often will have an emotional tie even to an abusive or neglectful parent. It is easy to think that children in foster care do not want to return home to far-from-perfect parents, but this is often not the case. Think back to Vernice Hill, in chapter 4. Although she faced many challenges as a parent, her children still loved her and wanted to return to the home they knew. As an adult, one of her children reflected, "[I] changed up my act" while in foster care to try to get returned home, alternating between behaving well and acting out: "I was so happy when I came home. My smile was so big."[10] Another said that "[f]oster care is not a place you want to be, because it's not your family."[11] He knew his mother had her problems, but he also felt that "[s]he tried her best."[12]

Parent-child relationships are complex, and children are capable of multiple, conflicting emotions. The idea is to recognize these different emotions and help the parent and the child see what is worth saving in the relationship, even if the parent must also learn to interact with the child differently. This recognition of the harm and the attempt to find a new path forward are essential for the health of the relationship that is likely to continue.

There is no certainty, of course, that adopting a more reparative mindset in family law will necessarily lead to reparations-like behavior. Litigants may feel there is too much at stake and so are unwilling to compromise. Parties may be unwilling or unable to move beyond their own narratives, perhaps rooted in earlier experiences, of being wronged. Serious mental illness may make a person unable to engage in a reparative process. Moreover, the time element of healing is important to respect— an individual may well not be ready to repair a relationship soon after a transgression. The immediate reaction to a transgression in an intimate relationship can be the desire for revenge and retaliation.[13] For these parties, a reparative approach is less about facilitating an immediate repair and more about creating the possibility for repair in the future. But by allowing more than transgression, a reparative approach leaves the door open to guilt and reparation, today or tomorrow.

In short, embracing the cycle of intimacy is central to the first two goals of restructuring families for the future and repairing relationships. Only by working through the various stages of intimacy can a family truly repair relationships and prepare for a future of continued relating.

Keeping family members safe

Restructuring families for the future and repairing relationships do not always take precedence. It is also essential to keep family members safe. Indeed, encouraging the law to take family violence seriously has been a hard-fought battle. Historically, violence between spouses and between adults and children was a private matter. This was true both as a matter of law and later as a matter of practice. Under Roman law, for example, a father had nearly complete control over his children, and the courts had no role in mediating this relationship.[14] This principle was embodied in the concept of *patria potestas*, the "authority held by the male head of a family...over his legitimate and adopted children, as well as further descendants in the male line, unless emancipated," authority that included power over "life and death."[15] In England, this parental power was moderated but still allowed for "reasonable" discipline, understood to include corporal punishment.[16] Similarly, at common law, husbands had the right to "correct" their wives through "domestic chastisement."[17] This tradition long persisted. During the colonial period in the United States, children were considered by divine authority to be the property of their fathers; and a father was presumptively entitled to the services and earnings of his children, provided he protected and educated them.[18] Although these legal conceptions changed over time, the understanding that husbands could discipline their wives and children with reasonable corporal punishment continued into the nineteenth century.[19]

The myth of family autonomy facilitates this violence. Although fathers and husbands no longer "own" their children and wives in the eyes of the law, it has been much harder to shift the cultural understanding that what happens behind closed doors is no one else's business. Some progress has been made on this front, although for child abuse and neglect, as described in chapter 2, the child-welfare system is focused almost exclusively on the lives of low-income families, particularly low-income families of color.

In the context of domestic violence, it was not until the 1970s that there was a fundamental shift in the conceptualization of physical abuse as a social problem worthy of public intervention.[20] Feminists fought hard to change laws and attitudes that viewed domestic violence as a private matter.[21] Mandatory arrest rules—which require the police to arrest a primary aggressor or both participants if the police cannot identify a clear perpetrator and victim[22]—were enacted to ensure greater law-enforcement participation and prevent the victim from protecting the perpetrator.[23] Similarly, "no-drop" prosecution policies mean that domestic-violence prosecutions continue even if the victim no longer wants to press charges.[24]

Despite this welcome focus on a long-ignored problem, there is concern about the effect of these laws, with some commentators worried that the laws and policies deprive victims of agency[25] and also work a particularly harsh judgment on men of color, who are systematically incarcerated, often against a victim's wishes.[26] Beginning with agency, advocates and scholars contend that the state should be available to victims of domestic violence but not take over all decision-making. Legal scholar and longtime advocate Leigh Goodmark, for example, believes that domestic-violence laws that encourage arrest and prosecution have brought much-needed public attention to the problem but that these policies often assume that the woman is incapable of making a choice for herself.[27] The heart of Goodmark's argument is that, too often, the legal system controls women in a way that mirrors the relationship they may have had with their abusers; instead, the legal system should empower women by expanding and developing alternatives that respect their ability to choose, even if the choice is inconsistent with the state's goal of safety.[28] This means that instead of restricting choices through mandatory arrests and no-drop prosecutions, the legal system should allow women to decide how to proceed and then recognize these choices without prejudice.[29] For example, a woman may choose to stay with her husband if he agrees to therapy. Knowing that she has the power to make this choice might encourage her to make a different choice should the circumstances change.

Turning to punishment of the perpetrator, some scholars contend that domestic-violence reformers have turned incarceration into the primary solution to domestic violence, rather than seeking to address the societal factors, such as economic inequity and sexist cultural attitudes, that significantly contribute to the problem of domestic violence.[30] The concern is that a myopic focus on incarcerating the perpetrator ignores the potentially devastating effects of incarceration on the family's structure and financial well-being.[31]

These are valid concerns. The point here is not to resolve difficult issues about who decides the course of a domestic-violence case and the appropriate response to perpetrators. Rather, the goal is to clarify that part of keeping family members safe is to continue the trajectory of breaking down the boundaries between public and private such that physical violence, sexual abuse, and neglect are not seen as matters of purely private concern and wrongdoing but are instead understood as social problems. While doing so, however, the state must also be attentive to the dangers of paternalism and the differential impact on families.

In particular, in all efforts to reduce family violence, it is essential to change the pattern of intervening mostly in the lives of poor, nonwhite families, largely to the exclusion of privileged families. Looking at child maltreatment, neglect is highly correlated with poverty, but sexual abuse is not. Consider one example. In the 1950s, the Van Derbur family of Colorado was at the center of Denver's social universe. Socially and economically successful, Van and Bootsie Van Derbur had four beautiful daughters. Their childhood was picture-perfect, with summers spent on the large family ranch, weekly trips to church, and regular visits with celebrities of the day. Each daughter excelled in her own way; the youngest, Marilyn, was crowned Miss America in 1958.[32]

In contrast to this beautiful public image, the reality behind closed doors was horrific. As Marilyn related in her 2004 autobiography, her father repeatedly raped her from ages five to eighteen.[33] She wrote about the "night child" who would wait, terrified, for her father to pad down the hallway into her bedroom.[34] She repressed the memories for years[35] and never told anyone until she was in her early twenties and a family friend guessed her secret.[36] She repeatedly noted the difficulty of living a dual life, because no one expected that her father—a charming and successful businessman—would rape his daughter.

Some members of the public may know that abuse happens in all families, but the state continues to intervene more readily in the lives of low-income families. This disserves both marginal families, who are subject to an intrusive state, and children of privileged families, who are left unprotected. Both situations call for a different approach.

CONCLUSION

Ruptures—large and small—are an inevitable part of family life, but these ruptures need not deprive children of the strong, stable, positive relationships essential for flourishing. By allowing the cycle of intimacy to run its course, dispute-resolution family law will help restructure families for ongoing relationships and also make it more likely that family members will be able to repair their relationships. Restructuring and repairing relationships between divorcing spouses would help them to co-parent their children after the divorce. Restructuring and repairing relationships in the adoption context would allow some adopted children to maintain ties with the important adults in their lives. And restructuring and repairing relationships in the child-welfare context would help heal the harm that was inflicted by the original abuse and neglect and would aid in a smoother reunification or, if parental rights are terminated, would make room for an ongoing relationship between parent and child, when appropriate. All of this would, in turn, help nurture strong, stable, positive relationships in the lives of children. Chapter 6 provides concrete examples of how to do so, showing that this is much more than wishful thinking.

6

Implementing the New Vision

SUSAN BURTON WAS thirteen years old when her parents divorced. As she describes it, her parents' divorce was the biggest event in her life. After the divorce, Burton moved with her mother and sister from Michigan to Colorado. Her grades began to drop, and one day, she went in search of her standardized test scores to remind herself that she had "once been smart." She checked the wet bar where her mother kept such things and found a green hanging folder with documents labeled "Divorce." She began to read her parents' divorce agreement and didn't find anything dramatic. No secret siblings or custody battle. Instead, what was most striking to her was the cover page, listing her mother as the plaintiff *versus* her father as the defendant. Burton talked about "the horrible wrongness of the 'v.' that divided them."[1]

After almost twenty years, she looked at the divorce agreement again. She thought it might not have the same effect on her as when she was a child, but it did. She compared the document to a murder mystery where the murder happens on the first page. She particularly disliked the brutality of the opening language of the divorce agreement: "There has been a breakdown in the marriage relationship to the extent that the objects of matrimony have been destroyed and there remains no reasonable likelihood that the marriage can be preserved. Now, therefore, it is ordered and adjudged that this marriage is hereby dissolved." To her, these words were not legalese but the "language of proclamations and founding documents." She felt the words reflected her own experience that her parents' divorce was an event that had changed her world.

As this one story illustrates, and as chapters 4 and 5 elaborated, the family-law system is not designed for mothers, fathers, parents, and children to resolve their most intimate disputes in a way that maintains strong, stable, positive relationships. Instead, it is an adversarial system developed to address commercial disputes and the like. When the existing approach to legal disputes is overlaid on families, there is tremendous collateral damage.

But there is another way. Return to Carol and Rick, and imagine a different path for their divorce. They are still ending their marriage, and there is still acrimony between the two of them. Instead of feeding these negative feelings, however, family law has adopted rules and processes and lawyer training that will help Carol and Rick restructure their family for the future and slowly repair their relationship to the point where they can function as co-parents. They will never be best friends, but that is not necessary for them to be effective co-parents. When Carol and Rick first consult lawyers, for example, each is told about a new law that will determine the custody of Julie with minimal fighting because it relies on verifiable evidence of their past decisions rather than subjective determinations made by "experts." The lawyers also tell them about a new process called collaborative law that is focused on constructive problem-solving. And the lawyers themselves take a very different tack, encouraging Carol and Rick to think about how their actions today will affect their ability to work together tomorrow. They also explain to Carol and Rick how their conflict will negatively affect Julie. When Carol or Rick suggests making an unreasonable demand as a strategic matter, the lawyers point out that this may well backfire in the long run, because it will hurt their co-parenting relationship and, ultimately, Julie. Through the collaborative process, Carol and Rick are able to reach an agreement about all the issues in the divorce. There are bumps along the way and plenty of hard feelings, but the process and the outcome are markedly different from the typical scenario described in the opening of chapter 5. When the divorce is finalized, Carol and Rick are much more inclined to work together, for the sake of seeing Julie thrive.

This chapter describes several promising reforms to the substance, process, and practice of dispute-resolution family law, showing that it is well within our reach to reform family law in a way that will help maintain, or recreate, strong, stable, positive relationships within the family, even after painful ruptures.

RESTRUCTURING FAMILIES WITH AN EYE TO THE FUTURE AND OPENING THE DOOR TO REPAIR

A devastating experience like Susan Burton's with her parents' divorce cannot be avoided completely. Family breakups are almost always painful. But there are some particularly encouraging reforms to the substance, process, and practice of family law that illustrate how the legal system can do much more to ensure that this pain does not undermine strong, stable, positive relationships. As these examples demonstrate, it is possible to change the law's approach to inevitable conflict and, instead of tearing families further apart, help restructure families for the future and open the door to the flourishing that comes from repairing relationships.

Substance

The substantive rules that form the body of family law itself need to facilitate ongoing relationships across the range of conflicts that families confront, including custody disputes, divorce, and child-welfare actions. A few examples show how this can look.

Child custody. Chapter 4 identified four problems with custody rules: pitting one parent against the other, failing to lay the groundwork for future co-parenting, presenting difficult judgments for outsiders, and making intrusive decisions. The first two concerns are directly related to restructuring the family for the future and repairing relationships, because when parents have not torn each other apart in a custody battle, it is much easier to work together to raise a child over the years to come.

A proposal for a new custody rule moves family law in this direction. In 1992, legal scholar Elizabeth Scott developed the approximation rule, which asks how the parents divided caretaking responsibilities before the divorce and then models the custody arrangement on this past practice.[2] If one parent did three-quarters of the caretaking work before the divorce, that parent would have the child three-quarters of the time following the divorce. Scott contends that this approach is a narrower inquiry than other custody rules, more accurately reflects the parents' preferences, better predicts how parents would arrange caretaking after the divorce in any event, and best serves the goal of maintaining stability for children.[3]

Beyond these important benefits, the rule also is a model for restructuring the family for the future and repairing relationships. Rather than setting one parent against the other in a battle to determine the "better" parent, the rule simply asks who did what before the marriage broke down. The parents are not on trial. Further, a rule that is predictable and relatively easy to apply helps decrease acrimony in the proceedings overall, because it presents less opportunity for one parent to introduce evidence that tears down the other parent and instead turns on verifiable facts. By reducing this kind of conflict and opportunity for denigrating the other party, the rule helps pave the way for future relating. It does not necessarily resolve the problems that led to the divorce, but it does not exacerbate the rupture in the family.[4]

Policymakers and at least one state legislature have embraced the approximation rule. In 2002, the American Law Institute (ALI) completed its *Principles of the Law of Family Dissolution*, an ambitious undertaking designed to reflect the changes in families and family law in the last decades of the twentieth century and to prompt further reforms. The ALI largely adopted Scott's proposal, with the Allocation of Custodial Responsibility rule. This rule stipulates that the court should allocate custodial responsibility so that the proportion of custodial time the child spends with each parent approximates the proportion of time each parent spent performing caretaking functions for the child prior to the parents' separation.[5] The rule specifies clear exceptions to this allocation standard, such as ensuring that the child has a relationship with each parent and an accommodation for the reasonable preferences of the child once the child reaches a certain age.[6] In 1999, West Virginia became the first state to adopt the approximation rule—indeed, it was the state's very first statutory guidance on child custody.[7] No other state has adopted the standard in full, although it is beginning to catch on.[8]

The rule does have downsides. For example, it penalizes a parent who contributes to the family financially and who may have close emotional ties to the child but does little day-to-day caretaking. This parent is free to negotiate a different settlement that would give the parent more time with the child, but if the couple does not agree, this parent is left with the approximation rule as the default. The approximation rule also freezes in place caretaking arrangements that derive from tradeoffs in a marriage that may look very different after divorce. One parent may not want or be able to provide three-quarters of the caretaking when the parent is on his or her own. Notwithstanding these concerns, its potential to facilitate postdivorce co-parenting is a vast improvement over the court-imposed, emotionally laden approach that now dominates the law of custody.

Economic consequences of divorce. One of the ways divorce adversely affects a parent's ability to provide children with strong, stable, positive relationships is that divorce can lead to tremendous financial stress for both parents, although typically more so for the custodial spouse. This economic strain can directly interfere with parenting. It can also lead to tremendous acrimony between the ex-spouses, often contributing to the noncustodial parent's disengagement after the divorce. How, then, can family law address the economic consequences of divorce?

Return to the discussion in chapter 2 about the division of paid and unpaid work in a household with children. Families with a full-time, stay-at-home parent are in the distinct minority, but in the typical opposite-sex, married family, both parents work, but the mother invests more in the family, at the cost of career development. For women who have left the workforce or who have chosen the so-called mommy track, this arrangement generally does not have dire economic consequences so long as the woman remains married. The problem with this trade-off surfaces at divorce, when she will likely find herself with limited spousal support and few marital assets, given the relatively low level of savings for most American families.[9] The main asset that most couples possess is their earning potential. The person who invested in a career walks away from the divorce with earning potential intact, whereas the person who invested in the family has a decidedly lower earning potential as a result of that investment, and the divorce provides little, if any, compensation for this.

This unequal position is then exacerbated by the reality that with two households to sustain instead of one, there is not enough money to support both families in the standard of living they had before the divorce. Child-support payments, spousal support, and even an unequal division of assets do not make up the difference. Neither spouse enjoys the same standard of living, but the custodial spouse typically bears more of the economic disadvantage and is in a worse position career-wise, because this person does not have the same earning potential as the spouse who invested in a career. Cue economic stress and bitterness between the ex-spouses.

One way to address this problem is with a better rule governing spousal support. As part of the *Principles of the Law of Family Dissolution*, the ALI proposed a rule for spousal support that would compensate spouses who have invested in the family.[10] There are interesting nuances and permutations in the ALI's proposal, but the central idea is that a spouse who forgoes investing in a career in order to care for children is entitled to compensation for that investment.[11] The rule applies where the caretaker spouse has shouldered a "disproportionate share" of the caretaking responsibility and has "substantially less" earning capacity at the end of the marriage.[12]

The animating concern underlying this proposal is the idea that the spouse who has invested in the family should not bear the brunt of the financial loss arising from divorce. The ALI calls these "compensatory spousal payments,"[13] highlighting the idea that the payments are intended to compensate for loss, not meet the needs of the payee.[14] This is a step in the right direction to ensure that caregivers are protected economically. Decreasing the economic stress of the custodial parent makes it more likely that the parent will be able to provide children with the strong, stable, positive relationships they need. And decreasing acrimony between ex-spouses makes it more likely that the noncustodial parent will remain involved in the lives of the children and thus will continue to provide the children with a strong, stable, positive relationship.

There are numerous arguments against a proposal such as this. For example, there is a concern that it might *increase* acrimony between the divorcing spouses because the career-investing spouse will resent the payments and not see them as compensation. Or the rule might reinforce gender norms by telling couples that an unequal division of labor is acceptable. Finally, some might argue that the state should not protect people from the consequences of their actions. These are adults who have entered into voluntary arrangements, and if they chose to conduct their relationship in a manner that may be unequal, then they must live with the consequences.

All rules present trade-offs, but it is worth exploring one of these concerns in greater detail to show the complexity of the issue. The problem with the view that people should live with the consequences of their actions is that we often make choices in positions of unequal power, without fully understanding the repercussions, and under the influence of various cognitive biases that affect judgment. And in light of the availability of no-fault divorce on demand, a marriage can end without the agreement of both spouses, thus leaving one spouse vulnerable to decisions of the other spouse.

To understand how cognitive biases may affect judgments in this area, consider a study by a law professor and a psychologist about young adults' views of divorce. The researchers wanted to know how young people perceived (1) the laws governing divorce, (2) the likely risk and consequences of divorce for the population at large, and (3) the likely risk and consequences of divorce for themselves.[15] The study surveyed two groups: marriage-license applicants and law-school students enrolled in a family-law course. The marriage-license applicants had relatively little knowledge of the laws governing divorce, but their perceptions of the frequency and effect of divorce in the population at large were mostly accurate, with them saying that roughly half of all marriages end in divorce, that courts do not always grant spousal support, and that spouses do not always pay child support.[16] When it came to estimating their own risks, however, they were much more optimistic. The couples estimated their own risk for divorce at zero and stated that if they did get divorced, they would have the benefit of both spousal and child support.[17] The law-school students were much more familiar with divorce laws, but this knowledge did not diminish the unrealistic optimism about their own lives. They, too, thought they would not get divorced and that if they did, they would receive sufficient spousal and child support.[18]

The technical term for this kind of discrepancy between the respondents' relatively accurate perceptions of the likelihood and effects of divorce in the population as a whole and their idealistic expectations for themselves is "representative bias"— the respondents considered themselves unrepresentative of the general population. Another bias at work is overoptimism, which leads people to perceive risks accurately but to believe unreasonably that they are not at risk. A student recognizes, for example, that divorce is widespread, but the student is convinced that he or she will not get divorced. The family-law course, while significantly improving the respondents' knowledge of divorce law, had no effect on the law students' representative or optimism biases. Although there are numerous reasons why only a few individuals entering marriage sign prenuptial agreements, the belief that divorce is unlikely is certainly a factor.[19]

This is not to suggest that all states should immediately adopt a rule authorizing compensatory spousal payments but rather to show that it is essential to rethink the substantive rules regarding the economic consequences of divorce and to do so with the goal of restructuring families for future relating and opening the door to repairing relationships.

Child welfare. One innovation in the substantive rules governing child welfare is an increased focus on guardianships as permanent placements for children. Unlike adoptive parents, guardians gain legal responsibility for a child without terminating the legal rights of the biological parents.[20] Guardianship is particularly appropriate for older children who do not want to sever ties with their parents but who cannot return home and for kinship caregivers who, for a variety of reasons, do not want to adopt.[21] Under the Fostering Connections to Success and Increasing Adoptions Act of 2008,[22] states are now allowed to use federal foster-care funds to subsidize these kinship guardianships.[23] Subsidized guardianships move children out of foster care more quickly and allow children to remain in permanent homes with family members who may not otherwise be able to afford to provide care.[24]

Subsidized guardianships do not address the underlying causes of abuse and neglect, but they are a superior alternative to foster care and can help mitigate the negative effects of the family rupture. By providing financial support for permanent care by family members, the state is less overtly involved in the lives of the family, increases stability and permanency in children's lives, and leaves the door open to contact between biological parents and children.[25] This makes it more likely that a child can have strong, stable, positive relationships with both parents and the family guardians.

Adoption. A fairly recent innovation is the growing use of open adoptions, in which birth parents and adoptive parents craft agreements to ensure some form of ongoing contact between the child and the birth parent. Approximately half the states make such agreements legally enforceable, although sometimes only in limited circumstances, such as adoptions from the child-welfare system, adoptions among relatives, or adoptions by stepparents.[26] Open adoptions are an important step forward in recognizing the particular needs of adoptive children. Rather than pretending that it is possible to erase one family and replace it with another, open adoptions acknowledge and can nurture the ties between children and both their birth parents and adoptive parents.

To be sure, open adoptions can be complicated for everyone involved. The arrangement, for example, poses difficult ethical questions about whether adoptive parents should include birth parents in their lives and, if so, how much contact is appropriate.[27] Over time, birth parents may want more contact, but adoptive parents may feel that the ongoing contact is making their family life too stressful and complex.[28] Additionally, when birth and adoptive parents do not agree about the terms of the open adoption, there are practical concerns about whether adoption agencies can mediate these conflicts and legal concerns about whether courts should enforce the agreements.[29]

The legal difficulty is that historically, adoption laws have transferred all parental rights and responsibilities to the adoptive couple. So if an adoptive couple later decides they do not want to honor a postadoption visitation agreement, a court order enforcing the agreement would interfere with the parental rights of the adoptive parents. This is particularly a problem for those agreements that expect some degree of shared time with the child, as opposed to simple updates about the child's progress.

It will not be easy to develop more flexible rules—and constitutional rights hang in the balance—but the goal is to restructure the adoptive family in a way that pays attention to the unique dynamics of adoption. This may well entail a new vision of parental rights, moving away from the current all-or-nothing understanding of parenthood.

New terminology. The names we use matter and can help reframe how family law approaches conflict. Increasingly, states are abandoning the win-lose terminology of "custody" and "visitation."[30] In 1999, for example, Colorado changed the legal term to "parental responsibilities."[31] Parental responsibilities are then broken down into "parenting time" and "decision-making authority."[32] Parenting time—which is counted by nights and can be split in any combination—is the actual time the child spends with each parent. Decision-making authority is the ability to make major life decisions for the child about religion, education, health, and so on. To differing degrees, most couples share both parenting time and decision-making authority. Colorado changed the labels to recognize the importance of the time both parents spend with their children after a divorce.[33] The concern was that "visitation" implies a more sporadic relationship between the noncustodial parent and the child. But even more important than semantic accuracy is that the new terms help focus the parents on what matters: not winning or losing custody but instead taking care of children and making important decisions.

Although no state has done so, another possibility is to develop a new legal status for family members who are no longer legally related but who, nonetheless, retain ongoing connections. When a couple divorces, for example, if the marriage produced a child and if, as is almost always the case, both parents retain at least some legal right to maintain a relationship with the child, the divorcing adults could receive a legal designation such as "co-parent." Instead of adhering to the legal fiction that the relationship has completely ended, this new legal status would acknowledge the ongoing connection that exists and the couple's joint responsibilities. Similarly, unmarried couples could receive this same legal designation for their children, underscoring their shared endeavor.

This proposal cuts against one of the central principles of the legal system—the value of clean lines—but it would better reflect real lives. Legal monikers recognize and give value to underlying relationships, thus legitimizing those connections. The designations would play an important expressive function by conveying societal acknowledgment of the ongoing ties, and it would be an official recognition that there is a place beyond rupture.

Process

Alternatives to litigation. Most reforms to family-law procedures have been in the field of marital dissolutions. Mediation provides families with a more cooperative and less adversarial alternative to litigation, and it has been shown to improve long-term psychological adjustment and postdivorce family relationships, particularly between noncustodial parents and their children.[34] When parents do not need to tear each other down to get their desired outcome, the parents are in a much better position to co-parent. (Chapter 9 addresses some concerns about mediation, particularly for women.)

Another promising approach comes from Australia and its recent introduction of "Family Relationship Centres" for both intact and separating families.[35] By providing parents with free or nearly free mediation services, the centers help separating parents make "the transition from parenting together to parenting apart" and help intact families work through difficult issues.[36] Built in easily accessible areas such as shopping malls, the centers provide relationship skills and family-law advice to couples, helping them build the skills they need to relate to each other and resolve disputes without going to court. The centers focus on issues relating to children, offering relationship counseling to the parents and referrals to outside services for specific needs, such as addiction and anger management.[37]

For couples who are separating, the goal is to help them develop a short-term workable plan that will help the family make the transition from one unit to two. The hope is that by forging a plan for the first year or two, the couple will get into the habit of working together, and then, as their lives inevitably change, they will be better positioned to adapt and continue their co-parenting. There are now Family Relationship Centres throughout the country, in every region.[38] The Australian government funds the centers, but they are run by nongovernmental organizations focused on counseling and mediation.[39] A group in Colorado has developed a pilot program to bring the idea of such centers to the United States.[40]

Perhaps the area that has seen the least procedural reform is the child-welfare system, which uses a rights-based model for decision-making rather than trying to solve the problems facing the families in the system. But rights will never be the primary way to produce good results for families, because a rights-based model creates, or at least perpetuates, an adversarial process for decision-making, impeding the thoughtful collaboration among parents, children, and the state that is essential to devising beneficial solutions

In lieu of a rights-based model, a problem-solving model better serves the goals of the child-welfare system. This model views abuse and neglect largely as products of poverty, not parental pathology, and it generates a new process that fosters collaboration between the state and families. To put it most simply, a rights-based model leads to an adversarial process, whereas a problem-solving model leads to a collaborative process, which is better suited to serving the interests of both parents and children.

Although a number of alternative processes could satisfy the problem-solving model, one relatively recent reform—family group conferencing—is particularly promising.[41] Unlike the case with mediation, many people in the United States are unfamiliar with the process, so it is worth describing it in some detail. Family group conferencing, also called "family team meetings," "family group decision-making," and "team decision-making," is part of the broader restorative-justice movement. This movement seeks to reform the justice system to incorporate victims and to allow the offender to "restore" the status quo and repair the damage that has been done to relationships, property, and communities.[42]

Family group conferencing originated with the Maori and other First Nations around the world. In response to several government reports documenting discrimination against Maori families in New Zealand's child-welfare system, New Zealand enacted the Children, Young Persons, and Their Families Act of 1989.[43] The law was intended to avoid the removal of Maori children to non-Maori families and to draw on the Maori tradition of involving extended-family members in decision-making, but the legislative changes were not limited to Maori families. Instead, the law required that all substantiated cases of child abuse and neglect be referred for family group conferencing.

Simplified descriptions of two cases, one receiving traditional child-welfare services and one receiving a family group conference, illustrate the marked differences between the two approaches. In the standard approach that now predominates in the United States, after a state agency receives a credible report of child abuse or neglect, a caseworker goes to the home and assesses the danger to the child. The caseworker—who likely is not from the same socioeconomic background as the family and may well be of a different race—may decide to work with the family while the child remains in the home, or the caseworker may decide that the child is in such imminent danger that he or she should be removed immediately. If this is the case, the agency removes the child from the home and places the child in foster care pending a more thorough investigation. Court proceedings oversee the agency's decision-making. In these proceedings, one lawyer represents the agency, a second lawyer represents the parents, and a third lawyer is typically assigned as a guardian ad litem to represent the child's interests.[44] Over the next several months, the caseworker develops a case plan for the parents, requiring them, for example, to obtain drug treatment and attend parenting classes. If the parents do not comply with this case plan within the specified period, then the state agency files for a petition for the termination of parental rights. If the court agrees that parental rights should be terminated, the child is freed for adoption. The majority of decisions in this model are made by professionals: caseworkers, therapists, guardians ad litem, lawyers, and judges. One of the dangers of this professional-driven approach is that caseworkers may too easily associate a safety risk with poverty and race and therefore remove children of color at higher rates than white children.[45]

In a family-group-conferencing case, the story and the decision-makers are decidedly different. After receiving a report of alleged abuse or neglect, a social worker conducts an initial investigation. If the social worker concludes that there is evidence of abuse or neglect, the social worker refers the case to a coordinator, who has the authority to convene a family group conference. The coordinator contacts the parents, the child (if the child is old enough to participate), extended-family members, social-family members, and significant community members who know the family. Before the conference, each potential conference participant meets separately with the coordinator to learn about the process. In these meetings, the coordinator screens for potentially complicating factors, such as a history of domestic violence, to determine whether the case is appropriate for family group conferencing and, if so, what additional support may be needed for the participants.

In its original form, there are three stages of the conference. (As described below, the process is often modified in the United States.) In the first stage, the coordinator and any professionals involved with the family, such as therapists, teachers, and the investigating social worker, explain the case to the family. In the second stage, the coordinator and the professionals leave the room while the family and community members engage in private deliberation. During the private deliberation, the participants acknowledge that the child was abused or neglected and develop a plan to protect the child and help the parents. If the participants reach an agreement, and they usually do, the group presents the plan to the social worker and the coordinator, who likely have questions for the participants. Parents, custodians, social workers, and coordinators can veto the plan produced by the conference and refer the case to court. In practice, this rarely occurs. The participants usually come to a decision, and the social worker and the coordinator accept the plan, perhaps with a few changes, if it meets predetermined criteria. In the final stage, the coordinator writes up the plan, sends it to all participants, and then sets a time for a subsequent conference to assess developments in the case.

The plan typically includes a decision about the safety of the child, including whether the child should be placed outside the home for a certain period of time and, if so, with whom. If the child is placed outside the home, this is almost invariably with a relative or other conference participant. The plan also identifies the services and supports needed by the parents. Finally, the plan determines which participants will both help the family and also check in on a regular basis to ensure that the child is safe and the parents are complying with the plan.

As is apparent from this description, several principles characterize the philosophy of family group conferencing:

- Children are raised best in their own families.
- Families have the primary responsibility for caring for their children, and these families should be supported, protected, and respected.
- Families are able to make reliable, safe decisions for their children, and families have strengths and are capable of changing the problems in their lives.
- Families are their own experts, with knowledge and insight into which solutions will work best for them.
- Families must have the freedom to make their own decisions and choices.[46]

The process of family group conferencing is intended to find and build on a family's strengths, rather than to place blame. One method for achieving this is to focus on the problem, rather than the person, and to concentrate on healing. Thus, family group conferencing facilitates a strengths-based practice—which focuses not on pathology and dysfunction but rather on resilience and potential for development—because it requires the family and the community to look within to find solutions. Family group conferencing also respects and values important cultural practices of the family. In the typical child-welfare case, the family is judged by outsiders who may be unfamiliar with a community's values and may misunderstand the real risk to the child. In a family group conference, the important decisions are made by those who share a history with the family and are more culturally aligned. Further, the conferences help develop a support network within the child's extended family and community—a crucial protective factor for children who grow up in high-risk environments—because conference participants play an active role in finding a solution for the troubles facing the family by providing, for example, child care, home furnishings, transportation, housing, and help with managing the household.

Family group conferencing thus represents a radical reorientation of child protection. Rather than relying on the impersonal nature of the decision-maker in the typical child-welfare case to "solve" the problem, family group conferencing directly involves a child's community in identifying the problem and crafting the solution. In this way, family group conferences are a partnership between the state, the family, and the community, with each party expected to play a role in planning and supporting the child and the family.[47] Family group conferences are not a means for child-protection officials to relinquish their responsibilities but rather are a different method for exercising those responsibilities.[48]

No country other than New Zealand requires the use of family group conferencing, but many countries have started to experiment with it. In the United States, child-welfare agencies have been using family group conferencing since the early 1990s, and now forty-five states have some form of conferencing,[49] although it is often implemented in a modified fashion, not giving families and communities control over the process.

Studies on programs implemented around the world and in the United States demonstrate that family group conferencing has had substantial success in improving child-welfare systems.[50] Studies suggest, but are not uniform in concluding, that families who participate in family group conferences have lower levels of subsequent abuse and neglect than in the typical child-welfare case.[51] Family group conferences are also associated with greater permanency for children. One study of twenty-seven thousand children in California and seventeen thousand children in five urban areas outside of California found that when the child-welfare system used family group conferencing instead of following the traditional path, children found a permanent home, either with their original families or with relatives, more quickly than children who did not have a family group conference.[52] Research also indicates that in the vast majority of cases, families are able to devise a plan for the care and protection of their children.[53] Family members, including fathers, participate in numbers far greater than in the traditional child-welfare model,[54] and children are more likely to be placed with a relative.[55]

Participants report satisfaction with the process and the result.[56] One mother described her experience as follows:

> There comes a time when you think "I can take control now" and that's when I think the normal way of running social services departments falls down. Yes people come initially because they do need a certain amount of support and a certain amount of help. But if you go on trying and nursemaid and suffocate that person then their growth isn't going to take place. The social services, the way it's run at the moment actually doesn't allow the person who has to . . . take control, they're very reluctant to give that person back the control of the family. So social services becomes the head of the family, and the mother and the

father, or one of them, becomes more or less like a child themselves, and they regress into no responsibility, because they're instructed all the way, what their responsibilities are. But they are not actually helped to rebuild their confidence to enable them to take up the full responsibility.[57]

This is not to say that family group conferencing is a panacea, and there have been some critiques of its theory and process. Of particular concern are victims of domestic violence, who may be required to interact or, worse, compromise with their batterers in an alternative dispute-resolution process. In the context of family group conferencing, there is considerable disagreement on the propriety of the process when there is a history of domestic violence. New Zealand mandates its use for all cases, including those with a history of domestic violence,[58] and some experts support this practice, arguing that with proper protections for the victim, family group conferencing can work effectively when domestic violence is part of the problem within the household.[59] Others, however, are more skeptical, arguing that domestic violence should be sanctioned with a clear message from the courts that violence is not tolerated.[60]

It is possible to develop a hybrid model. Typically, there is no legal representation in family group conferencing, but there are lay advocates for women and children within the conference. "Support persons" are identified by the coordinator for both adult and child victims, and these persons are supposed to protect victims who are emotionally and physically vulnerable.[61] Additionally, in some programs, lawyers, guardians ad litem, and court-appointed special advocates do participate in the conference.[62]

There is a similar disagreement about whether to use family group conferencing for cases involving child sexual abuse.[63] The concern is that the dynamics of sexual abuse can run across generations and reflect a deep denial within the family, thus undercutting the ability of family members in the conference to acknowledge the abuse and adequately protect the child.[64] On the other hand, the process provides a method for informing other family members about the abuse and thus protecting them from the perpetrator.[65] Again, there is no clear answer, but given the hidden nature of child sexual abuse, any process that helps bring it out into the open is a welcome development.

A final concern is whether a family challenged by serious issues such as substance abuse, chronic child abuse and neglect, and mental-health diagnoses can really make decisions. Practitioners have found, however, that there are healthy parts in almost all families, even those traditionally labeled dysfunctional.[66] Additionally, other conference participants, found in the extended family or the community, can help the family make decisions.[67] And if the community is dysfunctional, the coordinator can bring in members from a larger community where there are resources.[68] In this way, family group conferencing is able to adapt to each family's decision-making abilities.

Balancing out these concerns, it is important to put family group conferencing in perspective. The question is not whether it is a perfect process that resolves all the underlying issues facing families. Rather, the question is whether it is better than the current system, which is deeply alienating for families and does not even begin to address underlying issues.

Family group conferencing certainly has its limits. It does not tackle the larger structural reasons for families becoming entangled with the child-welfare system, particularly poverty. But it is a process that has the capacity to address many of the most profound theoretical and practical objections to the current child-welfare framework and is a marked improvement over the current legal framework. It is also a clear example of how a process can help repair family relationships.

Court-based reforms. Sometimes is it not possible or desirable to avoid the court system, but there are examples within the courts of more conciliatory approaches to conflict that can help restructure families and open the door to repairing relationships. For example, courts are increasingly using parenting coordinators for high-conflict divorces.[69] Usually a mental-health professional who is paid by the parents, a parenting coordinator works with the parents to develop a concrete plan for parenting and then helps the parents resolve the disputes that often come up under the plans.[70] The parenting coordinator can make decisions for the family, but more often the coordinator helps the parents negotiate their own compromise.[71] Similarly, some courts are adopting parenting programs to help parents learn how to work together after the divorce.[72] In one study, a program designed for noncustodial fathers showed that participants had a significant increase in co-parenting with a corresponding decrease in parental conflict after fathers participated in the program.[73]

It is also possible to rethink even the most seemingly banal details of litigation so that the court process reflects the importance of restructuring the family for the future and repairing relationships. Semantics matter deeply, as Susan Burton's experience reminds us. One advocate who has worked tirelessly to reform both the substance and the process of family law is Charles Asher, a former trial lawyer in Indiana who has committed his career to helping parents work through their issues with each other so that they can co-parent. Asher has advocated the removal of the "versus" in family-law cases so that the name of the case reads "In Re the Marriage of [x], mother, and [y], father."[74] This simple reframing reminds the litigants exactly what is at stake in the proceeding and avoids placing parents on opposite sides, at least at a semantic level.

Asher runs a website—www.UpToParents.org—that helps parents understand the impact of adversarial proceedings on their children. The website asks parents to enter into commitments regarding their behavior toward each other and their children.[75] The commitments are centered on the child, allowing the parents to highlight a positive aspect of their marriage and to work toward amicable relations that will benefit the child. After customizing the commitments with the child's name and the family's circumstances, the commitments might read as follows:

1. We know that Joey's one and only childhood is forming many of the gifts and problems he will carry into adulthood. Joey will experience any attack between us as an attack on him.

2. We realize conflict between us (his parents) can bring many bad things into Joey's life. Here are just a few: (a) blaming himself, (b) fear and depression, (c) hiding his feelings, (d) failure in school, (e) drugs and alcohol, (f) dangerous relationships.

3. We know that our cooperative relationship as his parents is Joey's best protection from the hurt and dangers in his life. It's peace and cooperation between us, his parents, that he cares deeply about.

4. Joey's only job is to be a child. And he can't be a child unless we're adults.
   a. Joey is not our witness or ally in any of our disagreements; it's our responsibility to reach good agreements for him.
   b. Joey is not our spy to find out about each other's personal life.
   c. Joey is not our whipping post; it's not his job to listen to us criticize each other.
   d. Joey is not our messenger to deliver checks, bills, messages, or anything else.
   e. Joey is not our counselor or confidant to help us with our hurt.

Asher's work illustrates how it is possible to reach parents who may be in the depths of litigation and help them adopt a mindset that focuses on restructuring the family for the future and opening the door to repairing relationships. His website is not mandatory, nor are the commitments legally enforceable, but they are nonetheless emblematic of a different approach to resolving conflicts in family law.

Other efforts at court-based reform include revamping court organization. One innovative approach is New York's Integrated Domestic Violence Court (IDVC).[76] The IDVC works to streamline the process for prosecuting domestic-violence offenders and providing relief for victims by pairing each family with a single judge.[77] Instead of multiple judges in separate courts addressing issues of, say, domestic violence, child support, and custody determinations, the "one family, one judge" approach allows all matters to be resolved by a judge with a comprehensive view of the multiple issues in a family. Each issue is still heard separately, sometimes on separate days, but the integrated court enables the judge to monitor compliance with the various court orders, helps the victim access comprehensive services for the entire family, and holds the perpetrator accountable.[78] Judges are trained to handle both civil and criminal cases relating to families and to address complex, interrelated family problems. Additionally, service providers give on-site assistance to families. The goal is not necessarily repairing the relationship between the batterer and the victim but rather protecting the victim and children and shoring up *their* relationship. This is essential for restructuring the family and keeping family members safe.

A final example is the Miami Child Well-Being Court, which uses a hands-on, positive approach to cases of abuse and neglect. The court engages mental-health experts to work closely with families, assess the relationship between parents and children, and provide timely progress reports to the court. The experts, the family, and the court then work together as a team to protect the child and respond to what led the family into court in the first place.[79]

Essential to the court's success is a reliance on child-development research. Studying the science of child development and the effect of trauma on children enables the team to understand the best way to help different families.[80] For example, many mothers in the court lack basic parenting skills and must learn how to interact positively with their children.[81] In one-on-one sessions, a mental-health expert works with a mother and her child, teaching the mother how to respond to the child, such as smiling at or holding the baby to form attachment bonds.[82] With the mother being taught specific skills, the family is often able to remain together without recurring episodes of maltreatment.[83] Other programs—such as the Nurse-Family Partnership, discussed in chapter 7—try to teach these skills to new parents as a way of preventing child abuse and neglect. But what is interesting about this court is that it has found that using the same approach—a positive, skills-based approach to parenting—even after a case has started is also effective.

The idea of reforming courts to better address problems within families is not new, and past experience gives some reason to be skeptical about the promises of court-based reform. As legal scholar Jane Spinak has shown, the historical antecedents of these modern problem-solving courts are in family law. The Children's Court, begun in 1902, sought to address the underlying social causes of juvenile delinquency.[84] The court was focused on the developmental needs of children and sought to treat rather than simply punish the child, embracing the ideal of rehabilitation.[85] Similarly, the introduction of family courts around the country sought to address the issues underlying child abuse and neglect and family dysfunction more generally.[86] But, as any practitioner will readily attest, family court is largely a failure. Consider one description:

> In many jurisdictions, particularly those in large urban areas, the courts are overwhelmed by the size of their caseloads: Overtaxed judges hear "lists" of up to 100 cases a day, giving each case a maximum of five minutes. Families are sworn in *en masse* at the bar of the court, with little sense that what they say to the judge thereafter constitutes sworn testimony, rather than a free-for-all conversation. Judges bark at the parties, calling parents "Mom" or "Dad," rather than by their names. Orders typically are entered without any articulation of findings of fact, conclusions of law, or even a recitation of the relevant legal standards in justification.[87]

Spinak argues that there are several reasons that problem-solving courts cannot deliver on their promise. First, she is skeptical about the ability of courts to effectively address the intractable social issues facing the parties, especially given overwhelmingly large caseloads. Second, she contends that the team approach leads to role confusion and places the defendant's counsel in a particularly difficult place, as it is unclear how best to protect the client's interests. Finally, when services are provided through courts, rather than the community, it creates a perverse incentive to initiate a court case, because this may be the most effective way to ensure that a client receives the help needed, and yet these services come with the intrusive surveillance of the court.[88]

These very real limitations for court reform are one of the reasons this book argues for strengthening families long before there is a crisis and then using alternative, noncourt processes, such as family group conferencing, for resolving disputes once they arise. It is true that there is only so much a court, or any other process, can do once a family has broken down. There are more and less effective ways to intervene, but all attempts are after-the-fact and therefore present a much harder, longer road to fostering strong, stable, positive relationships.

Even if a family does reach court, however, the criticisms of problem-solving courts are not necessarily reasons to return to the adversarial, winner-takes-all approach to family disputes. The question is always "As compared to what?" It may be true that the Miami Child Well-Being Court, for example, raises the concerns Spinak identifies. But its attempt to help parents gain the skills they need and keep families together, even at the cost of role confusion and creating an incentive to initiate a case, is preferable to the truly dismal outcomes in regular family courts. This may be a matter of choosing between two bad options, but given the clear problems with pitting family members against one another and the well-documented reality that family members are going to relate to one another after the court proceedings end, it is more important to *try* to resolve disputes collaboratively than to continue with a system that exacerbates conflict within families.

Practice

Lawyers can make an enormous difference in family-law cases. In the divorce context, if lawyers take a scorched-earth approach to the dispute, determined to prove that their client is "right" and setting out to "screw the bastard," it will be much harder for ex-spouses to co-parent after the case is over. Often a lawyer's client is hurt and angry over the end of the marriage and would prefer both retaliation and vindication, but the lawyer can help the client understand the costs—financial and emotional—of seeking revenge through the legal process. Family-law attorneys must remember that the "opposing side" is someone the client will have to work with for many years to come. The biggest challenge for lawyers, then, is to resist enacting and embodying the client's anger and resentment, which only exacerbates the conflict between the divorcing spouses. To help lawyers act differently, there are at least two exemplary reforms to the training of law students and to professional norms.

Beginning with law school, students need to understand that family law is not about winner-takes-all litigation but rather is about helping to restructure a family with an eye to the future. One way to inculcate this value is to teach law students about family-systems theory, described in chapter 1, and the idea that a family functions as a whole. Students need to appreciate that the family influences the emotional health of its members and that to understand any one person within the family, it is necessary to understand the family as a whole, with all its various dynamics.[89] Drawing on this body of work would help lawyers think about their clients and analyze their interests somewhat differently. Rather than isolate the individual and advocate zealously for that person as an individual, family-systems theory helps the lawyer understand that the client and the dispute are part of a larger system and that the client likely will continue to operate in that system (the family) in some form after the dispute is settled. The lawyer is still a zealous advocate, but in doing this, the lawyer is helping the client think more broadly about his or her goals and interests.

Helping lawyers think this way requires different training. A move in the right direction is the Family Law Education Reform (FLER) Project, begun in 2004 by family-law professors, family-court judges, practicing lawyers, mental-health professionals, mediators, and others.[90] The FLER Project recognized the inadequacy of legal representation in family courts and sought to adapt the law-school curriculum to prepare new lawyers for practicing family law, focusing on the interdisciplinary nature of modern practice, the variety of alternatives to litigation commonly used today, and teaching skills to law students such as being reflective and self-aware in family practice.[91] In 2006, the FLER Project released a report recommending numerous changes to family-law education. Of particular relevance to the idea of family-law practitioners working to restructure families with an eye to the future and leaving the door open to repairing relationships, the report recommended that law schools teach students about the emotional component of family-law cases and how to care for themselves in this highly charged field.[92]

But reforming family-law education is not enough—it is also critical to change how practicing lawyers approach their work. A study by legal scholars Ronald Gilson and Robert Mnookin found that in some contexts, particularly in smaller practicing communities, there are incentives for family-law attorneys to engage in cooperative behaviors and not practice scorched-earth litigation strategies, thus resisting the clients' urge to fight.[93] Their informal survey of matrimonial specialists in San Francisco, for example, found that because the lawyers knew one another better and were repeat players, a lawyer could develop a reputation for cooperation and thus could be trusted by the other side to work toward an amicable resolution.[94] By contrast, Gilson and Mnookin found that in larger legal communities, such as Los Angeles and New York, it was difficult for attorneys to establish a reputation as cooperative, because lawyers simply did not have enough repeat business with one another.[95] As a result, in these larger cities, there was a greater tendency for lawyers to engage in full-throated, adversarial litigation.[96]

Some practitioners have found ways to overcome these challenges. One particularly promising development is the growing field of collaborative law, first started by Stuart Webb, a lawyer in Minneapolis who practiced civil law for eight years and family law for another seventeen years. Over time, Webb became disillusioned with the law, particularly the adversarial approach to family conflict. He also felt that incivility was on the rise in family-law practice. After a brief stint taking psychology courses, Webb realized that he was not going to become a psychologist, and instead he decided to develop a model for family-law practice that would allow him to do the aspects of the practice that he enjoyed but not those he disliked.[97]

Most important, Webb realized that settlement should be the paramount goal, avoiding litigation whenever possible. He believed that litigation often marred attempts to settle cases because of its adversarial nature, and so he wanted to create a settlement climate that removed all adversarial undertones. When he invited other attorneys in the area to "play the collaborative game," he received a positive response.[98]

In a collaborative divorce, both parties and their lawyers agree to negotiate divorce settlements without litigation. The parties contract for the settlement-only representation through a limited retention agreement between each attorney and client. A key term in the agreement is that if the settlement talks fail and the case proceeds to trial, the attorney will withdraw from the case, thus creating a strong incentive for both the attorney and the client to continue with settlement efforts. Collaborative coaches trained in the field of mental health help couples address emotional issues underlying the divorce, issues that may undermine the collaborative process. Collaborative-law practitioners contend that the process is appropriate for a broad range of individuals, leads to far more creative and responsive settlements between the parties, is generally less expensive than traditional adversarial litigation conducted by attorneys, and is more satisfying for clients and attorneys.[99]

Although collaborative law is best known for its use in divorce proceedings, it is starting to be used in other settings, such as estate planning and probate, in which maintaining or repairing family relationships is at a premium and traditional litigation may threaten those relationships.[100] Since 1990, when Webb first sent his invitations, collaborative lawyers have grown from a small group of family-law practitioners in Minneapolis to an estimated eight thousand to nine thousand collaborative practitioners around the world.[101]

In short, collaborative law is a model for how family-law practice across a range of disputes can be reworked to reduce conflict, better acknowledge the challenging emotional stakes of family-law cases, and recognize the ongoing relationships that will continue long after the ink is dry on any final decree.

KEEPING FAMILY MEMBERS SAFE

Even with a focus on restructuring and repairing, it is essential not to lose sight of the goal that dispute-resolution family law must keep family members safe. The reforms described above, however, do not compromise safety. The central aim of family group conferencing is ensuring the safety of the child. The process just envisions a different method for doing so. Similarly, one of the animating purposes of the IDVC is to better integrate different kinds of court cases to ensure that one judge is not granting a civil order of protection while another judge is ordering joint custody between a batterer and a victim. Chapter 9 explores in greater detail the balance between repairing relationships and keeping family members safe.

CONCLUSION

These examples are by no means exhaustive, but they do demonstrate that there is much more that the law can and should be doing to restructure families and open the door to repair, reflecting the reality of ongoing relationships. Reforms like those outlined above are a first step toward dislodging the win-lose mentality that dominates family-law litigation and encouraging the development of strong, stable, positive relationships that endure after the conflict. Using the framework developed in chapter 5, it is possible for the state to build on these examples and develop even more far-reaching and innovative reforms.

It would be even better if the state could prevent as much conflict as possible. There is much more that the state can do through structural family law to nurture strong, stable, positive relationships from the beginning, avoiding the need for dispute-resolution family law. This is the subject of the next two chapters.

7

A New Vision for Structuring Family Relationships

THE AMERICAN PUBLIC is fixated on school reform. How much does class size matter? Should children have fewer standardized tests? It is better to teach girls and boys separately? Is tenure necessary? Do charter schools improve outcomes? What is the best method for evaluating teachers? And so on. Endlessly. But this angst and public debate ignores one of the most salient factors in school success. What happens at home, long before a child enters kindergarten, has a tremendous influence on a child's trajectory in school.

Consider a study started in the 1970s by researchers at the University of Minnesota looking at young, low-income, first-time mothers with low educational attainment.[1] Before this study, there had been considerable research on the predictors of dropping out of high school—difficult peer relations, low achievement, behavioral problems, and little parental involvement in schooling[2]—but the bulk of this research focused on children beginning in late elementary or middle school. By contrast, the Minnesota study began following the participating families when the mothers were still pregnant. With that depth of data, researchers were able to track the effect of early-childhood experiences on high school graduation rates.[3] The study is still tracking outcomes, with the children now adults.[4]

The results of the study are startling. Looking back at the data, the researchers could predict with 77-percent accuracy the chance of a three-and-a-half-year-old later dropping out of high school by looking at two factors: observations of the mother-child relationship and the quality of the home environment.[5] This remained true even after controlling for other variables, such as the child's IQ and the family's income level (although remember that nearly all the parents in the study were relatively low-income).[6]

As the authors readily acknowledge, there are reasons to be cautious about draw-ing causal conclusions from these findings. Later experiences and circumstances can change the predicted course. An anxious attachment between a child and caregiver predicted behavioral problems in kindergarten and beyond, but the study also found instances where the earlier attachment pattern did not result in later problems.[7] Interestingly, though, when positive outcomes followed a rocky start, there was typi-cally a moderating factor, such as an increase in social support and a corresponding decrease in family stress.[8] More often, the early patterns continued into childhood and, as elaborated below, set the child on a path to school success or difficulty. Notwithstanding some variability in the data at the margins, it is clear that families matter tremendously. This insight is the animating principle of flourishing family law.

THE BASIC ARGUMENT

Chapters 5 and 6 showed that it is possible to reform dispute-resolution family law so that inevitable conflicts can be resolved in a way that helps families main-tain the strong, stable, positive relationships they need to flourish. But this is still an after-the-fact approach. Rather than waiting for families to fall apart, the state should proactively foster strong, stable, positive relationships to avoid conflicts in the first place.

The starting point is recognizing that families and the state are mutually depen-dent. In a complex modern world, families of all income levels rely on the state. But just as families need the state, the state also needs families. The state cannot, and should not, directly undertake the essential work of raising children. Instead, the state relies on families to ensure the well-being of the next generation of citizens. This mutual dependency means that the state cannot absolve itself of responsibility for family well-being. If the state wants a flourishing society, it must nurture strong, stable, positive relationships within families.

The next step is acknowledging that the concept of family autonomy—as least as traditionally understood as freedom from the state—is both descriptively inac-curate and prescriptively unenlightening. It does not describe the actual relationship between families and the state, and it does not help policymakers think more care-fully and creatively about how best to structure family law to nurture strong, stable, positive relationships within the family.

The final step is that in lieu of family autonomy, the state should embrace four cornerstones for structural family law:

- To foster *strong* relationships, structural family law should recognize a broader range of families than simply the traditional nuclear family.

- To foster *stable* relationships, structural family law should encourage a long-term commitment between parents, to each other and to the joint enterprise of raising a child.
- To foster *positive* relationships, structural family law should alter the physical context for family life to enable greater family interaction and increase the social embedment of families.
- To put it all together, structural family law should support parents in their critical child-development work.

A structural family law built on these four cornerstones would help families avoid conflicts and ensure the well-being of both individuals and society. The next chapter describes concrete examples of reforms that embody these cornerstones, but first it is worth elaborating on the abstract ideas.

MUTUAL DEPENDENCY

In light of the long-standing belief that families are autonomous and that dependency is a sign of pathology and dysfunction, it is useful to elaborate on the concept of mutual dependency, as a practical and theoretical matter.

Families need the state

All families need the state, regardless of income level. Legal rules governing marriage and divorce and establishing parental authority vis-à-vis third parties clarify who has legal rights and responsibilities within the family. Similarly, most families benefit from the availability of public education, even if the quality of schools differs by community. Some state programs and legal rules particularly help middle- and upper-income families, such as default rules governing inheritance rights, the passage of protective legislation such as the Family and Medical Leave Act, and the availability of child-care tax credits, Social Security retirement benefits, and tax deductions for dependents. These programs are nominally available to all families but typically benefit only those families with at least a moderate income. Other state programs help lower-income families, such as subsidies for housing and child care, Supplemental Security Income for disabled individuals, the Earned Income Tax Credit, food stamps, and Medicaid.

As chapter 3 explained, the narrative that some families operate without state support—that they are independent—resonates because of the phenomenon of background and foreground noise, with familiar types of support, such as public education or tax deductions for dependents, not perceived as a massive governmental support program for families. Similarly, chapter 3 described the work of political scientist Suzanne Mettler, who has shown that people do not always realize they are receiving governmental support, particularly when the benefits are channeled through the tax code and do not require the beneficiaries to interact intensively with a state official.

The perception of zero support as the baseline has considerable implications for the development of social policy. When we believe that some families are independent, it is easier to pathologize those families who receive visible state support. But rather than pretending that some families are autonomous, acknowledging that the state supports *all* families means that we can have a far more productive conversation about the content and effectiveness of that support.

The state needs families

One way to think about the state's interest in strong, stable, positive relationships within families is Martha Nussbaum's capabilities approach.[9] A philosopher and legal scholar, Nussbaum emphasizes the conditions and goods needed for the capacity to function.[10] For each capability, a person needs both an internal capacity and the external conditions that allow a person to exercise that capability.[11] The idea of the capabilities approach is that it looks at what a person can do, not what the person has, and thus respects the basic decision-making power of an individual. Nussbaum contends that once a person has the capability to do something, whether he or she does it or not is the person's own choice and not something that should be forced. As she says, "The person with plenty of food may always choose to fast, but there is a great difference between fasting and starving."[12]

Nussbaum has identified the following central capabilities:

- *Life*: living until a natural death in old age.
- *Bodily health*: having good health, including reproductive health, having adequate nourishment and shelter.
- *Bodily integrity*: moving freely, being free from bodily assault, having opportunities for sexual satisfaction.
- *Senses, imagination, and thought*: being able to use the senses in a way informed by adequate education and in connection with self-expression.
- *Emotions*: having attachments to other people and things and being able to develop emotionally without overwhelming fear or anxiety.
- *Practical reason*: being able to form a conception of the good life and critically reflect about planning one's life.
- *Affiliation*: having connections with others, both socially and politically.
- *Connection with other species*: living in relationship to plants and animals.

- *Play*: being able to engage in recreation and play.
- *Control over our environment*: being able to engage in political decisionmaking and being able to control our material environment, such as having property rights.[13]

What is fascinating about this list is the important and sometimes irreplaceable role that families play in developing many of these capabilities, both cultivating the internal capability and also creating the external conditions that foster its development and expression. To establish a capability for affiliation and emotions, for example, a child needs a minimally functioning family environment, because early attachment between a child and a caregiver is essential to an individual's ability to relate well to others throughout life.[14] To establish a capability for bodily health, a child needs to grow up in a home with sufficient, nutritious food. To establish a capability for thought, a child needs to grow up in a home with at least some cognitive stimulation. To establish a capability for exerting control over the political environment, a child needs a home that helps children become, in the words of legal scholar Linda McClain, "capable, responsible, self-governing citizens."[15] And so on, with the family's role playing out in nearly all the capabilities. To be sure, schools, faith communities, and other institutions also help develop these capabilities, but families lay the essential groundwork.

To make the state's interest in strong, stable, positive relationships within families more concrete, return to the family's role in education. As chapter 2 explained, the rise of the information economy and the decline of the manufacturing base in the United States mean that educational attainment profoundly affects life opportunities. Without an education, it is much harder to find a job that pays decent wages. But whether a child will succeed in school has a lot to do with the child's experiences at home.

The Minnesota study, finding that relationships within the family affect later academic achievement, is hardly unique in establishing a connection between the family and educational outcomes.[16] There is considerable evidence that much of the disparity in test scores between white and African American children, for example, exists before a child enters school. Tests of the cognitive abilities of nine-month-old African American and white children show the same results, but by age two, differences begin to appear, and abilities in reading and math are well entrenched by the time children begin kindergarten.[17] Indeed, most of the gap in math achievement scores at age twelve existed at age six.[18] (This achievement gap, although often characterized as a black-white gap, turns more on income than on race. The achievement gap between children from high- and low-income families is more than twice as large as the black-white achievement gap,[19] a marked change from fifty years ago.[20])

How do families affect academic achievement? Beginning with brain architecture, recall the discussion in chapter 1 about the development of neural pathways and the importance of laying down, during the first few years of life, connections between various parts of the brain. Recall also the development of "executive functions," which allow a child to retain information for short periods of time, ignore distractions, and switch easily from one point of focus to another.[21] The development of these capacities turns on interactions with caregivers during the early years of life, particularly before a child reaches age five.

More broadly, families provide children with a foundation for their future experiences in school. In the Minnesota study, the researchers knew that broad demographic characteristics—low socioeconomic status, gender, and low parental education, for example—were correlated with dropping out, but these characteristics did not explain the process that led a student to drop out, nor were the characteristics wholly predictive, because even within these groups, there were considerable differences in dropout rates.[22] The researchers also knew that factors such as behavior problems, low academic achievement, difficulty getting along with peers, and low parental involvement in schooling were more direct causes of dropping out, but these factors did not suddenly appear in middle childhood; instead, the researchers knew these problems had roots in early childhood.[23] Rather than seeing these predictors as the causes of dropping out, then, the researchers conceived of a "lengthy developmental pathway" beginning very early in life and culminating with dropping out.[24]

In this developmental approach to dropping out, early-childhood experiences do not directly cause dropping out, but rather these childhood experiences set the child on a certain path, which is then reinforced throughout childhood and into the school years.[25] This hypothesis was confirmed by the data. The researchers found that the early-childhood measures (quality of the mother-child caregiving relationship and quality of the home environment) predicted the middle-childhood markers listed above (behavioral problems and so on), which then predicted dropping out.[26] Put another way, the researchers found that they could strongly predict dropping out by age three and a half by looking only at assessments of the quality of the caregiving and the home environment and, of course, controlling for other factors such as IQ.[27] Behavior problems and poor peer relations were also predictors, but adding these factors to the early-childhood factors did not increase the accuracy of the prediction.[28]

In trying to figure out more precisely how the early experiences affected dropping out, the researchers concluded that the early experiences had a snowball effect.[29] Through the parent-child relationship, for example, a child learns to self-regulate (or not) and relate to others (or not). These skills are enormously important in a school setting, where children must stay on task, work with other children and adults, and so on. Additionally, a child takes an early experience and uses it to choose or interpret later experiences. The researchers give the example of a child who has learned not to express herself emotionally, because when she does, her parent rejects her. This child continues this pattern when in the presence of others at school, even though other adults and children would not necessarily react in the same way as the parent. The child thus does not have a "corrective experience" that would change the earlier pattern and instead develops difficult relations with adults and peers.[30] In this way, the early experiences create "vulnerabilities or strengths with regard to later experiences."[31] The early experiences do not directly cause the later experiences, but they do set a child along a path.[32]

The influence of families does not end when a child begins school. A supportive family environment shapes a child's school experience in numerous ways, reinforcing or undermining the progress made during the school day.[33] Providing a safe home where a child's health and nutritional needs are met is essential, but beyond this, parents influence a child's academic performance by attending important school events such as parent-teacher conferences,[34] encouraging and helping children with homework, and cooperating with teacher requests for additional help at home.[35] As detailed in chapter 2, it is particularly challenging for families with limited economic and social resources to make these crucial investments in their children. Recall, for example, the gap in "developmental time," with college-educated parents spending fifty minutes more a day than non-college-educated parents reading to children, taking them to the library, and so on, with the gap most pronounced during the key early years of childhood.[36] Similarly, families with incomes in the top quintile spend $7,500 more than families in the bottom quintile on developmental activities such as summer camp and enriching after-school activities.[37] This is not to suggest that economically stable families always provide children with the strong, stable, positive relationships that prepare a child for school success. Ask any child who grew up with plenty of money but alcoholic or abusive parents for a story about a harrowing, lonely childhood. Rather, it is simply to highlight why low-income children, despite similar cognitive abilities, arrive in kindergarten significantly disadvantaged.

In sum, families—or, more precisely, strong, stable, positive relationships within families—are essential for nurturing a host of essential capabilities in children, from the capacity for practical reason and critical thought to the ability to relate to others. The state can play some direct role later in a child's life, particularly once the child begins school at age five, but before then, it is very difficult for the state to influence very young children directly. Even when children attend preschool programs, these typically start at age three or four, missing the critical development period between birth and age three. Other institutions—such as faith groups, schools, sports teams, and the like—can help develop capabilities, but in the very early years, families are where development begins or falters. And even after children enter school, families continue to play a large role.

There is no doubt that the state needs families.

A new conception of family-state relations: Mutual dependency

In light of the state's need for families and families' need for the state, the relationship between the two is really one of mutual dependency. The state cannot raise children itself and instead needs functioning families to do this work. But to raise children well in a modern society, families need the state. This frame of mutual dependency helps guide a new vision for the kind of relationship that family law should structure between families and the state. Rather than conceiving of families as atomistic, set apart from the state, families and the state are working together.

Mutual dependency still has a place for autonomy, but it is not the autonomy idealized as no need for others. Instead, in the context of mutual dependency, autonomy means the capacity for self-governance, that people are able to regulate their own behavior according to their own interests and values.[38] Relationships are not antithetical to self-governance but instead are essential to it.[39] Relationships deeply affect who we are, what we value, and what we are able to do. This is clearly true in the context of the parent-child relationship. Through strong, stable, positive relationships, parents are able to help children develop the capabilities they need for a full life and to be self-governing. But it is also true in the context of the family-state relationship.[40] The state can provide support in a way that allows recipients to make important decisions for themselves without undue intrusion or humiliation.[41] Or the state can undermine relationships and second-guess parenting choices. Recall chapter 3's comparison of Social Security survivor benefits, which foster self-governance, and Temporary Assistance to Needy Families, which decidedly does not. In supporting families in their critical work, the state should try to further, not hinder, the self-governance of families.

In sum, conceiving of families and the state as mutually dependent opens the doors to much more creative thinking about how the state can and should support families in their essential work of raising children. It also leads back to strong, stable, positive relationships. As this book has repeatedly demonstrated, these kinds of relationships help cultivate the necessary capabilities in children.

It is fine to understand this as a conceptual matter—and doing so alone would be progress for family law—but it is also important to understand what this means in practice. The remainder of this chapter explores the four cornerstones that would help the state encourage strong, stable, positive relationships within the family, particularly between parents and children and between adults with children.

CORNERSTONES FOR NURTURING STRONG, STABLE, POSITIVE RELATIONSHIPS

To realize the goal of nurturing strong, stable, positive relationships within families, the state should recognize a broader range of families, encourage a long-term commitment between parents, alter the physical context for family life to promote family interaction and social embedment, and support parents in their critical child-development work. A structural family law built on these cornerstones would help cultivate strong, stable, positive relationships within the family, which in turn would ensure that children grow up with the central capabilities they need in life, leading to both individual and societal well-being.

Fostering strong relationships by recognizing a broader range of families

Legal recognition can help strengthen family relationships. As a quick reminder of the harms flowing from nonrecognition (detailed in earlier chapters), consider the dignitary harm to a child who is told that his mothers are not good enough for the state institution of marriage. Why are they excluded? And why is his family any less important than the family of the child sitting next to him in school? As is often the case, children say this best. When James Steinman-Gordon was nine years old, his two mothers were legally married. They had been together for twenty-one years and had performed a commitment ceremony before they had children, but after New York changed its laws to allow same-sex couples to marry, the two women decided to marry legally. This is what James said during the ceremony:

> Hello everybody. Today is a very special day for me because my moms are finally getting legally married. I've had many experiences in the past with kids saying, "Isn't your family a little weird?" and I always say, "You bet!" We can't watch any TV or play video games.... We have our own language, Machala. We are constantly singing and dancing all over the house; that's why my sister always closes the shutters as soon as she gets home. We even asked our elderly next-door neighbor if we could use her backyard to raise a cow (she said no but we're still hoping she'll change her mind).
>
> But then the kids say, "No, I mean about your two Moms." And I say, "Oh that? No, they're pretty normal. I love my moms."

I only realized how much some people discriminate against gays and lesbians when, in school, I wrote a persuasive essay to convince people that gays and lesbians should be able to legally marry. My mom showed me one of the cases that decided gay marriage should not be allowed. The judge said that the only reason for marriage is to have children. I thought that was ridiculous. I bet the judge didn't marry *his* wife only so that she could pop out some kids!

The judge also said that it's harmful for kids to have gay parents. Do I look like I'm having a dark, depressing life? My moms are the greatest parents I could ever have gotten and I can't imagine loving any family more than this one. This is such a happy day for my moms and me and my sister, and they deserve it all the way. Thank you for coming to share this day with us.[42]

Adults care about legal recognition. And so do children.

Beyond families headed by same-sex couples, this book has described the many other ways people experience family ties outside the traditional family, including grandparents raising their grandchildren, donor siblings finding each other and forming ties, two women raising a child with the help of a friend who was also the sperm donor, adult children taking care of their elderly parents, birth mothers choosing adoptive parents but then remaining present in their children's lives, extended-family members living together, and so on.

Structural family law should not resist these changes in families. Rather than insist on the model of two opposite-sex, married parents with biological or adoptive children, family law must acknowledge that social and emotional families are forming in numerous configurations. Consider the parent-child relationship. In light of a child's need for a continuous relationship with an attentive adult, legal parenthood should continue to be a highly privileged legal status. Parents and children should both be confident that the law will protect their relationship against interference by the state and third parties. Parents need to know that their social, emotional, and economic investments in children are protected. And a child's long-term dependency needs make it important to clarify who is responsible for caring for a child. But these needs do not require a particularly narrow or traditional definition of a parent-child relationship. Chapter 8 discusses the implementation of this approach.

One question about family form is the degree to which the state should try to influence family choices. Even with a strong tradition of pluralism, nearly all laws embody a normative vision of family, as chapter 3 demonstrated. Recognizing the ubiquitous judgments about families already embodied in the law does not justify them, but it does demonstrate that it is almost impossible for any policy to be completely neutral with regard to family choices. So how should the state make these choices? Consider the following example. In 2009, New York's Mayor Bloomberg contemplated eliminating vouchers for after-school programs. The *New York Times* reported that although the vouchers are available to many families in need, the vouchers "overwhelmingly benefit" Orthodox Jews in certain Brooklyn neighborhoods.[43] A mother of eleven children said she used the vouchers to enroll five of her older children in after-school programs, enabling her to spend time with her younger children. She concluded, "If I didn't have [the vouchers], my head would spin."[44]

Is it the state's responsibility to make this woman's life more manageable when she has chosen, consistent with her religious and cultural tradition, to have a large family? Or should the state discourage large families by, for example, making benefits available only for the first two or three or even four children in a family? Many state welfare programs do just this,[45] and the U. S. Supreme Court has upheld these schemes, finding that they do not violate the Equal Protection Clause.[46]

These are difficult questions, but the goal of fostering strong, stable, positive relationships within families provides some guidance. How this goal plays out in any given policy choice about family form will not always be readily apparent. In this context, for example, policymakers will need to consider the evidence about family size and the quality of relationships within the family. If the evidence tends to show that children form more secure attachment relationships in relatively small families, then the state might be justified in encouraging smaller families by, for example, limiting the vouchers to a specified number of children. Conversely, if the evidence shows that other factors, such as the social and financial resources available to the parents and the degree of support from a community are more determinative of child outcomes, then the state should provide the vouchers to all in need, regardless of family size. Most likely, the evidence will fall somewhere in between, and there will be lots of caveats to any conclusions, but the essential step is asking whether a certain policy advances strong, stable, positive relationships within the family.

The intention of this book is not to answer every policy decision facing family law today but rather to articulate the guiding principles that should be used to debate the policy decisions. Sometimes this will clearly indicate preferred policies, and other times it will not. But it will ensure that we are having the right conversation.

Fostering stable relationships by encouraging a long-term commitment between parents

As the chapters in part one detailed, there is overwhelming evidence that a stable relationship between parents and children is essential to child development. This stability is the basis for attachment between parents and very young children, which has lifelong effects. As argued above, structural family law should continue to protect the parent-child relationship, clarifying who has rights and responsibilities and thus promoting the stability of these relationships.

But stability between a child's parents is also tremendously important to the child's outcomes. We know from chapter 2 that child well-being is positively correlated with two, married parents. But we also know that the evidence is incomplete, and the connection between marriage and child outcomes is complex. A considerable portion of the discrepancy in child outcomes is a result of the factors that tend to accompany family form, including income, parental education, parenting quality, and the mental health of parents. Even with these caveats, it appears that at least some of the difference can be attributed to family structure.

As Sara McLanahan and Irwin Garfinkel plausibly argued, the causal relationship between family structure and poor child outcomes can be traced to the decision to bear a child before finding a reliable long-term partner. Having a child in this situation increases the chance that the relationship will not last, that both parents will begin new relationships, and that these new relationships will lead to more children. This instability and multipartner fertility appear to be separate causes of the poor outcomes for children, because they interfere with the parent's ability to care for the child. Theoretically, a parent and a child can maintain a stable relationship regardless of whether the child lives with both parents, but in practice, this tends not to happen. Typically, children who do not live with both parents have far less contact with the nonresidential parent, especially if the parents were never married. Family instability, then, typically means that the child loses contact with one parent, almost always the father. Additionally, when parents have children by multiple partners, this family complexity interferes with the mother's ability to maintain a strong, stable, positive relationship with the child. As chapter 2 showed, switching partners is associated with increased maternal stress and harsh parenting strategies and a decrease in parent-child literacy activities. Transitions in partners also mean that a child is even less likely to see a biological father.

In short, family instability and multipartner fertility make it harder for parents and children to maintain strong, stable, positive relationships. For these reasons, the state has an interest in encouraging a long-term commitment between adults who are raising children. When parents stay together, a child is more likely to maintain relationships with both parents, and the child is less likely to experience multiple family transitions. This does not necessarily mean that the state has to promote marriage. Other kinds of legal recognition may also encourage a long-term commitment between parents, but this is really a "how to" question and so is addressed in much greater length in chapter 8.

As in so many other contexts, the interests of family members are not always aligned. It may be in a child's interests for the mother and father to stay together, for example, but not necessarily in the parents' interests. The child might benefit from having two adults in the home and from the stability in family form (particularly the absence of new partners), but staying together might not be what the parents want. Setting aside a case of domestic violence, where separation makes good sense, commitment between adults is one of the situations where family law should first try to align the interests of the family by encouraging the parents to develop a stronger relationship with each other. But in the absence of that, family law should still prioritize the child's needs. "Staying together for the sake of the children" may seem outdated, but given the alternatives for the child, there is something to this intuition. This is not to say that the state should require couples to stay together or make it particularly difficult for them to exit a relationship, but there are more indirect ways for the state to encourage long-term commitment, discussed in the next chapter.

Even when parents are no longer romantically involved, the state should encourage parents to make a commitment to the joint work of raising the child. As chapters 5 and 6 demonstrated, *how* the state restructures a family following a divorce matters tremendously to the continued relationship between family members. When the substance, process, and practice of dispute-resolution family law encourage family members to maintain a connection and leave the door open to repair, it is that much easier for a nonresidential parent to maintain a relationship with a child. Similarly, for parents who have never married and do not live together, the state should ensure that its policies encourage parents to cooperate in raising their child.

Fostering positive relationships by altering the physical context of family life to promote family interaction and social embedment

It is not enough that relationships within the family be strong and stable. Indeed, many abusive relationships between adults and between parents and children are very strong and very stable. Relationships must also be positive. To foster positive relationships within families, structural family law should ensure that the physical context of family life both increases the amount and quality of family interaction and also cultivates greater social embedment of families.

Beginning with family interaction, families need time and space together, but too often, modern life gets in the way. In particular, the dominant pattern of development in America is antithetical to family interaction. As chapter 1 explained, the simple exercise of picturing the triangle formed by home, workplace, and school says a lot about the quality of a family's life. The closer these three places are to one another and the easier it is to travel from one to the other, the more time family members have for each another. Similarly, access to playgrounds ensures that a child has an opportunity for exercise and developmental play[47] and also provides parents and children with a time to connect with each other, even if only on the walk over.

To address these structural obstacles to family interaction, the state should take direct measures, such as those described in chapter 8, to promote the development of physical environments that make it easier for families to conduct their daily business and still have enough time left over for one another. A parent's ability to get to work and then get home relatively quickly is essential for ensuring that the parent can earn money and also be available to parent the children.[48]

In addition to these direct measures, the state should pay greater attention to the impact of its actions on families and family interaction when pursuing other objectives. When the state is constructing new roads and highways, for example, the primary state goal might be to ease congestion or further commercial activity. But in pursuing these objectives, the state should consider the impact on families. Most governments engage in a cost-benefit analysis before undertaking major developments, but this should also include a determination of whether the proposed work will benefit or hinder family interaction.

Another aspect of fostering positive relationships within the family is ensuring ties outside of the family. As chapter 1 showed, the social context for family life affects family relationships tremendously. The saying "It takes a village to raise a child" is shopworn, but the basic idea is sound. Parents do not and cannot raise children alone. Instead, a web of care—including extended-family members, friends, neighbors, and babysitters—provides critical support for parents in their caregiving responsibilities. This support can be both concrete, such as taking a child for an afternoon, and emotional, such as commiserating with a new parent about sleep deprivation. When a parent is well supported, it is much easier for that parent to provide a child with a positive relationship.

The problem, however, is that too often families need to recreate this web every time they move, and too often the web is frayed by environments that do not help neighbors build social connections. As chapter 1 explained, the relationships that make up a web of care are more or less likely to develop depending on the physical structure of a neighborhood. When cities and towns are designed for cars and when neighborhoods do not include sidewalks and common areas that promote casual interaction, social isolation increases. By focusing on the physical context for family life, structural family law can enrich the social context. What this calls for is very similar to the prescription for increasing family interaction: a neighborhood that is designed with families in mind. It is worth noting an additional benefit of encouraging the development of webs of care: they are a way for the state to further pluralism. This is state support but through a diversified and defused mechanism that seeks to strengthen what exists at the community level rather than displacing it.

*Putting it all together: Supporting parents in their critical
child-development work*

Finally, the state should do much more to help parents in their critical job of raising children. The equation is fairly straightforward. The early years of a child's life
are crucial to the child's development, the relationship between the caregiver and
the child plays a central role in this development, but caring for a very young child is
exceptionally difficult, all the more so if a new parent has additional economic and
social stressors. To promote child development, then, the state must work *through*
parents, because the state cannot reach very young children directly.

To underscore the demands on parents, picture a day in the life of a new mother.
The baby has never really "gone to bed," so it is hard to say when the day begins, but
let's say six a.m. The child wakes up and needs to be fed. This mother is breastfeeding, so only she can feed the child, and this can take at least thirty minutes, if not
considerably longer. The baby's diaper then needs to be changed and new clothes
put on, because the infant spits up after feeding. The baby also needs other physical care, such as cleaning the umbilical-cord stump and swabbing the child's mouth
with gentian violet to treat a mild case of thrush, a common malady in newborns,
especially those whose mothers were put on antibiotics during delivery. At seven
a.m., the mother is able to get a quick bite of food for herself. She does this while
holding her baby, because the infant cries whenever she is put down. The infant has
an as-yet-undiagnosed case of acid reflux, and the acid comes up more readily when
the child is horizontal. After eating a piece of toast, the mother walks the baby up
and down the room, comforting her. She is lucky if she has time to brush her teeth,
let alone shower. By nine a.m., the child needs another feeding, and so the cycle of
care begins again, and then it repeats at noon, at three p.m., and so on. Evenings
can be particularly difficult for infants, and this baby, like many, cries uninterrupted
from six to eleven p.m. The mother and the baby finally fall asleep at eleven p.m.,
but both awaken again at three a.m. for yet another feeding. After this feeding, the
mother is able to squeeze in two more hours of sleep before the "day" begins again
at six a.m.

These incessant demands for caretaking can exhaust and enervate even the most
competent, economically stable, mature adult with considerable help from family
members and paid caregivers. A young person with limited emotional, social, and
economic resources faces truly extraordinary challenges. And the addition of older
children, with their own needs, makes parenting even more difficult. It is not surprising, then, that children younger than one are at the greatest risk for child abuse.[49]
But even after a child begins to sleep more regularly, parenting continues to be a challenge. A toddler may not wake up every few hours at night, for example, but caring

for a young child has its own set of issues, from dealing with the "terrible twos" to worrying constantly about the child's safety as she tests her newfound mobility.

To ensure that parents provide their children with the strong, stable, positive relationships that are essential to child development, the state should help parents choose when to have children, assist them in the transition to parenthood, encourage fathers to be involved even when they do not live with their children, provide opportunities in the preschool years, and address economic stressors. As this list shows, most of this state support comes in the first years of a child's life. This is because during the early years, parents, rather than the state, are having the most interaction with children. It is also because this is the time when investments are most cost-effective, the topic of chapter 9.

Choosing to become a parent. Given the rigors of parenthood and the high stakes for child development, becoming a parent should be a true choice. Too often, however, a combination of limited access to effective birth control, the absence of economic opportunities, and too little knowledge about sexuality means that some young people become parents long before they are ready. When researchers at the Centers for Disease Control looked at live births in the United States—a statistic that excludes pregnancies that end in miscarriage, abortion, or stillbirth—they found that 63 percent of the pregnancies were intended, 23 percent were mistimed, and 14 percent were unwanted.[50] But when they looked at the numbers divided by age, the percentages were even starker. Only 23 percent of births to women ages fifteen to nineteen were intended, as compared with 75 percent of births to mothers ages twenty-five to forty-four.[51] Fifty-one percent of the teen births were "seriously mistimed," meaning that the mother wanted to be pregnant more than two years in the future, and 19 percent were unwanted.[52]

The state has a strong instrumental interest in helping teens delay childbearing. The U.S. teen birth rate has steadily declined since the 1950s, but it is still higher than that in most other industrialized countries.[53] This remains a serious social and economic problem, because teen births are strongly associated with poor outcomes for both mother and child, as described in chapter 2. A central role for the state is ensuring that women and men, and especially teenage girls and boys, do not have children until they want to do so.

Beyond the teen years, as the Fragile Families Study demonstrates, having a child before finding a reliable partner contributes to poor outcomes for children, because it increases the likelihood of multipartner fertility and family complexity. Helping young people delay childbearing until they are in a stable, committed relationship is critical. This is much easier said than done and involves the complex interaction between poverty and family form, but the state should work toward this goal nonetheless.

Making a transition to parenthood. Parenting can be deeply rewarding and fulfilling, but it can also be boring and, at times, enraging. The stress of becoming a parent can, in turn, interfere with attachment. The problem is that too often the images of parenthood are idealized. A well-coiffed mother gazes adoringly into her baby's face. A father and son throw a baseball in the park, talking amiably. Two siblings fight in the back seat of the car but only over a trivial matter. The public images of family life—whether in popular culture, in advertisements, or simply on the subway and in the grocery store—are often deeply at odds with the lived reality of family life. Mothers yell at their children. Fathers are often absent. And sibling fights can be physically and emotionally brutal. There is very little truth in advertising when it comes to family life. New parents are not told that their marriages will suffer after the birth of a child. Stay-at-home parents often do not know the economic risks they are assuming by stepping off the career ladder. And parents are often unprepared for the sheer boredom and monotony of caring for a young child. In short, the discrepancy between the expectations of parenthood and its reality can be jarring.

Preparing parents for the emotional reality—good and bad—of parenthood is an important part of a successful transition. New parents with strong support networks can turn to others for help with this transition. Breastfeeding groups, faith-based or secular parenting classes, and play groups, for example, provide a space for parents to talk about their challenges candidly. But for new parents who are socially isolated and who have few supportive family members to turn to, the state can help foster support networks to aid in the transition to parenthood. By doing so, structural family law will take a proactive, not just reactive, stance toward attachment.

Encouraging involvement by nonresidential fathers. Even with efforts to encourage a long-term commitment between parents, some children will grow up in single-mother homes. Given the very strong connection between parental involvement and a child's outcomes, the state should take steps to encourage fathers to remain active in their children's lives, even if the fathers are no longer romantically involved with the mothers. This means encouraging a connection between the father and the child and a co-parenting relationship between the father and the mother. This co-parenting relationship is crucial, because the quality of the father's relationship with the child's mother is one of the most important factors determining whether a father stays involved with his child.[54]

Providing opportunities in the preschool years. Once a child reaches age three, the state should take a more direct role in encouraging child development. By providing quality preschool programs, the state can work with parents to ensure that children are receiving the stimulation and school preparation they need. Research has long shown that quality early-childhood education programs have tremendous long-term effects. Study after study documented that these programs improve educational outcomes for the participants (including higher test scores, less use of special education and grade repetition, and increased likelihood that participants will attend a four-year college), aid cognitive and social-emotional development, reduce rates of teen and adult incarceration, reduce rates of teen pregnancy, improve skilled-employment rates, and improve earnings as adults.[55] These programs are often criticized because some studies have found that cognitive benefits fade over time, but there is solid evidence that even if some academic achievement benefits do weaken, the programs have a long-lasting positive impact on educational progress and attainment overall, participation in the labor market, and pro-social behaviors such as decreased involvement in the criminal justice system and fewer teen pregnancies.[56] Additionally, long-term benefits are not limited to small, demonstration programs but are also found in large-scale programs run in multiple locations.[57] Investing in these programs is a key way the state can shoulder some of the responsibility for child development and help parents with this essential work.

Addressing economic stressors. Economic stress translates into familial stress. Responding to the seismic shifts in the economy outlined in chapter 2 is not easy, and the country is engaged in an extended dialogue about how best to do so, but it is essential in debates about the shrinking middle class and the appropriate path to economic growth to make the connection between economic stability and strong, stable, positive relationships. Parents who earn decent wages are in a much better position to form lasting relationships with each other and provide their children with the attention that is critical for child development.

In addition to rebuilding the middle class, it is essential to address poverty. For more than forty years, sociologist William Julius Wilson has been studying the problems of poverty, race, and families in the United States. In his 1987 classic, *The Truly Disadvantaged*, Wilson contended that economic restructuring and the end of de jure segregation separated, both spatially and socioeconomically, low-income African Americans from middle- and upper-income African Americans. He countered the prevailing view that a "culture of poverty" was partly to blame for the low incomes of inner-city African Americans. Instead, he argued, structural problems caused poverty. For example, the lack of employment opportunities both created lower incomes and encouraged single-parenthood, because there were not enough African American men with sufficient income to make suitable marriage partners for women.[58]

In a 2009 book, Wilson revisited the relationship between race and poverty and argued that a combination of structural *and* cultural forces is responsible for the continued poverty plaguing African Americans in urban areas.[59] For issues such as unemployment, Wilson emphasized structural problems, such as the decreasing demand for low-skilled labor and the decline of the manufacturing sector.[60] But for issues facing low-income African American families, Wilson contended that cultural forces are also at play, leading to a decline in marriage and long-term partnering.[61] Citing work by other researchers, Wilson did not blame families but rather noted that in the face of poverty and the dearth of marriageable men, low-income women are making both a rational and an understandable choice not to marry but still to pursue motherhood, because being a mother is central to a sense of identity and self-worth.[62] The problem, however, is that these women often underestimate the challenges of raising children alone.[63]

Putting the structural and cultural forces together, Wilson argued that poverty adversely influences an individual's chances throughout her life, because those individuals with the lowest educational development and the weakest job-related skills are most likely to raise their families with the same insufficient resources and life chances they had as children.[64] This creates a cyclical pattern, making economic and social mobility extremely difficult to obtain.

Too often, commentators and politicians argue that families should pull themselves up by their own bootstraps,[65] but this personal-responsibility approach to overcoming poverty seems like wishful thinking at best and dangerously naive at worst. Family stability is important for child outcomes, and two parents are generally better than one. But this does not mean that a clinically depressed mother with a history of domestic violence and very limited income is simply going to wake up one morning and decide that because she has no subsidized child care or health care, she will shake off her depression, kick out her abuser, interact meaningfully with her child that day, and obtain a job with decent pay and workable hours. The problems are far more complex, and the opportunities available to her are far too limited. Recall the statistic discussed in chapter 4 that low-income single mothers in the United States are typically employed but that they still earn less than their counterparts in other industrialized countries. It is not a question of hard work but rather excruciatingly difficult circumstances and very limited opportunities. By addressing the economic stressors, the state helps parents tremendously.

* * *

These four cornerstones work together. Socially embedded parents have greater emotional support, making it easier for them to provide the strong, stable, positive relationships that children need. Legal recognition encourages and protects relationships and thus encourages families to interact and build a web of care. A long-term commitment between parents makes it easier to build a web of care. And so on. When restructuring the relationship between families and the state, then, it is important to consider all four cornerstones together, but it also means that working on any one cornerstone will likely help advance another, in a potentially virtuous cycle.

CONCLUSION

This chapter ends where it began: talking about school. A dominant American myth
is that anyone can succeed given the right tools and enough hard work. This leads to
a focus on schools. If low-income children just had better schools, so the argument
goes, all children could succeed. This focus on schooling is appealing, because the
state has direct access to schoolchildren and does not need to work through parents,
blunting the criticism that the state is intervening in the family. It also avoids shining
a spotlight on family functioning, with all the attendant sensitivity of judging families. But academic achievement does not begin in kindergarten or even a preschool
program. It begins at home.

To nurture many of the most important capabilities in young children, parents
lay the essential foundation for child well-being. They do so through strong, stable,
positive relationships with each other and with their children. The state has a clear
interest in ensuring that family members are providing one another with these kinds
of relationships, which leads to a reconceptualization of the relationship between
families and the state. Families are not independent of the state. Families need the
state. And the state needs families. Recognizing this mutual dependency creates a
framework for rethinking structural family law.

Instead of waiting for a crisis, the state should actively encourage the development
of strong, stable, positive relationships within the family. The four cornerstones—
recognizing a broader range of families, encouraging a long-term commitment
between parents, altering the physical context for family life, and supporting parents in their critical child-development work—should inform this new structural
relationship between families and the state. Chapter 8 shows how this is possible,
providing concrete examples of how the state can build on these four cornerstones.

8

Implementing the New Vision, Part Two

THINKING ABOUT HOW to help new parents has been the life work of David Olds, a professor of pediatrics, psychiatry, and preventive medicine at the University of Colorado–Denver and the founder of the Nurse-Family Partnership.[1] Olds had a relatively happy childhood growing up in Ohio, but when he was eleven, his parents divorced, his father moved to Florida, and his grandmother, who had lived with his family, died. Olds's mother had to work in a factory to support Olds and his sister.[2] As a result of this difficult time, Olds decided he wanted to do something to help people when he grew up.[3] He entered Johns Hopkins University with a scholarship to study international relations, but by sophomore year, he realized he was drawn to social and behavioral sciences. Forfeiting the remainder of his scholarship because of this transition, Olds signed up for courses in developmental psychology with a focus on early infant attachment.[4] He had to work at a part-time job cutting grass for the city of Baltimore to pay his tuition, but Olds knew he had made the right decision.[5]

After graduating from Johns Hopkins in 1970, Olds secured his first full-time job, at the Union Square Day Care Center, operating out of a church basement in West Baltimore.[6] There he observed firsthand the many challenges facing low-income children. He also saw that some of his colleagues approached their work at the day-care center without hope for the future of the children or their parents.[7] Wanting to engage the children more, Olds began to invite parents to come into his classroom during nap time to discuss their children's behavior at school and to talk about activities the parents could try at home with their children.[8] For many of the children in his classes, however, Olds realized that to really make a difference, the children needed help much earlier in life, beginning at birth.[9]

Olds began to read books by Uri Bronfenbrenner, a professor at Cornell University who wrote about "human ecology" and the networks that form among parents and others who care for children.[10] Olds and Bronfenbrenner began a scholarly correspondence, and Olds ultimately earned his Ph.D. in developmental psychology from Cornell.[11] While studying at Cornell, Olds took a part-time job at the Comprehensive Interdisciplinary Development Services (CIDS), where he developed the elements of a program for new parents.[12] Olds wanted to work with first-time parents, in their homes, beginning in pregnancy and using nurses as in-home visitors. The goals of the program were to improve pregnancy outcomes by providing prenatal care, to enhance child health and development by fostering strong parenting skills, and to improve the lives of the mothers by developing educational and work plans and timing subsequent pregnancies.

These three goals became the core of the Nurse-Family Partnership, a program Olds subsequently piloted with different populations in Elmira (New York), Memphis, and Denver. Working slowly and using randomized, controlled studies, Olds refined the program until, in 1996, he was convinced that it was ready to be broadly replicated. With federal funding, Olds has expanded his program, now serving first-time mothers and their infants in forty-three states.[13] As detailed below, the Nurse-Family Partnership is a resounding success, dramatically lowering rates of child abuse and neglect, increasing mothers' participation in the workforce, and improving educational outcomes for children, to mention just a few of the benefits of the program. It is also cost-effective, saving the state considerable money in the long run. An example of how the state can nurture strong, stable, positive relationships, the Nurse-Family Partnership, is discussed in greater detail later in this chapter.

Chapter 7 laid out the new vision for structural family law, basing it on the four cornerstones of (1) recognizing a broader range of families, (2) encouraging a long-term commitment between parents, (3) altering the physical context for family life to increase family interaction and social embedment, and (4) supporting parents in their critical child-development work. A natural reaction to this project of rethinking the basic relationship between families and the state is to ask what this might look like in practice and to question how practical such a reform effort might actually be. As this chapter demonstrates, this new relationship between families and the state is not just a lofty ideal. There are practices already in place—albeit underfunded and not uniformly adopted—that reflect the four cornerstones.

This chapter describes several of these promising reforms to demonstrate that it is possible for family law to nurture strong, stable, positive relationships, serving the interests of both families and the state. Given the overlapping nature of the four cornerstones, the examples are not as functionally clean as the categories suggest. The Nurse-Family Partnership, for instance, supports parents in their critical child-development work and also increases social embedment. But the examples do embody the basic idea of each cornerstone.

FOSTERING STRONG RELATIONSHIPS: RECOGNIZING
A BROADER RANGE OF FAMILIES

Chapter 7 explained that recognizing a broader range of families will help strengthen relationships, but this begs the tricky question of how the state should open up legal categories. The challenge is to ensure that the legal definition of family better reflects the reality of modern American families but that family law still has coherent, workable definitions. Although there are numerous contexts in which family law needs to grapple with this issue, two examples will help demonstrate that it is possible to strike a balance.

Broadening the definition of a legal parent. Too often, it is challenging to find even one person who is willing to take on the responsibility of raising children. This is particularly true for children in the child-welfare system who have been freed for adoption and who are older, part of a sibling group, or disabled.[14] But there are situations where, in addition to a legally recognized parent or parents, another individual with close emotional, social, and economic ties to a child seeks legal recognition. Sometimes recognizing this additional individual would mean that a child would have three parents. The first question for structural family law is determining when a person should be granted parental rights and responsibilities, and the second question is whether the law should vest parental rights in more than two parents. As chapter 4 described, the dilemma stems from the law's all-or-nothing approach to parenthood. An individual is either recognized as a legal parent with the attendant rights and responsibilities or is considered a legal stranger with neither. There are a few exceptions, but as a general matter, the law treats parenthood as a binary proposition. Further, the law allows children only two parents at any one time, in what chapter 4 called family law's "rule of two."

Beginning with the question of who should be granted parental rights, the answer is fairly straightforward in the context of same-sex parents jointly raising children in a state that does not recognize their relationship. (If the state does recognize the adult relationship, then both parents typically will have rights to the child, at least if the child is born during the relationship.) To ensure that the child has a strong relationship with both adults who are acting as parents, the state should grant full parental rights and responsibilities to both adults.

One way to do this is to allow second-parent adoptions. Available in only some states,[15] second-parent adoptions allow an adult to adopt a child without the existing parent losing any parental rights. This requires a court order approving the

adoption, typically preceded by a home visit by a social worker to approve the placement. Although it is costly and time-consuming for the parents, all states should
provide this option. In this context, there is no reason to deny a legal relationship
to a person already acting as a parent who is willing to take on the responsibilities
of raising a child. By legally recognizing the parent-child relationship, the state will
help strengthen the relationship.

Another way to recognize a same-sex parent is through the doctrine of psychological parenthood. This is particularly useful when a couple has not—as many
parents have not—gone through the expensive and time-consuming process of exe-
cuting a second-parent adoption. To understand how this works, consider the case
of Cheryl Ann Clark, Elsey Maxwell McLeod, and the child known by her initials
as E.L.M.C.[16] Cheryl and Elsey were committed domestic partners. After several
years together, they made the decision to start a family. After beginning the process
of applying for the adoption of a child from China, Cheryl was informed by their
social worker that China would not permit a same-sex couple to adopt. Cheryl and
Elsey decided to complete the adoption process but to include only Cheryl's name
on the adoption forms. The application was approved, and Cheryl and Elsey trav-
eled to China together to adopt E.L.M.C. Upon their return, they sent an arrival
announcement to their friends and family about the adoption, saying that the girl
"now lives with two adoring moms."

Although Cheryl was the only parent listed on the adoption paperwork, both
Elsey and Cheryl were active parents. Shortly after the adoption, the two women
filed for and were awarded joint custody of E.L.M.C. The child's legal name was
changed to include the last names of both Cheryl and Elsey. Both women were listed
in the school directory as parents of E.L.M.C. And the child's nanny reported that
Cheryl and Elsey equally parented the child. When Cheryl and Elsey ended their
relationship in 2001, the Colorado trial court found that it was "abundantly clear"
that Cheryl and Elsey co-parented and raised E.L.M.C. together and thus should
share custody of her, despite Cheryl's claim that she was the sole legal parent. The
appellate court agreed. Apart from the sex of the two parents, the case was no different from the end of a relationship between a heterosexual couple. Both women, who
had raised E.L.M.C. together, deserved legal recognition.

To recognize Elsey, the Colorado courts used the doctrine of psychological parenthood, also called de facto parenthood in some states, which confers legal status
on individuals who act like parents.[17] A psychological or de facto parent is typically
defined as someone who, for at least two years, lives with a child, does a significant
portion of the care work for the child, is not paid for that care work, and forms a
parent-child relationship with the permission of the legal parent.[18] This is an important development in the law and one that should be more broadly adopted, with

courts and legislatures experimenting with the precise test. In recognizing these individuals, however, it is important that the would-be parent enjoys full rights to the child *and* full responsibilities. The parent should be able to visit the child but must also be liable for child support. An adult cannot choose benefits without responsibilities.

The harder cases for broadening the definition of legal parenthood are instances where it is not clear who should have rights and responsibilities. Instead of two parents jointly raising a child, perhaps it is one parent raising a child with the sporadic help of a friend who might live with the family for two years, helping financially and emotionally, but then leave for six months because of work. Should this friend be able to assert some right to the child? Should the parent be able to receive child support from the friend during the six-month absence? Should it matter that the two adults are not romantically involved?

There are not necessarily promising examples, beyond an odd court decision, but flourishing family law provides a lens through which to focus these difficult decisions. The basic principles of flourishing family law clarify that when granting rights and responsibilities, the inquiry should be focused on determining which individuals have the requisite strong, stable, positive relationship with the child. Once that relationship has been established, then the law should protect it. This will necessarily be a case-by-case inquiry, but rather than lay down an absolute rule, it is more useful to focus the inquiry on the nature of the relationship between the adult and the child. Admittedly, this is somewhat in tension with the custody rule endorsed in chapter 6, that as between two parents, custody should be determined based on past time with the child. But in this context, where it is unclear who should be recognized as a parent at all, the reality of family life is complex, and the legal rule will need to be flexible. Courts and legislatures will need to grapple with difficult cases, but the point here is that third parties who are not typically granted parental rights should be able to make a claim to a child, so long as there is a strong, stable, positive relationship between the adult and the child. Additionally, there is no reason to condition legal parenthood on a romantic relationship between the two parents. Whether adults jointly caring for a child have sex is simply irrelevant to whether they are adequate parents and want to take on the shared enterprise of raising a child. If two friends or two siblings want to raise a child and both be recognized as legal parents, they should be allowed to do so.

Looking at the quality of the adult-child relationship, however, will not always settle the matter. In the context of assisted reproductive technology, for example, it could be that a disagreement about legal parenthood will begin before a child is even born. If a sperm donor who did not waive his rights to the child decides during the pregnancy that he wants to be the child's parent after the birth, then the court will need to project into the future. In this context, the principles of flourishing family law again give some guidance. The inquiry should turn, at least in part, on each potential parent's ability to work with the other parents. If one parent is clearly unwilling to compromise and wants sole parental rights to the exclusion of the other adults, and there is no clear justification for this exclusion such as a history of violence or dysfunction, then this might be basis for some concern. As has been shown repeatedly in this book, parents need to work together to raise children. An adult relationship may be temporary, but co-parenting is permanent, and a court should be allowed to give greater weight to a parent who will facilitate an ongoing relationship with all the important adults in a child's life.

Turning to the question of whether the law should vest parental rights in more than two people, consider two situations in which this might arise. First, same-sex couples (and opposite-sex couples, although less frequently) sometimes choose to raise a child with three parents. Two lesbians, for example, will ask a close male friend to donate sperm, perhaps because they want a known donor or want the child to grow up with a male role model in addition to the two women.[19] If the donation is made informally and the friend never waives his rights to the child, as would be required if the donation was made in a fertility clinic, then it is an open question whether he retains parental rights. His claim would be strengthened if the three adults jointly raised the child, with the two women acting as the primary parents but the friend participating both financially and emotionally. The problem, however, is that family law's "rule of two" means that if the friend is a legal parent, then one of the mothers is not. Second, if an opposite-sex couple with children divorces and the mother remarries, family law does not allow the stepfather to adopt the children unless the rights of the biological father are terminated. But perhaps both fathers are playing an active role, emotionally and financially, in the children's lives. The stepfather wants to be a legal father, the biological father does not want to lose his rights, and the mother wants to have a legal claim against both men for child support because the family is able to stay afloat financially only with the support of all three parents.

In these situations and more, it would be better to recognize that the children have strong, stable, positive relationships with more than two adults. In 2012, California came close to allowing three legal parents. The California legislature passed a bill that would allow a court to recognize more than two legal parents if it "would serve the best interest of the child based on the nature, duration, and quality of the presumed or claimed parents' relationships with the child and the benefit or detriment to the child of continuing those relationships."[20] The responsibilities of custody, visitation, and child support would be allocated among all legal parents according to the same uniform guidelines used under existing law but simply adjusted to allow for more than two parents.[21] Governor Jerry Brown vetoed the bill so it never became law, but it does provide a blueprint for how the state can move beyond the rule of two.

The state should continue to develop these alternative categories, to move family law closer to recognizing the reality of our lived lives. But in doing so, the state should be careful not to dilute parental rights too much. To truly invest in a child, emotionally and financially, a legal parent needs some assurance that the parent-child relationship will be respected.[22] This could be at risk if third parties with weak ties to a child are able to claim a relationship or if too many individuals are able to assert rights to a child. As anyone who has tried to co-parent a child with another adult knows, differences of opinion about what is best for a child are inevitable. Allowing a large number of individuals into that conversation would not only complicate the discussion but might well undermine the current allocation of authority between parents and the state. As it stands, the state generally defers to parental decision-making absent egregious circumstances. If the law were to recognize many legal parents, conflicts would likely arise, and the individuals would turn to the state as arbiter, thus usurping the decision-making role of parents.

So how many parents are too many? This is difficult to say and is a question for reasoned policy making, but the considerations are clear. It is important to recognize the reality that in some families, more than two individuals maintain strong, stable, positive relationships with a child and act like parents. But this does not mean that every treasured aunt or babysitter should suddenly be considered a parent. Rather, only those who have invested—emotionally, socially, and financially—in the child should be recognized as parents under the law.

Setting aside the thorny questions of particular legal rules, the central point is that the state should concern itself more with nurturing strong, stable, positive relationships than with any one particular structure of child and adult relationships. State recognition—rights and responsibilities—should turn on the extent to which a relationship nurtures this kind of connection, not whether the particular configuration fits within an existing, familiar family form. For example, a court faced with a situation like E.L.M.C.'s should ask whether the woman seeking legal rights has a strong, stable, and positive relationship with the child, not whether the two mothers fit a preconceived category of family. Although the court reached the right decision in that case, it was only after much anguish for Elsey and the child. And where a child really does have three parents, say, the sperm donor who is treated like a father, then all three parents should have some legal protection.

Broadening access to marriage. Turning to marriage, for two individuals who want to marry, the state should allow them to do so, absent a clear showing of harm either to the adults or to children. The most gaping hole in access to marriage at the moment is the refusal of a majority of states to extend civil marriage to same-sex

couples. As discussed in chapter 4, there is no credible evidence that children growing up with parents of the same sex are harmed in any way, so there is no basis for
the state to discourage the formation of these kinds of families. On the contrary, the
state should accept the existence of same-sex couples and work to strengthen the
relationships within these families by allowing same-sex couples to marry.

Apart from arguing that religious institutions should not have to perform marriages for same-sex couples (and recent state laws allow this carve-out), the principal
objection voiced by opponents of marriage equality is that the state has an interest
in preserving the traditional meaning of marriage, both as the site for expressing
traditional gender roles and as the locus for procreative sex.[23] Although *individuals*
certainly may hold this view of marriage, it is an inappropriate basis for state action.
The Constitution permits distinctions to be drawn along the lines of sex only in
very limited circumstances, and it is never permissible to draw sex distinctions to
promote gender-specific roles.[24] Further, although some individuals may view procreative sex as the only "good" or permissible kind of sex, it is not the business of
the state to determine which kind of sex is acceptable. Indeed, the Supreme Court
recognized this in its decision in *Lawrence v. Texas*, where the Court held that the
Constitution prohibits criminalizing homosexual sodomy.[25] To be sure, the Court
there struck down a criminal statute and was not addressing marriage equality, but it
is still some basis for concluding that the Constitution does not permit the state, as
a prescriptive matter, to prefer one kind of sexual activity over another, so long as it
is between consenting adults.

Finally, it is true that marriages are more stable than cohabiting relationships
(with all the caveats explained in this book), and it is true that the state has some
interest in ensuring that children are raised in families with committed parents,
but this argues in favor of extending marriage to same-sex couples, to ensure that
the children these couples are *already* raising have the same benefits as children of
opposite-sex couples. Moreover, rather than diluting the meaning of marriage, marriage equality reinforces the importance of raising children within a committed relationship. The gender of the parents is not relevant to their ability to commit to each
other and to the challenging business of raising children together.

In short, there is no legitimate basis for the state to oppose marriage between
two men or two women, and there are very good reasons to support marriage for
same-sex couples to ensure the long-term stability and well-being of the family. The
states that have not extended civil marriage to same-sex couples should do so as
quickly as possible.

These examples demonstrate that it is possible for structural family law to reflect
the reality of American family life and strengthen family relationships. It will entail
some difficult line-drawing exercises and some inevitable trade-offs, but it is clear

that we need to move beyond the current status quo of imposing an increasingly archaic model of family on a rapidly changing social reality. Another aspect of changing families is the decline of marriage and the rise of cohabiting relationships, addressed in the next section.

FOSTERING STABLE RELATIONSHIPS: ENCOURAGING A LONG-TERM COMMITMENT BETWEEN PARENTS

As this book has repeatedly shown, overwhelming evidence establishes that a stable and committed relationship between parents affects the outcomes of children, but the real challenge is how to encourage this kind of relationship between the adults. As the introduction argued, simply taking an unmarried couple who have just become parents down to city hall and issuing them a marriage license will not necessarily produce a lasting relationship between the parents and ensure that they take on the difficult job of raising a child together. Instead, the state must first identify why some people do not get married or maintain long-term cohabiting relationships and then address these barriers to commitment.

Why parents do not commit to each other

One of the intriguing findings in the Fragile Families Study described in chapter 2 is that 80 percent of the women were romantically involved with the father at the time of the child's birth, and 50 percent were living with the father. Belying the stereotype of the uninvolved father good for only a one-night stand, most fathers in the study provided financial support during the pregnancy (81 percent) and visited the mother in the hospital (77 percent).[26] Despite these early ties, only 35 percent of the couples were still living together five years after the birth,[27] fewer than half of these couples had married,[28] and father involvement dwindled over time, with half of the children of the unmarried parents not seeing their fathers regularly by age five.[29]

McLanahan has identified numerous reasons for the Fragile Families participants not to get married or even stay together, including low incomes, government policies that contain marriage and cohabitation penalties, social norms that condone single-motherhood, an absence of appealing marriage partners, and a lack of relationship skills that help parents maintain healthy relationships.[30] As McLanahan says, "No single factor appears to be dominant."[31] It is worth considering each factor separately.

Beginning with economic resources, it is true that lower-income families have much lower marriage rates, and it makes intuitive sense that people may be making a rational choice not to marry a partner with little economic resources. But the role of income in encouraging marriage is complex, and there is little evidence that simply raising incomes will raise marriage rates. Conservatives tend to believe that people are poor because they are not married, and so they promote marriage as an important antipoverty policy.[32] By contrast, liberals tend to believe that it is the lack of economic opportunity that leads to low marriage rates and so encourage programs that try to raise incomes.

In truth, neither side is right. McLanahan has shown that when the state reduces support for single mothers, thus encouraging them to marry (or when the state removes the economic disincentives to marry), marriage rates do not go up.[33] On the other hand, when women have greater economic support, they also do not get married. When Minnesota and Connecticut experimented with programs that increased economic support to low-income families, for example, the programs did increase marriage among certain groups, but the overall effect was not particularly strong.[34] Economics may play a role in long-term commitments, but it is far from the only factor.

Turning to government policies that contain marriage or cohabitation penalties, as chapter 4 explained, means-tested programs typically ask a parent to list all sources of income. If the parent is married, then the state will count the income from both parents when calculating eligibility. And some programs, such as the Supplemental Nutrition Assistance Program (better known as the food-stamp program), count income from all household members, regardless of legal ties. Both kinds of means-tested programs discourage stability, because they create an incentive for couples to live apart rather than cohabit.[35] But, as discussed in chapter 4, the actual effect of these rules on the decision to marry or live together is uncertain.

Considering cultural norms that support single motherhood, a particularly insightful work is the six-year ethnographic study of 162 low-income, single mothers in Philadelphia by sociologists Kathryn Edin and Maria Kefalas. The women in the study *wanted* to be married—indeed, they thought single-parenthood was second-best[36]—but they were unwilling to settle for unreliable men who would not be satisfying financial or emotional partners. Despite the lack of marriageable men, the women were unwilling to forgo motherhood.[37] The women highly valued motherhood, saw it as essential to their sense of self and their place in the world, and they did not want to postpone it until their thirties, a strategy typically deployed by middle-class women. As Edin and Kefalas conclude, the women "rely on their children to bring validation, purpose, companionship, and order to their often chaotic lives—things they find hard to come by in other ways."[38] Thus, although they were well aware of the risks of getting pregnant, the women Edin and Kefalas interviewed did not try particularly hard to avoid pregnancy. Once they were in a minimally stable relationship, they stopped using birth control on a regular basis.[39] Edin's follow-up work with Timothy Nelson on low-income fathers, discussed in chapter 2, tells a similar story about men not trying very hard to avoid impregnating women but also not seeing pregnancy as a reason to get married.

The acceptance of single-motherhood overlaps with the next barrier to marriage: demographic factors that lead to shortages of marriageable men. As Edin and Kefalas describe, women are making rational choices not to marry men who are unreliable economic and social partners. Numerous factors, including high rates of incarceration and low rates of employment, mean that many fathers are not appealing long-term partners. Telling a woman to marry the father of her child may well be very poor advice.

Finally, McLanahan found that a dearth of relationship skills made it difficult for parents in the study to maintain healthy relationships. McLanahan found that at the time of a child's birth, both parents were optimistic about their relationship, but this optimism did not translate into a long-term commitment. Conducting regression analyses on the Fragile Families data set, McLanahan ran simulations to determine whether marriage rates would change if the unmarried parents in the data set were given, one at a time, the characteristics of the married parents. As would be expected, the earnings of the men made some difference in marriage rates. That is, if the unmarried men earned as much as the married men, the marriage rate would increase. But relationship factors, such as trust and relationship quality, made a larger difference in marriage rates.[40] This is not to suggest that these factors are easy to change but rather that they are a promising avenue for exploration.

What the state can do to encourage commitment

There are several steps the state can take to address each of these factors, together and combined. To begin, the state must address one of the largest structural barriers: the high incarceration rate, particularly of low-income African American men.[41] There is not room in this already-too-long chapter to engage in a lengthy discussion of criminal-justice reform, but the need to reform that system is clear. It is exceedingly difficult for a man to be a meaningful father or partner when he is locked up. A related structural barrier is the low economic resources of many men. Policies that focus on improving the employment prospects of low-income parents and increasing the value of work would help the economic prospects for parents. These policies are discussed more fully below, but it is important to note here that this is not an easy task and that multiple factors, including high rates of incarceration and low levels of educational attainment, make it challenging to improve economic prospects, particularly for men.

Considering government policies that contain marriage penalties, one way to ease these penalties is to raise eligibility levels for means-tested programs and phase out eligibility more slowly. Thus, a married or cohabiting couple would still be eligible for, say, child-care subsidies if both incomes were included, and the amount of the subsidy would decline more slowly, leaving an incentive for the couple to stay together and continue to increase earnings. This is not to argue that persuading a legislature to make this kind of additional investment would be easy but is rather to highlight the downside of means-tested programs with strict eligibility standards and to identify the need to mitigate disincentives.

Adopting universal support programs that are not means-tested would better address this problem, but in an age of scarce resources, it seems unlikely that the state will provide, say, child-care vouchers to parents of all income levels. A step in the right direction would be to eliminate the kinds of support programs that benefit only middle- and upper-income families, such as the dependent-care tax credit, which allows individuals to deduct up to $6,000 in child-care expenses from their income for federal tax purposes,[42] and replace these kinds of income-differentiated subsidies with one overall subsidy to all families, regardless of income and not structured as a tax deduction, which benefits only those with sufficient income.

Turning to cultural norms that support single-motherhood, this may be one of the harder areas to change, and the role of the state may be the most difficult to pinpoint. As discussed below, the goal is not necessarily to increase the number of marriages but rather to increase the long-term commitment between parents, whatever the form. As the work of Kathryn Edin and her two coauthors shows, one of the reasons the relationship between the two parents does not last is that the pregnancy occurs very early in the relationship and was not a conscious choice of the two adults, made after an extensive search for a compatible partner. A place to start, then, is to help women consider delaying childbirth. It is telling that many of the women in the Fragile Families study did find somewhat more appealing partners down the road.[43] So it is not entirely true that there are *no* marriageable men. If young women had both a reason to delay childbearing and access to effective long-term birth control, such as an IUD, then they might be less likely to take a laissez-faire attitude toward contraception and pregnancy and more inclined to wait for a more compatible partner. Both factors are discussed below, including model programs that effectively do both.

Finally, looking at the psychological factors that affect whether a couple can maintain a healthy relationship, there is evidence that relationship counseling can help adults build relationships skills, which may encourage them to stay together. Although economic factors are important, relationship factors are also important, and programs designed to build relationship skills may have a significant effect on increasing marriage rates or at least promoting long-term commitment.[44]

As chapter 1 elaborated, there is considerable research about the markers of strong relationships between adults, such as attribution style. The question is how the state can draw on this knowledge to foster these attributes in adult relationships. Although marital counseling is no panacea, it is possible to teach some of these skills. Numerous studies indicate that counseling can positively affect the relationship between couples and between couples and their children.[45] Couples counseling has been shown to decrease symptoms of depression among parents and the frequency of conflict.[46] Couples counseling during the transition to parenthood also has been shown to reduce the likelihood of intimate-partner violence.[47] Finally, one program designed specifically for low-income couples, the Supporting Father Involvement Program, which teaches parenting skills to fathers and relationship skills to couples, increased the involvement of fathers in their children's lives and improved the co-parenting relationship of the parents living together.[48]

Forms of commitment—not just marriage

Deciding that the state should encourage a long-term commitment between parents does not necessarily mean that the state should focus only on marriage. Elizabeth Scott argues that alternative relationship structures, such as cohabitation, are "underinstitutionalized," failing to provide the same stability and enduring support as married families.[49] She attributes the stability of relationships formalized through marriage to the labyrinth of social norms that encourage the couple to stay together and support each other and dependents.[50] More informal family relationships, such as cohabitation, are not supported legally or socially in the same way as marriage, and therefore behavioral expectations in such relationships often vary.[51]

This understanding of the social meaning of marriage is captured in the testimony of one of the plaintiffs in a California marriage-equality case. Explaining why the term "marriage" was so important, and thus why California's domestic-partnership scheme, which gives same-sex couples virtually all of the benefits of marriage but not the actual name, was inadequate, the woman said, "I'm a 45-year-old woman. I have been in love with a woman for 10 years and I don't have a word to tell anybody about that."[52]

But if the law began to grant greater recognition to cohabiting relationships, and these relationships benefited from the same state support as marriage, social norms might build up around cohabitation, encouraging cohabiting couples to stay together. The goal is to encourage a long-term commitment between parents, not marriage per se. Once we focus on what the state is trying to achieve—stability in the relationship between parents as a way of improving child outcomes—then we can begin to identify multiple ways to achieve this outcome.

It is possible, culturally, to separate commitment and marriage. Marriage is on the decline in Scandinavian countries, for example, but the cohabiting relationships there are more stable than those of cohabiting couples in the United States—they are also more stable than marriages in the United States.[53] Looking at cohabiting relationships in both countries, children of cohabiting parents in Sweden are far more likely to live with their fathers than children in cohabiting households in the United States. Ninety percent of nonmarital births in Sweden are to biological parents who are living together but have not married.[54] By contrast, 60 percent of nonmarital births in the United States are to single, noncohabiting mothers.[55] To be sure, cohabiting relationships in Sweden are not as stable as marriages in Sweden. Unmarried couples in Sweden are twice as likely to break up as their married counterparts,[56] but these relationships are still more stable than either cohabiting or marital relationships in the United States. Marriage, standing alone, is not the sole answer.

Thinking about the demographic group with the lowest rate of marriage, low-income African Americans, it is helpful to frame the question as legal scholar Robin Lenhardt suggests: instead of asking "why aren't Blacks doing better with marriage?" we should be asking "why isn't marriage doing better for Blacks?"[57] It could be that offering other forms of state-sanctioned relationships would be more appealing to different groups. Rather than maintaining the two extremes of marriage, with all the legal protections and social meaning, and cohabitation, with very little of either, the state would do better to offer alternatives to marriage that privilege the status of the relationship and offer much-needed stability. These alternatives may well appeal to different demographic groups and, over time, build up their own social norms of stability and commitment.

France, for example, has a system of registering partners called PACS (*pacte civil de solidarité*), which allows a cohabiting couple, either same-sex or opposite-sex, to draw up a contract outlining their legal rights and obligations toward each other and register it with the court.[58] A PACS is similar to marriage in that the two adults must be a couple, not friends or relatives, and must agree to support each other for the duration of the contract.[59] But beyond this, the couple can tailor their contract to reflect their preferred level of commitment. A set of default rules apply, but these default rules impose fewer obligations than marriage. There is no mention of parental obligations, property is presumed to be separate, rather than joint as in a marriage, and there is no obligation to pay spousal support at the end of the relationship.[60] A couple entering a PACS can contract for greater protection, choosing, for example, to impose an obligation of support at the end of the relationship, but this decision is left to the couple. This highly flexible model is very popular in France, with one PACS for every two marriages.[61]

There is no guarantee that these alternative forms would be any more appealing culturally to demographic groups that are eschewing marriage, but it would be worth experimenting with alternative forms of commitment that carry less cultural baggage than marriage. As the French example demonstrates, state recognition need not be limited to marriage. The state could grant far greater legal rights and benefits to cohabiting couples with children, with the goal of strengthening these relationships. This does not mean that the state can offer different forms of recognition to different populations but rather that the state can offer a variety of types of legal recognition to all couples and allow the couples to choose their preferred form.

A tricky implementation question is whether relationship recognition should happen as a default matter—after, say, a couple lives together for two years or bears a child together—or whether relationship recognition should always be on an opt-in basis, allowing couples to choose it but never forcing it on them without their active consent. British Columbia, for example, has chosen the former route. The Definition of Spouse Amendment Act there defines a spouse as someone who is married to another person or who has lived and cohabited with another person in a "marriage-like relationship" for at least two years.[62] This status takes hold without additional action taken by the couple.

This approach to relationship recognition solves the problem of coverage—it ensures that couples who act a certain way will be treated as legal couples—but it risks imposing an unwanted status, giving the state an opportunity to impose dominant norms on marginalized communities. Recall chapter 3's description of the experience of former slaves during Reconstruction. When the former slaves continued the practices they used during slavery, including serial relationships and informal divorce, the state brought criminal prosecutions, convicting the men in particular of adultery, bigamy, and fornication.[63]

There is no easy answer to this dilemma, but the insight that the state has a greater interest in couples with children does provide some policy guidance. It would be possible, for example, to structure an opt-in scheme of relationship recognition for couples without minor children but an automatic scheme for couples with minor children. This would reflect the instrumental interest of the state in the parents' relationship and would limit the state's more active role to adult relationships involving children. It would also send a clear message about the state's interest: adults can order their lives as they see fit when only the adults are affected, but when children are involved, the state will step in to promote family stability.

In sum, the state interest is ensuring not that the greatest number of people are married but rather that parents are committed to caring for their children, a task that is, generally speaking, easier to accomplish when there are two parents in the home rather than one. But flourishing family law does not require any single vision of the good family, even if so much of public policy assumes that there is such a thing. It is more important to determine the right goals and structure of family law than to prescribe a single, particular family form. Regardless of what the state calls it—marriage, cohabitation, domestic partnership, registered partnership, or other alternatives—the point of state recognition is to encourage stability and commitment between parents, so that the parents can meet the needs of their children.

The nascent efforts described above, from mentoring fathers to marriage counseling, could help make men more appealing long-term partners and encourage a commitment between parents. But even with additional supports for adult relationships, there will continue to be some single parents, by choice or by happenstance, and the state must also support these parents, a topic taken up below in the discussion of the fourth cornerstone, supporting parents in their critical child-development work.

FOSTERING POSITIVE RELATIONSHIPS: ALTERING THE PHYSICAL CONTEXT OF FAMILY LIFE

There are numerous ways the state can help families spend more time together and increase their social ties with a community. As the examples below demonstrate, by encouraging family interaction and social embedment, the state can help foster positive relationships within the family.

Direct efforts

The design of neighborhoods can have a tremendous impact on family interaction and the development of social ties, for better and for worse. Colorado, for example, is full of new developments, springing up across the dry prairies around Denver. Too many of these developments embody the worst of urban sprawl, with large homes built on large lots, far from public transportation and commercial centers. This kind of development is correlated with higher rates of obesity, increased costs for maintaining a car, and a large proportion of tax dollars spent on roads and highways.[64] This kind of development also means long commutes and lots of time in cars, which is vital time taken away from family interactions and the creation of social ties within the community.

But not all developments are like this. In 1989, the city of Denver decided to transform Stapleton, the old Denver airport near downtown, into a sustainable, forward-thinking neighborhood. By 1995, the city had created a comprehensive development plan modeled on Denver's historic neighborhoods, with an emphasis on a diversity of residents, homes, shops, businesses, and schools, built together to create a community that is "people-focused rather than car-focused."[65]

Stapleton stands out from other neighborhood-development projects because of several innovative features. The homes were designed in a mixture of styles to create an architectural dynamism, and the housing comes in a variety of combinations and costs, from single-family homes to affordable rental apartments, some of which are subsidized (10 percent of all homes and 20 percent of all rental apartments are set aside for low-income families and individuals). The neighborhoods were laid out to encourage casual interaction, along sidewalks and in the many common areas. High-quality schools were built within the community. The development prioritizes the ability to walk and bike, with trails and green paths throughout Stapleton, connecting residents to parks, schools, and the local farm in addition to transportation hubs and the commercial area. Easy access to public transportation means a short commute to Denver's downtown. Zoning regulations allow homeowners to build carriage houses, providing space for home offices, multigenerational housing, and rental apartments. The homes and neighborhoods are appealing, with homes built on north-south blocks to allow for maximum southern exposure, and views of both the nearby mountains and the urban downtown center preserved so that residents are visually connected to both nature and the city.[66]

In short, the development embodies the third cornerstone of structural family law. The neighborhood design increases family interaction by shrinking the size of the triangle created by work, home, and school. When children attend neighborhood schools and parents work nearby, there is more time in the day to prepare and eat a family dinner. When a safe, inviting playground is a short walk away, it is much easier for a parent to take a child to play. The development is a true alternative to suburban sprawl, with its negative impact on family interaction. In the words of one of the developers, "People don't necessarily want to live in sprawl, but they like having nice new parks and good schools nearby."[67]

The neighborhood design also helps families develop social ties. Chapter 1 described how neighborhood design can create chance encounters between neighbors, and that this in turn leads to greater connections. In particular, when a neighborhood has continuous sidewalks, front porches, and inviting common areas, the residents are more likely to develop ties with one another. In Stapleton, neighbors run into one another on sidewalks, on the way to the store, and at the local playground, helping with the creation of social ties and the reciprocity that is essential to a strong social web supporting a family.

Finally, on the economic front, the ready access to public transportation and jobs makes it easier for parents to earn a living. The flexible zoning allows multigenerational families to live together. And the mixed-housing and set-asides for low-income families decrease the concentration of poverty, providing low-income families with better access to jobs and good schools. On the job front, Stapleton has successfully wooed businesses. The connectivity of Stapleton allows for an easy commute and affordable housing for workers, two factors Denver has heavily advertised to encourage large businesses to relocate to the Stapleton area. To date, Stapleton has attracted the FBI, the U.S. Bank, and SMA Solar Technology, all large institutions that have established regional headquarters in Stapleton, creating numerous local jobs for residents.[68]

The principles of Stapleton will sound familiar to anyone who knows about the trend in development called New Urbanism. As an alternative to sprawling development, New Urbanism encourages the development of compact, urban, walkable, diverse, and sustainable communities that promote a sense of connectedness among residents. New Urbanism preserves the traditional neighborhood structure, with a large central public space, a range of homes, shops, and businesses within a ten-minute walking distance, and physically attractive surroundings and architecture intended to create a sense of enjoyment and belonging for residents.[69] Developing a walkable, well-connected neighborhood is essential, because it encourages residents to enjoy their neighborhoods from outside their cars and to interact with their neighbors.[70] New Urbanism also embraces the development of high-quality train systems to connect residents and workplaces, reducing commute times and making the commute more enjoyable, and opportunities for residents to get around using scooters, bicycles, and the like.[71] Charlotte, North Carolina, for example, has made a conscious effort to encourage development within urban areas and along a new rail line.[72]

This kind of neighborhood layout is possible both in new developments, such as Stapleton, and also in areas written off as victims of urban blight. Take, for example, a corner of East Oakland, California, which for years was the home to a decrepit public-housing complex located next to an industrial complex and rife with crime. In thinking about how to revitalize the area, the Oakland Housing Authority decided to try something new. Rather than simply rebuilding the housing, they engaged an architect, David Baker, known for his innovative designs for low-income residents that build a sense of community.[73] Baker's firm designed a 157-unit development on 7.5 acres, called Tassafaronga Village. The development has a mix of home designs, from small apartment buildings and single-family townhouses to a reclaimed pasta factory now housing a medical clinic and supportive housing and boasting a rolling green roof. The development includes pocket parks, open spaces, a community garden, sidewalks around and among the buildings, and a large central gathering space. The development was built in two years, under budget, and has already had an impact on surrounding real estate prices.

The design elements are paying off. The crime rate has declined 25 percent since the days of the old housing project, and residents gather regularly in the open spaces, with children working in the garden and block parties using the shared outdoor pizza oven.[74] As the director of the community garden said, "Things aren't perfect— there's still some crime—but people didn't used to want to leave their houses in the old days. Now parents feel safe dropping off their kids in the garden, and seniors help maintain the streets."[75] In other words, a community is building, and through these kinds of ties, families are able to develop support networks.

One final example will show how the ideas in this book also apply in other contexts, such as caring for the elderly, an increasingly important issue given the aging baby boom population. Land-use policies, zoning regulations, and social programs that enable older people to "age in place" go a long way toward ensuring that the elderly are well cared for, serving their needs and also easing the burden on adult children, who often shoulder enormous caregiving responsibility for aging parents. When older people can walk to stores and restaurants, for example, the loss of the ability to drive is less onerous.

Communities such as Park La Brea in Los Angeles espouse the aging-in-place model, with the goal of keeping people in their homes as they grow older, rather than moving them to nursing homes.[76] Aging in place recognizes the emotional value of a home where the residents may have lived for years, known as "place attachment," and the importance of independent living to seniors, but it also acknowledges that many residents will need some assistance.[77] Thus, Park La Brea was developed around pre-existing homes where many older people were already living[78] and built in a way that allows senior residents to age in place comfortably, with the age-specific resources they require.

The private apartment complex maintains nearly forty-two hundred units, and approximately fifteen hundred seniors have been living in the development for many years.[79] In 2003, the Jewish Family Service of Los Angeles implemented new programs in Park La Brea to engage the senior residents in activities with their neighbors, such as field trips to local museums and dance classes, and also addressed access to medical services, transportation, and daily caregivers.[80] When a resident in her seventies broke her rib and needed help getting around, for example, the Park La Brea staff arranged for transportation not only to her medical appointments but also to her weekly salon appointment.[81] The Park La Brea model allows seniors to feel safe, knowing that they will not be taken out of their homes and also will not be forced to live in isolation with their needs unmet. Park La Brea Senior Services director Susan Alexman describes the concept well: "You know the saying, 'It takes a village to raise a child'? Well, it takes a community to support an older adult."[82]

These kinds of developments do not simply happen. Denver made a conscious choice to create Stapleton. The Stapleton Foundation, a private nonprofit advocacy group, worked with Denver to develop a plan for the decommissioned airport.[83] The partnership published a 1995 report, *The Green Book*, to guide redevelopment; the city approved the plan that same year.[84] The city was engaged at every level of the process, first decontaminating the land of spilled jet fuel, clearing the old terminal buildings, and ensuring that the *Green Book* plan was put into place as a part of any

sale.[85] While most major redevelopment projects are sold by cities as a single purchase of land, Denver sold the forty-two-hundred-acre plot to the developer, Forest
City, in increments.[86] With the sale being permitted to take place over a five-year
period, Forest City was not forced to take on the kinds of loans that require quick
and cheap development projects.[87] Instead of building cookie-cutter homes on vast
lots, Forest City engaged in a more costly process, hiring twenty different home-
builders to build a variety of high-density homes.[88] Forest City was able to purchase
the land in four years after early building successes and strong sales. The sale also
included the developer's promise to build $44 million worth of parks, increasing the
acreage of Denver parks by 25 percent.[89]

Although the city received the purchase price for the land, it still needed to make
investments in the development, such as roads and sewer systems, estimated at more
than $346 million.[90] To finance these extra costs, Denver relied on tax-increment
financing, using bonds that bank on increased property and sales taxes.[91] The new
property taxes are paid by the residents of Stapleton, and the development raised the
property values of the surrounding neighborhoods, which previously had low-flying
jetliners landing beside houses, causing noise and pollution.[92] Additionally, new
retail developments, such as the shopping center Quebec Square, helped generate
property and sales taxes.[93]

Even if a state or local government cannot undertake this level of development
or revitalization, it could require all developers simply to install sidewalks and playgrounds. This would benefit family interaction by making it easier for parents to
spend time with their children, and it would increase social embedment by making
it more likely that neighbors interact and form relationships. Other smaller fixes
include local governments rezoning single-family areas to allow developers to build
new homes or renovate existing homes to accommodate the demand for multigenerational living. As chapter 4 explained, although there is an increasing demand for
such homes—and such homes would clearly help families address both social and
economic needs of multiple generations—too often developers run into roadblocks
from local zoning boards. As one developer found, once the developer explained the
problem to mayors and other city officials, they were willing to fix it.[94] It just takes
that first step of pointing out the problem.

Considering families even when acting in other areas

Beyond these direct efforts to increase family interaction and social embedment,
the state should pay greater attention to the impact of its actions on families when
pursuing other objectives seemingly unrelated to families. When designing large
public-works projects or issuing new rules governing workplaces, for example, the

state should undergo a review process that considers the impact of the project on family interaction and social embedment. This could be modeled on the National Environmental Policy Act, which requires all federal agencies to consider the impact of a proposed action on the environment before making a decision about whether to undertake that action.[95] That law has lots of subtleties,[96] but the central idea is what is relevant: considering the impact of a seemingly unrelated action on a particular aspect of society. This does not mean that the state must always act in a way that puts family interests first. Indeed, the National Environmental Policy Act does not require this. It only requires federal agencies to *consider* the impact of its actions, so that at least these are known. This may seem like a tremendous governmental intrusion and an invitation to more needless regulation and bureaucracy, but too often the state does not consider families, making it that much harder for families to develop and sustain positive relationships, which has enormous costs for society.

PUTTING IT ALL TOGETHER: SUPPORTING PARENTS IN THEIR CRITICAL CHILD-DEVELOPMENT WORK

It is essential for the state to support parents in their critical work of raising children, but this leaves open the question of how the state should do so. The key elements are helping individuals choose when to become parents, assisting parents in the transition to parenthood, encouraging involvement by nonresidential fathers, providing opportunities in the preschool years, and addressing economic stressors. In each category, there are excellent examples of promising programs and reforms.

Choosing to become a parent

We know from chapter 7 that many births, particularly for young women ages fifteen to nineteen, are unplanned and unwanted. The challenge is to help young people delay childbearing until they are ready for the responsibility and want to take it on. Researchers at the Brookings Institute have concluded that numerous factors influence teen pregnancy but that these factors can generally be grouped into three categories: the motivation to avoid pregnancy, knowledge about fertility and contraceptives, and access to contraceptives.[97] After reviewing numerous preventive programs, they concluded that there are several cost-effective measures for reducing teen pregnancy.

On the motivation front, abstinence-only education does not significantly reduce teen pregnancies, but programs that address youth development and provide improved educational and economic opportunities *are* effective.[98] On the knowledge front, both in-school and community-based education programs addressing issues such as condom use and HIV prevention reduce sexual interactions and increase the use of contraceptives.[99] Finally, on the access front, expanding eligibility for family-planning services increases the use of contraceptives.[100]

To detail one successful program that falls into the motivation category, the Teen Outreach Program works with ninth- through twelfth-graders and does not focus on teen pregnancy per se but rather on inculcating future-mindedness in the students. Through a structured program, the students work under the supervision of adults to perform community service, which is followed by a classroom discussion of students' life options, including career and relationship choices. The goal is to help students better know themselves and their values and help them cope with the stressors in their lives as they move into adulthood. The program places very little emphasis on pregnancy and educational performance and instead focuses on the social and emotional growth of the students.[101]

In a large-scale, controlled, randomized study, participating students were significantly less likely at the end of one year to become pregnant, as compared with similarly situated teenagers who did not participate in the program.[102] Participating students also were less likely to have failed a course or been suspended from school.[103] One theory about why the program is so successful is that it works on numerous fronts: keeping teenagers busy, creating opportunities for teens to feel useful and important, and fostering positive relationships between the teens and adults.[104]

A successful program that falls into the access category is the Contraceptive CHOICE Project, started in 2007 by a group of researchers in St. Louis, Missouri. The study recruited more than nine thousand women ages fourteen to forty-five in the St. Louis area and allowed them to choose their own form of reversible birth control for up to three years, free of cost.[105] The researchers began with the understanding that many pregnancies are unintended and that long-acting reversible contraceptives such as intrauterine devices (IUDs) and contraceptive implants are much less popular in the United States than other forms of birth control, such as oral contraceptives, even though the long-acting contraceptives are far more effective at preventing pregnancies.[106] The participating women received education about all forms of FDA-approved contraceptives, although the efficacy of the long-acting contraceptives was emphasized. Seventy-five percent of the participants chose a long-acting reversible contraceptive.[107]

The researchers monitored rates of births and abortions among the CHOICE participants for four years. Both rates plummeted for teens. The national birth rate for teens in 2010 was 34.3 teenage births per 1,000 women, but the birth rate for CHOICE participants was 6.3 per 1,000.[108] The researchers did not break out the abortion rates by age, but the abortion rate for all participants—which ranged from 4.4 to 7.5 per 1,000, depending on the year—was far below the national abortion rate of 19.6 per 1,000.[109] As this pilot program demonstrates, access to affordable, effective birth control is enormously important for both preventing unwanted births and reducing the abortion rate.

But when prevention programs and contraceptives do not work, there is a need for a Plan B, as it were. To the extent that teens will be sexually active—and some will—then a comprehensive program would first try to avoid pregnancies through programs aimed at motivation, knowledge, and access but would also make abortion available as a last resort. Abortion has long been a social and political flashpoint in the United States, but it clearly plays a role in preventing teenage *motherhood*. Looking at 2006, the teen pregnancy rate for girls and young women ages fifteen to nineteen who had ever had intercourse was 152.8 per 1,000, but the birth rate was 41.9 per 1,000.[110] Some of the pregnancies ended in miscarriages, but nearly one-third of the pregnancies ended in an abortion.[111] Without access to abortions, there would be far more teen mothers than there are today. This statistic is not going to change the mind of someone committed to outlawing abortions, but it does put the onus on those who oppose abortions to ensure that young women who do give birth are also given opportunities to develop their own lives and ensure the well-being of their children. Chapter 9 explores this in greater detail.

Beyond teens, it is also important to help young women delay childbearing until they have found more reliable partners. Edin and Kefalas contend that young, low-income women bear children partly to give meaning to their lives but also because there is little opportunity cost to having a child at a young age.[112] Low-income women living in impoverished neighborhoods have dismal economic prospects. Having a child does not derail a career, as it might for a middle-class young woman, because there are few career prospects in the first place. This is not an easy factor to address, because it involves poverty writ large, but it does underscore the interrelated nature of poverty and family form. To the extent that the state can create meaningful pathways out of poverty for both men and women, it can create an incentive to delay childbearing and increase the pool of eligible partners, in turn reducing multipartner fertility and family complexity.

Transitioning to parenthood

Once a person becomes a parent, whether by choice or by circumstance, it is essential to help that parent develop a strong, stable relationship with the child, because the basic attachment between a parent and a child is the groundwork for all the child development that follows. Becoming a parent is stressful, but this is particularly true for a very young parent who has few social, emotional, and economic resources. The Nurse-Family Partnership, described at the beginning of this chapter, is an excellent example of a program designed to work specifically with first-time, low-income mothers.[113] The average age of the mothers is twenty, the average household income is $7,500, and the vast majority (85 percent) are unmarried.[114]

During regular in-home visits beginning in pregnancy and lasting through the first two years of a child's life, visiting nurses help families in numerous ways. While mothers are still pregnant, the nurses work with them to improve prenatal health. After children are born, nurses help new mothers and fathers provide more competent care to children by teaching them basic parenting skills and working directly with parents and children. Nurses also address economic stability by helping mothers develop and accomplish goals related to staying in school and finding work. Finally, nurses help mothers plan any subsequent pregnancies.[115] Although the program focus is on mothers, nurse visitors also work with fathers, encouraging them to be active parents.

To understand how the program works, consider the true story of Irene, a fifteen-year-old girl who became pregnant by accident. The youngest of six children being raised by a single mother, Irene felt guilty about getting pregnant, because she had planned to graduate from high school and go to college. When the pregnancy center confirmed her pregnancy, it referred her to the Nurse-Family Partnership. Irene chose to participate in the program—participation was not mandatory or a condition of receiving any other form of support—and shortly thereafter, her visiting nurse, Wendy, began to visit Irene in her home. Irene's boyfriend could not attend these early meetings, but Wendy gave Irene a Spanish-language version of *What to Expect When You're Expecting* so Irene could go over it with him later. Irene says that the day her baby, Vanessa, was born was the hardest day of her life. She woke up in the middle of night and looked at Vanessa and thought, "What am I going to do?" But Wendy was an enormous help during this transition. She came to the hospital, giving Irene a hug and telling her, "You're going to be OK." Wendy helped Irene learn to breastfeed, and when this was difficult, Wendy said, "You need to be patient with yourself. You need to take this calm. Take the positive things and leave the negative things behind." As is typical, Wendy worked with Irene over the next two years, teaching her about child development and parenting skills and encouraging her to stay in school. When Irene graduated from high school and began working in a day-care center, she said she felt proud of what she had accomplished.[116]

As Irene's story illustrates, the program is intensive, with a nurse visiting once a week for the first six weeks after a baby is born, then every other week until the child is twenty-one months old, and then once a month until the child is two years old. An essential component of the program is that the nurse is not there to judge the mother but rather plays a supportive role, boosting the young mother's confidence by teaching her to care for the child.

Contrast this supportive, deferential approach with the more typical interaction a low-income parent has with "the authorities." For example, New York offers a program to decrease infant mortality and increase birth weight among babies born to low-income mothers. But to participate in the program, low-income women must go through an intensive intake process that requires them to divulge a tremendous amount of personal information that a woman with private insurance would not be required to tell her doctor. Khiara Bridges, a legal scholar and anthropologist, conducted a study of this program. She found that the women were asked questions about their immigration status, the source of their income including questions about criminal activity and working off the books, their prior involvement with the child-welfare system, and a host of other questions about their eating habits and psychosocial history. As Bridges describes it, although well-intentioned, the state stance toward the woman is inherently one of distrust.[117] This is not to say that the Nurse-Family Partnership is perfect and does not raise any of these issues, but the program has a fundamentally different orientation, working from the very beginning to establish a partnership between the visiting nurse and the mother.

The results of the Nurse-Family Partnership program are striking. Families receiving this kind of support experience child abuse and neglect at a rate half that of non-participating families.[118] Mothers increased their involvement in the labor force by 82 percent,[119] reduced their reliance on welfare and government assistance,[120] had fewer encounters with the criminal justice system,[121] and were more likely to be living with the fathers of their children three years after the visits ended.[122] Children in the program grew up to enjoy greater academic success and exhibit fewer behavioral problems than nonparticipating children.[123] Children also were less likely to become involved in the criminal-justice system as adolescents, reporting fewer arrests and convictions than nonparticipating children.[124] Another way to think about these benefits is to compare costs with estimated savings. The program costs $7,300 per child, but for every $1.00 invested in the program, society saves $5.70 in the long run.[125]

No program is a cure-all, of course, and there are some limitations to the success of the model. Researchers have found, for example, that there are no real benefits if the families are also experiencing domestic violence.[126] Similarly, a nineteen-year follow-up study of children born in the program found that the criminal-justice benefits were only for girls and not for boys. Participating girls had fewer arrests and convictions as compared with a control group, but participating boys showed no less criminal-justice involvement than boys in the control group.[127]

Despite these limitations, what makes the Nurse-Family Partnership such an excellent example of flourishing family law is that it helps forge a strong attachment between parents and children, rather than simply reacting after parents fail to do so. By making programs like the Nurse-Family Partnership available to all parents in need, the state can take a proactive stance toward family functioning while still not stepping into the shoes of parents.

Encouraging involvement by nonresidential fathers

The conventional wisdom about nonmarital families is that we have separated marriage and parenthood. Couples no longer feel obligated to be married before having a child. This may be true, but even if it is possible to separate marriage and parenthood, it is not possible to separate *relationships* and parenthood. As chapter 2 explained, whether unmarried fathers are able to maintain contact with their children depends in large part on the relationship between the father and the mother. When this relationship is functional enough, fathers see their children with some regularity, but when there is tension between the parents, then the father is much less likely to maintain an ongoing relationship with his child.

Kathryn Edin and Timothy Nelson described this dynamic in their work on inner-city fathers. The men in their study rejected "the old package deal," where men were husbands first and fathers second.[128] In the old model, the relationship between the adults bound the family together and kept the fathers committed to their children. But the men wanted "a new package deal," where their relationship with their children came first and the mothers were on the periphery.[129] Yet this was not how it worked in practice. The relationship between the adults still had a tremendous influence on the family, because the mothers would act as gatekeepers to the children, keeping the fathers away from their children.[130] Sometimes this was warranted, as when a father turned violent, but this was not always the case.[131] Instead, there were two main sources of friction. First, the mothers wanted the fathers to do more—pay more child support, or help more with the child care—and they became frustrated with the fathers' inability to do so. The fathers, by contrast, felt that they were doing the best they could, providing what little money they were able to earn and also giving the children an emotional relationship.[132] Second, when a mother began seeing another man, he was often jealous of the father. To maintain the new relationship, it was easiest for a mother to keep the father away from the family.[133]

In this way, the relationship between the mother and the father is still very much at the center of the family dynamic. The state should draw on this observation when trying to encourage greater involvement by nonresidential fathers. There are some lessons to be learned from those fathers who do maintain relationships with their children. As noted in chapter 2, contrary to the stereotype of the absent black father, the unmarried, nonresidential African American fathers in the Fragile Family Study were more likely to be involved with their children than the other fathers, and they were more likely to maintain better co-parenting relationships with the mothers of their children.[134] Edin and Nelson made the same observation.[135] Additionally, even though men are not always actively involved with all of their children, one study found that 70 percent of nonmarital fathers were intensively involved in the life of at least one child.[136]

Building on these observations, there are at least three lessons. First, time may help. The more experience a community has with nonmarital relationships, the greater chance it has had to build up alternative norms. Thus, for low-income African Americans, whose marriage rates declined before other groups, one way to understand the evidence of greater involvement is that the community has begun to develop norms of nonresidential fathering and co-parenting following a breakup. With more time, other demographic groups may well do the same.

Second, as described above, smoothing the relationship between mothers and fathers is essential to reducing maternal gatekeeping. If the two parents can get along and their relationship is not a source of stress to the mother, then it is more likely that the father will maintain a relationship with his children. One innovation described in chapter 6 would work well here: the Australian model of Family Relationship Centres, where a couple can easily find free or heavily subsidized mediation intended to help couples co-parent following a breakup. As that chapter explained, the idea is to find a workable solution for the short term to get parents into the habit of co-parenting. Then, when circumstances inevitably change down the road—say, the mother takes on a new partner—the parents can manage that change.

Finally, we need a broader and clearer notion of unmarried fatherhood, because there is no institutionalized role or expectations for this group of men.[137] For example, unless an unmarried father goes to court to get a visitation order, he does not have a set custody schedule, as would be typical for a divorcing father. Instead, the only thing the state seems to expect of unmarried fathers is that they pay child support. But fathers resent this monetization of their relationship with their children. As Edin and Nelson consistently found, the fathers in their study did not want to be "just a paycheck" and instead wanted recognition for the hands-on parenting they provided to their children.[138]

One way to encourage a social norm of low-conflict co-parenting following a breakup and to institutionalize unmarried fatherhood is to reform the child-support laws to better reflect the abilities and contributions of unmarried fathers. Tough child-support enforcement seems like an easy policy choice. Of course, men should support their children financially. No one likes a deadbeat dad. But the real story is more complicated, and there is a good argument that current policies do more harm than good.[139] As chapter 4 explained, many low-income fathers simply do not have the income to pay child support, and vigorous enforcement efforts only push them further into debt and increase friction with the mothers of their children. Part of the problem is that child-support rules do not credit in-kind payments made by fathers, such as the provision of diapers, formula, or clothing, even though studies have found that fathers and often mothers prefer these kinds of payments, because they are more tangible and give the sense that the father is really contributing to the family.[140] These kinds of contributions are often made in person, which means that the father is maintaining some form of contact with his child. These payments also reflect greater involvement in parenting. Rather than simply paying cash, in-kind support requires a father to go to a store, think about what his child needs, and bring that to the child's home.

One proposal that would address the problem with large child-support arrearages, encourage greater involvement by nonresidential fathers, and decrease friction between mothers and fathers is to set up a system that would credit these in-kind payments. Although presenting some bureaucratic challenges, the basic idea is that the law would recognize informal child support—such as diapers and formula and nonmonetary contributions such as spending significant time with the child—as a way for "deadbroke" fathers to meet their child-support obligations.[141] The point is not to excuse absentee fathers but rather to value the contributions that some fathers can make.[142] To encourage fathers to make monetary contributions, credit could be limited to those who cannot pay but are actively searching for a job and participating in a fathering program to improve their chances of providing financial support in the future.[143]

At the very least, those who cannot pay their child-support obligations through cash payments should not have to face incarceration for missed payments, especially if the payments they do owe are so minimal that they cannot meaningfully improve the child's standard of living.[144] Instead, the system should reward the parenting and in-kind support that the fathers can provide and that demonstrably improve a child's life.[145] By adopting this new system, the focus would shift away from valuing only financial contributions to favoring "involved fathering," where both formal and informal contributions count.[146] This is a reform that has not yet been adopted but would make tremendous sense to try.

Providing opportunities in the preschool years

Early-childhood-education programs are an important aspect of school readiness and a key way the state can help parents ensure healthy child development. What is less known about early-childhood-education programs is that there are distinct policy and program-design choices to be made about how they work, and certain designs are associated with improved parenting. The Chicago School District's Child-Parent Center (CPC), for example, provides early-childhood education to children beginning in preschool and either ending at kindergarten or continuing until third grade. The program provides services to children, including health screening and free meals. Unlike many programs, it also provides services to parents, including home visits, referrals to social-service agencies, and parenting skills and vocational training.[147]

A study of the CPC found that the rate of child abuse and neglect among children in the preschool program was 52 percent lower than the rate in a control group of similar but nonparticipating families.[148] The results were even better for those children who stayed in the program for at least four years. For these children, the child-abuse and neglect rate was 48 percent lower than the rate for children in the program for one to four years.[149]

Like the Nurse-Family Partnership program, there is evidence that the CPC is cost-effective. One study found that for a family enrolled in the program for eighteen months, the program cost $6,692 and generated $47,759 in benefits by the time the child turned 21.[150] This return included savings from lower rates of special-education enrollment and fewer arrests, coupled with higher taxes paid by the students when they graduated from high school. The calculations did not account for any savings from reduced involvement in the child-welfare system and thus are likely to be much higher.

Similarly, a congressionally mandated, randomized study of Head Start programs found that one of the benefits of the program, at least for children who entered at age three and thus had two years in the program, was that Head Start affected parenting practices. As compared with families who were not enrolled in Head Start (and instead were in another, usually lower-quality early-childhood program or at home with a caregiver), the Head Start parents were less likely to have spanked their children, more likely to read to their children, more likely to take their children to cultural-enrichment activities, and less likely to use harsh parenting strategies.[151] These benefits continued even after the child left the program and began elementary school, although the effect was not quite as strong.[152]

Addressing economic stress

Throughout this time—from birth through school—parents need support addressing economic challenges. The first key is providing subsidized, high-quality child care. Early-childhood-education programs are not the equivalent of child care, often running for only limited hours or only during the school year. Working parents need more hours of caregiving, and they need it for young children of all ages. Quality child care that runs all day serves the dual purpose of allowing parents to work and ensuring the healthy development of children.

To provide this care, the math is fairly simple, if also daunting: the state should invest far more money in child-care subsidies through programs such as the federal Child Care and Development Block Grant.[153] Current allocations help some families, but there is still a vast unmet need for subsidized child care, both during the preschool years and for after-school programs, as detailed in chapter 4. If the state did nothing else, subsidizing child care for all low-income parents would be an enormous step forward.

Subsidizing child care will help parents work, but there are additional aspects to economic stress. As chapter 2 explained, the U.S. economy is undergoing a seismic shift, with jobs congregating around two poles: low-wage service jobs on one end and high-wage professional jobs on the other. At the same time, men in particular are falling behind in educational attainment, meaning that fewer men are prepared for the higher-paying jobs available in an information economy.

Addressing this economic shift is perhaps the single biggest challenge facing the United States. There is no clear or easy answer, but there is no doubt that part of the solution is bolstering educational levels. If we want young people to be ready to participate in the higher end of the labor market, they must graduate not only from high school but also from college. And this brings us back to families. As this book has repeatedly argued, if we care about graduation rates from high school and college, we must focus on family functioning in the early years. The answer is not job training for eighteen-year-olds but rather nurse visitors for eight-week-olds.

Another part of the response to these shifts in the labor market is that the United States will need to provide income supports for families at the bottom end of the income spectrum. It is not the fault of these families that jobs with decent wages and benefits have simply disappeared. Those jobs are not coming back, and wages for service jobs are not going to rise radically. One way to support parents in low-wage jobs is through programs like the Earned Income Tax Credit (EITC), which bolsters the wages of low- and moderate-income workers and is more politically palatable than cash transfers. As described in chapter 4, the EITC is administered through the tax code and is a tax credit that individuals apply for when they would ordinarily file for taxes. Originally passed in 1975, the EITC was intended to offset the burden of Social Security taxes and increase the incentives to work. The program particularly helps families, as the income support is considerably higher for workers with qualifying children than it is for single workers.

Consider a real-life example: Julie is a single mother of three young children living in Des Moines, Iowa. She works full-time for a nonprofit organization while also attending college full-time. In 2011, she earned $33,173, and she received an EITC refund check for $2,279 in 2012. She used her annual EITC checks to make a down payment on a used car so she can commute to work and to school, to help pay her college tuition, and to help pay the preschool tuition for one of her children.[154]

In 2013, the maximum credit available was $6,044 for a worker with three qualifying children.[155] Some states and local governments also offer a similar program, further raising the income for families.[156] The EITC is no panacea, and it does not address the needs of adults who cannot work because of disability, but it does provide a prototype for the kind of program that could be used to raise the incomes for low-wage service workers.

In addition to work supports, there is also a place for traditional supports, such as subsidized housing. One pilot program, the Keeping Families Safe project, works with some of the most vulnerable families. The pilot program targeted twenty-nine very-low-income families shown to have long-term housing instability and a chronic condition such as mental illness or substance abuse; each family also had an open child-welfare case at the time. The program provides permanent housing to the families, along with onsite case managers who intensely supervise and address the needs of each family, with at least two visits to the home per month, directing the family to the various social-service programs available.[157]

Rather than providing only highly specialized assistance or temporary shelter, Keeping Families Together provides a permanent and stable home for families to have the consistency they need to address difficult issues and stay together. The program also promotes trusting relationships between caseworker teams and families through long-term assistance, ensuring that the families receive the support they need, such as a replacement mattress after a bedbug infestation or school supplies for the children. The majority of the child-welfare cases were favorably resolved, there were reduced incidences of child maltreatment, the parents struggling with substance abuse remained sober, twenty-six of the families stayed together, school-age children went to school more often and performed at a higher level, and many of the adult family members were employed at some point after job-readiness training.[158]

Although the program is expensive, costing slightly more than $33,000 per year for each family enrolled in supportive housing, the reduced need for foster care, child-welfare involvement, or shelter support saves more than $32,000 per year, making the total public cost for keeping each family together only $1,000 per year, or $3 per day.[159] Recognizing the success of this project, the U.S. Department of Health and Human Services recently issued a $35-million notice of funding availability to expand the pilot project and further show how supportive housing can help even the most vulnerable families, and keep children out of the foster-care system.

Doing It All: The Harlem Children's Zone

Geoffrey Canada is the visionary leader of the Harlem Children's Zone (HCZ) in New York City. Canada used to run after-school programs, but, like David Olds, he soon realized that the challenges facing low-income children need a much more holistic, and earlier, response. Recognizing the essential role of families, Canada founded HCZ, which embraces what he calls the conveyor-belt approach to fighting poverty—working with families before a child is born and continuing until the child graduates from high school.[160]

The first step is Baby College, for expecting parents or parents of children who are between the ages of birth and three years. Developed in collaboration with T. Berry Brazelton, a leading pediatrician and author on parenting and child development, Baby College is a nine-week course for parents held on Saturday mornings and covering topics such as brain development, immunization, safety, parental stress, parent-child bonding, lead poisoning, and asthma.[161] There is no charge for the course, and HCZ provides incentives to join, including complimentary meals and child care during the course.[162] There is even a raffle at the end of each class for $50 gift certificates, and at the end of the course, one parent wins a month of free rent.[163] In addition to preparing adults for parenthood, Baby College builds a supportive community by encouraging the participants to bond with one another.[164]

The next steps are for the families who have won the placement lottery for HCZ's charter school, Promise Academy. Beginning with the Three-Year-Old Journey, parents attend a multisession class that covers child development, parenting strategies, and language-development skills.[165] With an emphasis on scientific explanations, the program prepares parents for the challenges they may face as their children enter preschool.[166] The Get Ready for Pre-K program helps transition the three-year-olds to preschool through a six-week intensive summer program designed to ease the adjustment to full-day programming that begins at age four.[167]

The Harlem Gems prekindergarten is a full-year program for four-year-olds that runs from eight a.m. until six p.m.[168] With an adult-to-child ratio of one to four, the Harlem Gems program focuses in particular on language skills.[169] The children then enter the Promise Academy kindergarten and continue in the Promise Academy charter-school system until high school graduation. Classes run Monday through Friday, as does a regular school week, but the days are longer at the Promise Academy, beginning at eight a.m. and ending at four p.m., followed by after-school programs until six p.m. and with a school year that extends well into July.[170] During the school day, there is an emphasis on health, as students receive freshly prepared, healthy meals and engage in daily physical activities.[171] Classes offered include traditional courses plus chess, web design, and photography.[172] Children who need extra assistance with their English or math skills can go to the Promise Academy on Saturdays.[173] These extra hours add up: a Promise Academy student who is behind grade level spends twice as much time at school than the typical New York City public-school student, and a Promise Academy student who is at grade level spends 50 percent more time at school than the typical student.[174]

HCZ also focuses on the needs of parents and the broader community, including those children who are not enrolled in the Promise Academy. HCZ's Asthma Initiative, for example, responds to this widespread problem, which afflicts 30 percent of the children in Harlem, compared with only 6 percent nationally.[175] The Asthma Initiative educates families on asthma triggers, provides pest control to eliminate household triggers, ensures proper medical care with access to the right medications and appropriate testing, and helps families identify asthma attacks before they become severe.[176] HCZ also offers other programs, such as an employment and technology center, a debt-relief-management program, and a family-counseling center (the Family Support Center) that focuses on crisis intervention.[177]

HCZ recognizes that it is not only children but also parents and, critically, the larger community that must change. Indeed, Canada chose to locate his program in a specific geographic area—central Harlem—to create what he calls positive contamination, where an entire community is organized around the healthy development of children.[178] HCZ began as a one-block pilot project and has now expanded to nearly one hundred blocks of central Harlem.[179] Today the organization serves more than ten thousand children, including the twelve hundred children going through the Promise Academy, and seventy-four hundred adults.[180]

Early results from HCZ are promising. The parents who participated in Baby College report that they read more to their children after taking the class; 99.5 percent of the children in the Harlem Gems prekindergarten program, many of whom started the year with a school-readiness classification of delayed or very delayed, completed the program with a classification of average or better, and the percentage of four-year-olds who had a classification of advanced rose from 12 percent to 42 percent.[181] In the Promise Academy, the students are excelling on standardized tests, far outperforming children in regular schools in Harlem,[182] and in the 2010–2011 academic year, 90 percent of the seniors at the Promise Academy were accepted into college.[183] Looking beyond the students who are enrolled in the Promise Academy, the Asthma Initiative has resulted in children having fewer asthma-related hospital stays, spending less time in hospital when they do go, and missing fewer days of school because of asthma.[184] The Family Support Center served 152 families in 2009–2010, and 99 percent of the families remained intact.[185]

There is considerable debate about HCZ's results, asking, for example, whether the investment is worth the return, whether the wraparound services HCZ offers make a difference to academic achievement, and whether the students enrolled at the Promise Academy are self-selected because their parents must participate in a lottery. This last point is a perennial question for all charter schools, but it is worth noting that HCZ makes a strong effort to recruit children from all families in central Harlem and does not simply rely on parents showing up for the lottery. So there is some reason to believe that the population at the Promise Academy is at least somewhat representative of the children in central Harlem.[186]

To give just a flavor of the debate over HCZ's results, consider the work of two researchers who looked closely at the strong test scores for the middle school to determine whether the positive results were because of the Promise Academy or other factors. Under New York City regulations, students are admitted to the Promise Academy based on a lottery. This requirement means that the researchers could study two randomized groups: those who are admitted and those who are not. The researchers could then assume that these groups are substantially the same because they both self-selected into the charter school or at least tried to do so. In looking at these two groups—the group that won admission to the Promise Academy middle school and the group that did not—researchers found remarkable gains among the Promise Academy students. The test scores for lottery winners and losers were essentially the same before the students enrolled at the Promise Academy middle school and reflected the widespread black-white achievement gap. By the end of middle school, however, the students at the Promise Academy had more than overcome the black-white achievement gap in math (they now scored higher than their white counterparts) and reduced the gap in English language arts.[187] By comparison, the middle-school students who lost the lottery did not make any gains on the black-white achievement gap.[188]

This suggests that the Promise Academy is making a difference, but it is not clear whether the impressive gains by Promise Academy students are the result of the school alone or of HCZ's conveyor-belt approach. To figure this out, the researchers compared the test scores of the Promise Academy students who lived within the catchment area for HCZ programs and thus were eligible for all of HCZ's programming and students who lived outside the zone and thus received only the schooling. There was no meaningful difference in test scores. The children not receiving the HCZ community programming had the same advances as the children who did receive the programming.[189]

This does not mean that HCZ's comprehensive approach is flawed. The study considers only one measure of success—test scores—and does not ask how else students and their families might be benefiting from HCZ's approach. More important, the study gauges short-term results—middle-school test scores—rather than long-term results such as college graduation rates, increased earnings, decreased involvement in the criminal-justice system, and so on. The first student to go through the entire conveyor belt will graduate from the Promise Academy in 2020, so it is far too early to determine the cumulative impact of HCZ.[190]

The jury may still be out on the specifics of the HCZ programs, but early investments have been shown time and again to be cost-effective. It is essential to continue to think creatively about how to fortify families so they can prepare their children for the future.

THE FORM OF REGULATION

The final issue is how the state should implement these changes. Chapter 3 identified the numerous ways in which the state influences families, but some means are more effective and more politically palatable than others. It remains an open question precisely how the state should foster strong, stable, positive relationships.

The state has a number of options, from setting rules that apply to everyone (direct regulation), to subsidizing preferred behavior to induce certain behavior, to establishing default rules (choice architecture), to influencing social norms. In some areas, the state is not likely to relinquish its role in direct regulation. For example, the state could stop regulating marriage altogether, but it is unlikely to do so. In these contexts, the choice of the mode of regulation is fairly straightforward. The state will continue its monopoly on the rules of entry and exit from a family.

The more difficult question is how best to influence families, particularly parents, in contexts where there is little direct regulation. Consider the goal of encouraging parents to provide the kind of parenting that will help prepare a child for school. This means a strong enough attachment between caregiver and child and inculcating more specific skills, such as language development and self-regulation. There is little the state can or should do directly to require this kind of parenting. The state should not, for example, enact laws requiring parents to read to their children or engage them in conversation. Instead, encouraging parents to be more responsive to their children should be a matter of indirect regulation. This can be done in a variety of ways.

Subsidizing preferred behavior. Middle-class parents have access to a variety of resources that help them develop their children's skills and abilities, including libraries, parks, and neighborhood children's programs. Additionally, to develop effective parenting skills, middle-class parents buy parenting books and attend fee-based classes. To help level the playing field and ensure that all parents have access to these kinds of resources, the state can subsidize preferred behavior. When the state funds local libraries, for example, it makes it easier for a parent to nurture a child's language development. And when the state offers programs such as the Nurse-Family Partnership and Head Start, it helps interested parents develop parenting skills.

A key part of this kind of indirect regulation is the optional and early nature of the state program. These kinds of preventive programs aim to develop a positive, nonpunitive, and nonjudgmental relationship with "the state"—meaning a visiting nurse or a Head Start program—early on. David Olds says that one of the reasons he chose to begin working with women while they were still pregnant was that it was important to begin the relationship between the nurse and the woman before adding the pressures of new parenting.[191] Similarly, when the state makes resources such as public libraries available, it is not telling parents what to do; it is simply encouraging parents to engage in language activities with their children by making it easier for them to do so.

Establishing default rules (choice architecture). The state can also set up an incentive structure that encourages certain behavior. In Sweden, for example, when the state wanted to encourage more fathers to take paternity leave, it changed the already-generous rules governing parental leave. Under the new system, new parents have a total of sixteen months of paid leave if the father takes at least two months of that time. If the father does not take the two months, then the total is fourteen months.[192] As a result of the change in laws, the rate of paternity leave increased radically. In 1990, only 6 percent of Swedish fathers took parental leave, but when Sweden introduced the idea in 1995—with a one-month use-it-or-lose-it scheme—this number rose to 77 percent.[193] After Sweden implemented a second month of nontransferable leave in 2002, the percentage of Swedish fathers who participated in paternity leave rose to 90 percent.[194]

These kinds of laws do not *require* a change in behavior. Instead, they simply change incentives, encouraging preferred behavior but still allowing families to make their own choices. If the parents want to return to work sooner, they are free to do so.

Influencing social norms. One of the most promising possibilities is the idea of influencing social norms. As chapter 3 described, an extensive set of social norms governs parenting behavior. These parenting norms, however, are double-edged. Just as the norms can help encourage beneficial behavior, such as encouraging a pregnant woman not to drink or smoke, they are also a means of enforcing conformity and, in particular, judging low-income parents. Chris Gottlieb teaches students at NYU Law School to represent parents involved in the child welfare system. Gottlieb has written about her own experience being judged by others, including a story about riding the subway with an infant strapped to her front in a baby carrier and reading the newspaper. Another woman leaned over and said that placing the newspaper that close to the baby's eyes could cause eye strain. As if the tiny infant was following the latest shenanigans of Congress! This ludicrous story makes for a funny anecdote at a dinner party, but Gottlieb explains how the tendency to judge other parents harshly is anything but funny for the low-income women facing the scrutiny of the child-welfare system. For these women, social norms are enforced by social workers, judges, and lawyers, who are all forming judgments about the women's parenting and using these judgments to make decisions about whether the family will stay together or whether a child can return home.[195] This is norm enforcement run amok.

In thinking about social norms and the family, then, and particularly in thinking about how the state might influence these norms, it is important to remember that social norms are not an unmitigated good and that the state can use these norms to police the behavior of marginalized communities. Applying these insights to the goal of fostering strong, stable, positive relationships, the goal is to encourage parents to be attentive, responsive caregivers, while also trying to soften the tendency to judge parents, and especially low-income parents, harshly. Encouraging attentive parenting might take any number of specific forms, such as changing the norm that new couples quickly stop using birth control or inculcating a more widespread norm of parents reading to young children nightly and engaging in meaningful serve-and-return interactions with infants.

The state can influence these parenting norms in a variety of ways. To use the example of the gender norms surrounding paid work and parenting, by enacting and enforcing workplace-discrimination laws, the state sends the message that women belong in the workplace as much as men. And by making family leave available to both parents, the state sends a message that men play an important role in caring for dependents. Enacting *paid* parental leave would send an even stronger message that parenting young children is a difficult but essential task and that the entire society has a stake in the enterprise and therefore should share in the cost of creating a meaningful attachment between parents and newborns.

To play out this example of encouraging both mothers and fathers to be active caregivers, think back to the traditional family in chapter 3, and let the narrative continue. After picking up the sick child from school, the father immediately logs onto his home computer and checks in at work, in part to create the impression that he is not letting family obligations get in the way of his work. Although he is an "involved dad," he knows that in his workplace, most men have their wives do things like pick up a sick child from school. The father needs to care for his child on the sly, so as not to appear uncommitted at work. He is not alone in this worry. Men are typically less likely than women to take advantage of family-friendly policies at work, in part because they are concerned that doing so makes them seem insufficiently invested in their careers.[196]

The challenge, then, is to try to change these gendered norms. The Family and Medical Leave Act has not translated into real change in the United States in terms of caring for dependents. The majority of fathers did take some form of leave, but of those who did, 64 percent took only one week or less.[197] Additionally, fathers who take leave almost always use sick days, vacation days, or personal days instead of designated parental-leave programs.[198]

By contrast, Sweden's use-it-or-lose-it paternity-leave scheme has successfully changed behavior. Before the law, mothers were far more likely to be primary caregivers, but the new paternity-leave policy has affected social norms to such a degree that fathers with infants strapped into carriers and strollers are now a ubiquitous sight in Stockholm and elsewhere.[199] Indeed, the social norm has taken such a strong hold that instead of meeting resistance in the workplace, men can face social sanctions from coworkers if they do *not* take paternity leave.[200] Despite increased parenting by fathers, we are nowhere near this norm in the United States, and much work remains to be done.

In short, social norms can be a powerful tool for affecting individual behavior, but the relationship between laws and changes in social norms is not always clear. In the context of encouraging responsive parenting, the subsidy programs and structures discussed above will help create an environment where it is more possible to parent well. But a change in social norms is equally important, because it would lead to both internal and external pressure to be a responsive parent. Geoffrey Canada knows well the power of neighbors and communities, which is part of the reason he chose to base the Harlem Children's Zone in a geographically specific area. His goal is to transform the entire neighborhood, and he knows this will be easier if neighbors and friends are all making changes together.

CONCLUSION

There are many ways for the state to restructure family law to recognize a broader range of families, foster a long-term commitment between parents, alter the physical context for family life, and support parents in their critical child-development work. These efforts would, in turn, foster strong, stable, positive relationships within families. This chapter has described a few promising examples to inspire more thought and creativity around this issue and spur policymakers to adopt existing measures and develop new ones. The state need not, and in many cases should not, directly intervene in family life. Instead, the state will often be more successful, and likely meet less resistance, if it attempts to encourage this kind of relationship through indirect means such as subsidies, incentives, choice architecture, and influencing social norms.

If these measures so clearly benefit both families and society, why haven't we adopted them far more broadly? Politics and money—the topics of chapter 9.

9

The Limits of Flourishing Family Law

IN MAY 2012, New York City's Mayor Michael Bloomberg proposed a ban on the sale of soda and other sugary drinks in cups larger than sixteen ounces.[1] The political and cultural backlash was immediate and intense. Bloomberg had introduced the ban as a measure for combating obesity and diabetes, and Manhattan Borough President Scott Stringer commended the mayor for "taking on the soda cartel which is driving the obesity epidemic in this country."[2] But others saw the issue differently. The Center for Consumer Freedom, for example, ran a full-page ad in the *New York Times* with an image of Bloomberg dressed as a nanny with the taglines "You only thought you lived in the land of the free" and "New Yorkers need a mayor, not a nanny."[3] Criticisms also extended to left-leaning commentators. Jon Stewart mocked the proposal on TV's *The Daily Show*, saying that "it combines the draconian government overreach people love, with the probable lack of results they expect."[4]

Government regulation is often unpopular. There are rational, economic reasons for adopting the proposals set forth in the preceding chapters, but there will inevitably be strong resistance, at least in some political quarters, to reorienting the system of family law along the lines I have advocated. Fears of a nanny state resonate deeply across much of the country.

A different point of resistance is the fear that a change in state support will unleash a judgmental, discriminatory state that focuses too readily on personal failures rather than systemic causes of hardship.[5] There is a long history of equating poverty with laziness, particularly for people of color. Focusing on families, and particularly on what some families do not currently provide to their children, so this argument goes, gives the state another opportunity to blame marginalized families rather than take some responsibility for the inequalities that drive different family capabilities and child outcomes. This is a well-founded concern, because, as chapter 3 described, direct state support for low-income families almost inevitably means state control of families, even with well-intentioned programs. In my Poverty Law class, for example, I ask students to imagine a new governmental program that would offer support to low-income families. I then ask them what conditions, if any, they would attach to the benefits in the new program. It is astounding how many onerous and intrusive conditions the students, who are almost uniformly liberal, suggest. The tendency to control families who receive visible benefits is widespread and not necessarily limited by political commitments.

This chapter addresses these political realities and two other potential limits to the proposed reforms: limits of application and limits of what the law can achieve. There are some relationships and some situations where it is inappropriate to repair a relationship or facilitate ongoing contact. There are also limits to what the state can achieve, as opposed to nonstate institutions such as faith-based groups and other communities. This chapter explores both.

The central topic here, however, is the considerable political hurdles facing the proposed reforms, which will challenge both liberals and conservatives. Some of the changes this book proposes are not politically sensitive. Embracing collaborative law more fully, for example, would be a culture change for practicing lawyers accustomed to the adversarial system and might engender some resistance from the bar, but it is unlikely to register on the national or even local level as worthy of impassioned political debate. Other proposals, however, are highly sensitive politically and are likely to provoke considerable resistance, from both the left and the right.

Liberals will need to engage in a conversation about the place of families in ensuring healthy child development. As much as liberals might wish otherwise, there is mounting evidence that family structure is a causal factor, among others, affecting child outcomes. And conservatives, who are typically quite willing to talk about families, will need to do more than simply call for people to pull themselves up by their bootstraps. Focusing on the family means *investing* in the family. As this chapter elaborates, adopting the reforms this book proposes will cross political lines in interesting ways. It is essential, then, to think carefully about how to talk about the issues and craft reforms in a way that a broad range of Americans can relate to.

LIMITS OF POLITICS

Understanding the culture wars

Before exploring the resistance to any one proposed reform, it is useful to consider the culture wars over the family more broadly. Every political season, the headlines signal the continued strength of hot-button issues, including abortion, abstinence-only sex education, marriage equality, and single parenthood. In a fascinating book, *Red Families v. Blue Families: Legal Polarization and the Creation of Culture*, legal scholars Naomi Cahn and June Carbone explore why disagreements over the family and family law resonate so powerfully. In a telling anecdote, Cahn and Carbone recount how upon hearing that the rate of nonmarital births had risen yet again, a conservative commentator attributed this shift to the growing acceptance of same-sex marriage.[6] Cahn and Carbone relate their astonishment at this, given their certainty that the increase in nonmarital births was a result of the prevalence of abstinence-only sex education, the inaccessibility of contraception and abortion, and the poor economy.[7] They readily admit that they had no more evidence to back their conclusion than the conservative commentator had. Instead, both sides resorted to strongly felt, though unproven, intuition. As Cahn and Carbone sum it up, "Such is the nature of the culture wars."[8]

Their thesis is that there are two different family paradigms in the United States and that these paradigms track the familiar political divisions of red states and blue states. "Red families" espouse what are often called "traditional family values"— the idea that sex should not precede marriage, that children should be born only within marriage, that marriage is reserved for opposite-sex couples, and that sexuality should be controlled. The strongest marker of a red family, then, is early family formation, with relatively low average ages for marriages and first births.[9]

By contrast, "blue families" are more liberal in their attitudes toward family matters, believing that women should participate in the paid workforce and have the control over their fertility necessary to facilitate this participation, that men and women should play equal roles in the family and the workplace, and, perhaps most important, that childbearing should be delayed until a couple is financially and emotionally ready. Blue families, as a result, delay family formation until after completing college or graduate school.[10]

The actual families in these two groups, however, look quite different from the values each group espouses. Liberal blue states tend to have more traditional families, with low rates of divorce and teen pregnancy. Massachusetts, for example, with its early embrace of marriage equality and relatively easy access to abortion, has the lowest divorce rate in the country and relatively few teen births.[11] By contrast, Arkansas, with its opposition to marriage equality and dedication to abstinence-only sex education, has the second-highest divorce rate and a high rate of teen births.[12]

The gap between values and reality might not be a problem were it not for the considerable economic repercussions that flow from the different family practices. Cahn and Carbone argue that the red-family paradigm is inconsistent with the demands of the new information economy, which rewards investments in higher education. As long as unmarried young adults continue to be sexually active (and chances are that they will),[13] and as long as contraception and abortion are relatively difficult to obtain (and they are, for women in red states),[14] then young women will have unplanned pregnancies. These pregnancies complicate women's ability to continue with their education, so early family formation often means less education and lower incomes. Additionally, the pregnancies can lead to precipitous marriages, which are more likely to end in divorce. The end result is a less stable family.

By contrast, the blue-family approach to family life is consistent with the demands of the information economy. For blue families, a new middle-class ethic frames sexuality not in moral terms but instead in rational, instrumental terms. In light of the challenges of completing an education while also raising a family, so this ethic goes, postponing family formation is the key to succeeding in the new economy. Blue families embrace this approach to family life and thus benefit economically from the new economy. Postponing marriage and childbirth allows young people to finish their education, means they will be more mature when they do become parents, and raises the likelihood that their marriages will endure. Creating a cascade effect, blue families, with their greater economic stability, are able to invest in the earning potential of their children by sending them to college. These children, in turn, delay childbearing until after they have finished their education and are more emotionally mature and financially stable.

Returning to the question of why disagreements over family issues are so politically salient, Cahn and Carbone argue that red families resent that their approach to family life (early marriage and childbearing) is at odds with the new information economy. Blue-family values—comprehensive sex education, access to abortion when necessary, marriage equality, and shared roles within marriage—offend red families, in part because these values are antithetical to red-family values but also because these values are rewarded by the information economy, which demands workers with higher levels of education.[15] The red families thus feel embattled in attempts to maintain their family values. They are angry that their way of life is at odds with what it takes to succeed in America, and they are bitter that blue families benefit economically by espousing the offensive values. According to Cahn and Carbone, red families believe that the only way to address this conflict is by rigid adherence to traditional values.[16]

This reaction explains why issues such as abortion, marriage equality, and single-parenthood assume different meanings, symbolically and practically, in red-family regions and blue-family regions. For red families, these issues are a rear-guard action in an all-out effort to protect their way of life and their identity. For blue families, the focus is on preparedness for parenting, and if this means educating teenagers about contraception and even accepting abortion so that childbearing can be delayed, so be it. This means that the culture wars are not only about differing values and understandings, such as a disagreement about when life begins. The wars are also about the conflict between red and blue values, coupled with ever-increasing economic rewards for the blue paradigm, which have heightened the sense of moral alarm in red states, raising the stakes for everyone.

This red-families and blue-families frame does not capture some large segments of the American public—most notably lower-income African Americans and middle- and upper-income supporters of Republican candidates—for whom family form does not necessarily follow voting patterns. For example, according to exit polls, 52 percent of college graduates voted for Bush in 2004,[17] 48 percent voted for McCain in 2008,[18] and 47 percent voted for Mitt Romney in 2012.[19] It is unclear whether these individuals should fall within the red paradigm because they voted Republican or the blue paradigm because, as college graduates, their families are more likely to be founded on marriage to have delayed family formation, and to have low divorce rates.[20] Similarly, the frame does not accurately depict nonwhite Americans, particularly lower-income African Americans, whose voting patterns are overwhelmingly blue[21] but whose family form is more typically red.[22] Despite these limitations, the frame has the virtue of resonating with a generalized understanding of American politics and is a useful starting point for understanding the culture wars.

Opposing worldviews

Another reason debates about the family are politically salient is that disagreements over family values are rooted in deep belief systems about the world, which then inform political judgments about the kinds of issues that are the topic of this book. To better understand these opposing worldviews, it is helpful to tease out the two primary approaches to politics in our system: liberal and conservative. Of course, these are overly broad categories, and other approaches, such as libertarianism, do not fit neatly within either category. But in light of the two-party system and a general tendency to dichotomize political issues, these categories are sufficiently accurate that they can facilitate an exploration of potential resistance to family-law reform.

Psychologist Jonathan Haidt is interested in the moral foundations of political ideology. Haidt contends that there are five foundations of morality: concern about harm, fairness, loyalty, authority, and purity.[23] In his own research, he has found that liberals and conservatives both embrace the first two foundations as essential to society, but only conservatives also view the other three foundations—loyalty, authority, and purity—as necessary components.[24] Liberals reject these foundations as bases for state action and communal life.[25] What liberals fail to understand, according to

Haidt, is that the conservative embrace of the other three foundations is based on a view that "morality is not just about how we treat each other (as most liberals think); it is also about binding groups together, supporting essential institutions, and living in a sanctified and noble way."[26] Loyalty, authority, and purity, with their clear rules on who belongs and how groups should operate, are the ties that bind.[27]

In a somewhat more simplified scheme that draws on metaphors rooted in images of the family, linguist George Lakoff contends that there are two dominant moral systems. These images depict an idealized family—that of the strict father or the nurturant parent. In the strict-father system, the world is understood as a dangerous place, and the parent's role is one of protector and disciplinarian, instilling in the child a sense of right and wrong through strict rules and corresponding punishments.[28] A central value is self-reliance, taught by the parent.[29] In this moral system, authority plays an important role, gender roles are traditional and clearly delineated, and right is distinguishable from wrong.[30] Moral strength comes from self-discipline and overcoming external evils.[31] By contrast, in the nurturant-parent model of morality, the emphasis is on caring for others, empathy, and self-fulfillment.[32] Authority, particularly centralized and unquestioned authority, is deemphasized.[33] Parents thus make context-specific decisions (as opposed to fixed rules) that are geared to improving individual well-being. In this moral system, the parent's role is to inculcate responsibility indirectly and nurture the child.[34]

These moral systems translate into different political views, particularly about the appropriate role of government, with the strict-father and nurturant-parent metaphors informing an understanding of the relationship between the citizen and the state.[35] Views about the appropriate role of the government differ depending on the preferred moral system. In the strict-father moral system, the government's responsibility is to promote morality, self-discipline, and self-reliance. This is done largely through reward and punishment, with the government leaving self-disciplined individuals alone to pursue their own interests (thus the importance of the free market) and punishing those who do not care for themselves.[36] In the nurturant-parent moral system, the government's responsibility is to promote fairness and help those in need. Empathy reigns supreme.[37]

To understand how the two moral systems play out in matters of public policy, Lakoff explores divergent views on government-funded, low-interest college loans. For liberals, such loan programs are highly moral, because they help people in need who could not otherwise help themselves, increase self-fulfillment, strengthen the nation, and promote fairness by giving more people access to college. For conservatives, however, these programs are immoral, because they promote dependence on the government instead of self-reliance, interfere with the private market for loans thus hindering self-determination, and inappropriately redistribute money from those who have earned it, penalizing individuals who are self-reliant and self-disciplined.[38]

The red/blue divide, then, is not just about family values and family practices, but it is also fundamentally about competing visions of morality and the family-state relationship. As a result, state support has become one of the central battlegrounds in the culture wars, with its inflamed and culturally divisive iconography of "welfare queens" and oversexualized mothers.[39] Too often, any form of support for struggling families is likened to welfare—a clear death sentence in the current political environment.[40] To oversimplify the debate, conservatives oppose what they perceive as state handouts,[41] and liberals believe that supportive programs are the foundation of a just society.[42]

Two cultural scripts about state support flow from the differing worldviews described by Haidt and Lakoff. In red states, the dominant belief is that the state should be the strict father, not the nurturant parent, and certainly not the finger-wagging nanny. In this view, family autonomy is a critical value, with conservatives hewing closely to the belief that a stark line should separate the state and the family, a belief that resonates on cultural, political, and emotional registers. The strict-father state should foster independence, not dependence. State support symbolizes an important step away from independence and family autonomy, threatening the family and its role in society. The concern is that the state will take over for the family, telling parents how to raise their children, weighing in on every matter, from how much television children watch to what they eat and how to discipline them.

In blue states, the dominant belief is that the state should be the nurturant parent. Liberals generally do not feel threatened by state support, because their worldview is not predicated on the state as authority figure.[43] Rather, it is the absence of state support that threatens the future of children. In this cultural script, the state is simply helping parents raise their children by providing the necessary support. Parents are well-intentioned but not necessarily capable of raising their children without additional help (a central theme of this book).

Exacerbating these already-opposing worldviews is the tendency of individuals to discount factual information that might alter their beliefs. The Cultural Cognition Project at Yale has conducted numerous experiments demonstrating that for politically sensitive and symbolic issues, such as gun control and affirmative action, individuals perceive simple facts about these issues through their preformed commitments. A person who is inclined to support gun rights, for example, is not going to change his or her opinion based on new evidence about the number of accidental shootings among children.[44] Similarly, a person who is inclined to be suspicious of police behavior will look at a video of a high-speed police chase and conclude that the wildly erratic driving of the fleeing car did not merit the use of deadly force.[45] This is yet one more reason debates are not rational exchanges of information but rather are duels about opposing and inherently incompatible worldviews.

Although there may be strong policy arguments in favor of state investment in families, lessons from the Cultural Cognition Project indicate that this is not a rational issue. It is not, for example, a matter of aggregating more data about the effectiveness of certain programs. A person inclined to view state support skeptically is not going to be convinced by a study from the RAND Corporation showing that a program has the desired effect.

Further aggravating polarization is the growing tendency to self-segregate based on political viewpoint, with Americans increasingly likely to live and worship with people of similar political dispositions, thus reinforcing their beliefs and the larger political divisions.[46] People living in the thick bubbles of San Francisco, Portland, and brownstone Brooklyn often forget about the equally thick bubbles of Oklahoma City, Provo, and Colorado Springs. When like-minded people talk only to one another, they are more likely to reach extreme conclusions.[47] And the rise of niche news distribution—think Fox News and MSNBC, Drudge Report and Huffington Post—means that people get information from sources that are unlikely to challenge their preconceptions.

Understanding the origins of political attachments makes clear that disagreements are not going away. Deploying rational arguments, marshaling more facts, or simply yelling louder is not going to persuade the other side. Arguments such as "Hey, red-staters, you're getting divorced an awful lot and having lots of kids out of wedlock. This isn't good for your families" are unlikely to evoke responses such as "Oh, thanks for pointing that out. You're right. We should become more like Massachusetts." Attachments run deep, are rooted in personalities and worldviews, and are unlikely to be dislodged easily.

Moreover, these symbolic issues resonate on a deep emotional level. Both red and blue families want to transmit their values to the next generation. This sense of investment in family issues is not surprising given the level of emotion associated with families—our own and others. Referring to families as "private" is a common trope, but it does not account for the tremendous possessiveness some individuals and groups feel about other people's families. Small-scale examples of this are ubiquitous: fathers and mothers at the playground watching and judging the parenting decisions of other parents; long, and often fraught, conversations that friends have about parenting choices; even the intense interest people have about the families of politicians and celebrities.

There is an abiding sense that even though an issue may not reach our family personally, we are still somehow affected. And in many ways, we *are* affected. Children, of course, influence one another, thus moderating the lessons parents try to instill in their own children. The broader community also influences families, making it easier or harder for a family to maintain values that run counter to those of the majority. Think of a conservative Christian family in Berkeley or a same-sex couple in Provo. Each family knows it will be harder to pass on their values if they run counter to the values of other families in the community. Although some advocates of marriage equality deride opponents with such slogans as "Focus on Your Own Damn Family,"[48] this simplification fails to account for the influence families have on one another.

It is no surprise, then, that the culture wars engage an emotional center: families and the ability to pass along a heritage of values. These issues are deep-seated and go to the core of identity and belonging.

Talking purple

As with all cultural scripts, the schemas described above are stylized, but they help us see, if only with broad brushstrokes, the forces shaping the political landscape. The irony is that it is the red states with their abundance of fragile families that would most benefit from state investment in family relationships. And yet the ideology of these states creates opposition to supportive programs because of a confluence of libertarianism and family values that reflect the strict-father understanding of the family-state relationship. In practice, the red/blue divide means that Alabama, which has one of the highest poverty rates in the nation,[49] enrolls one of the lowest percentage of eligible children in Head Start programs,[50] while Massachusetts, with a much lower poverty rate,[51] became the first state to provide universal health care.[52]

To move forward, then, it is helpful to disaggregate the various reasons people favor or oppose governmental programs. Different kinds of support resonate in different ways. When the state allows an individual to deduct certain child-care expenses, for example, this is relatively uncontroversial, because it is understood as allowing the individual to retain more of what he or she "earned." By contrast, when the state subsidizes child care directly, say through the provision of vouchers, this is perceived as an affirmative transfer of resources from wealthy families to lower-income families and thus raises the specter of dependency and unworthiness. In both instances, however, the state is subsidizing the family. Even within programs that support low-income families, the design of the program matters. For example, the Earned Income Tax Credit (EITC) and Temporary Assistance for Needy Families (TANF) are both programs that provide income supports for low-income families, but because the EITC is tied to gainful employment and is administered through the tax code, it is not tainted in the same way as TANF, which has earned the pejorative term "welfare." Subsidized child care and TANF are nurturant-parent policies, because they are the state helping struggling families. Child-care deductions and the EITC are strict-father policies, because they reward independence.

To reach consensus, or even to have a civil discussion, requires creating a bridge such that red can talk to blue and blue can talk to red. To use shorthand, the question is how to build conservative support for the Nurse-Family Partnership and the Harlem Children's Zone (HCZ), both described in chapter 8, and liberal support for programs that promote long-term relationships between parents. This involves both reframing the issue and designing programs in ways that appeal to both liberals and conservatives.

Beginning with reframing, approaching the issue at a broad level of generality will only provoke responses based on cultural scripts that are unintentionally triggered in this conversation. For example, if we ask whether the state should support families, one answer will be "No, families should support themselves," and another answer will be "Of course we should." Instead of focusing on support, per se, the frame should be family functioning. The animating idea is that parents *are* responsible for their children, but all parents need some form of help to provide children with strong, stable, positive relationships. The shift in emphasis, then, is from the state to parents.

This reframing draws upon the moral foundations that register for conservatives: authority (following the rules of a good citizen by not relying on welfare) and purity (being a functional family, not corrupted by substance abuse and child abuse or neglect). Instead of highlighting programs as state support, they can be described as programs that foster responsible parenting and educational preparedness, for parents and children alike. Thus, to win greater support for the Nurse-Family Partnership, advocates should tie the program not necessarily to the prevention of child abuse and neglect—although this is certainly an additional benefit—but instead to responsible parenthood. Similarly, the Harlem Children's Zone's projects should be understood not to ameliorate poverty, even though that is certainly one goal, but rather to cultivate better parenting, in this generation and the next.

Both the Nurse-Family Partnership and the Harlem Children's Zone make considerable efforts to talk "purple"—across the red/blue divide—both in their program design and also in their marketing material, which may account for their relative success in garnering additional, if also insufficient, government funding. For example, the Nurse-Family Partnership website describes the program as follows: "Nurse-Family Partnership helps transform the lives of vulnerable first-time moms and their babies. Through ongoing home visits from registered nurses, low-income, first-time moms receive the care and support they need to have a healthy pregnancy, provide responsible and competent care for their children, and become more economically self-sufficient."[53] Similarly, the Harlem Children's Zone's website says: "the Harlem Children's Zone Project is a unique, holistic approach to rebuilding a community so that its children can stay on track through college and go on to the job market. The goal is to create a 'tipping point' in the neighbourhood so that children are surrounded by an enriching environment of college-oriented peers and supportive adults, a counterweight to 'the street' and a toxic popular culture that glorifies misogyny and anti-social behavior."[54]

This frame of responsible parenthood will likely be more effective with conservatives than arguments about the myth of family autonomy or the dire need for state support. Instead, this frame addresses the underlying concern that state support absolves parents of the responsibility of caring for their families (the authority foundation).

Similarly, Haidt's schema provides some insight into how to frame efforts to encourage a long-term commitment between parents. Liberals are likely to reject these efforts, claiming that the programs are simply another way to judge low-income families, perpetuate myths about racial inferiority, and privatize poverty. The challenge is to cast the programs in terms that resonate with liberals and particularly draw on the values of protecting against harm and promoting fairness. Addressing the ill effects of family structure is, admittedly, very sensitive, but one way to mediate the judgment inherent in any discussion of family form is to emphasize the unfairness that flows from different family structures. As this book has shown, children who come from families with complex family structures are less likely to do well in school and beyond. Teachers and others can tell children to work hard in school, but this message ignores the five years of uneven child development that occurred before kindergarten started. Focusing on family functioning, then, is a way of mitigating this unfairness. This does not excuse uneven investments in schools by the state. It is unconscionable for the state to spend more money in one school district than another, but it does address an important aspect of educational inequality: academic preparedness.

Turning to program design, the challenge is to identify the substantive components of a program that will garner the broadest support. The provision of more direct cash assistance will provoke tremendous resistance and is not a viable option. Thus, programs should focus on delivering in-kind assistance in a way that resonates with market incentives. In the context of both the Nurse-Family Partnership and the Harlem Children's Zone, the programs are designed to prepare parents to raise their children to succeed in the education-oriented workplace of the twenty-first century. Acknowledging the problems of early childbearing, both programs encourage a focus on existing children and careful planning for subsequent children. Similarly, both programs promote parental employment.

In sum, a "purple" approach to flourishing family law would pay close attention to both the framing and the design of programs. The goal of fostering flourishing families is best served by developing low-salience, high-impact interventions that appeal to a broad range of individuals.

Concerns about state control

Despite its benefits, state investment in families is not necessarily an unmitigated good, and state regulation of relationships entails considerable risks, as chapter 3 elaborated. Similarly, it is not necessarily clear what it means to "help" a family. In his dissenting opinion in *Planned Parenthood of Southeastern Pennsylvania vs. Casey*, where the Supreme Court struck down a provision of a Pennsylvania law that required a woman to give notice to her husband before having an abortion,[55] Chief Justice Rehnquist argued that the state law, in its own words, was "intended to promote the integrity of the marital relationship," which Rehnquist argued was an important state interest.[56] He viewed the spousal-notice requirement struck down by the Court as a "rational attempt by the State to improve truthful communication between spouses and encourage collaborative decisionmaking."[57] Reasonable people can disagree about how to improve relationships.

In the current political climate, there is a risk that any effort to work with families will reinforce cultural stereotypes about dysfunctional families, especially low-income families of color. Too often, the debate about poverty and race is boiled down to opposing characterizations of the problem: blaming either the family ("African American families are poor because they are dysfunctional") or the state ("African American families are dysfunctional because they are poor"). The reality is, of course, much more complicated. Individuals do make choices about their lives, but there is only so much a person can do given environmental constraints. For example, if there are no realistic pathways out of poverty for a young woman who barely made it out of high school, then it is harder to blame her for getting pregnant when the pregnancy and the child will bring a much-needed sense of purpose and self-worth.

In light of the racial and class history of state-sponsored programs for families, there is good reason to be skeptical about any project of state-sponsored cultural change. And yet there is a real need for families to function better. It may be tempting to think that a hands-off approach is preferable to yet another round of programs intended to help families, but this book has shown that taking a reactive approach to well-being has its own costs. It would be much better to find ways to nurture relationships effectively and respectfully, balancing state support with family self-determination.

Finally, it is important to clarify that supporting parents does not mean creating cookie-cutter parents. There is no one parenting style that works best for all children. The evidence suggests that different styles of parenting—from authoritative to authoritarian to permissive[58]—are effective for most racial, ethnic, and religious groups, as measured by rates of delinquency and emotional and behavioral problems.[59] The only style of parenting that is consistently correlated with higher rates of delinquency and emotional and behavioral problems is, unsurprisingly, the uninvolved parent.[60] As this book has argued, the focus of state support must be on helping parents draw on their own innate strengths and styles, not establishing parental mandates.

The Nurse-Family Partnership strikes just the right balance between providing support and fostering self-determination. One of the key elements of the program is that the nurse forges a relationship with the soon-to-be mother before the challenges of parenthood set in. Already a partner, the nurse is less likely to be perceived as a judgmental outsider if problems arise during the first two years of life. Additionally, the nurse is encouraging the mother to find and draw on her own strengths, rather than pointing out her deficits. As a coach, not a judge, the visiting nurse is teaching the mother to find her own approach to parenting.

Funding

Turning to a different concern, although one still rooted in politics, a common response to a proposed program is that there simply is not enough money to pay for it. But this is a shortsighted argument. As explained throughout this book, investing in family relationships during early childhood is far more cost-effective than investing in remedial programs later in a child's life. Chapter 7 described the overwhelming research establishing that early-childhood programs improve educational outcomes, skilled-employment rates, and adult earnings, while also reducing rates of incarceration and teen pregnancy.[61]

To take just one measure—the gain in earnings—consider the work of economist James Heckman. He has shown that early-intervention programs that target the years before a child enters school yield a 15-to-17-percent return on investment.[62] By contrast, investments in schools do not provide the same return on investment, and investments in remedial programs, such as job training for adults and adult literacy programs, do almost nothing to increase earnings.[63] Heckman's calculations do not include the additional savings from reductions in criminal-justice involvement and special-education use and other back-end programs. Or recall chapter 8's discussion of the long-term savings from the Nurse-Family Partnership and the Chicago School District's Child-Parent Center. For every dollar invested in the Nurse-Family Partnership, society saves $5.70 in the long run.[64] And for a family enrolled in the Chicago program for eighteen months, the program cost $6,692 but generated $47,759 in benefits by the time the child reached twenty-one.[65]

Despite the considerable savings to be had and despite what we know about the critical importance of the first few years of life, current funding patterns focus most heavily on school-age children rather than children younger than three. Federal, state, and local governments together spent $14,641 for each child age six to eleven[66] but only $5,415 for each child age zero to two and $8,602 for each preschool-age child.[67] The significant difference is the cost of public-school education.[68] In light of the $260-billion price tag for the criminal-justice system[69] and the approximately $50-billion price tag for special education,[70] the only question is whether we pay now or pay later.

Properly understood, then, the financial challenge is a short-term one. Investing in front-end programs such as the Nurse-Family Partnership requires investments today but will see returns only tomorrow, and meanwhile, the state must continue to pay for the back-end programs necessitated by yesterday's failure to invest in families. The real issue is how to shift away from our current reactive approach and toward a proactive approach to family relationships.

This is not to say that the funding issues are easy. Saving substantial amounts of money over the long run is appealing, but the funding streams are baroque. Investments made by one segment of the government (a health department providing prenatal care, for example), may be realized by another (the education system), but when budgets are in silos, there is little incentive for one institution to make investments that another institution will realize. This is difficult within one level of government—say, at the local or state level—but the problem is even more difficult in our federalist system of government. When a state government invests in early-childhood education, for example, this may result in fewer children placed in foster care, but the savings will be shared with the federal government. This is not an easy problem to solve, but it does clarify the need to think about costs and benefits more holistically and to create a funding scheme that provides the correct incentives to invest in family relationships.

Another challenge is that unlike the federal government, which can legally run a deficit, state and local governments are often required by law to balance their budgets every year. For this reason, a program that requires an outlay today but provides a return only in the future simply may not be feasible. There is no way around this problem of a delayed return on investment, and this is a reason centralized federal funding, even if it devolves control to states and localities, is essential.

LIMITS OF APPLICATION

A different limit of flourishing family law is that the state should not always seek to repair relationships and restructure the family for future relating. A clean and clear end to certain relationships has an important place in family law, and ignoring this can be counterproductive, if not outright dangerous. Take the example of domestic violence. There is a strong argument that a battered partner should never be asked to repair a relationship with the batterer and that any ongoing contact, such as joint custody, creates opportunities for the batterer to continue to control the victim. This is an important concern, and the response to it is complex.

It is useful to begin by describing the debate among domestic-violence researchers about typologies of violence between intimate partners. Sociologist Michael Johnson, among others, has argued that domestic violence is not a unitary phenomenon. Instead, Johnson believes there are four main categories of domestic violence among heterosexual partners: situational couple violence, intimate terrorism, violent resistance, and mutual violent control.[71] The categories are distinguished not by the type and severity of violence but rather by the degree of control one partner exerts over the other.[72]

Situational couple violence is the most common type and involves a disagreement that escalates into violence, which can be mild or severe. For most couples, the violence is isolated, although some couples repeat this pattern continuously. Situational couple violence is perpetrated by both men and women, although the violence inflicted by men is more serious. Situational couple violence does not typically involve one partner wielding complete control over the other. *Intimate terrorism* is a relationship where one partner, almost always the man, completely controls the other partner using violence and a number of other tactics, including economic control, psychological abuse, isolation, threats, and intimidation. *Violent resistance* occurs when a victim of intimate terrorism uses violence to resist the batterer. It is most often used by women against abusive men and is used infrequently. *Mutual violent control* is rare and involves both partners engaging in violent and controlling acts.[73]

The effort to categorize types of domestic violence is controversial, because some advocates worry that the categories are oversimplified and mask important differences among families and that the categories will be misused, intentionally or unintentionally, leading some families away from needed services while steering others toward unneeded intervention.[74] Regardless of whether Johnson's typology is the best way to describe the landscape, it provides an important insight that family law should not treat domestic violence as a single phenomenon. Recognizing that cases differ does not condone any kind of familial violence or imply that one type of violence is less serious than another. Instead, differentiation acknowledges the varied needs of families and can lead to more effective intervention and policies.[75]

It is clear, for example, that when the violence has the hallmarks of intimate terrorism, encouraging ongoing engagement and co-parenting is inappropriate. In these cases, a complete break is almost certainly warranted, and any restructuring of the family should be focused on keeping the family members safe and minimizing, to the greatest degree possible, any interaction between the parents. The focus is not on repairing the relationship but rather on paving the way for a different, nonviolent future, which will necessitate complete separation. This is one clear limit to the model suggested in chapter 5 and 6, and Johnson's typology helps underscore the necessity of treating these cases differently.

Even when a case does not clearly fall into the category of intimate terrorism, family law must still be cautious about repairing family relationships. Anecdotal accounts from advocates suggest that courts are using the typology to dismiss some claims of domestic violence as "mere" situational couple violence and thus are awarding joint custody where it is clearly inappropriate to do so and are refusing to apply statutory protections that are relevant to custody determinations in cases of domestic violence.[76] A court should treat any family with a history of violence differently from a family with no history of violence. Instead of simply dismissing the violence, a court or custody evaluator should pay particular attention to the nuances of the family dynamic. It is possible that the parents could learn to relate to each other without violence and could co-parent in the future, but it is also possible that any kind of ongoing contact is inappropriate and would compromise the safety of the family members. In short, any typology should be treated simply as one tool among many for determining how best to restructure a family.

Differentiation should also play an important role in child-welfare cases. For the approximately 10 percent of particularly egregious child-abuse and neglect cases, repairing the relationship probably is misguided.[77] But for the majority of cases involving poverty-related neglect, the state would do well to take a far more supportive and less adversarial stance toward the family. The child-welfare field has begun this work, distinguishing those families who should receive supportive interventions from families who should receive adversarial or coercive interventions.[78]

But even in cases of domestic violence or child abuse where the state should facilitate a complete break in the relationship, the victim of the violence will need to heal internally. Family law can and should account for the impact of an abusive relationship and attempt to foster repair within a single person. For example, in a case of severe domestic violence, family law can focus much more clearly on repairing the physical, psychological, and emotional damage to the survivor and bystander children. This recognition would provide a rationale for funding mental-health services. It would also provide a rationale for a different form of reparation, such as a disproportionate award of marital property to the victim. For example, in one New York case involving a lengthy history of horrific domestic violence (the kind Johnson would term intimate terrorism), the court found that the domestic violence was egregious marital conduct warranting a greater distribution of the marital estate to the wife.[79] This is a different but still appropriate form of repair.

Finally, turning to a different boundary of this book's approach, an often-raised concern with respect to mediation and other alternative processes is that they disadvantage women. Some scholars argue that mediation can require women to speak in inauthentic voices, such as a voice that suppresses anger, and that mediation may disadvantage the party with a more relational sense of self, arguably the woman, who will compromise to maintain a connection.[80] There is also a concern that the flexibility and lack of legal constraints in alternative dispute resolution settings can recreate existing power imbalances.[81]

These are valid concerns, but the relevant question is not whether an alternative process perfectly meets the needs of family members but rather whether it is an improvement over the current approach. In the child-welfare system, for example, the relevant comparator is the traditional adversarial system, which does little to help women regain custody of their children.[82] In the typical adversarial child-welfare proceeding, parents have very little voice and ability to give meaningful input. And there are serious power dynamics at play in the courtroom, with educated lawyers, judges, and social workers deciding what is "best" for the family. It may be that a parent feels somewhat pressured in a family group conference, but arguably the process is more attuned to the needs of the family members than the clearly dysfunctional family-court system. And in the context of marital mediation—which benefits family functioning postdivorce—there is evidence that women fare just as well in mediated custody agreements as they do in litigated custody agreements.[83]

Looking specifically at mediation and domestic violence, critics contend that abusers will not be held accountable for their abusive behavior, that the power imbalance in the relationship will lead the victim to compromise in the mediation, and that the confidential nature of the mediation will mean that there is no public condemnation or opportunity for prosecution.[84] But again, these concerns are not insurmountable. The confidentiality of mediation, for example, does not preclude a victim from choosing to file criminal charges against the abuser, and the privacy may allow the abuser to admit wrongdoing and agree to seek help.[85] To support this argument, advocates of mediation point to research suggesting that voluntary mediation prevents future violence.[86] Additionally, some experts believe that a less adversarial approach to domestic violence can benefit survivors and perpetrators. For example,

John Braithwaite, a leading scholar of restorative justice, has asserted that "court processing of family violence cases actually tends to foster a culture of denial, while restorative justice fosters a culture of apology," and that apology, "when communicated with ritual seriousness, is actually the most powerful cultural device for taking a problem seriously, while denial is a cultural device for dismissing it."[87]

When to use alternative processes is a complicated topic, and entire library shelves are dedicated to the subject. The point here is simply that there are reasons to be cautious about the attempt to repair relationships and that we should not do so in all cases.

LIMITS OF THE LAW

This book has focused on the role of the law in both undermining and strengthening family relationships, highlighting the pervasive, if often undetected, influence of the state in our most intimate relationships. But this is not to argue that the state can and should do everything. Other entities and institutions play a significant role in helping families flourish. For example, faith communities, informal support networks, and community groups play essential roles in nurturing strong, stable, positive relationships.

To give just one example, this book has emphasized the relevance of physical space to family functioning. The state can certainly try to build more family-friendly developments, but there is also a role for nongovernmental organizations. The nonprofit organization KaBOOM! has helped build more than two thousand playgrounds around the United States.[88] Its visionary leader, Darell Hammond, was raised in a group home after his father abandoned his family and his mother was unable to care for him and his siblings. Although "children's home" can call up Dickensian images, Hammond had a very positive experience in the home and always wanted to pay back society for taking care of him. In 1996, he read about two young siblings who had suffocated while playing in an abandoned car in a poor neighborhood in Washington, D.C. The children had nowhere else to play.[89] As chapter 2 described, this problem is far more widespread than many might think, with approximately half the children in the United States living in "play deserts," areas with no access to a park, playground, or community center.

The story of the suffocated children, his own formative experiences in playgrounds, and the broader problem of play deserts inspired Hammond to co-found KaBOOM!, which helps build playgrounds around the country. But it does so in a way that engages the neighborhood, creating a blueprint for further social change. Working with corporate partners such as Home Depot, KaBOOM! provides 90 percent of the funding for the cost of the playground and also a guide for planning the project.[90] The community raises the remaining 10 percent of the money and conducts all the planning for the project, which culminates in a one-day building effort that can involve as many as five hundred local participants.[91] The process takes far longer than if KaBOOM! simply built the playground itself. But the process is what transforms the community. Children help design the playground, community members learn about assets and skills they did not realize they had, and the entire community is mobilized around a common purpose.[92]

The history of the United States is replete with this kind of community effort. The most important role for the state in this context is to support, not supplant, this civic engagement. The state can do so by acting in the background by, for example, helping to build communities that facilitate interaction and continuing tax exemptions for nonprofit organizations.

To circle back to the political salience of state support, this kind of effort can appeal to both conservatives and liberals. Conservatives want the state out of the family, and one way to minimize at least the visibility of the state role is for the state to support intermediate institutions, such as community nonprofits. Liberals want the state to respect diversity in families, and one way for the state to foster pluralism is by supporting a variety of different nonprofit institutions, each reflecting different values.[93]

CONCLUSION

The most significant and daunting challenge to embracing flourishing family law is the highly charged political atmosphere. Debates about families and family law are not rational, fact-intensive exchanges about how to construct an effective system of family law. Instead, the emotional stakes are high, and each side, invoking its own contested view of morality, is certain it is right. In truth, there are no easy solutions, politically or socially. But a constructive starting point is for both liberals and conservatives to acknowledge that the other side is acting out of a sincerely held belief system and not resort to inaccurate caricatures that only fuel animosity and misunderstanding. Starting from this place of respect, it may be possible to find some common ground and reach compromise, with the public and policymakers alike engaging in a politics of pragmatism, not dogma.

Conclusion

AS A SOCIETY, we are faced with a choice. We can choose not to educate young people about sexuality, to make birth control scarce and expensive, and to make affordable abortions virtually unavailable. We can also choose not to provide supportive services to young parents, leaving any significant state investment until a child enters school at age five, and even then not challenging our public education system, which is rife with inequality, to truly make a difference. We can offer families few meaningful pathways out of poverty and leave the middle class to struggle economically. We can continue to build developments and zone neighborhoods so that parents live far from their jobs and families live in social isolation, cut off from neighbors and extended family, with few opportunities to develop the web of care that families need to thrive.

With this option, we will talk a lot about personal responsibility, the easy fix of getting married, and the importance of staying in school, but we will do little to change the circumstances and structures for millions of family lives. We know where this path takes us, because it is where we are: paying for expensive back-end programs, such as special education, the child-welfare system, and mass incarceration. As a society, we did not pay earlier, but we are paying now.

Or we can choose a different path. We can invest in families to foster strong, stable, positive relationships. This means preventing pregnancies and teen births by educating teens about sexuality and giving them meaningful after-school opportunities that a create sense of purpose and hope for the future. It also requires access to low-cost, effective birth control and, when necessary, affordable, safe abortions. For the women who choose to carry a pregnancy, planned or unplanned, to term, investing in families means providing early-intervention programs such as the Nurse-Family Partnership, to build parenting skills and plan for the future, and high-quality preschool programs. It also means providing relationship counseling so parents will have the skills they need to stay together, or at least co-parent effectively, and helping young men and women delay childbearing until they have found a reliable partner. And it means creating different physical environments that encourage casual interaction among families and facilitate social ties. This will cost money, but the investment would be sound.

Recall the story of Irene, described in chapter 8. Pregnant at fifteen, Irene could have become another depressing statistic, dropping out of school and failing to meet the needs of her daughter, virtually ensuring that they would both live in poverty. But with the timely intervention of a visiting nurse, Irene finished high school, learned how to care for her child, did not become pregnant again, and began working in a day-care center. Wendy, the nurse, was never judgmental but instead was there to help Irene, teaching her the skills she needed to develop a strong, stable, positive relationship with her daughter and keep on track with her own goals.

To foster these strong, stable, positive relationships, the state does not need to develop an all-encompassing, universal safety net. Instead, the state needs to adopt a fundamentally different approach to family law that carefully targets intervention at the most critical junctures where families need support. And when problems and changes do arise in families—from divorce to child abuse—a state response that restructures the family, opens the door to repair, and keeps family members safe would reduce acrimony and smooth the way for the continued interaction that will almost inevitably follow the end of any legal "resolution" of the problem.

Strong, stable, positive relationships are essential to society. Although it is neither possible nor desirable to legislate emotional outcomes—that a family *shall* live happily ever after—the state can play an important role in helping families flourish. It is time to begin.

NOTES

INTRODUCTION

1. Nearly half of all divorces involve children, so even after a divorce is finalized, the former couple must continue to co-parent. *See* Paul R. Amato, *The Consequences of Divorce for Adults and Children*, 62 J. MARRIAGE & FAM. 1269, 1269 (2000). Similarly, the dominant image of adoption is of infants placed in the homes of nonrelatives, but nearly half of the domestic adoptions in the United States are by someone who is related to the child or who knew the child before the adoption. *See* Sharon Vandivere, Karin Malm, & Amy McKlindon, *Adoption USA: Summary and Highlights of a Chartbook on the National Survey of Adoptive Parents* 2 (2010), *available at* http://basis.caliber.com/cwig/ws/library/docs/gateway/Blob/69117.pdf?w=NATIVE%28%27TITLE+ph+is+%27%27chartbook%27%27%27%29&upp=0&rpp=-10&order=native%28%27year%2FDescend%27%29&r=1&m=1 (describing survey sponsored by the federal government). Moreover, in 43 percent of domestic adoptions, the child lived with the biological family at some point before the adoption. *Id.* In the child-welfare system, a little more than half of all children removed from their homes eventually return to the custody of their parents. *See* CHILDREN'S BUREAU, ADOPTION AND FOSTER CARE ANALYSIS AND REPORTING SYSTEM (AFCARS) FY 2011 DATA, U.S. DEP'T HEALTH & HUM. SERVS., 3, *available at* http://www.acf.hhs.gov/sites/default/files/cb/afcarsreport19.pdf (in 2011, 53 percent of all children exiting foster care returned to their parents or primary caregivers).

2. JOYCE A. MARTIN ET AL., NAT'L CENTER FOR HEALTH STAT., CTRS. FOR DISEASE CONTROL & PREVENTION, BIRTHS: FINAL DATA FOR 2010, 61 NAT'L VITAL STAT. REP. 1, 8 (2012), *available at* http://www.cdc.gov/nchs/data/nvsr/nvsr61/nvsr61_01.pdf (Table C showing percentage of births to unmarried women).

3. ROSE M. KREIDER & RENEE ELLIS, U.S. CENSUS BUREAU, LIVING ARRANGEMENTS OF CHILDREN: 2009 3–4 (2011), *available at* http://www.census.gov/prod/2011pubs/p70-126.pdf (23.6 percent of children live with a single mother; 3.7 percent live with a single father).

4. According to 2010 U.S. census data, approximately 115,000 same-sex couple households reported having children. *See* DAPHNE LOFQUIST, U.S. CENSUS BUREAU, *Same-Sex Couple Households: American Community Survey Briefs* 2 (2011), *available at* http://www.census. gov/prod/2011pubs/acsbr10-03.pdf. There are reasons to believe, however, that the census significantly undercounts same-sex families. *See* DAVID M. SMITH & GARY J. GATES, HUMAN RIGHTS CAMPAIGN, GAY AND LESBIAN FAMILIES IN THE UNITED STATES: SAME-SEX UNMARRIED PARTNER HOUSEHOLDS 1-2 (2001), *available at* http://www.urban.org/ UploadedPDF/1000491_gl_partner_households.pdf (discussing the 2000 census and estimating that "gay and lesbian families could be undercounted as much as 62 percent").

5. *See* NAOMI CAHN, THE NEW KINSHIP: CONSTRUCTING DONOR CONCEIVED FAMILIES 2 (2013) (estimating that fifty thousand children a year are born from donated eggs and sperm).

6. *See* LEE RAINWATER & WILLIAM L. YANCEY, THE MOYNIHAN REPORT AND THE POLITICS OF CONTROVERSY 3–4 (1967).

7. DANIEL PATRICK MOYNIHAN, U.S. DEP'T LAB., THE NEGRO FAMILY: THE CASE FOR NATIONAL ACTION ch. 1 (1965), *available at* http://www.dol.gov/oasam/programs/history/ moynchapter1.htm#.UPh_j-h97eY.

8. *Id.* at ch. 5, *available at* http://www.dol.gov/oasam/programs/history/moynchapter5. htm#.UN9s_29pdmc.

9. *Id.* at ch. 2, *available at* http://www.dol.gov/oasam/programs/history/moynchapter2.htm.

10. *See* DAVID C. CARTER, THE MUSIC HAS GONE OUT OF THE MOVEMENT: CIVIL RIGHTS AND THE JOHNSON ADMINISTRATION, 1965–1968, at 67–73 (2009).

11. WILLIAM JULIUS WILSON, MORE THAN JUST RACE: BEING BLACK & POOR IN THE INNER CITY 95–108 (2009).

12. *Id.* at 115–28.

CHAPTER 1

1. *See Elsie Widdowson; Wartime Nutrition Expert*, LOS ANGELES TIMES (June 27, 2000), *available at* http://articles.latimes.com/2000/jun/27/local/me-45312.

2. Elsie M. Widdowson, *Mental Contentment and Physical Growth*, THE LANCET, June 16, 1951, at 1316–18.

3. *Id.* at 1318.

4. Another example is that of hedonic psychology. Around the same time Seligman was developing the idea of positive psychology, several other noted psychologists proposed the new field of hedonic psychology. *See* Daniel Kahneman, Ed Diener & Norbert Schwarz, *Preface to the First Edition* of THE RUSSELL SAGE FOUNDATION, WELL-BEING: THE FOUNDATIONS OF HEDONIC PSYCHOLOGY, at ix (Daniel Kahneman, Ed Diener & Norbert Schwarz eds., 1999). Arguing that psychology was overly focused on the negative, the founders of this field contended that in addition to studying negative emotions and circumstances, researchers should study positive emotions and circumstances. *See id.*

5. *See id.*

6. Positive psychology is not the simple study of happiness but rather the study of what makes life worth living, which involves far more than fleeting, superficial happiness. *See* Christopher Peterson, A Primer in Positive Psychology 7 (2006). This book uses the term "happiness" advisedly, because in the context of modern American society, happiness can be too simplistic, evoking a hammock on a beach at sunset rather than the more complex notions of satisfaction and fulfillment, which, positive psychology shows, typically come only with hard work and personal investment.

7. *Id.* at 4.

8. Ed Diener & Robert Biswas-Diener, Happiness: Unlocking the Mysteries of Psychological Wealth 47–67 (2008).

9. *See* Ctr. on the Developing Child, *In Brief: The Science of Early Childhood Development, available at* http://developingchild.harvard.edu/index.php/resources/briefs/inbrief_series/inbrief_the_science_of_ecd/; Nat'l Sci. Council on the Developing Child, *The Timing and Quality of Early Experiences Combine to Shape Brain Architecture* 1–4 (Working Paper No. 5, 2007), *available at* http://developingchild.harvard.edu/index.php/resources/reports_and_working_papers/working_papers/wp5/.

10. Genetics provide a blueprint for brain development, and the pre- and postnatal environment along with a child's relationships affect the expression of this genetic plan. The mechanism through which experiences affect the expression of genes is the epigenome. In a useful analogy, neuroscientists liken genes to the hardware of a computer, setting the limits of what the body can do but useless without an operating system. The epigenome is that operating system, determining which functions the hardware will perform. Experiences and environment shape the epigenome, leaving "signatures" on the epigenome that, in turn, affect which genes will be turned on and off. The example of identical twins helps explain this process. Although identical twins have the exact same genetic makeup, their different experiences in life will lead to different epigenomes, meaning that some genes will be expressed differently. Thus, although identical twins may be very similar in many aspects of their lives, their health, behavior, and skills can differ because of the different expressions of their genes. *See* Nat'l Sci. Council on the Developing Child, *Early Experiences Can Alter Gene Expression and Affect Long-Term Development* 1 (Working Paper No. 10, 2010), *available at* http://developingchild.harvard.edu/index.php/resources/reports_and_working_papers/working_papers/wp10/. Looking at the environment, if a fetus is exposed to certain toxins, such as alcohol, during pregnancy (and especially during particularly sensitive periods of the pregnancy), this harms the development of neural circuits. Similarly, after birth, the availability of nutrients and the absence of toxins also affect the construction of the neural circuitry. *See* Nat'l Sci. Council on the Developing Child, *supra* note 9, at 2.

11. Daniel Siegel & Jennifer McIntosh, *Family Law and the Neuroscience of Attachment, Part II*, 49 Fam. Ct. Rev. 513, 513 (2011).

12. *Id.*

13. *See* Center on the Developing Child, *supra* note 9; Nat'l Sci. Council on the Developing Child, *Young Children Develop in an Environment of Relationships* 1–3 (Working Paper No. 1, 2004), *available at* http://developingchild.harvard.edu/index.php/resources/reports_and_working_papers/working_papers/wp1/; Nat'l Sci. Council on the Developing Child, *Children's Emotional Development Is Built into the Architecture of Their Brains* 1 (Working Paper No. 2, 2004), *available at* http://developingchild.harvard.edu/index.

php/resources/reports_and_working_papers/working_papers/wp2/; Nat'l Sci. Council on the Developing Child, *supra* note 9, at 5.

14. Nat'l Sci. Council on the Developing Child, *supra* note 9, at 1–5.

15. *Id.* at 2–4.

16. *Id.*

17. Nat'l Sci. Council on the Developing Child, *Building the Brain's "Air Traffic Control" System: How Early Experiences Shape the Development of Executive Function* 1–8 (Working Paper No. 11, 2011), *available at* http://developingchild.harvard.edu/index.php/resources/reports_and_working_papers/working_papers/wp11/.

18. Nat'l Sci. Council on the Developing Child, *Excessive Stress Disrupts the Architecture of the Developing Brain* 1–4 (Working Paper No. 3, 2005), *available at* http://developingchild.harvard.edu/index.php/resources/reports_and_working_papers/working_papers/wp3/.

19. *Id.* at 1.

20. *See* Jack P. Shonkoff & Susan Nall Bales, *Science Does Not Speak for Itself: Translating Child Development Research for the Public and Its Policymakers*, 82 Child Dev. 17, 23–24 (2011) (describing the conscious effort to use metaphors and terms, including "toxic stress," to convey complex scientific methods to nonscientists).

21. Nat'l Sci. Council on the Developing Child, *supra* note 18, at 1. "Tolerable stress" falls between positive stress and toxic stress, and is the kind of stress that has the potential to affect brain architecture; it typically does not, however, either because the stressful period is brief or because there is a responsive caregiver who is able to help the child cope with the stressful event. Examples include the loss of a family member or a serious accident. *See id.* For further discussion of the effect of toxic stress on brain development, *see* National Scientific Council on the Developing Child, *Persistent Fear and Anxiety Can Affect Young Children's Learning and Development* (Working Paper No. 9, 2010), *available at* http://developingchild.harvard.edu/index.php/resources/reports_and_working_papers/working_papers/wp9/.

22. National Sci. Council on the Developing Child, *supra* note 10, at 1–2.

23. National Sci. Council on the Developing Child, *supra* note 18, at 2.

24. *Id.*

25. *Id.* at 2–3.

26. *Id.* at 1–4. Although adverse experiences such as abuse and neglect put all children at risk for poor outcomes, some children are genetically predisposed to be particularly affected by adverse experiences. For these children, toxic stress is particularly correlated with later physical and mental illnesses, such as clinical depression. *See* Nat'l Sci. Council on the Developing Child, *Establishing a Level Foundation for Life: Mental Health Begins in Early Childhood* 1 (Working Paper No. 6, 2008), *available at* http://developingchild.harvard.edu/index.php/resources/reports_and_working_papers/working_papers/wp6/.

27. Nat'l Sci. Council on the Developing Child, *supra* note 9, at 4.

28. *Id.* at 2.

29. *Id.*

30. Nat'l Sci. Council on the Developing Child, *Maternal Depression Can Undermine the Development of Young Children* 3 (Working Paper No. 8, 2009), *available at* http://developingchild.harvard.edu/index.php/resources/reports_and_working_papers/working_papers/wp8/.

31. *Id.*

32. *Id.*

33. *Id.* at 3–4.

34. *Id.* at 1.

35. *Id.* at 2 (citing calculations from the Early Childhood Longitudinal Study, Birth Cohort 9-month restricted use data [NCES 2006-004]).

36. *Id.* at 4.

37. *Id.*

38. Martin E. P. Seligman, Flourish: A Visionary New Understanding of Happiness and Well-Being 20 (2011) (and noting that "[v]ery little that is positive is solitary").

39. Positive psychologists define life satisfaction and happiness in slightly different ways. Martin Seligman speaks of "authentic happiness," which entails pursuing a pleasant, engaged, and meaningful life. *See* Martin E. P. Seligman, Authentic Happiness: Using the New Positive Psychology to Realize Your Potential for Lasting Fulfillment 262–63 (2002). A *pleasant* life means seeking positive emotions about the past, present, and future. In looking at the past, this means feeling satisfaction, contentment, and serenity. In looking at the future, this means optimism, hope, trust, faith, and confidence. And for the present, this means both pleasures and gratifications—pleasures being momentary emotions, such as sexual feelings or pleasing sounds and sights, gratifications falling into a higher order and usually involving intentional activities such as cooking or reading. Authentic happiness is not built on the intensity of these positive emotions but rather on the frequency of mild to moderate positive emotions. Positive emotions are balanced by, rather than exclusive of, negative ones. An *engaged* life is absorption in work, love, and leisure. Mihaly Csikzentmihalyi's concept of "flow" is relevant here. According to Csikzentmihalyi, flow is the experience of deep engagement in an activity that is marked by time passing quickly, the complete focusing of attention, and a sense of almost losing the self. The activity can be either physical or mental and can be felt by Olympic athletes and by everyday people in their day-to-day lives. The key to flow is the match between a person's perceived ability and the perceived challenge of a task. Flow is most often found when a person is working at the limits of but still within his or her abilities, using those abilities to a great degree. Csikzentmihalyi termed this experience "flow" because it *feels* effortless, although in fact a great deal of effort is expended. Experiencing flow is so deeply satisfying that seeking this feeling again becomes the motivation for engaging in the behavior, rather than any external outcome. *See generally* Mihaly Csikzentmihalyi, Finding Flow: The Psychology of Engagement with Everyday Life (1997); Mihaly Csikzentmihalyi, Flow: The Psychology of Optimal Experience (1990). A *meaningful* life is one in which we serve something larger than ourselves. Seligman posits that using our strengths to work toward this larger goal will help create a meaningful life that is deeply satisfying. *See* Tayyab Rashid, *Authentic Happiness, in* 1 A–K The Encyclopedia of Positive Psychology 73–75 (Shane J. Lopez ed., 2009).

Ed Diener believes that life satisfaction partially comes from feeling well emotionally, such as the joy that accompanies an afternoon with a close friend, or enjoying pleasurable aspects of life, such as dark chocolate, but it also comes from a broader sense of the person's whole life, including strong relationships, engaging work, spirituality, self-respect, and whether there is meaning and purpose in the person's life. Ed Diener and Robert Biswas-Diener call this "psychological wealth." Diener & Biswas-Diener, *supra* note 8, at 6.

There are numerous other ways to conceive of well-being. For example Carol Ryff and Burton Singer have identified six factors that constitute eudaimonia: autonomy, environmental mastery, personal growth, relationships with others, purpose in life, and self-acceptance. *See* Carol Ryff & Burton H. Singer, *Know Thyself and Become What You Are: A Eudaimonic Approach to Psychological Well-Being*, 9 J. HAPPINESS STUD. 13, 18–23 (2006). Corey Keyes has focused on social well-being, emphasizing a person's social condition, including social acceptance, social actualization, social coherence, social contribution, and social integration. *See* Matthew W. Gallagher, *Well-Being, in* 2 L–Z THE ENCYCLOPEDIA OF POSITIVE PSYCHOLOGY 1031–32. Although these articulations vary in their particulars, they have a strong constant theme of social connection.

40. Rashid, *supra* note 39, at 74.

41. Ed Diener & Martin E. P. Seligman, *Very Happy People*, 13 PSYCHOL. SCI. 81, 81 (2002).

42. *Id.* at 82–83 tbl.2.

43. Kelly Musick & Larry Bumpass, *Reexamining the Case for Marriage: Union Formation and Changes in Well-Being*, 74 J. MARRIAGE & FAM. 1, 3–4 (2012) (describing the qualifications to the marriage-benefit findings, particularly that the studies look only at ongoing marriages and thus do not account for divorce and that the benefits of marriage typically diminish, although do not disappear, over time).

44. Robert E. Emery, Erin E. Horn & Christopher R. Beam, *Marriage and Improved Well-Being: Using Twins to Parse the Correlation, Asking How Marriage Helps, and Wondering Why More People Don't Buy a Bargain, in* MARRIAGE AT THE CROSSROADS: LAW, POLICY, AND THE BRAVE NEW WORLD OF TWENTY-FIRST-CENTURY FAMILIES 126–27 (Marsha Garrison & Elizabeth S. Scott eds., 2012) (summarizing the research).

45. DIENER & BISWAS-DIENER, *supra* note 8, at 50.

46. Alois Stutzer & Bruno S. Frey, *Does Marriage Make People Happy, or Do Happy People Get Married?*, 35 J. SOCIO-ECON. 326, 326–28 (2006). (The German Socio-Economic Panel Study started in 1984 in West Germany and after unification included residents of the former East Germany.)

47. *Id.* at 330.

48. *Id.*

49. *Id.* at 334–35. The exception is for individuals around the age of thirty; for these individuals, the satisfaction levels of those who will be married in the future and those who will remain single are indistinguishable. *See id.*

50. *Id.* at 337.

51. *Id.* at 332. By contrast, looking at individuals who ultimately divorced, low levels of life satisfaction preceded the marriage and then remained present in the marriage. *Id.* at 337. Marriage is thus not necessarily a cure for low life satisfaction. The study excluded life-satisfaction reports soon before and for three years after the marriage, because these are known to be particularly high and therefore may not reflect the effect of marriage over time.

52. Emery, Horn & Beam, *supra* note 44, at 132–34.

53. *Id.*

54. Musick & Bumpass, *supra* note 43, at 3–4 (describing this body of research).

55. *Id.* at 9–14. This study found that when comparing intact marriages with intact cohabiting relationships, "there were no statistically significant differences between the married and cohabiting for depression.... Where there were statistically significant differences, marriage was not always more advantageous than cohabitation: The married fared better in health than cohabitors, but the opposite was true of happiness and self-esteem." *See id.* at 12–13.

56. Vincent J. Felitti et al., *Relationship of Childhood Abuse and Household Dysfunction to Many of the Leading Causes of Death in Adults: The Adverse Childhood Experiences (ACE) Study*, 14 AM. J. PREVENTIVE MED. 245 (1998). The ACE Study used a questionnaire mailed to 13,494 adults (70.5 percent responded) who had recently completed a standard medical evaluation.

57. To view the ACE questionnaire, *see* http://www.acestudy.org/yahoo_site_admin/assets/docs/ACE_Calculator-English.127143712.pdf.

58. Felitti et al., *supra* note 56, at 249–50.

59. *Id.* at 252–53.

60. Maxia Dong et al., *Insights into Causal Pathways for Ischemic Heart Disease: Adverse Childhood Experiences Study*, 110 J. AM. HEART ASS'N 1761, 1765 (2004), *available at* http://circ.ahajournals.org/content/110/13/1761.full.pdf (tbl. 4 showing a 3.1 incidence of ischemic heart disease for subjects with ACE scores of 7–8 versus 1.0 for subjects with ACE scores of 0, when controlling for both covariates and traditional risk factors).

61. For a layperson's discussion of this phenomenon, *see* Paul Tough, *The Poverty Clinic*, THE NEW YORKER, Mar. 21, 2011, at 25, 30. For a clinical discussion, *see* Dong et al., *supra* note 60, at 1765–66.

62. *See, e.g.,* Anuradha Paranjape et al., *Lifetime Exposure to Family Violence: Implications for the Health Status of Older African American Women*, 18 J. WOMEN'S HEALTH 171, 175 (2009), *available at* http://www.ncbi.nlm.nih.gov/pmc/articles/PMC2945718/pdf/jwh.2008.0850.pdf. ("[family violence] has effects on health that persist despite time, over and above other non-modifiable factors").

63. *Id.* at 174.

64. Amy E. Bonomi et al., *Medical and Psychosocial Diagnoses in Women with a History of Intimate Partner Violence*, 169 ARCH. INTERNAL MED. 1692, 1695 (2009) *available at* http://archinte.jamanetwork.com/data/Journals/INTEMED/20255/ioi90068_1692_1697.pdf. (tbl. 2, showing a higher risk of health problems for domestic violence sufferers).

65. Emmy E. Werner, *High-Risk Children in Young Adulthood: A Longitudinal Study from Birth to 32 Years*, 59 AM. J. ORTHOPSYCHIATRY 72, 72 (1989).

66. *Id.* at 73.

67. Emmy E. Werner, *Children of the Garden Island*, SCI. AM., Apr. 1989, at 106, 106–10; Werner, *supra* note 65, at 72–74.

68. MICHAEL PETERS, DAVID THOMAS & CHRISTOPHER ZAMBERLAN, U.S. DEP'T JUST., OFF. JUV. JUSTICE & DELINQUENCY PREVENTION, *Boot Camps for Juvenile Offenders: Program Summary*, 2–3 (1997) (describing common aspects of juvenile boot camps but also acknowledging diversity among programs), *available at* https://www.ncjrs.gov/pdffiles/164258.pdf.

69. *See* Anthony Petrosino et al., The Campbell Collaboration, *Scared Straight and Other Juvenile Awareness Programs for Preventing Juvenile Delinquency: A Systematic Review*, 9 CAMPBELL SYSTEMATIC REVIEWS 1 (David Wilson & Charlotte Gill eds., 2013), *available at* http://www.campbellcollaboration.org/lib/project/3/.

70. Youths who went through these types of programs had higher recidivism rates than youths assigned to regular juvenile case processing. *See* ELIZABETH S. SCOTT & LAURENCE STEINBERG, RETHINKING JUVENILE JUSTICE 218 (2008).

71. *See id.* at 217–18.

72. *Id.* at 217–20 (describing multisystemic therapy and the public savings it generates).

73. Bruce D. Perry & Maia Szalavitz, The Boy Who Was Raised as a Dog and Other Stories from a Child Psychiatrist's Notebook: What Traumatized Children Can Teach Us about Loss, Love, and Healing (2006).

74. *Id.* at 80.

75. Jane Jacobs, The Death and Life of Great American Cities (1961).

76. Robert D. Putnam, Bowling Alone: The Collapse and Revival of American Community (2000).

77. *Id.* at 20.

78. *Id.*

79. *Id.*

80. Carol B. Stack, All Our Kin 32 (1974).

81. *Id.* at 40.

82. *Id.* at 28.

83. For two book-length descriptions of these kinds of networks today, *see* Jason DeParle, American Dream: Three Women, Ten Kids, and a Nation's Drive to End Welfare (2004); Adrian Nicole LeBlanc, Random Family: Love, Drugs, Trouble, and Coming of Age in the Bronx (2003).

84. U.S. Dep't Health & Hum. Servs., Nat'l Center for Injury Prevention and Control, *Costs of Intimate Partner Violence against Women in the United States*, at 1–2 (2003), *available at* http://www.cdc.gov/ncipc/pub-res/ipv_cost/ipvbook-final-feb18.pdf.

85. *Id.*

86. *Id.*

87. *Id.* at 44.

88. Marga Vicedo, *The Evolution of Harry Harlow: From the Nature to the Nurture of Love*, 21 Hist. Psychiatry, at 2 (2010), *available at* http://individual.utoronto.ca/vicedo/vicedoca/Publications_files/Vicedo_HofP.pdf.

89. Deborah Blum, Love at Goon Park: Harry Harlow and the Science of Affection 143–44 (2002).

90. *Id.* at 145.

91. *Id.* at 145–46.

92. *Id.* at 147.

93. Harry F. Harlow, *The Development of Affectional Patterns in Infant Monkeys, in* Determinants of Infant Behavior: Proceedings of a Tavistock Study Group on Mother-Infant Interaction Held in the House of the CIBA Foundation 75, 77 (B. M. Foss ed., 1961) (fig. 12 showing that the cloth-fed and wire-fed monkeys spent approximately the same amount of time on each mother and that both showed a strong preference for the terry-cloth mother).

94. Harry Harlow, *Love in Infant Monkeys*, Sci. Am., 1959, at 68–74.

95. Vicedo, *supra* note 88, at 5.

96. *See generally* John Bowlby, Attachment (1969); John Bowlby, Separation: Anxiety and Anger (1973); John Bowlby, Loss: Sadness and Depression (1980); John Bowlby & Mary D. Salter Ainsworth, Child Care and the Growth of Love (Margery Fry ed., 2d ed. 1965); Mary D. Salter Ainsworth, Infancy in Uganda: Infant Care and the Growth of Love (1967); Mary Ainsworth et al., Patterns of Attachment: A Psychological Study of the Strange Situation (1978).

97. *See* Bowlby, Attachment, *supra* note 96, at 371–74.

98. *See id.* at 224–28.

99. John Bowlby, A Secure Base: Parent-Child Attachment and Healthy Human Development 24–25 (1988).

100. *Id.* at 124–25.

101. Mario Mikulincer & Phillip R. Shaver, Attachment in Adulthood: Structure, Dynamics, and Change 129–35 (2007).

102. These four styles are described in a number of books on attachment but are well summarized in Phillip R. Shaver, Mario Mikulincer & Brooke C. Feeney, *What's Love Got to Do with It? Insecurity and Anger in Attachment Relationships*, 16 Va. J. Soc. Pol'y & L. 491, 493–97 (2009).

103. Ainsworth, *supra* note 96, at 345–46; Ainsworth et al., *supra* note 96, at 255–60; Bowlby, *supra* note 99, at 11.

104. Mikulincer & Shaver, *supra* note 101, at 190–92, 194–218.

105. *Id.* at 22–25, 251–366.

106. James A. Coan, *Toward a Neuroscience of Attachment, in* Handbook of Attachment 242 (Jude Cassidy & Phillip R. Shaver eds., 2d ed. 2008).

107. *Id.* at 244.

108. *Id.* at 246–47, 251–52; *see also* Daniel Siegel, The Developing Mind: Toward a Neurobiology of Interpersonal Experience 88–91 (1999).

109. Coan, *supra* note 106, at 247–49; *see also* Siegel, *supra* note 108, at 88.

110. Daniel J. Siegel, The Mindful Brain: Reflection and Attunement in the Cultivation of Well-Being 166–68 (2007); Siegel, *supra* note 108, at 70–71; *see also* Allan Schore & Jennifer McIntosh, *Family Law and the Neuroscience of Attachment, Part I*, 49 Fam. Ct. Rev. 501, 501–02 (2011) (arguing that neuroscience demonstrates the scientific validity of attachment theory and that the child-caregiver relationship established in the prenatal period and continuing through the third year forms the basis for all future attachment relationships— "attachment drives brain development"); *see id.* at 502 (the brain "more than doubles by 12 months, and 40,000 new synapses are formed every second in the infant's brain. But, importantly, this brain growth is influenced by 'social forces,' and therefore is 'experience-dependent.' It requires not only nutrients, but the emotional experiences embedded in the relationship it co-creates with the primary caregiver.").

111. *See* Schore & McIntosh, *supra* note 110, at 506–07.

112. *See id.*

113. Bowlby, *supra* note 99, at 12, 27.

114. *Id.* at 26–27.

115. *Id.* at 27.

116. *Id.*

117. Mikulincer & Shaver, *supra* note 101, at 29–50.

118. *Id.* at 31, 39–42.

119. Coan, *supra* note 106, at 256.

120. James A. Coan, Hillary S. Schaefer & Richard J. Davidson, *Lending a Hand: Social Regulation of the Neural Response to Threat*, 17 Psychol. Sci. 1032, 1038 (2006).

121. Coan, *supra* note 106, at 255–57.

122. Coan, Schaefer & Davidson, *supra* note 120, at 1033–37.

123. Coan, *supra* note 106, at 256.

124. Darby Saxbe & Rena L. Repetti, *For Better or for Worse? Coregulation of Couples' Cortisol Levels and Mood States*, 98 J. PERSONALITY AND SOC. PSYCHOL. 92, 100–101 (2010); Benedict Carey, *Families' Every Fuss, Archived and Analyzed*, N.Y. TIMES, May 22, 2010, at A1, *available at* http://www.nytimes.com/2010/05/23/science/23family.html?ref=todayspaper&_r=0.

125. Susan M. Johnson, *Couple and Family Therapy: An Attachment Perspective, in* HANDBOOK OF ATTACHMENT 821 (Jude Cassidy & Phillip R. Shaver eds., 2d ed. 2008) (reviewing literature).

126. MIKULINCER & SHAVER, *supra* note 101, at 314.

127. *Id.* at 49, 251–366.

128. *See, e.g.,* Mario Mikulincer, Phillip R. Shaver & Keren Slav, *Attachment, Mental Representations of Others, and Gratitude and Forgiveness in Romantic Relationships, in* DYNAMICS OF ROMANTIC LOVE: ATTACHMENT, CAREGIVING, AND SEX 205–08 (Mario Mikulincer & Gail S. Goodman eds., 2006).

129. *See id.* at 207.

130. *See* Nancy L. Collins et al., *Psychosocial Vulnerability from Adolescence to Adulthood: A Prospective Study of Attachment Style Differences in Relationship Functioning and Partner Choice*, 70 J. PERSONALITY 965, 997–98 (2002) (finding that avoidant adolescents are prone toward anger, hostility, and verbal and physical aggression in their adult romantic relationships); Larry B. Rankin et al., *Mediators of Attachment Style, Social Support, and Sense of Belonging in Predicting Woman Abuse by African American Men*, 15 J. INTERPERSONAL VIOLENCE 1060, 1066, 1069–71 (2000) (finding that an insecure attachment style is correlated with more severe physical and sexual abuse in a study of adult males arrested for domestic violence); Amy Holtzworth-Munroe, Gregory L. Stuart & Glenn Hutchinson, *Violent versus Nonviolent Husbands: Differences in Attachment Patterns, Dependency, and Jealousy*, 11 J. FAM. PSYCHOL. 314, 319–20, 323–24, 327–29 (1997) (finding that violent husbands are less likely to be secure in their relationships, more fearful of intimacy, and prone to preoccupied, anxious-ambivalent, and disorganized attachment styles as compared with nonviolent husbands).

131. D. W. WINNICOTT, THE CHILD, THE FAMILY, AND THE OUTSIDE WORLD 17, 44 (1964).

132. D. W. Winnicott, *Transitional Objects and Transitional Phenomena—A Study of the First Not-Me Possession*, 34 INT'L J. OF PSYCHOANALYSIS 89, 93 (1953).

133. Harry T. Reis, & Phillip Shaver, *Intimacy as an Interpersonal Process, in* HANDBOOK OF RESEARCH IN PERSONAL RELATIONSHIPS 367, 376–83 (S. W. Duck ed., 1988).

134. Harry T. Reis & Brian C. Patrick, *Attachment and Intimacy: Component Processes, in* SOCIAL PSYCHOLOGY: HANDBOOK OF BASIC PRINCIPLES 523–63 (A. Kruglanski & E. T. Higgins eds., 1996).

135. JOHN HARVEY & JULIA OMARZU, MINDING THE CLOSE RELATIONSHIP: A THEORY OF RELATIONSHIP ENHANCEMENT 11 (1999).

136. *Id.* at 11–18. For a discussion of this second aspect—what psychologists call "attribution style"—*see* Thomas N. Bradbury & Frank D. Fincham, *Assessing Attributions in Marriage: The Relationship Attribution Measure*, 62 J. PERSONALITY & SOC. PSYCHOL. 457 (1992).

137. Amy Strachman, *Close Relationships, in* THE ENCYCLOPEDIA OF POSITIVE PSYCHOLOGY 181–82 (Shane J. Lopez ed., 2009).

138. For an extended discussion of this idea, *see* Clare Huntington, *Repairing Family Law*, 57 Duke L.J. 1245, 1247 (2008) (discussing the theories of Melanie Klein and other articulations of this cycle of intimacy).

139. *See, e.g.,* Nicholas Tavuchis, Mea Culpa: A Sociology of Apology and Reconciliation 37–44 (1991) (discussing the important tradition of apology, a form of repair, in Japanese culture); Michele Stephen, *Reparation and the Gift*, 28 Ethos 119, 127–38 (2000) (describing Kleinian themes of repair in numerous non-Western cultures, particularly in Melanesia and New Guinea).

140. *See, e.g.,* The New Encyclopedia of Judaism 89 (Geoffrey Wigoder et al. eds., 2002) (discussing Yom Kippur but noting that "the Day of Atonement can help bring atonement…only for offenses against God," whereas "[f]or those sins committed against one's fellow man, atonement is granted only after the sinner has made full restitution and sought the offended party's forgiveness"); Walpola Rahula, What the Buddha Taught 46 (2d ed. 1974) (describing compassion in Buddhist tradition); David B. Burrell, *Interfaith Perspectives on Reconciliation, in* The Politics of Past Evil 113, 122 (Daniel Philpott ed., 2006) ("the Islamic path of reconciliation becomes receiving one another under the canopy of God's prevailing mercy, to which all practicing Muslims feel themselves beholden. It is less a matter of making specific amends for personal injury than a mutual recognition that we are walking a path together, along which we all stumble, so that we are each empowered to welcome the other back, even when that means stepping across a divide exacerbated by personal injury"); *Matthew* 5:23–24 (King James) ("Therefore if thou bring thy gift to the altar, and there rememberest that thy brother hath ought against thee; Leave there thy gift before the altar, and go thy way; first be reconciled to thy brother, and then come and offer thy gift").

141. The reparative drive, for example, is an important aspect of the sociology of relationships, as sociologist Charles Tilly has explored in his work on narrative and conduct. *See* Charles Tilly, Why? 15 (2006). Tilly contends that a core human tendency is to provide reasons for conduct and that providing a reason is a way to confirm, establish, negotiate, or repair a relationship. *See id.* at 15, 19–20. Reasons fall into four categories: conventions, stories, codes, and technical accounts. *See id.* at 15. Depending on the context, it is possible to repair relationships using any of the four types of reasons, but stories are a particularly powerful way to do so, because they make the exceptional understandable and thus are particularly relevant in the context of unusual life events, such as marriage and divorce. *See id.* at 16, 95. Anthropologists likewise describe phases of conflict within a society, echoing the phases of human intimacy. In anthropological terms, a breach, in which a norm is violated, is followed by a crisis, in which the breach grows and taps into an underlying division within the society, and is later followed by redressive action, in which formal or informal mechanisms are used to restore peace and ensure reintegration. Victor Turner, Dramas, Fields, and Metaphors: Symbolic Action in Human Society 38–42 (1974). If the redressive action fails, the fourth phase becomes one of "irreparable schism." *Id.* at 41. Similarly, political scientists recognize the catalytic power of productive guilt in transitional justice efforts. *See generally* My Neighbor, My Enemy: Justice and Community in the Aftermath of Mass Atrocity (Eric Stover & Harvey M. Weinstein eds., 2004) (discussing the process of rebuilding after genocide and ethnic cleansing, including the role of trials and tribunals and offering a model of social reconstruction as an alternative).

142. Eli J. Finkel, Lauren E. Scissors & Jeni L. Burnette, *Vengefully Ever After: Destiny Beliefs, State Attachment Anxiety, and Forgiveness*, 92 J. Personality & Soc. Psychol. 871, 871 (2007) (listing these studies). Acting on these impulses, however, undermines the relationship. *See id.* Additionally, the cycle of emotions, and hence the reparative drive, can be hindered by other human tendencies, such as denial and rationalization. *See* R. D. Hinshelwood, Clinical Klein: From Theory to Practice 266 (1994).

143. This discussion relies on Robert G. Madden, *From Theory to Practice: A Family Systems Approach to the Law, in* Relationship-Centered Lawyering: Social Science Theory for Transforming Legal Practice 140–56 (Susan L. Brooks & Robert G. Madden eds., 2010).

144. *See* Naomi Schoenbaum, *Mobility Measures*, 2012 BYU L. Rev. 1169, 1194–1203 (2012); Melissa Murray, *The Networked Family: Reframing the Legal Understanding of Caregiving and Caregivers*, 94 Va. L. Rev. 385, 390–91 (2008); Ethan J. Leib, *Friendship and the Law*, 54 UCLA L. Rev. 631, 654–55 (2007).

145. Lucille Nahemow & M. Powell Lawton, *Similarity and Propinquity in Friendship Formation*, 32 J. Personality & Soc. Psychol. 205, 209–10 (1975).

146. *Id.* at 209.

147. *Id.* at 210 (residents who reported a friend of different age and race lived on the same floor as that friend 70 percent of the time, compared with living in different buildings only 12 percent of the time).

148. Frances E. Kuo et al. *Fertile Ground for Community: Inner-City Neighborhood Common Spaces*, 26 Am. J. Community Psychol. 823, 825 (1998).

149. *Id.* at 826.

150. *Id.* at 843.

151. Frances E. Kuo & William C. Sullivan, *Environment and Crime in the Inner City: Does Vegetation Reduce Crime?*, 33 Env't & Behav. 343, 358 (2001).

152. *Id.* at 348; *see also* Kuo et al., *supra* note 151, at 828.

153. *See* Stephanie E. Bothwell, Raymond Gindroz & Robert E. Long, Fannie Mae Foundation, *Restoring Community through Traditional Neighborhood Design: A Case Study of Diggs Town Public Housing*, 9 Housing Policy Debate 89, 90 (1998).

154. Amy Wilkerson et al., *Neighborhood Physical Features and Relationships with Neighbors: Does Positive Physical Environment Increase Neighborliness?*, 44 Env't & Behav. 595, 605–06 (2012).

155. *Id.* at 607.

156. *See* Katharine B. Silbaugh, *Women's Place: Urban Planning, Housing Design, and Work-Family Balance*, 76 Fordham L. Rev. 1797, 1818–35 (2007). I develop this idea in greater detail in chapter 3.

157. This is not a critique of positive psychology. Indeed, positive psychologists readily acknowledge the ancient roots of their ideas. *See* Seligman, *supra* note 38, at 11.

158. The Nicomachean Ethics of Aristotle book I, ch. II, at 5 (J. E. C. Welldon trans., 1892). This translation uses the word "happiness" instead of "eudaimonia."

159. *Id.* book I, ch. VI, at 15.

160. *Id.*

161. *Id.* book I, ch. IX, at 18–21.

162. *Id.* book IX, ch. IX, at 305.

163. *Id.* book VIII, ch. I, at 246; *id.* book VIII, ch. V, at 253–54; *id.* book VIII, ch. XIV, at 273–74.

164. *Id.* book VIII, ch. I, at 245.

165. Roy F. Baumeister & Mark R. Leary, *The Need to Belong: Desire for Interpersonal Attachments as a Fundamental Human Motivation*, 117 PSYCHOL. BULL. 497, 497 (1995).

166. *Id.* at 497, 501–03.

CHAPTER 2

1. DAPHNE LOFQUIST ET AL., U.S. CENSUS BUREAU, HOUSEHOLDS AND FAMILIES: 2010, at 5 (2012), *available at* http://www.census.gov/prod/cen2010/briefs/c2010br-14.pdf (tbl. 2, 20.2 down from 23.5 percent in 2000). This statistic overstates the number of "truly traditional" families, because the Census does not distinguish between a married couple raising their own biological or adopted children and a blended family, where the married couple may be jointly raising children from other marriages. The category is simply for "husband-wife households with own children," *see id.*, and the narrative makes clear that "[b]iological, adopted, and stepchildren of the householder who are under 18 are the 'own children' of the householder." *See id.* at 4.

2. James R. Wetzel, *American Families: 75 Years of Change*, MONTHLY LAB. REV., Mar. 1990, at 4, 10, *available at* http://www.bls.gov/mlr/1990/03/art1full.pdf (chart 4 showing "Composition of American Households").

3. D'VERA COHN, JEFFREY S. PASSEL & WENDY WANG, PEW RESEARCH CTR., BARELY HALF OF U.S. ADULTS ARE MARRIED—A RECORD LOW 1 (2011), *available at* http://media.al.com/bn/other/Marriage-report-Pew-Research-Center-Dec-2011.pdf (statistics from Pew Research Center analyses of U.S. Census data). The data are for all adults eighteen and older.

4. *Id.* at 8.

5. *Id.*

6. *Id.*

7. *Id.*

8. *2010 ACS Sample*, INTEGRATED PUBLIC USE MICRODATA SERIES (hereinafter *2010 ACS Sample*, IPUMS USA), *available at* http://usa.ipums.org/usa/index.shtml (follow "Analyze Data Online," select "2010 ACS," make table with "row" marst, "column" sex, "filter" age [18–*], inctot [*–12,000], race [2], and for "weight" select none]).

9. For marriage rates of African Americans, *see id.* (follow "Analyze Data Online," select "2010 ACS," make table with "row" marst, "column" sex, "filter" age [18–*],inctot [70,000–*], race [2], and for "weight" select none). For African Americans, marriage rates also vary by gender: 70 percent of upper-income African American men are married, but only 45 percent of upper-income African American women are married. *See id.* (marriage-rate data for gender filtered for age [18+], race [black], total personal income [>$70,000]). This pattern is reversed for low-income African Americans: 25 percent of low-income African American women are married as compared with only 20 percent of African American men. *See id.* (marriage-rate data for gender filtered for age [18+], race [black], total personal income [<$12,000]). For marriage rates of whites, *see id.* (follow "Analyze Data Online," select "2010 ACS," make table with "row" marst, "column" sex, "filter" age [18–*]; inctot [70,000–*], race [1], and for "weight" select none).

10. ROSE M. KREIDER, INCREASE IN OPPOSITE-SEX COHABITING COUPLES FROM 2009 TO 2010 IN THE ANNUAL SOCIAL AND ECONOMIC SUPPLEMENT TO THE CURRENT

POPULATION SURVEY 1 (U.S. Census Bureau, Working Paper, 2010), *available at* http://www.census.gov/population/www/socdemo/Inc-Opp-sex-2009-to-2010.pdf (citing the 2010 figure of 7.5 million); U.S. Bureau of the Census, 1960 Census of Population, PC(2)-4B, "Persons by Family Characteristics," tbl. 15, data available at www.census.gov/population/socdemo/hh-fam/uc1.xls (listing the 1960 census data on unmarried couples but also noting that the number is not entirely accurate because the 1960 census simply asked about the presence of two unmarried, opposite-sex adults and did not ask the respondent to specify whether the adults were partners); *see also* CATHERINE FITCH, RON GOEKEN & STEVEN RUGGLES, MINN. POP. CTR., THE RISE OF COHABITATION IN THE UNITED STATES: NEW HISTORICAL ESTIMATES, 2–3 (2005), *available at* http://www.hist.umn.edu/~ruggles/cohab-revised2.pdf (describing this flaw in the 1960 Census data collection and noting that it led to an overcount of cohabitants). Thus, the increase in cohabitation is even greater than the numbers in the text suggest. This increase in cohabitation is continuing. In 2010, 7 percent of American adults ages thirty to forty-four were cohabiting, as compared with only 3 percent in 1995. *See* RICHARD FRY & D'VERA COHN, PEW RESEARCH CTR., LIVING TOGETHER: THE ECONOMICS OF COHABITATION 7 (2011), *available at* www.pewsocialtrends.org/2011/06/27/living-together-the-economics-of-cohabitation/. The number of Americans who have *ever* cohabited is much higher. In 2009–2010, 65 percent of women ages nineteen to forty-four had ever cohabited, compared with 45 percent in 2005. WENDY MANNING, NAT'L CTR. FOR FAMILY & MARRIAGE RESEARCH, TRENDS IN COHABITATION: OVER TWENTY YEARS OF CHANGE, 1987–2010, at 1 fig.1 (2013), *available at* http://ncfmr.bgsu.edu/pdf/family_profiles/file130944.pdf.

11. Galena K. Rhoades, Scott M. Stanley & Howard J. Markman, *The Pre-Engagement Cohabitation Effect: A Replication and Extension of Previous Findings*, 23 J. FAM. PSYCHOL. 107, 107 (2009) ("Upwards of 70% of couples now" cohabitate before marriage).

12. PAULA GOODWIN, WILLIAM MOSHER & ANJANI CHANDRA, U.S. DEP'T HEALTH & HUM. SERVS., VITAL & HEALTH STATISTICS SER. 23 NO. 28, MARRIAGE AND COHABITATION IN THE UNITED STATES: A STATISTICAL PORTRAIT BASED ON CYCLE 6 (2002) OF THE NATIONAL SURVEY OF FAMILY GROWTH 12, fig.18 (2010), *available at* http://www.cdc.gov/nchs/data/series/sr_23/sr23_028.pdf (showing probability, by educational status, of transitioning from cohabitation to marriage within three years).

13. FRY & COHN, *supra* note 10, at 15–17 (describing the correlation between income and cohabitation); GOODWIN, MOSHER & CHANDRA, *supra* note 12, at 13 (noting that a white woman in her first cohabitation had a 27-percent chance of transitioning to marriage within one year, a Latino woman had a 21-percent chance, and an African American woman had a 14-percent chance).

14. ANDREW CHERLIN, THE MARRIAGE-GO-ROUND: THE STATE OF MARRIAGE AND THE FAMILY IN AMERICA TODAY 17 (2009).

15. STEPHANIE VENTURA, NAT'L CENTER FOR HEALTH STATISTICS, CTRS. FOR DISEASE CONTROL & PREVENTION, DATA BRIEF NO. 18, CHANGING PATTERNS OF NONMARITAL CHILDBEARING IN THE UNITED STATES 1 (2009), *available at* www.cdc.gov/nchs/data/databriefs/db18.htm (fig. 1 showing percentage of births to unmarried women, United States, 1940–2007).

16. JOYCE A. MARTIN ET AL., NAT'L CTR. FOR HEALTH STATISTICS, CTRS. FOR DISEASE CONTROL & PREVENTION, BIRTHS: FINAL DATA FOR 2010, 61 NAT'L VITAL STATS. REP. 1, 8 (2012), *available at* http://www.cdc.gov/nchs/data/nvsr/nvsr61/nvsr61_01.pdf (tbl. C showing percentage of births to unmarried women).

17. U.S. Dep't Health & Hum. Servs., Ctrs. for Disease Control and Prevention, Vital Stats—Births, *available at* http://www.cdc.gov/nchs/data_access/vitalstats/VitalStats_Births.htm (follow "National" hyperlink under "Birth Tables," "Characteristics of Mother"; then select "Demographic Characteristics of Mother—2010") (458,637 out of 636,425 African American births were to unmarried mothers [72.1 percent], 504,411 out of 945,180 Latino births were to unmarried mothers [53.4 percent]).

18. Betzaida Tejada-Vera & Paul D. Sutton, Nat'l Ctr. for Health Statistics, Births, Marriages, Divorces, and Deaths: Provisional Data for 2009, 58 Nat'l Vital Stats. Rep. 1, 1–2 (2010), *available at* http://www.cdc.gov/nchs/data/nvsr58/nvsr58_25.pdf (explaining reporting processes).

19. *See, e.g.*, Americans for Divorce Reform, http://www.divorcereform.org/about.html ("[T]he constant question is, what do you use as the denominator of the fraction or ratio? Do you weigh people getting divorced per year against the number of people who are getting married that same year, or against people who got married when the divorcing people got married, or against everyone who is married, or whoever has been, or do you try to project how many people who are getting married will divorce in the future, disregarding older people who are in more stable marriages?").

20. Diana B. Elliot & Tavia Simmons, U.S. Census Bureau, Marital Events of Americans: 2009, at 8 (2011), *available at* http://www.census.gov/prod/2011pubs/acs-13.pdf (tbl. 2, Characteristics of Those Married, Divorced, and Widowed in the Last 12 Months, by Sex: 2009).

21. Matthew D. Bramlett & William D. Mosher, Ctrs. for Disease Control & Prevention, Advance Data No. 323, First Marriage Dissolution, Divorce, and Remarriage: United States 5 (2001), *available at* http://www.cdc.gov/nchs/data/ad/ad323.pdf ("After 10 years of marriage, 48 percent of marriages of women under age 18 years at marriage have disrupted compared with 40 percent of marriages of women who were 18–19 years of age at marriage, 29 percent of marriages of women who were 20–24 years of age at marriage, and 24 percent of marriages of women at least 25 years of age at marriage").

22. Pew Research Ctr., The Decline of Marriage and Rise of New Families 38 (2010), *available at* http://www.pewsocialtrends.org/files/2010/11/pew-social-trends-2010-families.pdf.

23. Fragile Families and Child Wellbeing Study, Fact Sheet, *available at* http://www.fragilefamilies.princeton.edu/documents/FragileFamiliesandChildWellbeingStudyFactSheet.pdf; Sara S. McLanahan, *Fragile Families and the Marriage Agenda, in* Fragile Families and the Marriage Agenda 1–2 (Lori Kowaleski-Jones & Nicholas H. Wolfinger eds., 2006).

24. Rose M. Kreider & Renee Ellis, U.S. Census Bureau, Living Arrangements of Children: 2009 3–4 (2011), *available at* http://www.census.gov/prod/2011pubs/p70-126.pdf (23.6 percent of children live with a single mother; 3.7 percent live with a single father).

25. David T. Ellwood & Christopher Jencks, *The Spread of Single-Parent Families in the United States since 1960, in* The Future of the Family 35 (Daniel P. Moynihan, Timothy M. Smeeding & Lee Rainwater eds., 2004).

26. *2010 ACS Sample*, IPUMS USA, *supra* note 8, http://usa.ipums.org/usa/index.shtml, (follow "Analyze Data Online," select "2010 ACS," make table with "row" race, "filter" marst [3–6], nchild [1–*], and for "weight" select "perwt"). Data filtered for unmarried people living with one or more of their own children, showing 23.5 percent of this population is African American. For data on

race and the overall population, here and in the subsequent notes, *see* U.S. CENSUS BUREAU, USA PEOPLE QUICKFACTS (2013), *available at* http://quickfacts.census.gov/qfd/states/00000.html.

27. *Id.* (follow "Analyze Data Online," select "2010 ACS," make table with "row" hispan, "filter" marst [3–6], nchild [1–*], and for "weight" select "perwt"). Data filtered for unmarried people living with one or more of their own children, showing 19.4 percent of this population is Latino.

28. *Id.* (of the unmarried people living with one or more of their own children, 64 percent of this population is white; follow "Analyze Data Online," select "2010 ACS," make table with "row" race, "filter" marst [3–6], nchild [1–*], and for "weight" select "perwt"), but 80.6 percent of this "white" category is not Latino (for these data, follow "Analyze Data Online," select "2010 ACS," make table with "row" hispan, "filter" marst [3–6], nchild [1–*], and for "weight" select "perwt"), meaning that the non-Latino white population accounts for 53 percent of the single-parent population).

29. *Id.* (follow "Analyze Data Online," select "2010 ACS," make table with "row" race, "filter" marst [3–6], nchild [1–*], and for "weight" select "perwt"). Data filtered for unmarried people living with one or more of their own children, showing 3.3 percent of this population is of Asian descent, compared with 5 percent of the population at large. For general percentage of Asian Americans in the United States, *see id.* (follow "Analyze Data Online," select "2010 ACS," make table with "row" race).

30. TIMOTHY S. GRALL, U.S. CENSUS BUREAU, CUSTODIAL MOTHERS AND FATHERS AND THEIR CHILD SUPPORT: 2007, at 4 (2009), *available at* http://www.census.gov/prod/2009pubs/p60-237.pdf (fig. 1 showing Poverty Status of Custodial Parents).

31. U.S. CENSUS BUREAU, POV07: FAMILIES WITH RELATED CHILDREN UNDER 18 BY NUMBER OF WORKING FAMILY MEMBERS AND FAMILY STRUCTURE: 2010, http://www.census.gov/hhes/www/cpstables/032011/pov/new07_200_01.htm (below 200 percent of poverty). The statistic is for single-mother families with related children younger than eighteen.

32. CHERLIN, *supra* note 14 at, 16–19.

33. *Id.* at 17.

34. *Id.* at 18.

35. *Id.* at 19–20.

36. Cynthia Osborne et al., *Instability in Fragile Families: The Role of Race-Ethnicity, Economics, and Relationship Quality* 13, 36 (Ctr. for Family and Demographic Research, Bowling Green State Univ., Working Paper No. 2005-02, 2005), *available at* www.bgsu.edu/downloads/cas/file35693.pdf.

37. Gunnar Andersson, *Children's Experience of Family Disruption and Family Formation: Evidence from 16 FFS Countries*, 7 DEMOGRAPHIC RES. 343, 353 (2002), *available at* http://www.demographic-research.org/volumes/vol7/7/.

38. *Id.* Additionally, the amount of time a child will spend with a single parent is also higher: Children born to cohabiting parents spend approximately 25 percent of their childhood with a single parent, 25 percent with two cohabiting parents, and 50 percent with married parents, whereas children born to married parents spend 84 percent of their childhood in a two-parent family. *See* Larry Bumpass & Hsien-Hen Lu, *Trends in Cohabitation and Implications for Children's Family Contexts in the United States*, 54 POPULATION STUD. 29, 37–38 (2000).

39. For a good overview, *see* http://www.freedomtomarry.org/states/.

40. United States v. Windsor, 133 S. Ct. 2675, 2695 (2013) (holding that the Defense of Marriage Act is unconstitutional as a deprivation of liberty).

41. *See* DAPHNE LOFQUIST, U.S. CENSUS BUREAU, SAME-SEX COUPLE HOUSEHOLDS 2 (2011), *available at* http://www.census.gov/prod/2011pubs/acsbr10-03.pdf. There are reasons to believe that the census significantly undercounts same-sex families. *See* DAVID M. SMITH & GARY J. GATES, HUMAN RIGHTS CAMPAIGN, GAY AND LESBIAN FAMILIES IN THE UNITED STATES: SAME-SEX UNMARRIED PARTNER HOUSEHOLDS 1–3 (2001), *available at* www.urban. org/UploadedPDF/1000491_gl_partner_households.pdf (estimating that "gay and lesbian families could be undercounted as much as 62 percent").

42. Gary J. Gates, *Family Formation and Raising Children among Same-Sex Couples*, FAM. FOCUS (Nat'l Council on Fam. Relations, Minneapolis, Minn.), Winter 2011, at F3.

43. *See* NAOMI CAHN, THE NEW KINSHIP: CONSTRUCTING DONOR CONCEIVED FAMILIES 2 (2013) (estimating that 50,000 children a year are born from donated eggs and sperm).

44. *Id.* at 53.

45. *Id.* at 52–54.

46. *Id.* at 55.

47. *Id.* at 54.

48. *Id.* at 66, 78.

49. *Id.* at 62, 84–85.

50. *Id.* at 84.

51. Wendy Sigle-Rushton & Sara McLanahan, *Father Absence and Child Well-Being: A Critical Review*, in THE FUTURE OF THE FAMILY 116, 120–21 (Daniel P. Moynihan, Timothy M. Smeeding & Lee Rainwater eds., 2004).

52. *Id.* at 121; *see also* Thomas E. Smith, *Parental Separation and the Academic Self-Concepts of Adolescents: An Effort to Solve the Puzzle of Separation Effects*, 52 J. MARRIAGE & FAM. 107, 113, 116 (1990).

53. Sigle-Rushton & McLanahan, *supra* note 51, at 121.

54. *Id.* at 122–23.

55. Sigle-Rushton & McLanahan, *supra* note 51, at 123.

56. *Id.* at 124.

57. *See id.* at 124–25; Jane Waldfogel, Terry-Ann Craigie & Jeanne Brooks-Gunn, *Fragile Families and Child Wellbeing*, 20 FUTURE OF CHILDREN 87, 97–99 (2010).

58. Sigle-Rushton & McLanahan, *supra* note 51, at 125.

59. For just one example, *see* Robert L. Flewelling & Karl E. Bauman, *Family Structure as Predictor of Initial Substance Use and Sexual Intercourse in Early Adolescence*, 52 J. MARRIAGE & FAM. 171, 178 (1990) (finding that children growing up in single-parent households are almost twice as likely to have sex at an earlier age than their counterparts growing up in two-parent households). There is some evidence that the poor outcomes for adolescents in single-parent homes are mediated in multigenerational homes when the single mother lives with her parents who also help care for the child. Two researchers found that even after controlling for income, parenting behavior, and home and school characteristics among the study participants, the outcomes for adolescents in multigenerational homes (measured by high school graduation, college attendance, and substance abuse) were at least as good as for adolescents in married families. *See* Thomas Deleire & Ariel Kalil, *Good Things Come in Threes: Single-Parent Multigenerational Family Structure and Adolescent Adjustment*, 39 DEMOGRAPHY 393, 407–11 (2002). Most of the multigenerational families in the data set were low-income and African American. The researchers looked at two types of multigenerational homes: never-married single mothers living with their parents and

divorced single mothers living with their parents. The outcomes were best for the never-married single mothers in the multigenerational households, although the researchers note that their sample size was small. In these families, the children had better outcomes than children in married homes. For the divorced single mothers in multigenerational households, the outcomes were not different from those for children in married homes. *See id.* This study should be taken as only preliminary evidence of the beneficial effect of multigenerational homes, because, as the authors readily acknowledge, they had to omit a large portion of the participants in the data set because there was no information on the family structure, and yet these individuals, as a group, had poorer outcomes. *See id.* at 395–96. For a study concluding that the differences in child outcomes are attributable to factors other than family structure, *see* Kevin Lang & Jay L. Zagorsky, *Does Growing Up with a Parent Absent Really Hurt?* 36 J. Hum. Resources 253 (2001).

60. Andrea J. Sedlak et al., U.S. Dep't Health & Hum. Servs., Fourth National Incidence Study of Child Abuse and Neglect (NIS-4): Report to Congress, Executive Summary 12 (2010), *available at* http://www.acf.hhs.gov/sites/default/files/opre/nis4_report_exec_summ_pdf_jan2010.pdf.

61. Susan L. Brown, *Family Structure and Child Well-Being: The Significance of Parental Cohabitation*, 66 J. Marriage & Fam. 351, 355, 357 (2004). The study asked questions about children's relationships with others, performance in school, ability to concentrate, behavioral maturity, tendency to lie, feelings of depression, and so on.

62. *Id.* at 364.

63. *Id.*; Susan D. Stewart, *How the Birth of a Child Affects Involvement with Stepchildren*, 67 J. Marriage & Fam. 461, 462 (2005) (summarizing the literature); Sandra L. Hofferth & Kermyt G. Anderson, *Are All Dads Equal? Biology versus Marriage as a Basis for Paternal Investment*, 65 J. Marriage & Fam. 213, 227, 230 (2003) (examining the engagement and availability of residential fathers, biological and nonbiological, in married and cohabiting families and finding that in both types of families, the nonbiological fathers spent less time with the children than in families with married, biological fathers); Wendy Manning & K. A. Lamb, *Adolescent Well-Being in Cohabiting, Married, and Single-Parent Families*, 65 J. Marriage & Fam., 876, 879, 890 (2003) (using data from the National Longitudinal Study of Adolescent Health to look at outcomes for children in cohabiting stepfamilies and single-mother homes and finding that they are largely the same; children living with cohabiting stepparents score lower on tests for social and emotional well-being, and stepparents are less involved in their stepchildren's lives than biological parents in intact households, sharing fewer meals, reading less often, and participating in fewer outside activities).

64. Sigle-Rushton & McLanahan, *supra* note 51, at 124.

65. *See* E. Mavis Hetherington, *Should We Stay Together for the Sake of the Children?*, in Coping with Divorce, Single Parenting, and Remarriage 99 (E. Mavis Hetherington ed., 1999); Donna R. Morrison & Mary Jo Coiro, *Parental Conflict and Marital Disruption: Do Children Benefit When High-Conflict Marriages Are Dissolved?*, J. Marriage & Fam. 626, 634–35 (1999) ("parents remaining married is not a better alternative for children when conflict between the parents is high. Indeed, the largest increase in scores on the Behavior Problems Index were observed for the children whose parents remained in such marriages"). There is an exception, however, for couples who continue to fight after the divorce. In this context, divorce researcher Mavis Hetherington, a sociologist, has found that "if conflict is going to continue [postdivorce], it is better for children to remain in an acrimonious two-parent household than to divorce." Hetherington, *supra*, at 101.

66. *See* Paul R. Amato & Alan Booth, A Generation at Risk: Growing Up in an Era of Family Upheaval 219–20 (1997) (noting that when divorces are preceded by a long period of interpersonal conflict, children tend to have positive outcomes once these parents divorce and the children are removed from the highly contentious environment and that young adults who perceived their parents' marriage as conflicted had less psychological distress and higher levels of overall life satisfaction if their parents divorced); Hetherington, *supra* note 65, at 114–15.

67. Hetherington, *supra* note 65, at 114.

68. E. Mavis Hetherington & John Kelly, For Better or for Worse: Divorce Reconsidered 3, 157–59, 94 (2003).

69. *Id.*, at 94–96, 114; Amato & Booth, *supra* note 66, at 219.

70. Hetherington, *supra* note 65, at 94, 114–15.

71. Judith Wallerstein, Julia Lewis & Sandra Blakeslee, The Unexpected Legacy of Divorce: A 25 Year Landmark Study 299 (2000) ("it's in adulthood that children of divorce suffer the most. The impact of divorce hits them most cruelly as they go in search of love, sexual intimacy, and commitment. Their lack of inner images of a man and a woman in a stable relationship and their memories of their parents' failure to sustain the marriage badly [hobble] their search, leading them to heartbreak and even despair. They cried, 'No one taught me'…they have no good models on which to build their hopes").

72. Paul R. Amato, *Reconciling Divergent Perspectives: Judith Wallerstein, Quantitative Family Research, and Children of Divorce*, 52 Fam. Rel. 332, 338–39 (2003).

73. Janet R. Johnston, *High-Conflict Divorce*, 4 Future of Children 165, 166 (1994), *available at* www.princeton.edu/futureofchildren/publications/docs/04_01_09.pdf.

74. *Id.* at 173 ("parents whose joint custody arrangements were court-ordered or court recommended were more likely to be classified as 'failed' or 'stressed,' and their children were more likely to be symptomatic or at high risk in terms of their behavioral, emotional, and social adjustment").

75. Robert Emery, *The Consequences of Divorce for Children: Postdivorce Family Life for Children, in* The Postdivorce Family: Children, Parenting, and Society 16 (Ross A. Thompson & Paul R. Amato eds., 1999).

76. *Id.*

77. Amato & Booth, *supra* note 66, at 219.

78. Robert E. Emery, Marriage, Divorce, and Children's Adjustment 52 (1999).

79. E. Mark Cummings & Christine E. Merrilees, *Identifying the Dynamic Process Underlying Links between Marital Conflict and Child Adjustment, in* Strengthening Couple Relationships for Optimal Child Development: Lessons from Research and Intervention 27, 28–32 (Marc S. Schulz et al. eds., 2010). The authors distinguish constructive marital conflict from destructive marital conflict, noting that "it is not whether couples fight but how they fight that is most pertinent to the well-being of adults, children, and families." *Id.* at 36. Constructive marital conflict does not threaten the physical safety of family members or the stability of the family; further, it maintains emotional bonds throughout the conflict. *See id.; see also* E. Mark Cummings et al., *Interparental Discord and Child Adjustment: Prospective Investigations of Emotional Security as an Explanatory Mechanism*, 77 Child Dev. 132 (2006).

80. Judith A. Seltzer, *Father by Law: Effects of Joint Legal Custody on Nonresident Fathers' Involvement with Children*, 35 Demography 135, 144 (1998) (citing "the consistent finding of a positive effect of joint legal custody on frequency of visits").

81. Mindy E. Scott et al., *Postdivorce Father-Adolescent Closeness*, 69 J. MARRIAGE & FAM. 1194, 1195 (2007) (summarizing research).

82. E. Mavis Hetherington, Martha Cox & Roger Cox, *Effects of Divorce on Parents and Children, in* NONTRADITIONAL FAMILIES: PARENTING AND CHILD DEVELOPMENT 233, 246 (Michael E. Lamb ed., 1982) (noting that fathers who had been highly involved before divorce "reported that they could not endure the pain of seeing their children only intermittently, and by 2 years after divorce had coped with this stress by seeing their children infrequently although they continued to experience a great sense of loss and depression"); HETHERINGTON & KELLY, *supra* note 68, at 120 (citing a longitudinal study of fourteen hundred families, in which researchers found that "a surprising number of men stay away because they find being all the way out of a child's life less painful than being halfway in it").

83. Hetherington, Cox & Cox, *supra* note 82, at 246.

84. Solangel Maldonado, *Beyond Economic Fatherhood: Encouraging Divorced Fathers to Parent*, 153 U. PA. L. REV. 921, 983 (2005) (referring to "sociolegal forces that discourage paternal involvement and fail to provide incentives for them to remain involved").

85. Judith Stacey & Timothy J. Biblarz, *(How) Does the Sexual Orientation of Parents Matter?*, 66 AM. SOC. REV. 159, 167–72 (2001). For additional studies reaching the same conclusion, *see* Michael J. Rosenfeld, *Nontraditional Families and Childhood Progress through School*, 47 DEMOGRAPHY 755, 770 (2010) (using Census data to perform a large-scale, nationally representative analysis of school outcomes for children of same-sex couples and finding that after controlling for parental socioeconomic status and student characteristics such as learning disabilities, there were no educational differences between children of same-sex couples and children of opposite-sex couples through primary school); Stephen Erich et al., *Gay and Lesbian Adoptive Families: An Exploratory Study of Family Functioning, Adoptive Child's Behavior, and Familial Support Networks*, 9 J. FAM. SOC. WORK 17, 21, 27–28 (2005) (studying adoptive families, forty-seven with same-sex parents and sixty-eight with opposite-sex parents, and finding that same-sex partners were able to meet the demands of effective family functioning and access effective support networks, further finding no significant differences in behavioral problems among the children raised by same-sex parents).

86. Jennifer L. Wainright, Stephen T. Russell & Charlotte J. Patterson, *Psychosocial Adjustment, School Outcomes, and Romantic Relationships of Adolescents with Same-Sex Parents*, 75 CHILD DEV. 1886, 1895 (2004).

87. Nanette Gartrell & Henny Bos, *US National Longitudinal Lesbian Family Study: Psychological Adjustment of 17-Year-Old Adolescents*, 126 PEDIATRICS 1, 6–7 (2010), *available at* http://pediatrics.aappublications.org/content/early/2010/06/07/peds.2009-3153.full.pdf+html.

88. Consider the women who gave birth in 2011. Beginning with age, of all the women ages fifteen to nineteen who gave birth that year, 86 percent of the births were nonmarital, and of the women ages twenty to twenty-four, 62 percent of the births were nonmarital. RACHEL M. SHATTUCK & ROSE M. KREIDER, U.S. CENSUS BUREAU, SOCIAL AND ECONOMIC CHARACTERISTICS OF CURRENTLY UNMARRIED WOMEN WITH A RECENT BIRTH: 2011, at 4 (2013), *available at* http://www.census.gov/prod/2013pubs/acs-21.pdf. By contrast, for women aged thirty to thirty-four, only 19 percent of the births were nonmarital. *Id.* Turning to income, for women who had a household income of less than $10,000, 69 percent of the births were nonmarital; for women with a household income between $10,000 and $14,999, 61 percent of the

births were nonmarital. *Id.* The rate stays above the national average up to an income of $49,999. *Id.* By contrast, for women who had incomes between $150,000 and $199,999, only 14 percent of the births were nonmarital, and for women with a household income of at least $200,000, only 9 percent of the births were nonmarital. *See id.* Finally, considering education, of all the births by women with no high school diploma, 57 percent were nonmarital; and of all the births by women with only a high school diploma, 49 percent were nonmarital. *Id.* By contrast, only 9 percent of the births to women with a college degree were nonmarital. *Id.*

89. Hetherington, *supra* note 65, at 107–08.

90. *Id.* at 103.

91. For an example of the rare study focusing on middle- and upper-income single-mother families, *see* Elizabeth J. Kjellstrand & Melanie Harper, *Yes, She Can: An Examination of Resiliency Factors in Middle- and Upper-Income Single Mothers*, 53 J. Divorce & Remarriage 311, 323–24 (2012) (finding that middle- and upper-income mothers in the study were generally resilient but also noting considerable limitations in the study design).

92. Pew Research Ctr., *supra* note 22, at 11–12, 23.

93. Susan L. Brown, *supra* note 61, at 364. For the younger children, the differences in family income and parental resources explained the divergent outcomes for behavioral and emotional problems but not the level of school engagement. For the older children, the differences explained the level of school engagement but not the worse outcomes for behavioral and emotional problems.

94. To give another example, one review of empirical research found that income differences account for 30 to 50 percent of the differential in high school graduation rates but that family structure remained a salient factor. Sigle-Rushton & McLanahan, *supra* note 51, at 137.

95. Waldfogel, Craigie & Brooks-Gunn, *supra* note 57, at 92–93.

96. For more information about the ongoing Fragile Families Study, *see About Fragile Families*, Fragile Families and Child Wellbeing Study, http://www.fragilefamilies.princeton.edu/about.asp; McLanahan, *supra* note 23, at 6. The births are representative of all births in cities with populations of at least two hundred thousand. The animating study questions were trying to identify the resources and abilities of unmarried parents, with a particular focus on fathers, exploring the relationship between the unmarried parents, assessing the well-being of the children in the families, and gauging the effect of different policies and environmental conditions on both parents and children.

97. One of the factors the study is following is whether a couple marries soon after the birth of the child. Thus, the study is really tracking three groups: married at birth, married soon after birth, and never married. The findings in the text sometimes conflate the "unmarried at birth" and "married soon after birth" categories, because these groups have similar characteristics and similar outcomes, with a few exceptions not particularly relevant here, unless noted.

98. *See* McLanahan, *supra* note 23, at 6–14; Fact Sheet, *supra* note 23. The researchers found that the fathers who were married at the time of the birth of the child or who married shortly thereafter were more likely to be working than the fathers who did not marry; the married fathers also earned more money than the unmarried fathers who worked. Similarly, married mothers made significantly more money than unmarried mothers (an average of $12.50 per hour as opposed to $7 to $8 per hour). Looking at age, the unmarried parents were generally in their early twenties at the time of birth, as compared with the married parents, who tended to be in their late twenties and thirties.

99. Waldfogel, Craigie & Brooks-Gunn, *supra* note 57, at 100–04.

100. *See id.* at 87, 89. One way researchers try to do this is through longitudinal studies, such as the Fragile Families Study, which looks at families over time. This kind of study allows the researchers to identify events early in a child's life, such as a high-conflict parental relationship, that predate a family breakup and might separately influence the child's outcomes. *See* Sigle-Rushton & McLanahan, *supra* note 51, at 127.

101. The following description of the various factors possibly affecting child outcomes draws on the characteristics of the families in the Fragile Families Study and other data sets. *See* Waldfogel, Craigie & Brooks-Gunn, *supra* note 57, at 87 nn. 6–29.

102. GRALL, *supra* note 30, at 4–5 (fig. 1 showing Poverty Status of Custodial Parents).

103. *See* U.S. CENSUS BUREAU, STATISTICAL ABSTRACT OF THE UNITED STATES: 2012, at 463, tbl. 709 (2012), *available at* http://www.census.gov/compendia/statab/2012/tables/1280709.pdf.

104. ANNETTE LAREAU, UNEQUAL CHILDHOODS: CLASS RACE, AND FAMILY LIFE 248 (2003). Seventy-five percent of white children in the top income quartile participate in nonathletic extracurricular activities, compared with only 55 percent in the bottom income quartile. Robert D. Putnam, Carl B. Frederick & Kaisa Snellman, *Growing Class Gaps in Social Connectedness among American Youth, 1975–2009*, at 12–13 (July 12, 2012) (unpublished student paper, Harvard Kennedy School of Government), *available at* http://www.hks.harvard.edu/var/ezp_site/storage/fckeditor/file/SaguaroReport_DivergingSocialConnectedness_20120808.pdf. Sports participation has also diverged along income lines, with nearly 50 percent of the wealthier students participating in a sport compared with fewer than 25 percent of the lower-income students. *See id.* at 13. Participation in sports and other extracurricular clubs is correlated with academic performance and college attendance. *See id.* For a detailed portrait of two families—one headed by a single mother and the other by a married, opposite-sex couple—and the differences in their lives, *see* Jason DeParle, *Two Classes, Divided by "I Do,"* N.Y. TIMES, July 14, 2012, at A1, *available at* http://www.nytimes.com/2012/07/15/us/two-classes-in-america-divided-by-i-do.html?pagewanted=all.

105. Greg J. Duncan & Richard J. Murnane, *Economic Inequality: The Real Cause of the Urban School Problem*, CHI. TRIB., Oct. 6, 2011, *available at* http://articles.chicagotribune.com/2011-10-06/news/ct-perspec-1006-urban-20111006_1_poor-children-graduation-rate-gap.

106. *See generally* Doris R. Entwisle & Karl L. Alexander, *Summer Setback: Race, Poverty, School Composition, and Mathematics Achievement in the First Two Years of School*, 57 AM. SOC. REV. 72 (1992).

107. U.S. DEP'T EDUC., THE CONDITION OF EDUCATION 2013, at 80–81 (2013), *available at* http://nces.ed.gov/pubs2013/2013037.pdf. The concentration is particularly marked in urban areas, where 37 percent of students attend schools where at least 75 percent of students receive free or reduced-cost lunch. *Id.* at 81.

108. Lisa Black, *Spending Gap between State's Rich, Poor Schools Is Vast*, CHI. TRIB., Nov. 7, 2011, *available at* http://articles.chicagotribune.com/2011-11-07/news/ct-met-school-funding-gaps-20111107_1_spending-gap-taft-s-district-poorest-schools.

109. *Id.*

110. For data on Taft Elementary School, *see Taft Elementary School (K-5)*, ILLINOIS INTERACTIVE REPORT CARD, http://iirc.niu.edu/School.aspx?schoolid=560990860052020. For data on Rondout Elementary School, *see Rondout Elem School (K-8)*, ILLINOIS INTERACTIVE REPORT CARD, http://iirc.niu.edu/School.aspx?schoolid=340490720022001.

111. *Taft Elementary School (K–5)*, Illinois Interactive Report Card, http://iirc.niu.edu/School.aspx?schoolid=560990860052020; *Rondout Elementary School (K–8)*, Illinois Interactive Report Card, http://iirc.niu.edu/School.aspx?schoolid=340490720022001.

112. For a discussion of Lareau's methodology, including her definition of class, *see* Lareau, *supra* note 104, at app. A. The "middle-class" families included upper-middle-class families. *Id.* at 3.

113. *See id.* at 45.

114. *See id.* at 66.

115. *See id.* at 76.

116. *See id.* at 62. The concerted cultivation approach maps the skills needed for success in the modern workplace. *See id.* at 62, 81. Of course, part of this is circular: middle-class individuals are the workplace supervisors, and so it is their culture that becomes the dominant norm of the workplace.

117. Betty Hart & Todd R. Risley, Meaningful Differences in the Everyday Experience of Young American Children 29–30, 132 (1995).

118. *Id.* at 132.

119. *Id.* at 125–26 ("A major difference associated with social strata was in the amounts of prohibition parents gave their children. The professional parents gave their children an average of 5 prohibitions per hour; the welfare parents gave their children an average of 11.... There was a striking difference, too, in affirmative feedback. The professional parents gave their children affirmative feedback every other minute, more than 30 times per hour, twice as often as the working-class parents gave their children affirmative feedback and more than 5 times as often as parents in welfare families gave their children affirmative feedback. The children in welfare families heard a prohibition twice as often as they heard affirmative feedback").

120. *Id.*

121. *Id.* at 133–34 ("In the professional families the extraordinary amount of talk, the many different words, and the greater richness of nouns, modifiers, and past-tense verbs in parent utterances suggested a culture concerned with names, relationships, and recall. Parents seemed to be preparing their children to participate in a culture concerned with symbols and analytic problem solving. To ensure their children access to advanced education, parents spent time and effort developing their children's potential, asking questions and using affirmatives to encourage their children to listen, to notice how words refer and relate, and to practice the distinctions to be made among them....In the welfare families, the lesser amount of talk with its more frequent parent-initiated topics, imperatives, and prohibitions suggested a culture concerned with established customs. To teach socially acceptable behavior, language rich in nouns and modifiers was not called for; obedience, politeness, and conformity were more likely to be the keys to survival").

122. For an excellent summary of the effect of income and parental education on children's achievement, *see* Julia Isaacs & Katherine Magnuson, Ctr. On Children & Families at Brookings, Income and Education as Predictors of Children's School Readiness (2011), *available at* http://www.brookings.edu/~/media/research/files/reports/2011/12/15%20school%20readiness%20isaacs/1214_school_readiness_isaacs.pdf. As described in the text and this source, these factors are related. Income is correlated with other socioeconomic factors, like parents with higher levels of education and two-parent households, factors that might separately contribute to the higher levels of achievement, rather than the income itself.

123. *See* Waldfogel, Craigie & Brooks-Gunn, *supra* note 57, at 90.

124. Putnam, Frederick & Snellman, *supra* note 104, at 10–13 (noting the developmental time invested by mothers and fathers as classified by educational attainment of the mothers).

125. *Id.* at 11.

126. *See* Waldfogel, Craigie & Brooks-Gunn, *supra* note 57, at 90–91; John Mirowsky & Catherine E. Ross, *Depression, Parenthood, and Age at First Birth*, 54 Soc. Sci. & Med. 1281, 1293 (2002) (finding that maternal depression is greatest when the mother's first birth is before age twenty-three and the least likelihood of depression in first-time mothers around the age of thirty).

127. Kristin Turner & Marcia J. Carlson, *Multipartnered Fertility and Depression among Fragile Families*, 73 J. Marriage Fam. 570, 577–80, 583 (2011).

128. *Id.* at 583.

129. Jacinta Bronte-Tinkew et al., *Symptoms of Major Depression in a Sample of Fathers of Infants: Sociodemographic Correlates and Links to Father Involvement*, 28 J. Fam. Issues 61, 81–84 (2007).

130. Sara S. McLanahan & Irwin Garfinkel, *Fragile Families: Debates, Facts, and Solutions*, *in* Marriage at the Crossroads: Law, Policy, and the Brave New World of Twenty-First Century Families 148 (Marsha Garrison & Elizabeth S. Scott eds., 2012); Sara McLanahan, *Diverging Destinies: How Children Are Faring under the Second Demographic Transition*, 41 Demography 607, 621–22 (2004); *see also* Waldfogel, Craigie & Brooks-Gunn, *supra* note 57, at 91–92.

131. *See* Waldfogel, Craigie & Brooks-Gunn, *supra* note 57, at 91.

132. Kathryn Edin & Timothy J. Nelson, Doing the Best I Can: Fatherhood and the Inner City 202–03 (2013).

133. *Id.*

134. *Id.* at 62–64, 68–69.

135. *Id.* at 143, 164, 169–70, 208.

136. McLanahan & Garfinkel, *supra* note 130, at 148.

137. *Id.*

138. Sara McLanahan and Audrey N. Beck, *Parental Relationships in Fragile Families*, 20 Future of Children 17, 22 (2010) (finding that only 51 percent of children at age five had seen their fathers in the past month).

139. Laura Tach et al., *Parenting as a "Package Deal": Relationships, Fertility, and Nonresident Father Involvement among Unmarried Parents*, 47 Demography 181, 197–201 (2010) (noting several reasons for this, including the absence of a formal custody or visitation agreement and the social norm that unmarried parents have more fluid and frequent transitions to new partners, who then "crowd out" the old partners).

140. Grall, *supra* note 30, at 9 (showing that 39.6 percent of never-married custodial parents received child support as compared with 51.2 percent of divorced custodial parents).

141. McLanahan & Beck, *supra* note 138, at 27; *see also* Robert I. Lerman, *Capabilities and Contributions of Unwed Fathers*, 20 Future of Children 63, 75 (2010).

142. Waldfogel, Craigie & Brooks-Gunn, *supra* note 57, at 100–04. For details on the differences, *see id.* at 106 app. 2.

143. *Id.* at 98. The findings contain considerable nuance, however, and show that at least for some outcomes, family stability is an important factor. Cognitive outcomes, for example, were strongly correlated with the consistency of the family form, regardless of whether that form was

marriage, cohabitation, or single-parenthood. *See id.* at 97. By contrast, behavioral and health outcomes turned on the type of family structure, even when that family structure was stable. *See id.* at 98 (noting these findings and also that children of cohabiting parents had worse outcomes than children of married parents on some but not all measures).

144. McLanahan & Garfinkel, *supra* note 130, at 151.

145. *Id.*

146. *Id.* at 152.

147. *Id.* at 152–53.

148. *Id.* at 153.

149. *Id.* at 153–54.

150. Waldfogel, Craigie & Brooks-Gunn, *supra* note 57, at 93–94. Moreover, in unmarried families where there was a man who was not the biological father of all the children in the home, there was an increase in risk for child abuse and neglect. *See id.* at 99.

151. McLanahan & Garfinkel, *supra* note 130, at 154.

152. *Id.*

153. *Id.*

154. *Id.* at 151–54.

155. *See* Patricia Tiaden & Nancy Thoennes, U.S. Dep't Just., Extent, Nature, and Consequences of Intimate Partner Violence: Findings from the National Violence against Women Survey 1 (2000), *available at* http://www.ncjrs.gov/pdffiles1/nij/181867.pdf.

156. *See id.* at 9.

157. *See id.* at 9–10 (exhibit 1 displaying the survey statistics for intimate-partner violence).

158. Shannan Catalano, U.S. Dep't Just., Intimate Partner Violence, 1993–2010, at 1 (2012), *available at* http://bjs.ojp.usdoj.gov/content/pub/pdf/ipv9310.pdf (finding that between 1994 and 2010, "the overall rate of intimate partner violence in the United States declined by 64 percent, from 9.8 victimizations per 1,000 persons age 12 and older to 3.6 per 1,000").

159. *Id.*

160. U.S. Dep't Just., Crime in the United States 2010, Expanded Homicide Data Table 10, http://www.fbi.gov/about-us/cjis/ucr/crime-in-the-u.s/2010/crime-in-the-u.s.-2010/tables/10shrtbl10.xls (adding the total number of wives and girlfriends murdered). Additionally, 241 men were killed by intimate partners. *Id.* (adding the total number of husbands and boyfriends murdered).

161. U.S. Dep't Health & Hum. Servs., Admin. on children, Youth & Families, Child Maltreatment 2011, at 19 (2012), *available at* http://www.acf.hhs.gov/sites/default/files/cb/cm11.pdf (hereinafter Child Maltreatment 2011). The numbers in the text reflect only those cases investigated by the child-welfare system. The actual rate of child maltreatment is much higher, as captured (at least in part) by the National Incidence Study. The most recent iteration of this periodic study, in 2006, found a maltreatment rate of 17.1 per 1,000 children. *See* Sedlak et al., *supra* note 60, at 3–4. This rate is based only on the stringent harm standard for maltreatment (and not the broader category of endangerment) and is defined to include incidents where "through the purposive acts or marked inattention to the child's basic needs, behavior of a parent/substitute or other adult caretaker caused foreseeable or avoidable injury or impairment to a child or materially contributed unreasonable prolongation or worsening of an existing injury or impairment." *See* U.S. Dep't Health & Hum. Servs., Study Findings: National Study

OF THE INCIDENCE AND SEVERITY OF CHILD ABUSE AND NEGLECT 4 (1981). The narrow definition thus does not include the behavior of a noncaretaker unless the parent "knowingly permitted" the acts or omissions. *See id.* The National Incidence Study uses a sentinel survey methodology, which looks far beyond the reported cases by surveying community professionals who work with children in a variety of settings, from police stations and hospitals to schools and emergency shelters. It thus sweeps in numerous cases that are not investigated through the child-welfare system. Indeed, the child-welfare system investigated only 32 percent of the total number of maltreatment incidents found in the 2006 iteration of the study. *See* SEDLAK ET AL., *supra* note 60, at 16.

162. U.S. DEP'T HEALTH & HUM. SERVS., ADMIN. ON CHILDREN, YOUTH & FAMILIES, *supra* note 161, at 21.

163. *Id.* (78.5 percent of cases involve neglect); JANE WALDFOGEL, THE FUTURE OF CHILD PROTECTION: HOW TO BREAK THE CYCLE OF ABUSE AND NEGLECT 124–125 (1998) (describing the relationship between poverty and neglect).

164. U.S. DEP'T HEALTH & HUM. SERVS., ADMIN. FOR CHILDREN & FAMILIES, THE AFCARS REPORT 1 (2012), *available at* http://www.acf.hhs.gov/sites/default/files/cb/afcarsreport19.pdf.

165. *Id.* at 2.

166. U.S. CENSUS BUREAU, USA PEOPLE QUICKFACTS (2013), *available at* http://quickfacts.census.gov/qfd/states/00000.html.

167. For example, legal scholar Elizabeth Bartholet contends that African American children are disproportionally maltreated because African American families are disproportionally living in poverty, unemployed, living in poorly resourced neighborhoods, and struggling with substance abuse and are frequently single-parent households, all factors that are highly correlated with maltreatment. *See* Elizabeth Bartholet, *The Racial Disproportionality Movement in Child Welfare: False Facts and Dangerous Directions,* 51 ARIZ. L. REV. 877, 899–908 (2009). Bartholet advocates for a proportionality comparison with maltreatment rates rather than race. *See id.* at 899. She believes that any maltreated child should be removed from an unsafe home, giving African American children the same protection from maltreatment that white children are afforded. *See id.* at 920–21. By contrast, legal scholar Dorothy Roberts argues that there is disproportionate state intervention in the lives of African American families, resulting in a disproportionate number of African American children in the welfare system. *See* DOROTHY ROBERTS, SHATTERED BONDS: THE COLOR OF CHILD WELFARE, at vii (2002). She contends that government policies exacerbate the issues of poverty and single parenting, welfare reform keeps needy families living in cycles of poverty, and harsh police practices targeting black young adults further separate parents from children. These factors lead to more African American children being removed from their struggling families, even if their parents are not maltreating them. *See id.* at 173–200. Once children are removed, governmental efforts have shifted away from preserving families and instead have moved toward more easily terminating parental rights, leaving black children stranded in the foster-care system. *See id.* at 23–25.

168. U.S. DEP'T HEALTH & HUM. SERVS., ADMIN. ON CHILDREN, YOUTH & FAMILIES, *supra* note 161, at 21.

169. *See* DAVID FINKELHOR ET AL., U.S. DEP'T JUST., NATIONAL INCIDENCE STUDIES OF MISSING, ABDUCTED, RUNAWAY, AND THROWNAWAY CHILDREN, SEXUALLY ASSAULTED CHILDREN: NATIONAL ESTIMATES AND CHARACTERISTICS 1–4, 9 (2008), *available at* www.

ncjrs.gov/pdffiles1/ojjdp/214383.pdf (concluding, after addressing various methodological concerns, that "[i]t may be inherently impossible to get a complete and unbiased accounting of all child sexual assaults close to the time they occur").

170. *See* Ryan C. W. Hall & Richard C. W. Hall, *A Profile of Pedophilia: Definition, Characteristics of Offenders, Recidivism, Treatment Outcomes, and Forensic Issues*, 82 MAYO CLINIC PROC. 457, 460 (2007), *available at* http://download.journals.elsevierhealth.com/pdfs/journals/00256196/PIIS0025619611610744.pdf (using the following definition of sexual abuse: "any sexual act directed against another person forcibly and/or against that person's will or not forcibly or against the person's will in which the injured party is incapable of giving consent"); *see also* David Finkelhor et al., *Sexual Abuse in a National Survey of Adult Men and Women: Prevalence, Characteristics, and Risk Factors*, 14 CHILD ABUSE & NEGLECT 19, 20–21 (1990) (reporting the results from a large survey and finding that 27 percent of the women and 16 percent of the men responding to the survey reported being victims of sex abuse during their childhood). A more conservative estimate—although one that is limited because it identifies sexual abuse only by a parent or a caretaker—can be found in the National Incidence Study. *See* SEDLAK ET AL., *supra* note 60, at 3-1 to 3-4 (finding that 135,300 children were sexually abused by a parent or caretaker in the 2005–2006 study year). Incidence studies, however, will never capture the extent of the problem, because one of the hallmarks of child sexual abuse is that the child often does not tell anyone about the abuse at the time, or even if the child does tell someone, the family will keep the incident secret.

171. *See* REBECCA BOLEN, CHILD SEXUAL ABUSE: ITS SCOPE AND OUR FAILURE 91–101 (2001) (discussing studies finding that abuse by strangers accounted for only 7 percent of all sexual abuse and listing other types of extrafamilial offenders, including family friends, acquaintances, and people in positions of authority who are known to the family).

172. *See id.* at 113–14. Within the family, the offender is most often an uncle, *see id.* at 114, although in African American families, the most common offender is a stepfather, *see id.* The next-most-common offender for all groups is a father or cousin. *See id.* In the case of male victims, the offender is less likely to be a family member, with only 11 to 12 percent of all abuse of males occurring within the family. *See id.* at 114. To be clear, then, in the majority of cases for both girls and boys, the perpetrator is a nonfamily member though not a stranger to the child.

173. SHERRY HAMBY ET AL., U.S. DEP'T JUST., CHILDREN'S EXPOSURE TO INTIMATE PARTNER VIOLENCE AND OTHER FAMILY VIOLENCE, 1 (2011) *available at* https://www.ncjrs.gov/pdffiles1/ojjdp/232272.pdf.

174. U.S. DEP'T HEALTH & HUM. SERVS., SUBSTANCE ABUSE & MENTAL HEALTH SERVS. ADMIN., NSDUH REPORT: CHILDREN LIVING WITH SUBSTANCE-DEPENDENT OR ALCOHOL-ABUSING PARENTS: 2002 TO 2007 (2009), *available at* http://www.oas.samhsa.gov/2k9/SAparents/SAparents.htm.

175. *Id.*

176. *Id.*

177. U.S. DEP'T HEALTH & HUM. SERVS., SUBSTANCE ABUSE & MENTAL HEALTH SERVS. ADMIN., RESULTS FROM THE 2011 NATIONAL SURVEY ON DRUG USE AND HEALTH: DETAILED TABLES, *available at* http://www.samhsa.gov/data/NSDUH/2011SummNatFindDetTables/ NSDUH-DetTabsPDFWHTML2011/2k11DetailedTabs/Web/HTML/ NSDUH-DetTabsTOC2011.htm (tbl. 1.23B, Illicit Drug Use in Lifetime, Past Year, and Past Month among Persons Aged 18 or Older, by Demographic Characteristics: Percentages, 2010 and

2011; illicit drugs include marijuana, cocaine, heroin, hallucinogens, inhalants, prescription psycho-therapeutics used for nonmedical purposes, and methamphetamine). When asked about the use of illegal drugs within the previous year, however, African American rates were slightly higher than those for whites, and rates for Latinos remained the lowest. *Id.* (15.5 percent for African Americans, as compared with 14.7 percent for whites and 13.7 percent for Latinos).

178. *See* CARMEN DeNAVAS-WALT ET AL., U.S. CENSUS BUREAU, INCOME, POVERTY, AND HEALTH INSURANCE COVERAGE IN THE UNITED STATES: 2012, at 13 (2013) (reporting an official poverty rate of 15.0 percent in 2012, up from 12.5 percent in 2007, before the recession).

179. *Id.* at 17.

180. ALISHA COLEMAN-JENSEN ET AL., U.S. DEP'T AGRIC., HOUSEHOLD FOOD SECURITY IN THE UNITED STATES IN 2011, at 4 (2012) (14.9 percent of households were food-insecure).

181. U.S. DEP'T LAB., BUREAU LAB. STAT., NEWS RELEASE, THE EMPLOYMENT SITUATION—NOVEMBER 2013 1 (Dec. 6, 2013), *available at* http://www.bls.gov/news.release/pdf/empsit.pdf.

182. *Id.* (tbl. A-15).

183. JULIA ISAACS, URBAN INST., UNEMPLOYMENT FROM A CHILD'S PERSPECTIVE 2 (2013), *available at* http://www.urban.org/UploadedPDF/1001671-Unemployment-from-a-Childs-Perspective.pdf.

184. U.S. DEP'T HEALTH & HUM. SERVS., CTRS. FOR DISEASE CONTROL AND PREVENTION, STATE INDICATOR REPORT ON PHYSICAL ACTIVITY, 2010, at 13 (2010), *available at* http://www.cdc.gov/physicalactivity/downloads/PA_State_Indicator_Report_2010.pdf.

185. *What Is a Play Desert?*, KABOOM!, http://kaboom.org/map_play/what_play_desert.

186. *See* Richard Freeman, *Is a Great Labor Shortage Coming?*, *in* RESHAPING THE AMERICAN WORKFORCE IN A CHANGING ECONOMY (H. Holzer & D. Nightingale eds., 2007); Allan C. Ornstein, *Class Counts: Education, Inequity, and the Shrinking Middle Class* 225 (2007); DAVID AUTOR, CTR. FOR AM. PROGRESS, THE POLARIZATION OF JOB OPPORTUNITIES IN THE U.S. LABOR MARKET 5–6 (2010), *available at* http://www.brookings.edu/research/papers/2010/04/jobs-autor (suggesting that the recession of 2007–2009 supported the trends of computerizing middle-skill jobs and sending many of these jobs offshore; following the recession, there was no change in unemployment rates for high-skill occupations or low-skill service jobs, but employment dropped 8 percent for mid-level sales and office jobs and 16 percent for blue-collar manufacturing and operative jobs).

187. U.S. DEP'T LAB., BUREAU LAB. STAT., NEWS RELEASE, "EMPLOYMENT PROJECTIONS—2010–20," available at http://bls.gov/news.release/ecopro.nro.htm.

188. High-skill jobs require the problem-solving and intuitive abilities that are usually developed in higher education and cannot be mechanized or easily taught to employees abroad. On the other end of the spectrum, low-skill manual jobs such as home health aides, cab drivers, and janitors require little education but do demand an ability to communicate with others, an ability to adapt to a variety of situations, physical presence, and, often, physical strength, none of which can be replicated by a computer or by workers who are located in other countries. *See* AUTOR, *supra* note 186, at 5–6.

189. *Id.* The middle class continues to shrink as the disparity between wages for those who have graduated from college and those who have not widens. Autor reports: "Real hourly earnings of college-educated workers rose anywhere from 10 to 37 percent between 1979 and 2007, with the greatest gains among workers with a postbaccalaureate degree. Simultaneously, real

earnings of workers with high school or lower educational levels either stagnated or declined significantly. These declines were especially steep among males: 12 percent for high school graduates and 16 percent for high school dropouts." *Id.* at 6. He further found that "[c]ollege graduates work more hours per week and more weeks per year than high school graduates, spend less time unemployed, and receive a disproportionate share of nonwage fringe benefits, including sick and vacation pay, employer-paid health insurance, pension contributions, and safe and pleasant working conditions." *Id.* at 5.

190. Harry J. Holzer & Marek Hlavac, *A Very Uneven Road: US Labor Markets in the Past 30 Years, in* THE LOST DECADE? SOCIAL CHANGE IN THE U.S. AFTER 2000, tbl. 5b (John R. Logan ed., forthcoming 2013), *available at* http://www.irp.wisc.edu/publications/dps/pdfs/dp140012.pdf.

191. AUTOR, *supra* note 186, at 6.

192. *Id.* at 25.

193. *Id.*

194. *Id.*

195. Target Hourly Pay, Glassdoor: An Inside Look at Jobs and Companies, http://www.glassdoor.com/Hourly-Pay/Target-Cashier-Hourly-Pay-E194_D_KO7,14.htm.

196. U.S. DEP'T LAB., BUREAU LAB. STAT., HOME HEALTH AND PERSONAL CARE AIDES: OCCUPATIONAL OUTLOOK HANDBOOK, *available at* http://www.bls.gov/ooh/healthcare/home-health-and-personal-care-aides.htm.

197. U.S. DEP'T LAB., BUREAU LAB. STAT., FOOD AND BEVERAGE SERVING AND RELATED WORKERS: OCCUPATIONAL OUTLOOK HANDBOOK, *available at* http://www.bls.gov/ooh/food-preparation-and-serving/food-and-beverage-serving-and-related-workers.htm.

198. U.S. DEP'T LAB., BUREAU LAB. STAT., TEACHER ASSISTANTS: OCCUPATIONAL OUTLOOK HANDBOOK, available at http://www.bls.gov/ooh/education-training-and-library/teacher-assistants.htm.

199. Holzer & Hlavac, *supra* note 190, at 8.

200. Catherine Rampell, *The Mancession*, N.Y. TIMES ECONOMIX BLOG (Aug. 10, 2009), http://economix.blogs.nytimes.com/2009/08/10/the-mancession/.

201. The growth in pink-collar jobs and the trend toward dual-income families have resulted in gains for women overall. *See* Holzer & Hlavac, *supra* note 190, at 8.

202. Richard Florida, *The Crisis in Male Wages*, THE ATLANTIC, June 9, 2011, *available at* http://www.theatlantic.com/business/archive/2011/06/the-crisis-in-male-wages/240160/; *see also id.* ("for the past several years the combination of technology and globalization has...reduced the number and share of low-skill production jobs that were once the province of male breadwinners").

203. UNITED NATIONS OFFICE ON DRUGS AND CRIME, TOTAL PERSONS HELD IN PRISONS, PENAL INSTITUTIONS OR CORRECTIONAL INSTITUTIONS (2011), *available at* http://www.unodc.org/unodc/en/data-and-analysis/statistics/data.html (follow "Persons detained" link; then select "CTS 2011 Total Persons held" tab).

204. LAUREN E. GLAZE, BUREAU JUST. STAT., U.S. DEP'T JUST., CORRECTIONAL POPULATION IN THE UNITED STATES, 2010, at 8 (2011), *available at* http://bjs.ojp.usdoj.gov/content/pub/pdf/cpus10.pdf (app. tbl. 3).

205. U.S. DEP'T JUST., CRIME IN THE UNITED STATES 2011, TABLE 43A, *available at* http://www.fbi.gov/about-us/cjis/ucr/crime-in-the-u.s/2011/crime-in-the-u.s.-2011/tables/table-43.

206. U.S. Dep't Just., Prisoners in 2011, at 9 tbl. 9 (2012), *available at* http://www.bjs.gov/content/pub/pdf/p11.pdf (of the 237,000 prisoners under state jurisdiction sentenced for drug crimes, 105,600 were African American).

207. *See, e.g.*, Illinois Disproportionate Justice Impact Study Commission, Key Findings and Recommendations (2011), *available at* http://www.senatedem.ilga.gov/phocadownload/PDF/Attachments/2011/djisfactsheet.pdf (discussing the findings of a comprehensive study documenting the disproportionately harsh treatment of racial minorities involved in drug crimes).

208. Marc Mauer & Tracy Huling, The Sentencing Project, Young Black Americans and the Criminal Justice System: Five Years Later 1, 3 (1995), *available at* http://www.sentencingproject.org/doc/publications/rd_youngblack_5yrslater.pdf.

209. E. Ann Carson & Daniela Golinelli, U.S. Dep't Just., Prisoners in 2012 – Advance Counts 8 tbl. 7 (2013), *available at* http://www.bjs.gov/content/pub/pdf/p12ac.pdf. The incarceration rate for women has increased from 61 female prisoners for every 100,000 women in 2002 to 63 female prisoners for every 100,000 women in 2012. Although the female incarceration rate is higher today than it was in 2002, it has declined in recent years. The female incarceration rate reached a high of 69 female prisoners for every 100,000 women in 2007–2008 and has decreased each year since. *See id.*

210. Paul Guerino, Paige M. Harrison & William J. Sabol, U.S. Dep't Just., Prisoners in 2010, at 27 app. tbl. 15 (rev. 2012), *available at* http://www.bjs.gov/content/pub/pdf/p10.pdf.

211. Lauren E. Glaze & Laura M. Maruschak, Bureau Just. Stat., U.S. Dep't Just., Parents in Prison and Their Minor Children 1–2 (rev. 2010), *available at* www.bjs.gov/content/pub/pdf/pptmc.pdf.

212. *Id.* at 3.

213. *Id.* at 2.

214. Brady E. Hamilton & Stephanie Ventura, Nat'l Ctr. for Health Stat., Data Brief No. 89, Birth Rates for U.S. Teenagers Reach Historic Lows for All Age and Ethnic Groups 2 (2012), *available at* http://www.cdc.gov/nchs/data/databriefs/db89.pdf.

215. *Id.* The rate of teen births is also much lower than in the past: 34.3 teen births per 1,000 births as compared with 96.3 per 1,000 in 1957.

216. *Id.* (fig. 3 showing number of births for women ages fifteen to nineteen by race and Latino origin, United States, 1940–2010; showing the 2010 birth rate for African American women as 51.5 per 1,000, for Latino women as 55.7 per 1,000, and for white women as 23.5 per 1,000).

217. U.S. Dep't Health & Hum. Servs., Ctrs. for Disease Control & Prevention, About Teen Pregnancy, *available at* http://www.cdc.gov/TeenPregnancy/AboutTeenPreg.htm.

218. Rebecca A. Maynard & Saul D. Hoffman, *The Costs of Adolescent Childbearing, in* Kids Having Kids: Economic Costs and Social Consequences of Teen Pregnancy 381–82 (Saul D. Hoffman & Rebecca A. Maynard eds., 2008).

219. *Id.* at 362.

220. *Id.*

221. U.S. Dep't Health & Hum. Servs., Ctrs. for Disease Control & Prevention, *supra* note 217; *see also* Lauren S. Scher & Saul D. Hoffman, *Consequences of Teen Childbearing*

for Incarceration among Adult Children, Updated Estimates through 2002, in KIDS HAVING
KIDS: ECONOMIC COSTS AND SOCIAL CONSEQUENCES OF TEEN PREGNANCY, *supra* note
218, at 315–19 ("Our most conservative estimate, based on a family fixed-effect approach, finds
that a delay of a teen birth would decrease the probability of incarceration by 10.6 percent and
years in jail by 13.4 percent. A less conservative approach, based on mother's age at first birth,
rather than at the respondent's birth, implies that delay would reduce the probability of incarceration by almost 33 percent and years in jail by 38 percent. Thus our estimates strongly confirm the
impact of a teen birth on the incarceration of sons").

222. SUZANNE M. BIANCHI, JOHN P. ROBINSON & MELISSA A. MILKIE, CHANGING
RHYTHMS OF AMERICAN FAMILY LIFE 171 (2006) (these parents did nine hours of paid work
per week more in 2000 than in 1965).

223. *Id.* at 173.

224. BRIAN MCKENZIE, U.S. CENSUS BUREAU, OUT-OF-STATE AND LONG
COMMUTES: 2001, at 3 (2013), *available at* http://www.census.gov/hhes/commuting/files/2012/
ACS-20.pdf.

225. *Id.*

226. *Id.* at 6 tbl. 4.

227. Nick Paumgarten, *There and Back Again*, THE NEW YORKER, Apr. 16, 2007, *available at*
http://www.newyorker.com/reporting/2007/04/16/070416fa_fact_paumgarten?printable=
true.

228. Larry Long, *Residential Mobility Differences among Developed Countries*, 14 INT'L
REGIONAL SCI. REV. 133, 139 (1991). The only two countries that are more mobile than the
United States are Canada and New Zealand. *See id.* at 137.

229. DAVID K. IHRKE, CAROL S. FABER & WILLIAM K. KOERBER, U.S. CENSUS
BUREAU, GEOGRAPHIC MOBILITY: 2008 TO 2009, at 3 (2011), *available at* www.census.gov/
prod/2011pubs/p20-565.pdf.

230. From 2008 to 2009, more than 26 percent of families living below the poverty line moved,
compared with 12 percent of families living at or above 150 percent of the poverty level. *See id.* at 8.

231. BIANCHI, ROBINSON & MILKIE, *supra* note 222, at 46.

232. The labor-force-participation rate (individuals working or looking for work) for all mothers with children younger than eighteen was 70.5 percent in 2012, and the participation rate for
married mothers with a spouse present was 68.3 percent. U.S. DEP'T LAB., BUREAU LAB. STAT.,
NEWS RELEASE, EMPLOYMENT CHARACTERISTICS OF FAMILIES—2012 (Apr. 26, 2013), *available at* http://www.bls.gov/news.release/pdf/famee.pdf.

233. U.S. DEP'T LAB., BUREAU LAB. STAT., NEWS RELEASE, MARRIED PARENTS' USE OF
TIME, 2003–06 (May 8, 2008), *available at* http://www.bls.gov/news.release/pdf/atus2.pdf (tbl.
2, Time Spent in Primary Activities [1] by Married Mothers and Fathers with Own Household
Children under 18 by Employment Status of Self and Spouse, Average for the Combined Years
2003–06).

234. In dual-earner, married couples, both parents tend to work the same total number of
hours a week when paid and unpaid work are combined, Kim Parker & Wendy Wang, Pew
Research Ctr., *Modern Parenthood: Roles of Moms and Dads Converge as They Balance Work
and Family* 4 (Mar. 14, 2013) (married mothers spend a total of fifty-nine hours a week on paid
and unpaid work, and married fathers spend a total of fifty-eight hours a week), but the difference is in the breakdown of these hours. Mothers spend thirty-one hours a week on paid work,

sixteen hours on housework, and twelve hours on child care. *Id.* at 4. By contrast, fathers spend forty-two hours a week on paid work, nine hours on housework, and seven hours on child care. *Id.* Fathers spend more time on leisure activities than mothers (twenty-eight hours a week as compared with twenty-five hours), a category that includes exercising, watching TV, and socializing. Id. at 7.

235. John Monahan & Jeffrey Swanson, *Lawyers at Mid-Career: A 20-Year Longitudinal Study of Job and Life Satisfaction*, 6 J. Empirical Legal Stud. 451, 465–66 (2009).

236. *Id.*

237. Ann Crittenden, The Price of Motherhood: Why the Most Important Job in the World Is Still the Least Valued 150, 164–65 (2001).

238. *Id.* at 150.

239. Joanna L. Grossman & Lawrence M. Friedman, Inside the Castle: Law and the Family in 20th Century America 201–05 (2011).

240. Sondra E. Solomon et al., *Money, Housework, Sex and Conflict: Same-Sex Couples in Civil Unions, Those Not in Civil Unions, and Heterosexual Married Siblings*, 52 Sex Roles 561, 572 (2005).

241. *Id.*; Timothy J. Biblarz & Everen Savci, *Lesbian, Gay, Bisexual, and Transgender Families*, 72 J. Marriage & Fam. 480, 487 (2010).

242. Charlotte J. Patterson, Erin L. Sutfin & Megan Fulcher, *Division of Labor among Lesbian and Heterosexual Parenting Couples: Correlates of Specialized versus Shared Patterns*, 11 J. Adult Dev. 179, 183 (2004).

243. *Id.* at 188.

244. Cohabiting couples tend to split labor more equally, but the sample may be subject to a selection bias, suggesting that couples choosing cohabitation over marriage desire autonomy rather than interdependence and therefore naturally avoid the "specialization" that occurs in most marriages. Deborah A. Widiss, *Reconfiguring Sex, Gender, and the Law of Marriage*, 50 Fam. Ct. Rev. 205, 210 (2012). Alternatively, it is possible that because cohabiting couples have uncertain legal recourse should they break up, it is a rational response to maintain separate finances and push for a more equal division of unpaid labor. Julie Brines & Kara Joyner, *The Ties That Bind: Principles of Cohesion in Cohabitation and Marriage*, 64 Am. Soc. Rev. 333, 335–36 (1999).

245. Glaze & Maruschak, *supra* note 211, at 6 tbl. 10.

246. *Id.* at 18 app. tbl. 10.

247. *Id.*

248. Christopher J. Mumola, U.S. Dep't Just., Incarcerated Parents and Their Children 5 (2000), *available at* http://www.bjs.gov/content/pub/pdf/iptc.pdf (62 percent in state prisons and 84 percent in federal prisons).

249. Donald Braman, Doing Time on the Outside: Incarceration and Family Life in Urban America 102 (2007).

250. *Id.* at 105–09.

251. *Id.* at 109.

252. *Id.* at 109-10.

253. *Id.* at 111.

254. *Id.* at 110–11.

255. *Id.* at 156.

256. *Id.*

257. GLAZE & MARUSCHAK, *supra* note 211, at 5.

258. *Id.*

259. *Id.*

260. *Id.*

261. Naomi Schoenbaum, *Mobility Measures*, 2012 BYU L. REV. 1169, 1177 (2012).

262. *Id.* at 1169.

263. *See id.* at 1195; Melissa Murray, *The Networked Family: Reframing the Legal Understanding of Caregiving and Caregivers*, 94 VA. L. REV. 385, 390–91 (2008); Ethan J. Leib, *Friendship & the Law*, 54 UCLA L. REV. 631, 654–55 (2007).

264. Schoenbaum, *supra* note 261, at 1197.

265. *Id.* at 1202; Stephanie Coontz, Op-Ed, *Too Close for Comfort*, N.Y. TIMES, Nov. 7, 2006, at A17.

266. STEPHANIE COONTZ, THE WAY WE NEVER WERE: AMERICAN FAMILIES AND THE NOSTALGIA TRAP 25–26 (2000).

267. *Id.* at 28–29.

268. *Id.* at 29, 76.

269. *Id.* at 13.

270. *Id.* at 27.

271. *Id.* at 29.

272. *Id.* at 30–31.

273. *Id.* at 31–32.

274. *Id.* at 34–35.

275. *Id.* at 35–36.

276. *Id.* at 39.

277. HAMILTON & VENTURA, *supra* note 214, at 1 ("The U.S. teen birth rate declined 9 percent from 2009 to 2010, reaching a historic low at 34.3 births per 1,000 women aged 15–19").

278. COONTZ, *supra* note 266, at 39.

CHAPTER 3

1. *See* 42 U.S.C. §§ 601–02 (2006) (describing the purpose of Temporary Assistance for Needy Families [TANF] and discussing some of its requirements).

2. TANF does not affirmatively authorize family caps, but neither does it prohibit them, and the law's flexibility allows states to enact them at their choosing. Approximately nineteen states have family caps. NAT'L CONFERENCE OF STATE LEGISLATURES, WELFARE REFORM: FAMILY CAP POLICIES (2009), *available at* http://www.ncsl.org/issues-research/human-services/welfare-reform-family-cap-policies.aspx. For example, in California, if a child is born to a woman who has been receiving assistance for the ten previous months, the woman will not receive additional support for the child unless the pregnancy was the result of rape, incest, or "contraceptive failure if the parent was using an intrauterine device, a Norplant, or the sterilization of either parent." CAL. WELF. & INST. CODE § 11450.04(b) (2006). For more on family caps, *see generally* Rebekah J. Smith, *Family Caps in Welfare Reform: Their Coercive Effects and Damaging Consequences*, 29 HARV. J.L. & GENDER 151 (2006).

3. *See, e.g.*, FLA. STAT. ANN. § 765.401 (West 2003).

4. *See* Tara Siegel Bernard & Ron Lieber, *The High Price of Being a Gay Couple*, N.Y. TIMES, Oct. 3, 2009, at A1, *available at* http://www.nytimes.com/2009/10/03/your-money/03money.

html?pagewanted=all&_r=0 (finding that gay couples paid an additional $12,300 in tax-preparation fees over the forty-six years they were together). This calculation was done before the Supreme Court struck down the federal Defense of Marriage Act. *See* United States v. Windsor, 133 S. Ct. 2675 (2013).

5. 7 C.F.R. § 246.2 (2011).

6. U.S. Dep't Health & Hum. Servs., Admin. for Children & Families, Office of Head Start—Services Snapshot, National All Programs (2011–2012), at 1, *available at* http://eclkc.ohs.acf.hhs.gov/hslc/mr/psr (showing that 45.6 percent of Head Start enrollees are in a part-day program, and only 16 percent of enrollees attend a program that is available for a full working day).

7. *See* Bernard & Lieber, *supra* note 4. This analysis is based on a legal regime where neither an individual state nor the federal government recognizes same-sex relationships. After the U.S. Supreme Court's decision in 2013 striking down the federal Defense of Marriage Act, *see supra* note 4, the federal government now recognizes valid same-sex marriages. Many of the costs discussed in this analysis, however, are at the state level and would still be incurred by this couple.

8. *See* Joan Williams, *The Daddy Dilemma: Why Men Face a "Flexibility Stigma" at Work*, WashingtonPost.com (Feb. 11, 2013), http://www.washingtonpost.com/national/on-leadership/the-daddy-dilemma-why-men-face-a-flexibility-stigma-at-work/2013/02/11/58350f4e-7462-11e2-aa12-e6cf1d31106b_story.html; Joan Williams, Mary Blair-Loy & Jennifer Berdahl, *The Flexibility Stigma: Work Devotion vs. Family Devotion*, Rotman Mag., Winter 2013, at 34, 36, 39.

9. For a discussion of the effect of urban planning on family life, see Katharine B. Silbaugh, *Women's Place: Urban Planning, Housing Design, and Work-Family Balance*, 76 Fordham L. Rev. 1797 (2007).

10. *See, e.g.*, Cal. Fam. Code § 7540 (West 2013); Neb. Rev. Stat. § 42-377 (2012); Iowa Code Ann. § 252A.3 (West 2013); Kan. Stat. Ann. § 23-2208 (West 2012); N.M. Stat. Ann. § 40-11A-204 (West 2013). Vt. Stat. Ann. tit. 15, § 308 (West 2013).

11. Lehr v. Robertson, 463 U.S. 248, 261–62, 266–68 (1983) (upholding such a state law as a constitutional matter).

12. *Compare In re* T.J.S., 419 N.J. Super. 46 (N.J. Super. Ct. App. Div. 2011), aff'd, 212 N.J. 334 (2012) (holding that the wife of the biological father of a child born of a gestational surrogate cannot be listed as the mother on the child's birth certificate and that the wife may only establish a parental relationship with the child through adoption) *with In re* Marriage of Buzzanaca, 61 Cal. App. 4th 1410 (1998) (declaring that a husband and a wife are the lawful parents of a child not biologically related to them but born on their behalf by a gestational surrogate).

13. For a book-length treatment of this subject, *see generally* Cynthia Bowman, Couples, Law, and Public Policy (2010).

14. Elizabeth S. Scott, *A World without Marriage*, 41 Fam. L.Q. 537, 550 (2007).

15. *Id.* at 547–50.

16. Andrew Sullivan, *Why Gay Marriage Is Good for America*, Newsweek, July 25, 2011, *available at* http://www.newsweek.com/andrew-sullivan-why-gay-marriage-good-america-68453.

17. For a contrary view, *see* Solangel Maldonado, *Illegitimate Harm: Law, Stigma, and Discrimination against Nonmarital Children*, 63 Fla. L. Rev. 345, 379 (2011) ("Although courts have repeatedly held that nonmarital children should not be penalized for their parents' behavior, the law's discriminatory treatment of nonmarital children in certain contexts may serve to

reinforce any remaining social stigma of illegitimacy. As shown in the context of citizenship, intestate succession, and post-secondary educational support, the law's distinction between marital and nonmarital children suggests that there are meaningful differences between marital and nonmarital children and that parents' responsibilities toward their children differ based on the child's status as marital or nonmarital").

18. *See* U.S. Dep't Health & Hum. Servs., Admin. for Children & Families, How the Child Welfare System Works 1 (2013), *available at* https://www.childwelfare.gov/pubs/factsheets/cpswork.pdf#page=1&view=Introduction.

19. *See* Jeannie Suk, At Home in the Law: How the Domestic Violence Revolution Is Transforming Policy 14, 36 (2009); Leigh Goodmark, A Troubled Marriage: Domestic Violence and the Legal System 106–10 (2012).

20. *See* Suk, *supra* note 19, at 14, 36–37; Goodmark, *supra* note 19, at 111–13.

21. *See* Suk, *supra* note 19, at 37–41.

22. *See id.* at 38.

23. *See id.* at 42–43.

24. *See* Goodmark, *supra* note 19, at 88.

25. *See* Suk, *supra* note 19, at 14.

26. *See, e.g.,* 750 Ill. Comp. Stat. Ann. 60/214 (West 2013) (allowing protection orders to be issued in cases where one "has been abused by a family or household member"); N.H. Rev. Stat. Ann. § 1.F (2012) (specifying that the range of potential plaintiffs for whom a protective order can be issued is broad and includes intimate partners and those in a dating relationship); Ohio Rev. Code Ann. § 3113.31 (West 2013) (allowing the court to grant any protection order to prevent violence against "family or household members"); *see also* 18 U.S.C. § 2266 (2006) (including a person who cohabits in the definition of "spouse or intimate partner").

27. *See* Michael Puma et al., U.S. Dep't Health & Hum. Servs., Admin. for Children & Families, Head Start Impact Study Final Report: Executive Summary, xx, xxii (2010).

28. *See* U.S. Dep't Agric., Access to Affordable and Nutritious Food— Measuring and Understanding Food Deserts and Their Consequences: Report to Congress 52–53 (2009), *available at* http://www.ers.usda.gov/publications/ap-administrative-publication/ap-036.aspx#.UfrK9-CEzdm; *see also* Sarah Treuhaft & Allison Karpyn, *The Grocery Gap: Who Has Access to Healthy Food and Why It Matters,* at 7–8 (2010), *available at* http://www.policylink.org/atf/cf/%7B97C6D565-BB43-406D-A6D5-ECA3BBF35AF0%7D/FINALGroceryGap.pdf (low-income Census tracts have half as many supermarkets as higher-income tracts; low-income zip codes have 30 percent more convenience stores than middle-income zip codes).

29. As of 2012, there was approximately $166 billion in 529 accounts, up from $10.8 billion in 2001. (The "529" label refers to the section of the Internal Revenue Code where the plan is located.) *See* Morningstar, 529 College-Savings Plan Industry Survey 1 (2013), *available at* http://corporate.morningstar.com/us/documents/529Reports/529Landscape2013.pdf; Jennifer Ma & Douglas Fore, TIAA-CREF Institute, Saving for College with 529 Plans and Other Options: An Update 2–3 (2001); Internal Revenue Service, *529 Plans: Questions and Answers, available at* http://www.irs.gov/uac/529-Plans:-Questions-and-Answers.

30. Richard H. Thaler & Cass R. Sunstein, Nudge: Improving Decisions about Health, Wealth, and Happiness 3 (2008).

31. Nine states have "community property" rules, which require an even greater degree of sharing. *See* Alicia Brokars Kelly, *Money Matters in Marriage: Unmasking Interdependence in Ongoing Spousal Economic Relations*, 47 U. LOUISVILLE L. REV. 113, 115 (2008) (describing community-property regimes).

32. *Id.* at 123 (describing studies).

33. Silbaugh, *supra* note 9, at 1818–35.

34. *Id.* at 1825–26.

35. *Id.* ("Suburban residents drive either to urban workplaces or to workplaces in neighboring and similarly car-dependent suburbs, both requiring extensive travel time").

36. *Id.* at 1807.

37. *Id.* at 1827.

38. *Id.* at 1843.

39. *Id.* at 1845.

40. *Id.* at 1847.

41. *See, e.g.*, Elizabeth F. Emens, *Intimate Discrimination: The State's Role in the Accidents of Sex and Love*, 122 HARV. L. REV. 1307, 1366–74 (2009).

42. *Id.* at 1367–68.

43. Emens notes possible solutions, such as Virginia's tax-incentive program, which provides a $500 tax credit for making a private home accessible to disabled individuals. Elizabeth F. Emens, *Intimate Discrimination: The State's Role in the Accidents of Sex and Love*, 122 HARV. L. REV. 1307, 1394–95 (2009).

44. AYELET WALDMAN, BAD MOTHER: A CHRONICLE OF MATERNAL CRIMES, MINOR CALAMITIES, AND OCCASIONAL MOMENTS OF GRACE 58 (2009).

45. U.S. DEP'T LAB., CHILDREN'S BUREAU, INFANT CARE 41 (1938), *available at* http://mchlibrary.info/history/chbu/3121-1938.PDF.

46. *See, e.g.*, ELIZABETH M. SLOAN CHESSER, CHILD HEALTH AND CHARACTER 30–31 (1927). Instead, experts instructed that "a few minutes before feeding, [a child] should be taken up and held quietly in his mother's arms, in a variety of positions, so that no one set of muscles may become overtired." U.S. DEP'T LAB., *supra* note 45.

47. *See, e.g.*, WILLIAM SEARS ET AL., THE BABY BOOK: EVERYTHING YOU NEED TO KNOW ABOUT YOUR BABY—FROM BIRTH TO AGE TWO 281–83, 301–11 (2d ed. 2003) (advocating "babywearing" as beneficial to both mother and infant by promoting attachment and "harmony," enhancing learning and cognitive development, and reducing crying and colic); *see generally* WILLIAM SEARS & MARTHA SEARS, THE ATTACHMENT PARENTING BOOK (2001).

48. *See* BENJAMIN SPOCK, DR. SPOCK TALKS WITH MOTHERS: GROWTH AND GUIDANCE 110–12 (1961).

49. *See* BENJAMIN SPOCK & STEVEN PARKER, DR. SPOCK'S BABY AND CHILD CARE 687 (9th ed. 2012).

50. *Id.* at 688. For further discussion of the historically contingent nature of parenting advice, *see generally* ANN HULBERT, RAISING AMERICA: EXPERTS, PARENTS, AND A CENTURY OF ADVICE ABOUT CHILDREN 360–70 (2003).

51. When legal scholars first began to study social norms, many considered these norms to stand apart from the law, *see, e.g.*, ROBERT C. ELLICKSON, ORDER WITHOUT LAW: HOW NEIGHBORS SETTLE DISPUTES 15–81 (1991), but more recently, we have begun to understand that law and social norms work together, along with other influences, to shape behavior, *see*

Lawrence Lessig, *The New Chicago School*, 27 J. LEGAL STUD. 661, 673 (1998). Social norms, this latter view holds, are one of several forces—including markets and social institutions—that influence behavior, all of which are, in turn, shaped by law, at least to some extent. *Id.* at 662–63. In this way, law and social norms supplement, rather than replace, each other. *See* Saul Levmore, *Norms as Supplements*, 86 VA. L. REV. 1989, 1997–2008 (2000) ("Norms can supplement legal rules by coloring around the rules in a way that informs actors as to whether a rule is a serious signal, or 'sanction,' or is instead a mere price"). Even when a law is not enforced, the law can support a desirable norm by "expressing" it. *See* Cass R. Sunstein, *On the Expressive Function of Law*, 144 U. PA. L. REV. 2021, 2024 (1996) (exploring "the function of law in 'making statements' as opposed to controlling behavior directly"). The relationship between the expressive function of the law and social norms is quite complex. *See* Robert E. Scott, *The Limits of Behavioral Theories of Law and Social Norms*, 86 VA. L. REV. 1603, 1614–30 (2000) (describing this relationship). An often-used example is the pooper-scooper law. Although rarely enforced, the mere passage of such a law conveys the community's belief that dog owners should clean up after their dogs. Such a law also allows members of the community to sanction one another, emboldening one person to tell another that they really should scoop the poop.

52. *See* KRISTIN LUKER, ABORTION AND THE POLITICS OF MOTHERHOOD 192–215 (1984) (describing the role of the norm of motherhood in abortion debates).

53. *See* ARK. CODE ANN. § 20-16-1103 (2005) (requiring a medical provider to tell a patient that information regarding the "unborn child['s]" pain is available); *id.* at § 20-16-1104 (requiring a physician to inform a patient whether an analgesic or anesthetic would lessen or eliminate the "unborn child['s]" pain caused by the abortion).

54. Several other states have similar laws. *See, e.g.,* GA. CODE ANN. § 31-9A-3 (West 2013) (requiring that informed consent include telling the patient about the availability of information on "fetal pain"); GA. CODE ANN. § 31-9A-4 (Supp. 2005) (requiring that information on pain potentially experienced by an "unborn child" be available via printed materials and the state's website); LA. REV. STAT. ANN. § 1299.35.6 (2012) (requiring that the patient be informed of anesthesia or analgesics that could alleviate or eliminate pain to the "unborn child"); MINN. STAT. ANN. § 145.4242 (West 2013) (requiring that the patient be informed that information has been provided on "fetal pain" and whether an anesthetic or analgesic would eliminate or alleviate pain to the "unborn child"); OKLA. STAT. ANN. tit. 63, § 1-738.8 (West 2013) (requiring that the patient be informed that materials are available about pain and the "unborn child").

55. *See* Carol Sanger, *Infant Safe Haven Laws: Legislating in the Culture of Life*, 106 COLUM. L. REV. 753, 753 (2006).

56. *See id.* at 773.

57. *See id.* at 755–56. The laws of a few states also allow other specified individuals to leave the child, with the mother's permission. *See id.* at 765.

58. *See id.* at 754–55.

59. *See id.* at 760, 809.

60. *See supra* note 2 (describing family-cap laws).

61. According to the Government Accountability Office, the federal interest-mortgage deduction is "the third most expensive federal income tax expenditure, with the government expected to forgo about $80 billion of revenue for the deduction in 2009." *See* U.S. GOV'T ACCOUNTABILITY OFFICE, HOME MORTGAGE INTEREST DEDUCTION: DESPITE CHALLENGES PRESENTED BY

Complex Tax Rules, IRS Could Enhance Enforcement and Guidance 1 (2009), *available at* http://www.gao.gov/products/GAO-09-769.

62. *See* 8 U.S.C. § 1151(2)(A)(i) (2006); 8 U.S.C. § 1153(a); Kerry Abrams, *Immigration Law and the Regulation of Marriage*, 91 Minn. L. Rev. 1625, 1629 (2007) (describing how "federal immigration law *is* family law" for noncitizens and for citizens who marry noncitizens).

63. This historical description relies on William G. Ross, *A Judicial Janus:* Meyer v. Nebraska *in Historical Perspective*, 57 U. Cin. L. Rev. 125, 131–32 (1988). The use of German was declining even before World War I, but it was still used in social clubs, newspapers, and parochial schools. *See id.* at 132.

64. *Id.* at 133.

65. *Id.* at 135.

66. *Id.*

67. *Id.* at 139–40.

68. *Id.* at 145.

69. *Id.* at 145–46.

70. *Id.* at 146.

71. *Id.* at 127–51.

72. Meyer v. State of Nebraska, 262 U.S. 390, 400 (1923).

73. *Id.* at 399.

74. David B. Tyack, *The Perils of Pluralism: The Background of the* Pierce *Case*, 74 Am. Hist. Rev. 74, 74 (1968).

75. Paula Abrams, Cross Purposes: *Pierce v. Society of Sisters* and the Struggle over Compulsory Public Education 8 (2009).

76. *Id.* at 1.

77. *Id.* at 3.

78. Pierce v. Soc'y of Sisters, 268 U.S. 510, 535 (1925).

79. *Id.* at 534–35.

80. The two other cases typically cited as part of the core doctrine finding a liberty interest for parents and recognizing family autonomy are Wisconsin v. Yoder, 406 U.S. 205 (1972), and Prince v. Massachusetts, 321 U.S. 158 (1944).

81. For all these examples, there are considerable nuances and also differences among the levels of government. Rather than exhaustively detailing these nuances and differences, the point is simply to show that as a general matter, there are multiple ways the state indirectly influences educational decisions.

82. This is a complicated area of the law, and each state's formulation differs somewhat. Consider the decision of an Ohio court: "the authority of the parents must yield to that of the state...because the faith of the parents, as firm and clear as it is, does not permit them, under the law of this state and the nation, to expose [their child] to progressive ill health and death." *In re* Willman, 24 Ohio App. 3d 191, 199 (OH App. 1986).

83. *See, e.g.*, Cal. Penal Code § 11165.7, § 11166 (West 2012); N.Y. Soc. Serv. Law § 413 (McKinney 2012); Fla. Stat. Ann. § 39.201 (West 2012).

84. Suzanne Mettler, The Submerged State: How Invisible Government Policies Undermine American Democracy 37 (2011) (citing the Social and Governmental Issues and Participation Study of 2008, Cornell Survey Research Institute, data to be made publicly available as of 2015).

85. Suzanne Mettler & Julianna Koch, *Who Says They Have Ever Used a Government Social Program?: The Role of Policy Visibility*, at 34 (2012), *available at* http://government.arts.cornell.edu/assets/faculty/docs/mettler/PerceptionGovt-KochMettler-022812.pdf.

86. A person who identified himself or herself as "extremely liberal" was 20 percent more likely to answer yes on the initial question than someone who identified himself or herself as "extremely conservative." Suzanne Mettler, *Our Hidden Government Benefits*, N.Y. TIMES, Sept. 19, 2011, at A31.

87. *Id.*

88. METTLER, *supra* note 84, at 4.

89. ORLANDO PATTERSON, RITUALS OF BLOOD: CONSEQUENCES OF SLAVERY IN TWO AMERICAN CENTURIES 27–28, 32, 34–36 (1998); PEGGY COOPER DAVIS, NEGLECTED STORIES: THE CONSTITUTION AND FAMILY VALUES 28–80 (1997).

90. *See* Katherine M. Franke, *Becoming a Citizen: Reconstruction Era Regulation of African American Marriages*, 11 YALE J.L. & HUMAN. 251, 288–89 (1999).

91. *See id.* at 258.

92. Social Security Act of 1935, Pub. L. No. 74-271, 49 Stat. 620 (1935) (codified as amended in scattered sections of 42 U.S.C.).

93. RICKIE SOLINGER, PREGNANCY AND POWER: A SHORT HISTORY OF REPRODUCTIVE POLITICS IN AMERICA 146 (2005); Roland J. Chilton, *Social Control through Welfare Legislation: The Impact of a State "Suitable Home Law,"* 5 LAW & SOC'Y REV. 205, 205–08 (1970).

94. Chilton, *supra* note 93, at 206.

95. LINDA GORDON, PITIED BUT NOT ENTITLED: SINGLE MOTHERS AND THE HISTORY OF WELFARE 1890–1935, at 298 (1994). Georgia was the first state categorically to deny welfare to all unwed mothers with more than one illegitimate child. *See* RICKIE SOLINGER, WAKE UP LITTLE SUSIE: SINGLE PREGNANCY AND RACE BEFORE *ROE V. WADE* 22 (1992). During the 1960s, nineteen additional states passed or attempted to pass similar laws, denying public assistance to thousands of illegitimate children. In Louisiana, more than twenty thousand children and six thousand unwed mothers were rendered ineligible. *See id.* Other states tried preventive measures such as sterilization or even imprisonment of women who seemed likely to conceive additional illegitimate children. *See* THOMAS LITTLEWOOD, THE POLITICS OF POPULATION CONTROL 107–32 (1977); WINIFRED BELL, AID TO DEPENDENT CHILDREN 70–71 (1965).

96. SOLINGER, *supra* note 95, at 22.

97. GORDON, *supra* note 95, at 298.

98. *See supra* note 2 (describing family-cap laws).

99. *See id.* (describing TANF's silence on family caps).

100. *Id.* § 608(b)(2)(A).

101. Jill Elaine Hasday, *Parenthood Divided: A Legal History of the Bifurcated Law of Parental Relations*, 90 GEO. L.J. 299, 370–71 (2002).

102. 26 U.S.C. §§ 151–152 (2006).

103. *Victims of State Sterilization Tell Their Stories: Hearing before the N.C. Justice for Sterilization Victims Found.* (June 30, 2011), http://www.wral.com/news/video/9755940/#/vid9755940; Adam Owens, *N.C. Dedicates Marker to Eugenics Program*, WRAL.COM (June 22, 2009), http://www.wral.com/news/local/story/5406081/.

104. DANIEL J. KEVLES, IN THE NAME OF EUGENICS: GENETICS AND THE USES OF HUMAN HEREDITY 92–94 (1985).

105. Kim Severson, *Thousands Sterilized, a State Weighs Restitution*, N.Y. Times, Dec. 10, 2011, at A1.

106. Clarence J. Gamble, *Eugenic Sterilization in North Carolina*, 12 N.C. Med. J. 550, 550–51 (1951).

107. Severson, *supra* note 105.

108. *Id.*

109. Linda Gordon, Heroes of Their Own Lives: The Politics and History of Family Violence Boston 1880–1960, at 27–58 (1988).

110. *Id.* at 14–16, 32–55.

111. *Id.* at 46–47.

112. *Id.* at 36.

113. Hasday, *supra* note 101, at 342.

114. *Id.* at 335–41.

115. *Id.*

116. *Id.* at 307.

117. *See* Charles Murray, Coming Apart: The State of White America, 1960–2010, at 143–208 (2012).

118. *See id.* at 130–40, 149–208.

119. *See id.* at 149–208.

120. *See id.* at 281. Murray does not uncritically laud the top 20 percent. Instead, he contends that there is a hollowness to this group. *See id.* at 285–95 ("Personally and as families, its members are successful. But they have abdicated their responsibility to set and promulgate standards. The most powerful and successful members of their class increasingly trade on the perks of their privileged positions without regard to the seemliness of that behavior").

121. *See id.* at 282.

122. *See id.* at 281.

123. *See id.* at 282.

124. *See id.* at 279–81.

125. *See* Frances E. Olsen, *The Myth of State Intervention in the Family*, 18 U. Mich. J.L. Reform 835, 835 (1985). Mary Ann Glendon has made a similar point: "debates framed in terms of choice between intervention and nonintervention are as simplistic and unhelpful as those which try to distinguish sharply between individual and societal interests. These false dichotomies tend to obscure the facts that modern governments cannot avoid influencing families, directly and indirectly, in countless ways and that individuals benefit, not only from having 'rights,' but also from being surrounded by certain kinds of social arrangements." Mary Ann Glendon, The Transformation of Family Law 307–08 (1989).

126. *See* Olsen, *supra* note 125, at 863.

127. *See id.* ("The protective intervention argument misperceives the problems caused by unfortunate social policies. For example, the problem with state officials taking children away from poor parents is not really a problem of state 'intervention,' but a problem of the substance of that state behavior").

128. *See, e.g.*, Fox News Debate, on Martin Luther King Day, in Myrtle Beach, South Carolina, OnTheIssues.org (Jan. 16, 2012), http://www.issues2000.org/2012_GOP_SC_MLK.htm.

129. Rick Santorum on Fox News Debate on MLK Day at Myrtle Beach, OnTheIssues.org (Jan. 16, 2012), http://www.issues2000.org/Archive/2012_GOP_SC_MLK_Rick_Santorum.htm.

130. METTLER, *supra* note 84, at 4–5.

131. *Id.* at 5.

132. *Id.* at 69–71.

133. *Id.*

134. *Id.*

135. REPUBLIC NATIONAL COMMITTEE, 2012 REPUBLIC PLATFORM: RENEWING AMERICAN VALUES TO BUILD HEALTHY FAMILIES, GREAT SCHOOLS AND SAFE NEIGHBORHOODS, GOP.COM, *available at* http://www.gop.com/2012-republican-platform_ Renewing/.

136. METTLER, *supra* note 84, at 42–43.

137. Federal Agriculture Improvement and Reform Act of 1996, Pub. L. No. 104–127, 110 Stat. 88 (1996); Sarah Cohen et al., *Farm Subsidies over Time,* WASH. POST, July 2, 2006, *available at* http://www.washingtonpost.com/wp-dyn/content/graphic/2006/07/02/ GR2006070200024.html.

138. Food, Conservation, and Energy Act of 2008, Pub. L. No. 110-234, 122 Stat. 923 (2008) (codified in various sections of 7 U.S.C.).

139. 43 U.S.C. § 315 (2006). Some commentators criticize the grazing program for creating the "welfare cowboy" at the expense of environmental concerns. Michelle M. Campana, Student Article, *Public Lands Grazing Fee Reform: Welfare Cowboys and Rolex Ranchers Wrangling with the New West,* 10 N.Y.U. ENVTL. L.J. 403, 404 (2002).

140. ADENIKE ADEYEYE ET AL., ENVTL. LAW INST., ESTIMATING U.S. GOVERNMENT SUBSIDIES TO ENERGY SOURCES: 2002–2008, 9–21 (2009) (describing these subsidies).

141. Katherine M. Franke, *Longing for Loving,* 76 FORDHAM L. REV. 2688 (2008).

142. *Id.* at 2701.

143. MARTHA ALBERTSON FINEMAN, THE AUTONOMY MYTH: A THEORY OF DEPENDENCY 67, 121 (2004); MARTHA ALBERTSON FINEMAN, THE NEUTERED MOTHER, THE SEXUAL FAMILY AND OTHER TWENTIETH CENTURY TRAGEDIES 47–48, 161–66, 226–36 (1995).

CHAPTER 4

1. This description is based on a newspaper account. *See* N. R. Kleinfield, *The Girls Who Haven't Come Home,* N.Y. TIMES, July 7, 2013, at A20.

2. *Id.*

3. *Id.* at A21.

4. Four of the children were once in foster care for twenty-two months, which is not a short period, but there is no indication that Hill had tremendous difficulty regaining custody.

5. Edward Z. Tronick & Jeffery F. Cohn, *Infant-Mother Face-to-Face Interaction: Age and Gender Differences in Coordination and the Occurrence of Miscoordination,* 60 CHILD DEV. 85, 90 (1989).

6. Edward Z. Tronick & Andrew F. Gianino, *The Transmission of Maternal Disturbance to the Infant,* 1986 NEW DIRECTIONS FOR CHILD & ADOLESCENT DEV. 5, 8 (noting that for one out of three initial misattunements, the mother corrects the error).

7. Nancy S. Weinfield et al., *Individual Differences in Infant-Caregiver Attachment: Conceptual and Empirical Aspects of Security, in* HANDBOOK OF ATTACHMENT: THEORY, RESEARCH, AND

CLINICAL APPLICATIONS 84 (Jude Cassidy & Phillip R. Shaver eds., 2d ed. 2008); Tronick & Cohn, *supra* note 5, at 90.

8. Tronick & Gianino, *supra* note 6, at 9–10.

9. *See* ROBERT E. EMERY, RENEGOTIATING FAMILY RELATIONSHIPS: DIVORCE, CHILD CUSTODY, AND MEDIATION 215 (1994) (stating that only a spouse's death is ranked higher than divorce with respect to stress and noting that divorce involves numerous negative emotions, such as anger, regret, and sadness).

10. *See id.* at 42–48 (discussing a cyclical theory of grief in divorce).

11. *See* CHILD PROTECTION: USING RESEARCH TO IMPROVE POLICY AND PRACTICE (Ron Haskins et al. eds., 2007) (examining the effects of abuse and neglect on children); CYNTHIA CROSSON TOWER, UNDERSTANDING CHILD ABUSE AND NEGLECT 255 (3d ed. 1996); ANTHONY J. URQUIZA & CYNTHIA WINN, U.S. DEP'T HEALTH & HUM. SERVS., TREATMENT FOR ABUSED AND NEGLECTED CHILDREN: INFANCY TO AGE 18, at 71–80 (1994), *available at* http://www.childwelfare.gov/pubs/usermanuals/treatmen/acknow.cfm.

12. *See generally* JOHN BOWLBY, ATTACHMENT 24–34 (2d ed. 1982) (documenting the psychological and emotional trauma children experience when separated from their mothers); JOHN BOWLBY, LOSS: SADNESS AND DEPRESSION 7–14, 397–411, (1980); JOHN BOWLBY, SEPARATION: ANXIETY AND ANGER 13, 245–57 (1973); Wendy L. Haight et al., *Parent-Child Interaction during Foster Care Visits*, 46 SOC. WORK 325, 337–38 (2000) (discussing a study on parent-child visitation during separation that indicated the importance of reducing the time the parent and child are separated because of the disruptive impact of separation on the parent-child relationship and the risk of attachment-related issues for the child).

13. TOWER, *supra* note 11, at 255.

14. *See* Annette R. Appell, *The Endurance of Biological Connection: Heteronormativity, Same-Sex Parenting and the Lessons of Adoption*, 22 BYU J. PUB. L. 289, 295–96 (2008) ("It is common for adoptees to experience a deep and ongoing desire for 'roots, for existential continuity, and for a sense of completeness.' This 'genealogical bewilderment' is common among adoptees, regardless of the quality of their adoptive family relationships, and do not detract from those relationships.... This interest in connections is not limited to adoptees; birth parents and adoptive parents experience them as well. Birth parents often feel deep and ongoing or episodic connection to the children they relinquished. Adoptive parents too experience the gap between their child's original family or community and the child's adopted one and have their own curiosities about the child's birth family").

15. *See* Joan Heifetz Hollinger, *Adoption and Aspiration: The Uniform Adoption Act, the DeBoer–Schmidt Case, and the American Quest for the Ideal Family*, 2 DUKE J. GENDER L. & POL'Y 15, 38–40 (1995) (describing the primal-wound narrative of adoption in American culture).

16. *See* ANN FESSLER, THE GIRLS WHO WENT AWAY: THE HIDDEN HISTORY OF WOMEN WHO SURRENDERED CHILDREN FOR ADOPTION IN THE DECADES BEFORE *ROE V. WADE* (2006) (describing the pre-*Roe* years, when large percentages of young unmarried women were sexually active but had little access to birth control and further describing the secrecy of the adoption system in which young women who "went away" to have babies were typically pressured into surrendering their children for adoption, experiencing grief and guilt for years afterward but also describing a range of emotional reactions to the experience).

17. ADMIN. FOR CHILDREN & FAMILIES, U.S. DEP'T HEALTH & HUM. SERVS., THE AFCARS REPORT 6 (2012), *available at* http://www.acf.hhs.gov/sites/default/files/cb/

afcarsreport19.pdf (hereinafter AFCARS Report) (31 percent of children adopted out of the foster-care system in 2011 were adopted by a relative).

18. Sharon Vandivere et al., U.S. Dep't Health & Hum. Servs., Adoption USA: A Chartbook Based on the National Survey of Adoptive Parents 58, tbl. 2 (2009), *available at* http://aspe.hhs.gov/hsp/09/NSAP/chartbook/index.pdf. These statistics exclude adoptions from the child-welfare system.

19. Naomi R. Cahn & Joan Heifetz Hollinger, *Adoption and Confidentiality, in* Families by Law: An Adoption Reader 123 (Naomi R. Cahn & Joan Heifetz Hollinger eds., 2004) ("Adult adoptees cite health-related, medical, and psychological reasons for wanting to know the identity of their birth parents. Many are searching to fill in what they claim are missing parts of their identity, for an explanation of why they were relinquished for adoption, or to reassure their birth parents that they are well"); *see also* Annette Ruth Appell, *Blending Families through Adoption: Implications for Collaborative Adoption Law and Practice*, 75 B.U. L. Rev. 997, 998–1013 (1995) (describing unique characteristics of adoptive families and the need to recognize, not obscure, this uniqueness).

20. *See* Mark E. Courtney et al., Chapin Hall Ctr. for Children, Midwest Evaluation of the Adult Functioning of Former Foster Youth: Outcomes at Age 19, at 13–14 (2005), *available at* http://www.chapinhall.org/sites/default/files/Chapin HallDocument_4.pdf.

21. Andrew Cherlin, The Marriage-Go-Round: The State of Marriage and the Family in American Today 17 (2009).

22. The adversarial nature of the proceedings is intended to protect the rights of the parties, increase accuracy in fact-finding, ensure the integrity of the decision-making process, and instill a sense of legitimacy in the process. In a typical case, this means that parties have a right to be represented by a lawyer who advocates for only that party and no one else, that parties can call witnesses to support their version of events, that basic rules of evidence are used to ensure that testimony and documents are reliable, that lawyers can challenge evidence introduced by the other side, and so on. Although there are some important countercurrents, in its essence, dispute-resolution family law embraces these values.

23. In a highly fractured 2000 decision, the U.S. Supreme Court struck down a Washington state law that would have allowed a third party to petition a court for visitation with a child. The case was brought by two grandparents, who had sought visitation with their grandchildren, against the wishes of their daughter-in-law, after the children's father had died. The case generated multiple opinions by the justices, and no single opinion garnered a majority. The opinions did affirm that parents stand in a preferred position vis-à-vis nonparents when it comes to making important decisions for a child, but the plurality opinion, written by Justice O'Connor, did not adopt a categorical approach. Instead, the opinion merely stated that the parent's decision about visitation should be given "special weight" by a court. *See* Troxel v. Granville, 530 U.S. 57, 70 (2000).

24. *See generally* J. Herbie DiFonzo, Beneath the Fault Line: The Popular and Legal Culture of Divorce in Twentieth-Century America (1997).

25. Ira Mark Ellman et al., Family Law: Cases, Text, Problems 267 (5th ed. 2010).

26. Linda D. Elrod & Robert G. Spector, *A Review of the Year in Family Law: Parentage and Assisted Reproduction Problems Take Center Stage*, 39 Fam. L.Q. 879, 917 chart 1 (2006) (showing state-by-state comparison).

27. For a recent case exemplifying the kind of dispute that can arise between adoptive and biological parents, *see Adoptive Couple v. Baby Girl*, 133 S. Ct. 2552 (2013).

28. *See* Katharine B. Silbaugh, *Money as Emotion in the Distribution of Wealth at Divorce, in* Reconceiving the Family: Critique on the American Law Institute's Principles of the Law of Family Dissolution 234 (Robin Fretwell Wilson ed., 2006) (contending that the ALI Principles wrongly distinguish financial from nonfinancial matters, "fail[ing] to appreciate how emotional financial issues can become within marriages and at the time of marital dissolution. Finances are not distinct from emotions in relationships, but are an avenue through which spouses express emotions").

29. *See* Andrea K. Schneider & Nancy Mills, *What Family Lawyers Are Really Doing When They Negotiate*, 44 Fam. Ct. Rev. 612, 617 (2006). There may be several reasons for family-law attorneys to engage in this type of behavior. For example, clients may push their lawyers to engage in negative behavior, the emotional content of the subject matter may lead to negative behavior, and cases with lawyers may be disproportionately hard, thus requiring adversarial behavior.

30. *See id.* at 613, 617.

31. For example, between 1980 and 1992, joint-custody awards in Wisconsin increased from 18 percent to 81 percent of all custody awards. *See* Marigold S. Melli, Patricia R. Brown & Maria Cancian, *Child Custody in a Changing World: A Study of Postdivorce Arrangements in Wisconsin*, 1997 U. Ill. L. Rev. 773, 778 (1997); *see also id.* at 787 (noting that joint custody was most likely when the parties had fewest appearances before the court, indicating that these were instances in which the parties were able to resolve the issue largely without court intervention, whereas the couples with unequal and split custody had the highest number of court appearances, indicating that these were high-conflict cases).

32. States differ on their standards for reviewing settlement agreements on custody. In most states, judges are required to consider settlement agreements as one factor in determining what is in the best interests of the child but not necessarily to defer to parental agreements. *See* Linda Jellum, *Parents Know Best: Revising Our Approach to Parental Custody Agreements*, 65 Ohio St. L.J. 615, 624 (2004). In other states, judges are required to presume that settlement agreements are in the best interests of the child but must set aside any agreements that the judge determines are not in the child's best interests. *See id.* At least one state, Oregon, requires judges to enforce parental agreements for joint custody. *See id.* at 625.

33. If the couple cannot agree on custody at the outset of the case, they often do so through mediation or by settling the case at some point in the litigation, before it reaches the trial stage in front of a judge. In a study of 1998 data for an urban county, researchers found that 9 percent of cases proceeded through a trial and required a judicial adjudication. *See* T. K. Logan et al., *Divorce, Custody, and Spousal Violence: A Random Sample of Circuit Court Docket Records*, 18 J. Fam. Violence 269, 273 (2003). An older study found lower numbers. Examining more than nine hundred divorce cases in California from 1984 to 1987, this study found only 3.7 percent of cases proceeded to a trial, and only 1.5 percent failed to be settled before being decided by a judge. *See* Eleanor E. Maccoby & Robert H. Mnookin, Dividing the Child: Social and Legal Dilemmas of Custody 137–38 (1992) (fig. 7.2 showing breakdown of resolution types).

34. For the classic discussion of the indeterminacy of the best-interests standard, *see* Robert H. Mnookin, *Child-Custody Adjudication: Judicial Functions in the Face of Indeterminacy*, 39 L. & Contemp. Probs. 226 (1975).

35. Elizabeth S. Scott & Robert E. Emery, *Gender Politics and Child Custody: The Puzzling Persistence of the Best Interest Standard* 7 (Columbia Law Sch. Pub. Law & Legal Theory, Working Paper No. 9200, 2011), *available at* http://lsr.nellco.org/cgi/viewcontent.cgi?article=1092&cont ext=columbia_pllt, to be published at 77 L. & CONTEMP. PROBS. (forthcoming 2014).

36. *Id.* at 32.

37. *Id.* at 32–33.

38. *Id.* at 33.

39. Jeanne Wright, *Disorder in Court: Violence against Attorneys and Judges Is Increasing; Tighter Security Is One Solution; Another Is Knowing Self-Defense,* L.A. TIMES, Sept. 24, 1992, *available at* http://articles.latimes.com/1992-09-24/news/vw-1188_1_defense-attorney (present-ing anecdotal evidence of dangers for family-law judges and attorneys; "Legal experts say family law has the highest risk for violence. Attorneys are often dealing with clients who are experiencing the most traumatic events of their lives").

40. Mark Hansen, *Lawyers in Harm's Way,* 84 A.B.A. J. 93, 93 (1998) (describing results of ABA's family-lawyer violence survey).

41. SARAH FASS, NAT'L CTR. FOR CHILDREN IN POVERTY, PAID LEAVE IN THE STATES: A CRITICAL SUPPORT FOR LOW-WAGE WORKERS AND THEIR FAMILIES 3 (2009).

42. *See* 29 U.S.C. §§ 2601–2654 (2006).

43. Meloney Barney, *Upward Bound in Foster Care: What Worked for Me and What Remains to Be Done, in* GROWING UP IN THE CARE OF STRANGERS: THE EXPERIENCES, INSIGHTS AND RECOMMENDATIONS OF ELEVEN FORMER FOSTER KIDS 97, 97–110 (Waln K. Brown & John R. Seita eds., 2009).

44. *See* JANE WALDFOGEL, THE FUTURE OF CHILD PROTECTION: HOW TO BREAK THE CYCLE OF ABUSE AND NEGLECT 124–25 (1998). These percentages are not hard numbers. Indeed, as Waldfogel acknowledges, the percentages vary "a great deal by jurisdiction and over time." *See id.* at 124.

45. *See id.* at 125 (describing the connection between poverty and neglect); ADMIN. ON CHIL-DREN, YOUTH & FAMILIES, U.S. DEP'T HEALTH & HUM. SERVS., CHILD MALTREATMENT 2011, 21 (2012), *available at* http://www.acf.hhs.gov/sites/default/files/cb/cm11.pdf (in 2011, "Four-fifths (78.5%) of (unique count) victims were neglected, 17.6 percent were physically abused, and 9.1 percent were sexually abused").

46. PETER J. PECORA ET AL., CASEY FAM. PROGRAMS, IMPROVING FAMILY FOSTER CARE: FINDINGS FROM THE NORTHWEST FOSTER CARE ALUMNI STUDY 32 (2005), *avail-able at* http://www.casey.org/Resources/Publications/pdf/ImprovingFamilyFosterCare_FR.pdf (citing government sources when pointing out, "The prevalence of PTSD within the previous 12 months was significantly higher among alumni [25.2%] than among the general U.S. popula-tion [4.0%]. As a comparison, American war veterans have lower rates of PTSD [Vietnam: 15%; Afghanistan: 6%; and Iraq: 12% to 13%]").

47. *Id.* at 34 (tbl. 7.1, showing significantly higher rates among former foster children than the general population for depression, panic syndrome, social phobia, anxiety, alcohol dependence, drug dependence, and eating disorders).

48. *See, e.g.,* NAN P. ROMAN & PHYLLIS WOLFE, NAT'L ALLIANCE TO END HOMELESSNESS, WEB OF FAILURE: THE RELATIONSHIP BETWEEN FOSTER CARE AND HOMELESSNESS 9 (1995), *available at* http://b.3cdn.net/naeh/0322dc703428f347f3_s3m6iiv34 (finding that in a nationwide survey of homeless families in shelters, 77 percent of those parents who had once

been in foster care had at least one child who was or had been in foster care, as compared with 27 percent of parents in the shelters who did not have such a history). For an anecdotal account of the intergenerational cycle, *see* NINA BERNSTEIN, THE LOST CHILDREN OF WILDER (2001).

49. *See* COMM. ON WAYS & MEANS, U.S. HOUSE OF REPRESENTATIVES, GREEN BOOK 2012, at ch. 11: *Child Welfare Introduction and Overview* (providing statistics for state fiscal year 2010). A little more than half of the money came from state and local sources and the remainder from the federal government. *See id.* ($15.8 billion, or 54 percent of the total, was from state and local sources; $13.6 billion, 46 percent of the total, was from the federal government).

50. *See* CTR. FOR LAW & SOC. POL'Y, FEDERAL POLICY RECOMMENDATIONS FOR 2010 AND BEYOND 9–10 (2010), *available at* www.clasp.org/admin/site/publications/files/antipov-ertyagenda.pdf (hereinafter FEDERAL POLICY RECOMMENDATIONS FOR 2010 AND BEYOND) (estimating costs of physical and mental-health problems, including incarceration and lost productivity).

51. Wendy L. Haight, Jill Doner Kagle & James E. Black, *Understanding and Supporting Parent-Child Relationships during Foster Care Visits: Attachment Theory and Research*, 48 SOC. WORK 198, 198 (2003) ("A child's move into foster care and separation from the primary care-giver is likely to be stressful or traumatic for both parties. Visits may cause the parent and child to repeatedly re-experience difficult emotions associated with reunion and separation"); *id.* ("Infants and young children who are separated from their attachment figures through foster care not only experience significant emotional stress and sadness, but also may experience a decrease in the enrichment and structure important for continued social, cognitive, and communicative development").

52. AFCARS Report, *supra* note 17, at 3 (52 percent of children exiting foster care in 2011 were returned to a parent or primary caregiver).

53. Clare Huntington, *Welfare Reform and Child Care: A Proposal for State Legislation*, 6 CORNELL J.L. & PUB. POL'Y 95, 110 (1996) (citing a Carnegie Corporation study on the indi-vidual and societal productivity gains that come from high-quality subsidized child care; also citing the Committee for Economic Development's findings of child care's strengthening effect on the national economy).

54. CHILDREN'S DEFENSE FUND, CHILD CARE BASICS 2 (2005), *available at* http://www.childrensdefense.org/child-research-data-publications/data/child-care-basics.pdf (hereinafter CHILD CARE BASICS). By contrast, children enrolled in lesser-quality child-care settings have delayed language and reading skills and are more aggressive to other children and adults. *See id.*

55. *Id.*

56. CHILDREN'S DEFENSE FUND, THE STATE OF AMERICA'S CHILDREN HANDBOOK 2012, at 32 (2012), *available at* http://www.childrensdefense.org/child-research-data-publications/data/soac-2012-handbook.pdf (hereinafter STATE OF AMERICA'S CHILDREN HANDBOOK 2012).

57. FEDERAL POLICY RECOMMENDATIONS FOR 2010 AND BEYOND, *supra* note 50, at 8. For a break down state by state, *see* STATE OF AMERICA'S CHILDREN HANDBOOK 2012, *supra* note 56, at 35.

58. FEDERAL POLICY RECOMMENDATIONS FOR 2010 AND BEYOND, *supra* note 50, at 8.

59. *Child Care Arrangements of Grade School Children Ages 5–14 with Employed Mothers by Age, Selected Years 1995–2010*, CHILDSTATS.GOV, http://www.childstats.gov/americaschildren/tables/fam3c.asp?popup=true.

60. Huntington, *supra* note 53, at 115–17 (describing the funding shortfalls).

61. *Compare Fiscal Year 2013 Federal Child Care and Related Appropriations*, ADMIN. FOR CHILDREN & FAMILIES, U.S. DEP'T HEALTH & HUM. SERVS. (May 30, 2013), *available at* http:// www.acf.hhs.gov/programs/occ/resource/fy-2013-federal-child-care-and-related-appropriations, *with* U.S. DEP'T HEALTH & HUM. SERVS., CHILD CARE AND DEVELOPMENT FUND (CCDF) REPORT TO CONGRESS FOR FY 2006 AND FY 2007, at 3 (2011), *available at* http://www.acf. hhs.gov/sites/default/files/occ/rtc_2006_2007.pdf ("For both Fiscal Years (FY) 2006 and 2007, approximately $5 billion in Federal CCDF funding was available").

62. AMY BELASCO, CONG. RESEARCH SERV., THE COST OF IRAQ, AFGHANISTAN, AND OTHER GLOBAL WAR ON TERROR OPERATIONS SINCE 9/11, at 3 (2011), *available at* http:// www.fas.org/sgp/crs/natsec/RL33110.pdf (tbl. 1, Estimated War Funding by Operation: FY2001– FY2012 War Request).

63. NAT'L INST. FOR EARLY EDUC. RESEARCH, THE STATE OF PRESCHOOL 2011, at 5 (2012), *available at* http://www.nieer.org/sites/nieer/files/2011yearbook.pdf (citing the extensive cuts in the "What's New?" section of the Executive Summary).

64. Kate Taylor, *Budget Cuts May Threaten City Programs for Children,* N.Y. TIMES, Mar. 5, 2012, at A15, *available at* http://www.nytimes.com/2012/03/05/nyregion/mayors-budget-cutbacks-may-threaten-city-programs-for-children.html ("The number of children from low-income working families who attend city-subsidized child care has dropped by more than 9,000 since 2009, from 51,712 to 42,215. And the number of children attending after-school programs…has declined even more sharply, from 85,513 in 2009 to 52,000 in 2012—a drop of almost 40 percent").

65. Lee Rainwater & Timothy M. Smeeding, *Single-Parent Poverty, Inequality, and the Welfare State, in* THE FUTURE OF THE FAMILY 96, 97 (Daniel P. Moynihan, Timothy M. Smeeding & Lee Rainwater eds., 2004).

66. *Id.* at 105.

67. *Id.* at 98. Another difference is that in the United States, 30 percent of children living with single mothers live in extreme poverty, as compared with 6 percent in the United Kingdom and 2 percent in Sweden. *See id.* at 102 (defining extreme poverty as less than 30 percent of median income).

68. *Id.* at 99–101 (tracking spending and dividing countries into different regional groups, noting that the United Kingdom and Canada, combined with Australia, average more than 6 percent GDP, and Sweden is part of a group of Nordic Scandinavian countries that spends more than 12 percent of GDP).

69. *Id.* at 110.

70. *Id.* at 108–09. Single mothers in the United Kingdom also work these kinds of jobs, partially accounting for the difference in poverty rates between the United Kingdom and Sweden.

71. *Id.* at 108.

72. OWEN D. GUTFREUND, TWENTIETH CENTURY SPRAWL: HIGHWAYS AND THE SHAPING OF THE AMERICAN LANDSCAPE 58–59 (2005).

73. Katharine B. Silbaugh, *Women's Place: Urban Planning, Housing Design, and Work-Family Balance,* 76 FORDHAM L. REV. 1797, 1825–29 (2007); David Leonhardt, *In Climbing Income Ladder, Location Matters,* N.Y. TIMES, July 22, 2013, at A1, *available at* http://www.nytimes. com/2013/07/22/business/in-climbing-income-ladder-location-matters.html?_r=2&.

74. Penelope Green, *Under One Roof, Building for Extended Families,* N.Y. TIMES, Nov. 29, 2012, at A1, *available at* http://www.nytimes.com/2012/11/30/us/building-homes-for-modern-multigenerational-families.html.

75. Kim Parker, Pew Research Ctr., The Boomerang Generation: Feeling OK about Living with Mom and Dad 10 (2012), *available at* http://www.pewsocialtrends.org/files/2012/03/PewSocialTrends-2012-BoomerangGeneration.pdf.

76. *Id.* at 1–2.

77. *Id.* at 1.

78. Green, *supra* note 74.

79. Michelle Ernst et al., Transp. for Am., Dangerous by Design 2011: Solving the Epidemic of Preventable Pedestrian Deaths 11 tbl. 1 (2011), *available at* http://t4america.org/docs/dbd2011/Dangerous-by-Design-2011.pdf.

80. *Id.* at 5, 10.

81. *Id.* at 25.

82. Raj Chetty et al., The Economic Impacts of Tax Expenditures: Evidence from Spatial Variation across the U.S. 10, 19 tbl. 6 (July 2013) (unpublished draft, on file with the Equality of Opportunity Project, Harvard University), *available at* http://obs.rc.fas.harvard.edu/chetty/tax_expenditure_soi_whitepaper.pdf.

83. Leonhardt, *supra* note 73; *Mobility in the 100 Largest Commuting Zones*, Equality of Opportunity Project, *available at* http://www.equality-of-opportunity.org/index.php/city-rankings/city-rankings-100.

84. Chetty et al., *supra* note 82.

85. T. H. Marshall, *Citizenship and Social Class* (1963), *reprinted in* The Citizenship Debates 93, 94 (Gershon Shafir ed., 1998).

86. *Id.*.

87. *Id.* at 99–100 ("The Poor Law treated the claims of the poor, not as an integral part of the rights of the citizen, but as an alternative to them").

88. *Id.* at 107.

89. *Id.* at 108.

90. Will Kymlicka & Wayne Norman, *Return of the Citizen: A Survey of Recent Work on Citizenship Theory*, 104 Ethics 352, 355–56 (1994).

91. Kristy M. Krivickas & Daphne Lofquist, U.S. Census Bureau, Fertility & Family Statistics Branch, Demographics of Same-Sex Couple Households with Children 3 (Working Paper No. 2011–11, 2011), *available at* http://www.census.gov/population/www/socdemo/Krivickas-Lofquist%20PAA%202011.pdf (finding 150,000 same-sex couples in marital relationships).

92. The availability of second-parent adoptions to same-sex partners varies widely by state. For an excellent visual depiction of legal protections, *see* Am. Civil Liberties Union, States Where Same-Sex Couples Are Able to Get Joint and/or Second Parent Adoptions Statewide (2012), *available at* http://www.aclu.org/files/assets/aclu_map4.pdf.

93. *In re* Marriage Cases, 188 P.3d 384 (Cal. 2008).

94. John M. Hubbell, *Coalition Seeks Male-Female Marriage Definition: New Ballot Push for Constitutional Amendment*, S.F. Chron. (Apr. 28, 2005), *available at* http://www.sfgate.com/bayarea/article/CALIFORNIA-Coalition-seeks-male-female-marriage-2677038.php.

95. Proposition 8, Initiative Constitutional Amendment (California, 2008), *available at* http://vig.cdn.sos.ca.gov/2008/general/pdf-guide/Props/title-summary-analysis/prop8-title-summ-analysis-pg54-55.pdf.

96. Hollingsworth v. Perry, 558 U.S. 183 (2013).

97. Perry v. Brown, 671 F.3d 1052, 1078 (9th Cir. 2010).

98. Robert I. Lerman, *Capabilities and Contributions of Unwed Fathers*, 20 FUTURE OF CHILDREN 63, 64 (2010).

99. *Id.*

100. Ann Cammett, *Deadbeats, Deadbrokes, and Prisoners*, 18 GEO. J. ON POVERTY L. & POL'Y 127, 145 (2011).

101. Esther Griswold & Jessica Pearson, *Twelve Reasons for Collaboration between Departments of Correction and Child Support Enforcement Agencies*, 65 CORRECTIONS TODAY 87, 87 (2003).

102. 42 U.S.C. § 608(a)(2) (2012).

103. 42 U.S.C. § 608(a)(3) (2012).

104. *See* Laurie S. Kohn, *Engaging Men as Fathers: The Courts, the Law, and Father-Absence in Low-income Families*, 35 CARDOZO L. REV. 102 (2013).

105. As legal scholar Kristin Collins has documented at length, the federal government provided cash assistance to military widows throughout the nineteenth century. *See* Kristin A. Collins, *"Petitions without Number": Widows' Petitions and the Early Nineteenth Century Origins of Public Marriage-Based Entitlements*, 31 L. & HIST. REV. 1, 7–14 (2013) (summarizing her work on this topic). These programs were designed only for widows and, in practice, were limited to white widows. *See id.* Later versions of cash assistance programs in the twentieth century, notably Aid to Dependent Children and then Aid to Families with Dependent Children, were not limited to widows, but men and married couples were ineligible. *See* Angela Onwuachi-Willig, *The Return of the Ring: Welfare Reform's Marriage Cure as the Revival of Post-Bellum Control*, 93 CAL. L. REV. 1647, 1665–73, 1685 (2005) (describing this history).

106. Known as the "man in the house rules," in the 1950s and 1960s, state welfare-eligibility rules either disqualified a woman cohabiting with a man or counted the man's income in the income eligibility calculation, thus pushing thousands of families off the welfare rolls. *See* William E. Forbath, *Lincoln, the Declaration, and the "Grisly, Undying Corpse of States' Rights": History, Memory, and Imagination in the Constitution of a Southern Liberal*, 92 GEO. L.J. 709, 764–67 (2004) (describing these rules and their effect). The U.S. Supreme Court struck down these rules as a violation of equal protection. *See* Lewis v. Martin, 397 U.S. 552, 559 (1970); King v. Smith, 392 U.S. 309, 321–27 (1968).

107. INTERNAL REVENUE SERVICE, *Earned Income Tax Credit for 2012; Do I Qualify? available at* http://www.irs.gov/uac/Newsroom/Earned-Income-Tax-Credit-for-2012;-Do-I-Qualify%3F.

108. For tax year 2013, the maximum possible payment was $6,044. INTERNAL REVENUE SERVICE, PREVIEW OF 2013 EITC INCOME LIMITS, MAXIMUM CREDIT AMOUNTS AND TAX LAW UPDATES, *available at* http://www.irs.gov/Individuals/Preview-of-2012-EITC-Income-Limits,-Maximum-Credit--Amounts-and-Tax-Law-Updates.

109. INTERNAL REVENUE SERVICE, PREVIEW OF 2013 EITC INCOME LIMITS, MAXIMUM CREDIT AMOUNTS AND TAX LAW UPDATES, *available at* http://www.irs.gov/Individuals/Preview-of-2012-EITC-Income-Limits,-Maximum-Credit—Amounts-and-Tax-Law-Updates. For a nuanced discussion of the potential marriage penalty or marriage bonus, *see* David Ellwood, *The Impact of the Earned Income Tax Credit and Social Policy Reforms on Work, Marriage, and Living Arrangements*, 53 NAT'L TAX J. 1063, 1070–72, 1987–97 (2000).

110. *See* U.S. DEP'T AGRIC., SUPPLEMENTAL NUTRITION ASSISTANCE PROGRAM PARTICIPATION AND COSTS, *available at* http://www.fns.usda.gov/pd/snapsummary.htm (46,609,000 recipients).

111. 7 C.F.R. § 273.1(b)(1)(i).

112. 7 C.F.R. § 273.1(a)(3).

113. *See* Anne Alstott, *The Earned Income Tax Credit and the Limitations of Tax-Base Welfare Reform*, 108 HARV. L. REV. 533, 559–564 (1995) (discussing the difficulty of assessing the impact of marriage penalties).

114. KATHRYN EDIN & TIMOTHY J. NELSON, DOING THE BEST I CAN: FATHERHOOD AND THE INNER CITY 88 (2013) (describing the response of a woman to one study participant's proposal of marriage: "she turned him down flat, saying she didn't want to lose her freedom, her food stamps, or her subsidized apartment").

115. *See* Ellwood, *supra* note 109, at 1100 (studying the expansion of the EITC to determine whether its greater availability affected marriage or cohabitation rates and not finding "any real evidence that the EITC marriage penalties were reducing marriage" rates).

116. *See* Alstott, *supra* note 113, at 559–564 (describing the inevitable trade-off between avoiding marriage penalties and targeting programs to those most in need; noting, for example, that if income was treated on an individual, not a pooled, basis, then a couple with one spouse earning $200,000 and the other earning $10,000 would qualify for the EITC on the basis of the second spouse's earnings, even though the children in the family are not nearly in the same situation as the children of an unmarried single worker who earns $10,000).

117. JOSEPH GOLDSTEIN ET AL., IN THE BEST INTERESTS OF THE CHILD (1986); JOSEPH GOLDSTEIN ET AL., BEFORE THE BEST INTERESTS OF THE CHILD (1979); JOSEPH GOLDSTEIN ET AL., BEYOND THE BEST INTERESTS OF THE CHILD (1973).

118. *See, e.g.*, Adoption and Safe Families Act of 1997, Pub. L. No. 105-89, § 302, 111 Stat. 2115 (requiring the state either to return a child in foster care home as quickly as possible or find a new, permanent home, to ensure that the child has stability and continuity in his or her relationships).

119. There are some historical antecedents to the efforts described here, such as conciliation courts, which began in the 1930s. *See* J. Herbie DiFonzo, *Coercive Conciliation: Judge Paul W. Alexander and the Movement for Therapeutic Divorce*, 25 U. TOL. L. REV. 535, 543–44 (1994) (describing various state initiatives from the 1930s and 1940s); *see also* MARTHA ALBERTSON FINEMAN, THE ILLUSION OF EQUALITY: THE RHETORIC AND REALITY OF DIVORCE REFORM 151 (1991) (describing the expanding role of social workers in divorce). Additionally, no-fault divorce was originally conceived of as a method for decreasing hostility between divorcing spouses by putting these actions in family courts with specialized judges and trained staff available to help families resolve their disputes. *See* Herma Hill Kay, *Equality and Difference: A Perspective on No-Fault Divorce and Its Aftermath*, 56 U. CIN. L. REV. 1, 4–14 (1987) (providing an overview of the no-fault-divorce movement).

120. One study found that approximately 15 percent of all cases involve joint physical custody, *see* Suzanne Reynolds, Catherine T. Harris & Ralph A. Peeples, *Back to the Future: An Empirical Study of Child Custody Outcomes*, 85 N.C. L. REV. 1629, 1667 (2007), and the vast majority of cases involve joint legal custody, *see id.* at 1674–75 (finding that 70 percent of all custody cases involved joint-custody cases, and, looking only at mediated cases, 90 percent involved joint legal custody).

121. *See* JUNE CARBONE, FROM PARENTS TO PARTNERS: THE SECOND REVOLUTION IN FAMILY LAW 180–94 (2000).

122. *See* Elizabeth S. Scott, *Parental Autonomy and Children's Welfare*, 11 WM. & MARY BILL RTS. J. 1071, 1072–74 (2003) (arguing that substantive and procedural changes to child custody

"can be understood as unplanned but coherent efforts to encourage divorcing parents to function more like parents in intact families rather than in the traditional role of divorced parents," by, for example, encouraging more postdivorce contact).

123. *See* Hill Kay, *supra* note 119, at 4–5.

124. *See* Ben Barlow, *Divorce Child Custody Mediation: In Order to Form a More Perfect Disunion?*, 52 Clev. St. L. Rev. 499, 500–01 (2004) (discussing the prevalence, application, and future of divorce child-custody mediation in the United States); Ann L. Milne, Jay Folberg & Peter Salem, *The Evolution of Divorce and Family Mediation: An Overview, in* Divorce and Family Mediation: Models, Techniques, and Applications 3, 6 (Jay Folberg, Ann L. Milne & Peter Salem eds., 2004) ("Since its inception in the early 1970s, the landscape of the mediation field has evolved as more programs and services have been established. Mediation is now used in thousands of divorce-related disputes annually").

125. As detailed in chapter 6, collaborative law was first devised by a practitioner, Stuart Webb, in Minneapolis. Pauline H. Tesler, Collaborative Law: Achieving Effective Resolution in Divorce without Litigation xxx n. 1 (2d ed. 2008). Pauline Tesler, a practitioner in California, has been one of its leading advocates.

126. Juliana M. Sobolewski & Valarie King, *The Importance of the Coparental Relationship for Nonresident Fathers' Ties to Children*, 67 J. Marriage & Fam. 1196, 1197, 1200–01 (2005).

127. *Id.* at 1209. The study measured father-child contact by examining both face time and phone calls. The study measured father-child relationship quality through the child's responses to a series of questions, including the amount and type of comments and feedback the child received from the father, the likelihood that the child would communicate feelings to the father, and how much the child looked up to the father. The study measured responsive fathering by looking at how much the child felt the father responded to the child's thoughts and feelings and whether the child felt included in the decision process for issues that would affect the child. *See id.* at 1202. The researchers controlled for several variables, such as how far the child lived from the father, household income, and so on.

128. *Id.* at 1202.

129. *Id.*

130. *See* Tresa Baldas, *Taking Combat Out of Custody*, Nat'l L.J. (Nov. 21, 2005), *available at* http://www.law.com/jsp/article.jsp?id=1132580126868 (describing the perceived increase in high-conflict cases); *see also* Neela Banerjee, *Religion Joins Custody Cases, to Judges Unease*, N.Y. Times, Feb. 13, 2008, at A1 (quoting Ronald William Nelson, chair of the custody committee of the American Bar Association, as saying, "There has definitely been an increase in conflict over religious issues. Part of that is there has been an increase of conflicts between parents across the board, and with parents looking for reasons to justify their own actions").

131. Robert E. Emery, David Sbarra & Tara Grover, *Divorce Mediation: Research and Reflections*, 43 Fam. Ct. Rev. 22, 30 (2005).

132. *See* Robert E. Emery et al., *Child Custody Mediation and Litigation: Custody, Contact, and Co-parenting 12 Years after Initial Dispute Resolution*, 69 J. Consulting & Clinical Psychol. 323, 325–31 (2001).

133. *See* Colo. Bar Ass'n Ethics Comm. & Continuing Legal Educ. in Colo., Inc., Formal Ethics Opinion 115, Ethical Considerations in the Collaborative and Cooperative Law Contexts, at 4-392 (2007), *available at* http://www.cobar.org/repository/Ethics/FormalEthicsOpion/FormalEthicsOpinion_115_2011.pdf. The committee found

that the four-way agreement that some collaborative-law practitioners used violated the rule of professional conduct that bars a lawyer from representing a client if that representation is materially limited by the lawyer's responsibility to a third party.

134. *See* ABA COMM. ON ETHICS & PROF'L RESPONSIBILITY, FORMAL OPINION 07-447, ETHICAL CONSIDERATIONS IN COLLABORATIVE LAW PRACTICE 3–5 (2007) (disagreeing with the Colorado opinion and finding four-way agreements permissible limitations on the scope of representation). For an excellent discussion of the ethical issues at stake, *see* Scott R. Peppet, *The Ethics of Collaborative Law*, 2008 J. DISP. RESOL. 131, 131–132 (arguing that both the Colorado and the ABA opinions oversimplify the process of collaborative law and the relevant ethical issues but ultimately concluding that although difficult ethical issues are at stake, the process of collaborative law can satisfy rules of legal ethics).

135. For an argument that the reforms are more comprehensive, *see* Jana B. Singer, *Dispute Resolution and the Postdivorce Family: Implications of a Paradigm Shift*, 47 FAM. CT. REV. 263 (2009).

CHAPTER 5

1. AUSTIN SARAT & WILLIAM L. F. FELSTINER, DIVORCE LAWYERS AND THEIR CLIENTS: POWER AND MEANING IN THE LEGAL PROCESS 28 (1995).

2. Barbara Bennett Woodhouse, *Sex, Lies, and Dissipation: The Discourse of Fault in a No-Fault Era*, 82 GEO. L.J. 2525, 2531 (1994).

3. ROBERT E. EMERY, THE TRUTH ABOUT CHILDREN AND DIVORCE: DEALING WITH THE EMOTIONS SO YOU AND YOUR CHILDREN CAN THRIVE 29–34, 160–61 (2004).

4. *Id.* at 69, 139–40.

5. This book uses the term "reparative" to refer to the idea of mending or repairing relationships in preparation for the ongoing relationships that will continue after the end of the legal action. The term is also used in other contexts, such as reparations to African Americans for slavery, where the idea is to compensate a victim for an injury inflicted by a wrongdoer, or reparative therapy, the idea that it is possible to "repair" a person's sexual orientation. Neither of these meanings is intended here.

6. *See* HANS-WERNER BIERHOFF, PROSOCIAL BEHAVIOUR 139 (2002).

7. *See* MELANIE KLEIN & JOAN RIVIERE, LOVE, HATE, AND REPARATION 66–68 (1964).

8. *See, e.g.,* S.C. CODE ANN. § 20-3-90 (2006).

9. *See* Annette Ruth Appell, *Blending Families through Adoption: Implications for Collaborative Adoption Law and Practice*, 75 B.U. L. REV. 997, 998–1001 (1995) (describing the feelings of loss experienced by all parties in an adoption).

10. N. R. Kleinfield, *The Girls Who Haven't Come Home*, N.Y. TIMES, July 7, 2013, at A21.

11. *Id.*

12. *Id.*

13. Eli J. Finkel et al., *Vengefully Ever After: Destiny Beliefs, State Attachment Anxiety, and Forgiveness*, 92 J. PERSONALITY & SOC. PSYCHOL. 871, 871 (2007) (listing studies making this finding). Acting on these impulses undermines the relationship. *See id.*

14. *See* 1 WILLIAM BLACKSTONE, COMMENTARIES *452.

15. BLACK'S LAW DICTIONARY 1206 (8th ed. 2004). This authority was located solely in the father. *See* Sibylla Flügge, *On the History of Fathers' Rights and Mothers' Duty of Care*, 3 CARDOZO

Women's L.J. 377, 383 (1996). The descriptions of the absolute rights (and concomitant duties) of fathers pertained only to children born in a marriage. *See* Kristin Collins, Note, *When Fathers' Rights Are Mothers' Duties: The Failure of Equal Protection in* Miller v. Albright, 109 Yale L.J. 1669, 1682–85 (2000) (describing the common-law tradition that fathers owed no obligation to, and had no parental rights over, children born outside of marriage).

16. Blackstone, *supra* note 14, at *452.

17. *Id.* at *444 ("The husband . . . might give his wife moderate correction. For, as he is to answer for her misbehavior, the law thought it reasonable to intrust him with this power of restraining her, by domestic chastisement, in the same moderation that a man is allowed to correct his apprentices or children"); *see also id.* at *445 (noting that "this power of correction began to be doubted" with the reign of Charles II but that "the courts of law will still permit a husband to restrain a wife of her liberty, in case of any gross misbehavior").

18. *See id.* at *452–53 (describing the common-law right of a father to the custody, labor, and earnings of his minor children); Steven Mintz & Susan Kellogg, Domestic Revolutions: A Social History of American Family Life 1–16 (1988) (discussing the role of the "Godly" family in Puritan New England).

19. Diane Kiesel, Domestic Violence: Law, Policy, and Practice 21–26 (2007). An interesting exception to this was in the Masschusetts Bay and Plymouth colonies, where the Massachusetts *Body of Liberties* of 1641 guaranteed wives the right to be free from physical chastisement by their husbands. *See* Elizabeth Pleck, Domestic Tyranny: The Making of Social Policy against Family Violence from Colonial Times to the Present 21–22 (1987). Pleck describes how although these laws were rarely enforced, they did encourage informal enforcement from fellow citizens and the church, although even that enforcement was spotty and often blamed the wife as much as the husband. *See id.* at 17–31.

20. *See* Aya Gruber, *The Feminist War on Crime*, 92 Iowa L. Rev. 741, 748–50 (2007).

21. *See id.* at 753–56.

22. *See* Donna Coker, *Shifting Power for Battered Women: Law, Material Resources, and Poor Women of Color*, 33 U.C. Davis L. Rev. 1009, 1043–45 (2000).

23. *See* Gruber, *supra* note 20, at 760–61.

24. *See* Cheryl Hanna, *No Right to Choose: Mandated Victim Participation in Domestic Violence Prosecutions*, 109 Harv. L. Rev. 1849, 1850–1910 (1996).

25. *See* Gruber, *supra* note 20, at 749–50.

26. *See id.* at 805–06.

27. Leigh Goodmark, A Troubled Marriage: Domestic Violence and the Legal System 121–24 (2012).

28. *Id.* at 122–24.

29. *Id.* at 125; Leigh Goodmark, *Autonomy Feminism: An Anti-Essentialist Critique of Mandatory Interventions in Domestic Violence*, 37 Fla. St. U. L. Rev. 1, 31 (2009).

30. *See* Gruber, *supra* note 20, at 765–66.

31. Aya Gruber, *A "Neo-Feminist" Assessment of Rape and Domestic Violence Law Reform*, 15 J. Gender Race & Just. 583, 599–600 (2012).

32. *See* Marilyn Van Derbur, Miss America by Day: Lessons Learned from Ultimate Betrayals and Unconditional Love 9–20 (2004).

33. *See id.* at 21–28 (describing this abuse and noting that it happened at least once a week for thirteen years). Van Derbur does not reveal whether her father sexually abused her two middle

sisters, *see id.* at 12 (noting that her two middle sisters asked not to be included in the story), but she does describe his ten-year sexual abuse of her eldest sister, *see id.* at 192.

34. *See id.* at 21–22.

35. *See id.* at 35 ("I had no conscious memories of my nights").

36. *See id.* at 101–04.

CHAPTER 6

1. Susan Burton, *386: Fine Print—Act Four; May Be Hazardous to Children, This American Life,* WBEZ Chicago (July 24, 2009), http://www.thisamericanlife.org/play_full.php?play=386&act=4.

2. Elizabeth S. Scott, *Pluralism, Parental Preference and Child Custody,* 80 CALIF. L. REV. 615, 616–18 (1992).

3. *Id.* at 617–18, 631–37.

4. Turning to the other two concerns—that a custody rule draw upon verifiable information and mirror the deference afforded intact and divorcing-but-agreeable families—the approximation rule also does well. By removing the subjective element of custody decisions, the rule decreases the role of outsiders and supposed experts. Instead, the information needed to apply the rule is relatively easy to obtain and verify. The couple may not like the result, but at least the custody determination is a function of their own past decisions. The rule also mimics the deference given to intact families and divorcing-but-agreeable families by simply putting into a court order what the parties had presumably agreed upon as private actors in their marriage: who would do what amount of caretaking. *See* Elizabeth S. Scott & Robert E. Emery, *Gender Politics and Child Custody: The Puzzling Persistence of the Best Interest Standard* 42–44 (Columbia Law Sch. Pub. Law & Legal Theory, Working Paper No. 9200, 2011), *available at* http://lsr.nellco.org/cgi/viewcontent.cgi?article=1092&context=columbia_pllt, to be published at 77 L. & CONTEMP. PROBS. (forthcoming 2014).

5. PRINCIPLES OF THE LAW OF FAMILY DISSOLUTION § 2.08 (2002).

6. *Id.*

7. *See* John D. Athey, Note, *The Ramifications of West Virginia's Codified Child Custody Law: A Departure from Garska v. McCoy,* 106 W. VA. L. REV. 389, 390 (2004). The statute instructs courts to "allocate custodial responsibility so that the proportion of custodial time the child spends with each parent approximates the proportion of time each parent spent performing caretaking functions for the child prior to the parents' separation." W. VA. CODE § 48-9-206 (2011).

8. *See* Katharine T. Bartlett, *Prioritizing Past Caretaking in Child Custody Decisionmaking,* 77 L. & CONTEMP. PROBS. (forthcoming 2014) (describing how numerous states list past caretaking as a factor to consider when deciding best interests and discussing other ways states have incorporated the approximation rule into custody law).

9. *See* ANN CRITTENDEN, THE PRICE OF MOTHERHOOD: WHY THE MOST IMPORTANT JOB IN THE WORLD IS STILL THE LEAST VALUED 149–61 (2001). Even if the spouse who invests in the family gets a disproportionate share of marital assets, this is rarely enough to support the family. *See id.*

10. Under the ALI rule, there are five bases for spousal compensation: (1) loss of marital standard of living in a marriage exceeding a certain duration, (2) earning-capacity loss caused by taking care of marital children or children of either spouse, (3) earning-capacity loss caused by taking

care of a third party in fulfillment of a moral obligation, (4) marital dissolution that precedes the realization of an investment in the other spouse's earning capacity, and (5) a significant disparity in the ability to return to the premarital standard of living after the end of a short-term marriage. *See* PRINCIPLES OF THE LAW OF FAMILY DISSOLUTION § 5.03 (2002). The text addresses only the second basis for compensatory payments.

11. *Id.* § 5.03(b)(2).

12. *Id.* § 5.05(1), (2)(c). Courts have cited this provision to support an award to a caregiving spouse when that spouse left the workforce for a significant period of time to care for children and, in so doing, helped the other spouse's career. *See, e.g.,* Simonds v. Simonds, 886 A.2d 158, 175 (Md. Ct. Spec. App. 2005).

13. PRINCIPLES OF THE LAW OF FAMILY DISSOLUTION, ch. 5 (2002) ("Compensatory Spousal Payments").

14. *See id.* § 5.02 cmt. a.

15. Lynn A. Baker & Robert E. Emery, *When Every Relationship Is Above Average: Perceptions and Expectations of Divorce at the Time of Marriage*, 17 LAW & HUM. BEHAV. 439, 440 (1993).

16. *Id.* at 442–43 (marriage-license applicants acknowledged that courts do not always grant alimony, but their approximations for how often alimony is awarded were very optimistic—they thought that alimony was awarded in 40 percent of cases, when the actual figure is more like 10 percent; respondents thought child support was paid in full 40 percent of the time, when the actual figure is approximately 50 percent).

17. *Id.* at 443 (approximately 81 percent of the women thought they would receive alimony; 83 percent of the men thought the court would award alimony; 100 percent of the women thought their husbands would comply with the alimony award; 98 percent thought their spouses would pay child support in full).

18. *Id.* at 447–48.

19. *Id.*

20. Cynthia Godsoe, *Parsing Parenthood*, 17 LEWIS & CLARK L. REV. 113, 145 (2013).

21. *Id.* at 146.

22. Pub. L. 110-351 (2008), 122 Stat. 3949 (codified at scattered sections of 42 U.S.C., 26 U.S.C., and 31 U.S.C.).

23. Godsoe, *supra* note 20, at 145.

24. *See* U.S. DEP'T HEALTH & HUM. SERVS., CHILDREN'S BUREAU, SUBSIDIZED GUARDIANSHIP: CHILD WELFARE WAIVER DEMONSTRATIONS ii, 18 (2011) *available at* http://www.acf.hhs.gov/sites/default/files/cb/subsidized.pdf (finding that in some states, subsidized guardianship has reduced length of time in foster care by 22 to 43 percent).

25. Godsoe, *supra* note 20, at 145.

26. *See* U.S. DEP'T HEALTH & HUM. SERVS., ADMIN. for CHILDREN & FAMILY, CHILD WELFARE INFORMATION GATEWAY, POSTADOPTION CONTACT AGREEMENTS BETWEEN BIRTH AND ADOPTIVE FAMILIES 2–3 (2011), *available at* http://www.childwelfare.gov/system-wide/laws_policies/statutes/cooperative.pdf. The Uniform Adoption Act, promulgated by the National Conference of Commissioners on Uniform State Laws in 1994 and endorsed by the American Bar Association in 1995, is skeptical of open adoptions, except in the context of step-parent adoptions. *See* Joan Heifetz Hollinger, *The Uniform Adoption Act: Reporter's Ruminations*, 30 FAM. L.Q. 345, 345, 372–77 (1996) (discussing various views on open adoptions and the compromise struck not to sanction it but also not to forbid it in all circumstances).

27. Anita L. Allen, *Open Adoption Is Not for Everyone, in* ADOPTION MATTERS: PHILOSOPHICAL AND FEMINIST ESSAYS 47–51 (Sally Haslanger & Charlotte Witt eds., 2005).

28. *Id.* at 50.

29. *Id.* at 48–49.

30. *See, e.g.*, ARIZ. REV. STAT. ANN. § 25-403 (2012) ("legal decisionmaking" and "parenting time"); Minn. Stat. § 518.175 (2012) ("parenting time"); NEB. REV. STAT. § 43-2923 (2012) ("parenting arrangement[s]"); N.H. REV. STAT. ANN. § 461-A:6 (2012) ("parental rights and responsibilities"); N.D. CENT. CODE § 14-09-06.2 (2011) ("parental rights and responsibilities"); OHIO REV. CODE ANN. § 3109.04 (West 2013) ("allocation of parental rights and responsibilities" and "shared parenting"). *See* ANNE ENDRESS SKOVE, NAT'L CTR. FOR STATE COURTS, PARENTING TIME (2000), *available at* http://ncsc.contentdm.oclc.org/cdm/singleitem/collection/famct/id/231/rec/1, for a list of other states.

31. COLO. REV. STAT. § 14-10-103 (2013).

32. *Id.*

33. *See* SKOVE, *supra* note 30.

34. Robert E. Emery, David Sbarra & Tara Grover, *Divorce Mediation: Research and Reflections, in* RESOLVING FAMILY CONFLICTS 151–53 (Jana B. Singer & Jane C. Murphy eds., 2008).

35. PATRICK PARKINSON, FAMILY LAW AND THE INDISSOLUBILITY OF PARENTHOOD 187 (2011).

36. Patrick Parkinson, *The Idea of Family Relationship Centres in Australia*, 51 FAM. CT. REV. 195, 195 (2013).

37. PARKINSON, *supra* note 35, at 187–88.

38. *Id.* at 187.

39. *Id.*

40. *See* INST. FOR THE ADVANCEMENT OF THE AM. LEGAL SYS., THE RESOURCE CENTER FOR SEPARATING AND DIVORCING FAMILIES AT THE UNIVERSITY OF DENVER: EXECUTIVE SUMMARY, *available at* http://iaals.du.edu/images/wygwam/documents/publications/Resource_Center_Overview.pdf.

41. For more details on family group conferencing and a survey of the research on the process, *see* Clare Huntington, *Rights Myopia in Child Welfare*, 53 UCLA L. REV. 637 (2006).

42. *See* Mark S. Umbreit, *What Is Restorative Justice?, in* U.S. DEP'T JUST., FAMILY GROUP CONFERENCING: IMPLICATIONS FOR CRIME VICTIMS 1 (2000), *available at* http://www.cehd.umn.edu/ssw/rjp/resources/rj_dialogue_resources/Training_Resources/Family_Group_Conferencing.pdf (describing the restorative justice movement as an attempt to reform the justice system to incorporate victims and allow the offender to "restore" the status quo); John Braithwaite & Heather Strang, *Restorative Justice and Family Violence, in* RESTORATIVE JUSTICE AND FAMILY VIOLENCE 1, 4 (Heather Strang & John Braithwaite eds., 2002) ("The most general meaning of restorative justice is a process where stakeholders affected by an injustice have an opportunity to communicate about the consequences of the injustice and what is to be done to right the wrong"). Usually in lieu of traditional courtroom proceedings (although sometimes in addition to such proceedings), restorative justice "is a process whereby all the parties with a stake in a particular offense come together to resolve collectively how to deal with the aftermath of the offense and its implications for the future." John Braithwaite, *Restorative Justice: Assessing Optimistic and Pessimistic Accounts*, 25 CRIME & JUST. 1, 5 (1999) (citations and internal quotation marks omitted).

43. *See* Children, Young Persons, and Their Families Act 1989 (N.Z.).

44. There is considerable variability among states in this regard, with some states assigning a disinterested, responsible adult rather than a lawyer. Further, states differ in their conception of the guardian ad litem's role. In some states, the lawyer is supposed to represent the child's best interests; in other states, the lawyer is supposed to represent the child's *expressed* interests. In still other states, the lawyer plays a hybrid role, often depending on the age of the child.

45. Donald. J. Baumann et al., Am. Humane Ass'n, The Decision-Making Ecology 11 (2011), *available at* www.americanhumane.org/assets/pdfs/children/cprc-dme-monograph. pdf. Chapter 2 described the debate about overrepresentation of children of color in the child-welfare system.

46. Donald N. Duquette, *Non-adversarial Case Resolution, in* Child Welfare Law and Practice: Representing Children, Parents, and State Agencies in Abuse, Neglect, and Dependency Cases 354 (Marvin Ventrell & Donald N. Duquette eds., 2005).

47. See Gale Burford & Joe Hudson, *General Introduction: Family Group Conference Programming, in* Family Group Conferencing: New Directions in Community-Centered Child and Family Practice, at xix, xix (Gale Burford & Joe Hudson eds., 2000).

48. One study has found that family group conferences are more likely to be successful if there are several key factors: (1) community partners invited by the agency participated, (2) family members and friends invited by the family participated, (3) the meeting was held somewhere other than the agency, (4) service providers from other agencies participated, (5) a placement decision was made during the meeting, (6) the parents participated, (7) multiple agency staff participated, and (8) a dedicated and trained facilitator guided the discussion. *See* David S. Crampton et al., *Does Community and Family Engagement Enhance Permanency for Children in Foster Care? Findings from an Evaluation of the Family-to-Family Initiative*, 90 Child Welfare 61, 65–73 (2011). The findings varied by race and also by the number of key elements involved. Interestingly, when more key elements were present, the children were less likely to exit care, although the authors hypothesized that this might be because these were particularly complex cases. *See id.* at 71.

49. Sara Munson & Madelyn Freundlich, Am. Humane Ass'n, Families Gaining Their Seat at the Table: Family Engagement Strategies in the First Round of Child and Family Services Reviews and Program Improvement Plans 6 (2008), *available at* http://www.americanhumane.org/assets/pdfs/children/fgdm/pc-fgdm-cfsr-pip-review. pdf (noting that many states use different terms to describe family-engagement strategies, such as family group conferencing, team decision-making, and family-planning conferences, ideally meeting at crucial stages to develop an action plan, sometimes meeting every six months; however, often these strategies are not put into action or end up ineffectively monitored). One positive step in the United States has been the passage of the Fostering Connection to Success and Increasing Adoptions Act of 2008, which requires states to increase their efforts to find and engage immediate- and extended-family members, notify all adult relatives within thirty days of a child's removal, and tell these relatives of their legal rights to participate in the child's care and placement. *See* Pub. L. 110-351, 129 Stat. 3949 (codified as amended in scattered sections of 42 U.S.C.). Although notification is not the same as meaningful involvement, a study of a demonstration project found that when an agency did take this commitment seriously and made considerable efforts to identify and engage family members by assigning a "search and engagement specialist" to the case, children were more likely to be reunified with their parents or placed

with a relative than children who received only the standard child-welfare services. *See* Miriam J. Landsman & Shamra Boel-Studt, *Fostering Families' and Children's Rights to Family Connections*, 90 CHILD WELFARE 19, 26–37 (2011).

50. One cautionary note about the studies discussed in the text: there are no large, randomized trials comparing family group conferencing with traditional approaches, perhaps because family group conferencing requires large-scale, systemic change to be effective, and therefore it is difficult to maintain a control group within the same community. *See* Crampton et al., *supra* note 48, at 62–63. Despite this concern, one study (discussed in the text) of the majority of cases of foster-care placement in six large urban jurisdictions found positive outcomes for the problem-solving approach to child welfare. *Id.* at 74–76.

51. *See* NANCY SHORE ET AL., INT'L INST. FOR RESTORATIVE PRACTICES, LONG TERM AND IMMEDIATE OUTCOMES OF FAMILY GROUP CONFERENCING IN WASHINGTON STATE 1 (2002), *available at* canada.iirp.edu/uploads/article_pdfs/fgcwash.pdf (finding that "[c]hildren who had a conference experienced high rates of reunification or kinship placement, and low rates of re-referral to CPS. These findings generally remained stable as long as two years post-conference"); Joan Pennell & Gale Burford, *Family Group Decision Making: Protecting Women and Children*, 79 CHILD WELFARE 131, 145–47 (2000) (finding a decrease in abuse and neglect after a family group conference: the number of events triggering intervention declined from 233 to 117 for participating families; by contrast, nonparticipating families experienced an increase in triggering events, from 129 to 165). For other positive studies, *see* Charles E. Wheeler & Sabrina Johnson, *Evaluating Family Group Decision Making: The Santa Clara Example*, 18 PROTECTING CHILD. 65, 68 (2003); Melissa M. Litchfield et al., *Empowering Families in Child Protection Cases: An Implementation Evaluation of Hawai'i's 'Ohana Conferencing Program*, TECHNICAL ASSISTANCE BULL. (Nat'l Council of Juvenile & Family Court Judges, Reno, NV), Apr. 2003, at 64–65, *available at* http://www.ncjfcj.org/resource-library/publications/empowering-families-child-protection-cases-implementation-evaluation-0. Not all studies have found these results. *See* Stephanie Cosner Berzin, *Using Sibling Data to Understand the Impact of Family Group Decision-Making on Child Welfare Outcomes*, 28 CHILD. & YOUTH SERVICES REV. 1449, 1455–56 (2006) (finding either neutral outcomes for children after family group decision-making or negative outcomes comparable to child-welfare services, calling into question the effectiveness of such programs); Knut Sundell & Bo Vinnerljung, *Outcomes of Family Group Conferencing in Sweden: A 3-Year Follow-Up*, 28 CHILD ABUSE & NEGLECT 267, 282–83 (2004) (noting higher rates of re-referral for child-welfare agencies following a family group conference than with comparison group but also noting multiple explanations for higher rates).

52. Crampton et al., *supra* note 48, at 65–73.

53. *See* Burford & Hudson, *supra* note 47, at xix, xxi. Although not addressed in the text, family group conferencing is also used for juvenile offenses. *See* U.S. DEP'T JUST., FAMILY GROUP CONFERENCING: IMPLICATIONS FOR CRIME VICTIMS 2 (2000), *available at* https://www.ncjrs.gov/ovc_archives/reports/restorative_justice/restorative_justice_ascii_pdf/ncj176347.pdf (describing the process for addressing crimes of juveniles).

54. *See* William Vesneski & Susan Kemp, *The Washington State Family Group Conference Project*, *in* FAMILY GROUP CONFERENCING, *supra* note 47, at 312, 315; SHORE ET AL., *supra* note 51, at 4–5 (noting that in service plans, 80 percent of parents mentioned mental-health services, 61 percent mentioned substance-abuse treatment or prevention, 61 percent mentioned behavioral interventions, and 30 percent mentioned housing resources).

55. Joan Pennell, Myles Edwards & Gale Burford, *Expedited Family Group Engagement and Child Permanency*, 32 CHILD. & YOUTH SERVS. REV. 1012, 1013 (2010) (noting that "family group conferencing reinforces children's connections to their families and communities").

56. Jackie D. Sieppert, Jose Hudson & Yvonne Unrau, *Family Group Conferencing in Child Welfare: Lessons from a Demonstration Project*, 8 FAMILIES IN SOCIETY: J. CONTEMP. HUM. SERVS. 382, 388–89 (2000) (finding that 65 percent of family-conference participants were highly satisfied with conference decisions and 72 percent were highly satisfied with the plan made during the conference).

57. PETER MARSH & GILL CROW, FAMILY GROUP CONFERENCES IN CHILD WELFARE 169–70 (Olive Stevenson ed., 1998). Outside the specific context of family group conferencing, practitioner-based research by social workers has identified several key components of effectively working with families: (1) building trusting relationships with clients, especially given the understandable concern by parents that the social worker will remove a child; (2) communicating honestly and clearly about the concerns of the agency and the process that will be followed; (3) working with all family members; (4) including family members in case conferences, ensuring that decisions were not made ahead of time and the conference was just pro forma; and (5) including family members in writing up reports, to ensure that their point of view is included and the language is plainly understandable. *See* Michael Gallagher et al., *Engaging with Families in Child Protection: Lessons from Practitioner Research in Scotland*, 90 CHILD WELFARE 117, 122–29 (2011).

58. *See* Lisa Merkel-Holguin, *Diversions and Departures in the Implementation of Family Group Conferencing in the United States, in* FAMILY GROUP CONFERENCING, *supra* note 47, at 224–25.

59. Joan Pennell & Gale Burford, *Family Group Decision-Making and Family Violence, in* FAMILY GROUP CONFERENCING, *supra* note 47, at 171, 175–76. John Braithwaite has asserted that "court processing of family violence cases actually tends to foster a culture of denial, while restorative justice fosters a culture of apology," and that apology, "when communicated with ritual seriousness, is actually the most powerful cultural device for taking a problem seriously, while denial is a cultural device for dismissing it." John Braithwaite, *Restorative Justice and Social Justice*, 63 SASK. L. REV. 185, 189 (2000).

60. Ruth Busch, *Domestic Violence and Restorative Justice Initiatives: Who Pays if We Get It Wrong?, in* RESTORATIVE JUSTICE AND FAMILY VIOLENCE, *supra* note 42, at 223, 223–34.

61. *See* Merkel-Holguin, *supra* note 58, at 221, 227; GALE BURFORD, JOAN PENNELL & SUSAN MACLEOD, MANUAL FOR COORDINATORS AND COMMUNITIES: THE ORGANIZATION AND PRACTICE OF FAMILY GROUP DECISION MAKING 91 (1995). Some communities also offer support persons for offenders.

62. *See* Merkel-Holguin, *supra* note 58, at 221, 224, 227.

63. *See id.* at 225.

64. *See id.*

65. *See* MARK HARDIN ET AL., ABA CENTER ON CHILDREN & THE LAW, FAMILY GROUP CONFERENCES IN CHILD ABUSE AND NEGLECT CASES: LEARNING FROM THE EXPERIENCES OF NEW ZEALAND 22–23 (1996). Moreover, distinguishing cases presents difficulties, because some cases that appear to present "only" physical abuse or neglect may well involve sexual abuse, a fact that comes to light during the process. *See* GALE BURFORD & JOAN PENNELL, FAMILY GROUP DECISION MAKING: NEW ROLES FOR "OLD" PARTNERS IN RESOLVING FAMILY VIOLENCE: IMPLEMENTATION REPORT SUMMARY 19 (1995).

66. David Moore & John McDonald, *Guiding Principles of the Conferencing Process, in* Family Group Conferencing, *supra* note 47, at 49, 50.

67. *Id.*

68. *Id.*

69. *See* Nora Tooher, *Parent Coordinators Help Divorced Couples Who Won't Stop Fighting*, Law. USA (Nov. 20, 2006), http://lawyersusaonline.com/blog/2006/11/20/parent-coordinators-help-divorced-couples-who-wont-stop-fighting/; Christine A. Coates et al., *Parenting Coordination for High-Conflict Families*, 42 Fam. Ct. Rev. 246, 247 (2004).

70. *See* Tooher, *supra* note 69.

71. *See id.*

72. In addition to voluntary classes, courts are sometimes authorized to mandate participation. Colorado, for example, authorizes courts to require a divorcing couple to attend a parenting class to teach them how to co-parent after the divorce. *See* Colo. Rev. Stat. § 14-10-123.7 (2006).

73. *See* Jeffery T. Cookston et al., *Effects of the Dads for Life Intervention on Interparental Conflict and Coparenting in the Two Years after Divorce*, 46 Fam. Process 123, 132–35 (2007).

74. *See* Charles Asher, The *UpToParents* Model Rule for Family Cases 2 (2010), *available at* http://www.uptoparents.org/professionals.aspx ("In marital dissolution and separation cases where the parties have one or more children under the age of 20 on the date of the initial filing, all pleadings shall be captioned, 'In Re the Marriage of _____, father [or mother], and _____, mother [or father].' The party filing the initial petition shall be named first").

75. *FAQs*, Up To Parents, *available at* http://www.uptoparents.org/faq.aspx.

76. These courts are part of a larger movement to reform courts to address underlying issues facing the parties. Under the umbrella of "problem-solving courts," there are numerous specialized courts, from drug court to mental-health court. The IDVC, for example, is a project of the Center for Court Innovation, founded after the successful implementation of the Midtown Community Court in Manhattan. Ctr. for Court Innovation, See Who We Are, *available at* http://www.courtinnovation.org/who-we-are. The basic idea in a problem-solving court is that the judge is the head of a team of professionals working to identify and resolve the issues underlying, say, a misdemeanor drug violation, such as substance abuse, mental illness, and domestic violence. The defendant is often called a client and is supposed to work with the team on various goals, including staying sober or taking medication. For clients who do not comply, the court can impose certain sanctions, including jail time. The premise of these courts is that the surface issue is only a symptom of larger issues and that it is better for the individual and society to address the underlying issue. For a description of problem-solving courts in the criminal context, *see* Allegra M. McLeod, *Decarceration Courts: Possibilities and Perils of a Shifting Criminal Law*, 100 Geo. L.J. 1587 (2012).

77. Ctr. for Court Innovation, Integrated Domestic Violence Court Overview, *available at* http://www.courtinnovation.org/project/integrated-domestic-violence-court.

78. Ctr. for Court Innovation, Integrated Domestic Violence Courts: Key Principles 3, *available at* http://www.courtinnovation.org/research/integrated-domestic-violence-courts-key-principles?url=project%2Fintegrated-domestic-violence-court&mode=project&project=Integrated%20Domestic%20Violence%20Court.

79. Cindy S. Lederman, *From Lab Bench to Court Bench: Using Science to Inform Decisions in Juvenile Court*, Cerebrum 1, 5 (Sept. 2011), *available at* http://dana.org/WorkArea/showcontent.aspx?id=34228.

80. *Id.* at 5–6.

81. *Id.* at 2.

82. Cindy S. Lederman, *Healing in the Place of Last Resort: The Role of Dependency Court with Community-Based Efforts to Prevent Child Maltreatment, in* PREVENTING CHILD MALTREATMENT: COMMUNITY APPROACHES 176–77 (Kenneth A. Dodge & Doriane Lambelet Coleman eds., 2009).

83. *Id.* at 178–79. One study of the court found that for families who reached the therapeutic goals, there were no instances of substantiated maltreatment. *See id.* at 178.

84. Jane M. Spinak, *Romancing the Court*, 46 FAM. CT. REV. 258, 258–59 & n. 6 (2008).

85. *Id.* at 259.

86. *Id.*

87. Emily Buss, *Parents' Rights and Parents Wronged*, 57 OHIO ST. L.J. 431, 434–35 (1996) (describing the cursory proceedings in family court).

88. Spinak, *supra* note 84, at 260–69.

89. This discussion relies on Robert G. Madden, *From Theory to Practice: A Family Systems Approach to the Law, in* RELATIONSHIP-CENTERED LAWYERING: SOCIAL SCIENCE THEORY FOR TRANSFORMING LEGAL PRACTICE 140–56 (Susan L. Brooks & Robert G. Madden eds., 2010).

90. Mary E. O'Connell & J. Herbie DiFonzo, *The Family Law Education Reform Project Final Report*, 44 FAM. CT. REV. 524, 524 (2006).

91. *Id.* at 525.

92. *Id.* at 529–30. Many schools have started incorporating new skills and competencies into their family-law course offerings. In the Survey of Family Law Curricula by the New York State Bar, all nine law schools in the state offered family-law-related clinical opportunities, exposing students to real-life examples and providing the opportunity to work with real families; 89 percent of the schools had courses that discussed practical skills such as special training in representing children; and 78 percent of schools addressed alternative dispute-resolution methods, family-court structure and process, and recent family-law reform. *See* N.Y.C. BAR ASS'N COMM. ON FAM. CT. & FAM. L., SURVEY OF FAMILY LAW CURRICULA IN NEW YORK CITY AND LONG ISLAND LAW SCHOOLS 8 (2010). For one school's experience, *see* Andrew Schepard & J. Herbie DiFonzo, *Hofstra's Family Law with Skills Course: Implementing the FLER (The Family Law Education Reform Project)*, 49 FAM. CT. REV. 685 (2011).

93. *See* Ronald J. Gilson & Robert H. Mnookin, *Disputing through Agents: Cooperation and Conflict between Lawyers in Litigation*, 94 COLUM. L. REV. 509, 542, 547 (1994).

94. *Id.* at 546.

95. *Id.* at 547–48.

96. *See id.* at 547.

97. Stu Webb, *Collaborative Law: A Practitioner's Perspective on Its History and Current Practice*, 21 J. AM. ACAD. MATRIM. L. 155, 155–56 (2008).

98. *Id.* at 156–57.

99. PAULINE TESLER & PEGGY THOMPSON, COLLABORATIVE DIVORCE 8–9, 55–56, 203–47 (2006); PAULINE H. TESLER, COLLABORATIVE LAW: ACHIEVING EFFECTIVE RESOLUTION IN DIVORCE WITHOUT LITIGATION 9–17 (2d ed. 2008).

100. As one proponent of collaborative law in estate planning sums up the alternatives, "If anyone thinks about his or her own family and what would happen if there were a disagreement

about who's going to get the dining room table or $400,000 of annuities, would you prefer to go to court and cause as much humiliation and expense as possible, or would you prefer to resolve it, and talk to your siblings and parents at Thanksgiving?" Nora L. Tooher, *Estate Planners Put Trust in Collaborative Law*, LAW. USA (June 5, 2006), http://lawyersusaonline.com/blog/2006/06/05/estate-planners-put-trust-in-collaborative-law/ (quoting collaborative-law practitioner John Raskin).

101. Webb, *supra* note 97, at 157.

CHAPTER 7

1. *See* Shane Jimerson et al., *A Prospective Longitudinal Study of High School Dropouts Examining Multiple Predictors Across Development*, 38 J. SCH. PSYCHOL. 525, 529 (2000). The Minnesota Longitudinal Study of Parents and Children was initiated by developmental psychologist Byron R. Egeland. Egeland and several colleagues at the University of Minnesota began the study in 1975, recruiting a sample of 267 (180 would remain in the study for the long term) disadvantaged first-time mothers in their third trimester of pregnancy. The characteristics of the children, the mothers, and their parent-child interactions were extensively assessed at birth and at three, six, and twelve months. Assessments were later conducted every six months until age two and a half, yearly through the third grade, three times between ages nine and thirteen, and at ages sixteen, seventeen and a half, nineteen, twenty-three, twenty-six, and twenty-eight. *Minnesota Longitudinal Study of Risk and Adaptation*, INST. CHILD DEV., UNIV. MINN., http://www.cehd.umn.edu/icd/research/parent-child/.

2. *See* Jimerson et al., *supra* note 1, at 526.

3. The original focus of the study was on early-childhood maltreatment, but over time, researchers have used the longitudinal data to trace individual development and understand the factors that influence both positive outcomes, such as high-quality adult romantic relationships, *see* L. ALAN SROUFE ET AL., THE DEVELOPMENT OF THE PERSON: THE MINNESOTA STUDY OF RISK AND ADAPTATION FROM BIRTH TO ADULTHOOD 290–91 (2005), and negative outcomes, such as school dropouts, aggression, and attention problems, *see id.* at 209–11, 250–59.

4. *See* L. Alan Sroufe, Brianna Coffino & Elizabeth A. Carlson, *Conceptualizing the Role of Early Experience: Lessons from the Minnesota Longitudinal Study*, 30 DEV. REV. 36, 37 (2010).

5. *See* SROUFE ET AL., *supra* note 3, at 210; *see also* Jimerson et al., *supra* note 1, at 539 (reporting the same 77-percent figure for the combination of gender and the other two factors). The home environment was assessed with a well-known measure: Home Observations for Measurement of the Environment (HOME). The quality of the mother-child relationships was assessed using a number of different measures. *See id.* at 530–31.

6. *See* Jimerson et al., *supra* note 1, at 539; Sroufe, Coffino & Carlson, *supra* note 4, at 41.

7. *See* Sroufe, Coffino & Carlson, *supra* note 4, at 44.

8. *See id.*

9. In this effort, Nussbaum has collaborated with economist Amartya Sen. Sen uses the approach primarily as a basis for comparing the quality of life between two groups—a capabilities approach asks what people are able to be or do, not about their material resources. *See generally* AMARTYA SEN, DEVELOPMENT AS FREEDOM (1999); AMARTYA SEN, COMMODITIES AND CAPABILITIES (1985).

10. For a good summary of this argument, *see* Amartya Sen, *Capability and Well-Being, in* THE QUALITY OF LIFE 30–50 (Martha Nussbaum & Amartya Sen eds., 1993).

11. MARTHA NUSSBAUM, WOMEN AND HUMAN DEVELOPMENT: THE CAPABILITIES APPROACH 84–85 (2000). Nussbaum uses the capabilities approach to argue that the goal of governmental policies should be to nurture the central human capabilities needed for human dignity. *See id.* at 5, 12, 70–75.

12. *Id.* at 87.

13. *Id.* at 75–80.

14. By including love and affiliation in the list of central human capabilities, Nussbaum argues that she better accounts for the role of caregivers. And by making capabilities the focus of her inquiry, she does not, as many traditional liberal theories do, define the family as "private" and thus free from public scrutiny. *See id.* at 245–46. Instead, she contends that although *individuals* have privacy rights, institutions (e.g., families) do not have such rights, and thus it is proper to explore how the law has shaped institutions such as the family and then ask how the law might better influence these institutions to further the development of central human capabilities. The family, as such, holds no moral claim of protection or worth. Rather, the inquiry concerns what the family does for each individual's capabilities. *See id.* at 251–52.

15. *See* LINDA C. MCCLAIN, THE PLACE OF FAMILIES: FOSTERING CAPACITY, EQUALITY, AND RESPONSIBILITY 3, 17–18, 20–21 (2006). For more on the state's interest in a citizenry capable of engaging in a participatory democracy, *see* HANNAH ARENDT, THE HUMAN CONDITION 46 (1958); CAROLE PATEMAN, PARTICIPATION AND DEMOCRATIC THEORY 103–11 (1970); Will Kymlicka & Wayne Norman, *Return of the Citizen: A Survey of Recent Work on Citizenship Theory*, 104 ETHICS 352, 352–53 (1994); *see also* Prince v. Massachusetts, 321 U.S. 158, 168 (1944).

16. The insight that academic achievement is not the sole product of the quality of the school has its roots in the Coleman Report, a groundbreaking study of inequality in American education, commissioned by the U.S. Office of Education in accordance with the Civil Rights Act of 1964 and led by sociologist James Coleman. Published in 1966, the report was based on a study of six hundred thousand students, teachers, and principals across the country and was one of the first to use a child's test scores to gauge academic achievement. Coleman was a pioneer in considering the social context of education, and his report concluded that the social composition of the school (the educational backgrounds and aspirations of the students), the student's sense of control over his or her environment and future, the verbal skills of the teacher, and a student's family background were more closely related to academic achievement for African American students than factors such as per-pupil spending and class size. JAMES S. COLEMAN ET AL., U.S. DEP'T HEALTH, EDUC. & WELFARE, EQUALITY OF EDUCATIONAL OPPORTUNITY 22–23 (1966). The study was based on a nationally representative sample of test scores and questionnaires of students in first, third, sixth, ninth, and twelfth grades, along with questionnaires of teachers and principals. Coleman found that African American children entered school at a serious disadvantage because of a combination of poverty, community attitudes toward education, and low educational attainment by parents and that schools did very little to mitigate these disadvantages. *See id.* at 20.

17. For a discussion of this research, *see* Will Dobbie & Roland G. Fryer, Jr., *Are High-Quality Schools Enough to Increase Achievement among the Poor? Evidence from the Harlem Children's Zone*, 3 AM. ECON. J.: APPLIED ECON.158, 158–59 (2011).

18. James Heckman, *Skill Formation and the Economics of Investing in Disadvantaged Children*, 312 SCIENCE 1900, 1900–01 (2006).

19. Sean F. Reardon, *The Widening Academic Achievement Gap between the Rich and the Poor: New Evidence and Possible Explanations, in* WHITHER OPPORTUNITY? RISING INEQUALITY, SCHOOLS, AND CHILDREN'S LIFE CHANCES 93 (Greg J. Duncan & Richard J. Murnane eds., 2011) (comparing test scores for children from families in the ninetieth percentile of family income and children from families in the tenth percentile). For an excellent summary of the effect of income and parental education on children's achievement, *see generally* JULIA ISAACS & KATHERINE MAGNUSON, BROOKINGS INST., CTR. ON CHILDREN AND FAMILIES, INCOME AND EDUCATION AS PREDICTORS OF CHILDREN'S SCHOOL READINESS (2011), *available at* http://www.brookings.edu/~/media/research/files/reports/2011/12/15%20school%20readiness%20isaacs/1214_school_readiness_isaacs.pdf.

20. Reardon, *supra* note 19, at 93 ("fifty years ago the black-white gap was one and a half to two times as large as the income gap"). This income-achievement gap does not narrow as the child progresses through school, *see id.*, and it is becoming more pronounced over time—the income-achievement gap is 30 to 40 percent higher for children born in 2001 than for children born in 1976, *see id.*.

21. *See* NATIONAL SCI. COUNCIL ON THE DEVELOPING CHILD, *Building the Brain's "Air Traffic Control" System: How Early Experiences Shape the Development of Executive Function* 1–8 (Working Paper No. 11, 2011), *available at* http://developingchild.harvard.edu/index.php/resources/reports_and_working_papers/working_papers/wp11/.

22. Jimerson et al., *supra* note 1, at 526.

23. *Id.* at 526–27.

24. *Id.* at 527.

25. *Id.* at 527–28.

26. *Id.* at 528, 542–44.

27. *Id.* at 528, 542.

28. *Id.* at 528, 542–43.

29. Sroufe, Coffino & Carson, *supra* note 4, at 38–39; Jimerson et al., *supra* note 1, at 527, 544.

30. Sroufe, Coffino & Carson, *supra* note 4, at 38–39.

31. *Id.* at 38.

32. Jimerson et al., *supra* note 1, at 544. For an interesting discussion of the relationship between attachment and the development of social skills, *see* Sroufe, Coffino & Carson, *supra* note 4, at 46.

33. P. Lindsay Chase-Lansdale et al., *Neighborhood and Family Influences on the Intellectual and Behavioral Competence of Preschool and Early School-Age Children, in* 1 NEIGHBORHOOD POVERTY: CONTEXT AND CONSEQUENCES FOR CHILDREN 79, 80 (Jeanne Brooks-Gunn, Greg J. Duncan & J. Lawrence Aber eds., 1997).

34. ANNETTE LAREAU, HOME ADVANTAGE: SOCIAL CLASS AND PARENTAL INTERVENTION IN ELEMENTARY EDUCATION 2–3, 145 (2d ed. 2000).

35. *Id.*

36. Robert D. Putnam, Carl B. Frederick & Kaisa Snellman, Harvard Kennedy Sch. of Gov't, *Growing Class Gaps in Social Connectedness among American Youth* 11 (2012), *available at* http://www.hks.harvard.edu/var/ezp_site/storage/fckeditor/file/SaguaroReport_DivergingSocialConnectedness_20120808.pdf (fig. 3 showing little class difference in developmental time spent with children in 1975–1976 compared with a large gap in 2003–2010; classifying families by mothers' educational attainment).

37. Greg J. Duncan & Richard J. Murnane, *Economic Inequality: The Real Cause of the Urban School Problem*, Chi. Trib., Oct. 6, 2011, http://articles.chicagotribune.com/2011-10-06/news/ct-perspec-1006-urban-20111006_1_poor-children-graduation-rate-gap.

38. Guy Roth & Edward L. Deci, *Autonomy, in* 1 A–K The Encyclopedia of Positive Psychology 79–80 (Shane J. Lopez ed., 2009).

39. *See* Jennifer Nedelsky, Law's Relations: A Relational Theory of Self, Autonomy, and Law 123–24 (2011).

40. *See id.* at 124–27.

41. *See id.* at 39–40.

42. Copy of remarks on file with the author.

43. Julie Bosman, *Families Urge Bloomberg to Save After-School Vouchers*, N.Y. Times, June 13, 2009, at A13.

44. *Id.*

45. Chapter 3 discussed this in greater detail.

46. Dandridge v. Williams, 397 U.S. 471, 475 (1970).

47. Play allows children to learn without an adult mediating the social or physical environments. Karen Malone & Paul Tranter, *Children's Environmental Learning and the Use, Design and Management of Schoolgrounds*, 13 Children, Youth and Env'ts 87, 90–91 (2003). More specifically, play helps children develop three skill sets: physical and motor skills, such as coordination, strength, agility, and endurance; social skills, including sharing and cooperating, expressing feelings and needs, and negotiating with peers; and cognitive skills, such as pattern recognition, imaginative fantasy building, and developing a sense of interconnectedness in systems and environments. *See id.*

48. For a fascinating study finding that income mobility depends, at least in part, on the physical layout of a city, *see* David Leonhardt, *In Climbing Income Ladder, Location Matters*, N.Y. Times, July 22, 2013, at A1.

49. U.S. Dep't Health & Hum. Servs., Admin. for Children and Families, Child Maltreatment 2011, at 33–38 (2012), *available at* http://www.acf.hhs.gov/sites/default/files/cb/cm11.pdf (tbl. 3-4 showing a much higher rate of child maltreatment for children younger than one as compared with all other ages).

50. William D. Mosher et al., U.S. Dep't Health & Hum. Servs., Ctrs. for Disease Control and Prevention, Intended and Unintended Births in the United States: 1982–2010, at 6 (2012), *available at* http://www.cdc.gov/nchs/data/nhsr/nhsr055.pdf. The standard measure of an intended or unintended pregnancy is the mother's intention just before the time of conception. *See id.* at 1.

51. *Id.* at 7 fig. 2.

52. *Id.* at 7, 18 tbl. 2. The remaining 6 percent were mistimed (as opposed to "seriously mistimed"), meaning that the mother wanted to be pregnant less than two years in the future. *See id.*

53. Brady E. Hamilton & Stephanie J. Ventura, U.S. Dep't Health & Hum. Servs., Ctrs. for Disease Control and Prevention, Birth Rates for U.S. Teenagers Reach Historic Lows for All Age and Ethnic Groups 1 (2012), *available at* http://www.cdc.gov/nchs/data/databriefs/db89.pdf.

54. Kathryn Edin & Timothy J. Nelson, Doing the Best I Can: Fatherhood and the Inner City 208 (2013); Jennifer F. Hamer, *What African-American Non-Custodial*

Fathers Say Inhibits and Enhances Their Involvement with Children, 22 W. J. BLACK STUD. 117, 118, 120–23 (1998). For a description of the relationship between family complexity (multiple partners) and father involvement, and particularly the negative impact of a mother's multiple partners on father involvement, *see* Sara S. McLanahan & Irwin Garfinkel, *Fragile Families: Debates, Facts, and Solutions, in* MARRIAGE AT A CROSSROADS: LAW, POLICY, AND THE BRAVE NEW WORLD OF TWENTY-FIRST CENTURY FAMILIES 153–54 (Marsha Garrison & Elizabeth S. Scott eds., 2012).

55. *See, e.g.*, LYNN A. KAROLY, M. REBECCA KILBURN & JILL S. CANNON, EARLY CHILDHOOD INTERVENTIONS: PROVEN RESULTS, FUTURE PROMISE 55–78, 128–29 (2005) (looking at the results for twenty early-childhood intervention programs, including many preschool programs, and finding that for "cognition and academic achievement, behavioral and emotional competencies, educational progression and attainment, child maltreatment, health, delinquency and crime…and labor market success…[there were] statistically significant benefits…in at least two out of every three programs…that measured outcomes in that domain"); MICHAEL PUMA ET AL., U.S. DEP'T HEALTH & HUM. SERVS., ADMIN. FOR CHILDREN AND FAMILIES, HEAD START IMPACT STUDY FINAL REPORT: EXECUTIVE SUMMARY iv–v, xxv (2010) (finding that Head Start programs positively affect a child's vocabulary, letter-word identification, preacademic skills, letter naming, parent-reported emergent literacy, applied problems, and social issues such as hyperactive behavior, health status, parent reading to child, and family cultural-enrichment activities; Head Start also has positive effects on cognitive, social-emotional, health, and parenting outcomes; "On nearly every measure of quality traditionally used in early childhood research, the Head Start group had more positive experiences than those in the control group"); ECONOMIC OPPORTUNITY INST., THE LINK BETWEEN EARLY CHILDHOOD EDUCATION AND CRIME AND VIOLENCE REDUCTION, *available at* http://www.eoionline.org/early_learning/fact_ sheets/ELCLinkCrimeReduction-Jul02.pdf. For a study of one specific program, *see* Frances A. Campbell et al., *Early Childhood Education: Young Adult Outcomes from the Abecedarian Project*, 6 APPLIED DEVELOPMENTAL SCI. 42, 47–52 (2002).

56. KAROLY ET AL., *supra* note 55, at 128.

57. *Id.* at 114–15.

58. WILLIAM JULIUS WILSON, THE TRULY DISADVANTAGED: THE INNER CITY, THE UNDERCLASS, AND PUBLIC POLICY 81–84 (2d ed. 1987).

59. WILLIAM JULIUS WILSON, MORE THAN JUST RACE: BEING BLACK AND POOR IN THE INNER CITY 2 (2009).

60. *Id.* at 70–78.

61. *Id.* at 106–07.

62. *Id.* at 126–27.

63. *Id.* at 108–32.

64. *Id.* at 46.

65. Chapter 3 described this in greater detail.

CHAPTER 8

1. NURSE-FAMILY PARTNERSHIP, PROGRAM HISTORY, *available at* http://www.nursefamilypartnership.org/about/program-history.

2. Andy Goodman, Robert Wood Johnson Fdtn., The Story of David Olds and the Nurse Home Visiting Program 6 (2006), *available at* http://www.rwjf.org/content/dam/farm/reports/program_results_reports/2006/rwjf13780.

3. *Id.*

4. *Id.*

5. *Id.*

6. *Id.* at 7.

7. *Id.*

8. *Id.*

9. *Id.*; Nurse-Family Partnership, *supra* note 1.

10. Goodman, *supra* note 2, at 7.

11. *Id.* at 7–8.

12. *Id.* at 8.

13. Nurse-Family Partnership, *supra* note 1.

14. U.S. Dep't Health & Hum. Servs., Admin. for Children & Families, Adoption Assistance by State, *available at* https://www.childwelfare.gov/adoption/adopt_assistance/questions.cfm?quest_id=1. It is also harder to find adoptive homes for African American children. *See* Kerry DeVooght et al., *Trends in Adoptions from Foster Care in the Wake of Child Welfare Reforms*, FosteringConnections.org, Analysis No. 4 at 7 (Feb. 3, 2011), *available at* http://www.fosteringconnections.org/tools/assets/files/Connections_Adoption.pdf.

15. The availability of second-parent adoptions to same-sex partners varies widely by state. For an excellent visual depiction of legal protections, *see* Am. Civil Liberties Union, States Where Same-Sex Couples Are Able to Get Joint and/or Second Parent Adoptions Statewide (2012), *available at* http://www.aclu.org/files/assets/aclu_map4.pdf.

16. *In re* E.L.M.C., 100 P.3d 546 (Colo. App. 2004).

17. I have written elsewhere about the downsides of basing legal recognition on how a parent "acts." *See* Clare Huntington, *Staging the Family*, 88 N.Y.U. L. Rev. 589 (2013). Although psychological parenthood is an important protection for same-sex parents, I continue to be troubled by the notion that legal recognition would turn on faithfulness to a set script, as I explored in the article cited above.

18. Principles of the Law of Family Dissolution § 2.03(1)(c) (2002); *see also* Lindsy J. Rohlf, *The Psychological-Parent and De Facto-Parent Doctrines: How Should the Uniform Parentage Act Define "Parent"?*, 94 Iowa L. Rev. 691, 694–705 (2009) (describing the de facto and psychological parenthood doctrines and the states that recognize these doctrines and the states that reject them). Typically, it is the individual asserting legal rights who uses a de facto or psychological-parent doctrine, but there is a similar doctrine for a legal parent to use when the parent wants to ensure that another party is held to the obligations of legal parents, particularly child support. In this context, a legal parent might claim that the other party is a parent by estoppel, meaning that the other party held himself or herself out to the world as the child's parent and assumed full parental responsibilities with the agreement of the legal parent. Principles of the Law of Family Dissolution, *supra* § 2.03(1)(b)(iv).

19. For examples, *see generally* John Bowe, *Gay Donor or Gay Dad?*, N.Y. Times, Nov. 19, 2006, Magazine, at 66, *available at* http://www.nytimes.com/2006/11/19/magazine/19fathering.html?pagewanted=all&_r=0.

20. S.B. 1476, 2011–2012 Reg. Sess. (Cal. 2012).

21. *Id.*

22. *See* Elizabeth S. Scott & Robert E. Scott, *Parents as Fiduciaries*, 81 VA. L. REV. 2401, 2417 (1995).

23. Transcript of Oral Argument at 23, Hollingsworth v. Perry, 558 U.S. 183 (2013) (No. 12-144) (Charles J. Cooper, on behalf of Proposition 8 proponents, stating that "The concern is that redefining marriage as a genderless institution will sever its abiding connection to its historic traditional procreative purposes, and it will refocus…the purpose of marriage and the definition of marriage away from the raising of children and to the emotional needs and desires of adults, of adult couples"); *see also* Ralph R. Banks, *Why Do So Many People Oppose Same-Sex Marriage?*, 5 STAN. J. C.R. & C.L. 409, 413–22 (2009).

24. United States v. Virginia, 518 U.S. 515, 533–34 (1996) ("'Inherent differences' between men and women, we have come to appreciate, remain cause for celebration, but not for denigration of the members of either sex or for artificial constraints on an individual's opportunity. Sex classifications may be used to compensate women for particular economic disabilities they have suffered to promote equal employment opportunity, to advance full development of the talent and capacities of our Nation's people. But such classifications may not be used, as they once were, to create or perpetuate the legal, social, and economic inferiority of women") (citations omitted) (internal quotation marks omitted). For further discussion of the argument that restricting marriage to opposite-sex couples is impermissible sex-based discrimination, *see* Mary Anne Case, *What Feminists Have to Lose in Same-Sex Marriage Litigation*, 57 UCLA L. REV. 1199 (2010).

25. Lawrence v. Texas, 539 U.S. 558 (2003).

26. *See* Sara S. McLanahan, *Fragile Families and the Marriage Agenda, in* FRAGILE FAMILIES AND THE MARRIAGE AGENDA 7–8 (Lori Kowaleski-Jones & Nicholas H. Wolfinger eds., 2006).

27. FRAGILE FAMILIES AND CHILD WELLBEING STUDY, FACT SHEET, *available at* http://www.fragilefamilies.princeton.edu/documents/FragileFamiliesandChildWellbeingStudyFactSheet.pdf.

28. *Id.*

29. Sara McLanahan & Audrey N. Beck, *Parental Relationships in Fragile Families*, 20 FUTURE CHILD. 17, 22 (2010) (finding that only 51 percent of children at age five had seen their fathers in the past month).

30. Sara S. McLanahan et al., *Introducing the Issue*, 20 FUTURE CHILD. 3, 6 (2010).

31. *Id.*

32. In 2006, for example, the Bush administration created new federal grant programs to promote marriage and fatherhood. *See* Deficit Reduction Act of 2005, Pub. L. No. 109-171, § 7103(a), 120 Stat. 4 (amending 42 U.S.C. 603[a][2]). Grantees could promote marriage in a variety of ways, including public advertising campaigns on the value of marriage, education in public high schools, marriage skills training programs, and premarital education.

33. Sara S. McLanahan, *Single Mothers, Fragile Families, in* ENDING POVERTY IN AMERICA: HOW TO RESTORE THE AMERICAN DREAM 85 (Sen. John Edwards et al. eds., 2007). For further discussion of the mixed evidence on the relationship between income and marriage, *see* McLanahan & Beck, *supra* note 29, at 28–29 (describing studies finding an effect between changes in income and marriage rates and studies finding little to no effect).

34. McLanahan, *supra* note 33. Two to four years after the increase in economic support to low-income families, marriages rates of the participant groups varied from 4 percent to 16 percent. Lisa A. Gennetian & Virginia Knox, *Staying Single: The Effects of Welfare Reform Policies on*

Marriage and Cohabitation 15 (The Next Generation Working Paper Series, Paper No. 13, 2003), *available at* http://www.mdrc.org/sites/default/files/full_513.pdf. However, the average marriage rate was 10.6 percent, which was roughly equivalent to the 10.9 percent for the control group. *See id.*

35. Sara S. McLanahan & Irwin Garfinkel, *Fragile Families: Debates, Facts, and Solutions, in* MARRIAGE AT A CROSSROADS: LAW, POLICY, AND THE BRAVE NEW WORLD OF TWENTY-FIRST CENTURY FAMILIES 155–56 (Marsha Garrison & Elizabeth S. Scott eds., 2012).

36. KATHRYN EDIN & MARIA KEFALAS, PROMISES I CAN KEEP: WHY POOR WOMEN PUT MOTHERHOOD BEFORE MARRIAGE 135–36 (2005).

37. *Id.* at 130–31.

38. *Id.* at 172.

39. *Id.* at 7.

40. Marcia Carlson, Sara McLanahan & Paula England, *Union Formation in Fragile Families,* 41 DEMOGRAPHY 237, 249–55 (2004).

41. Jessica Dixon Weaver, *The First Father: Perspectives on the President's Fatherhood Initiative,* 50 FAM. CT. REV. 297, 297 (2012) (arguing that addressing the rates of incarceration of African American men would positively affect the number of absent fathers; further arguing that the state should focus on the family network to help strengthen the bonds between all family members).

42. *See* INTERNAL REVENUE SERVICE, TEN THINGS TO KNOW ABOUT THE CHILD AND DEPENDENT CARE CREDIT (Mar. 7, 2011), *available at* http://www.irs.gov/uac/Ten-Things-to-Know-About-the-Child-and-Dependent-Care-Credit.

43. *See* Sharon H. Bzostek, Sara S. McLanahan & Marci J. Carlson, *Mothers' Repartnering after a Nonmarital Birth,* 90 SOC. FORCES 817 (2012).

44. McLanahan & Beck, *supra* note 29, at 23–24; Carlson, McLanahan & England, *supra* note 40, at 256–57.

45. Philip A. Cowan, Carolyn Pape Cowan & Virginia Knox, *Marriage and Fatherhood Programs,* 20 FUTURE CHILD. 205, 213–25 (2010).

46. *Id.* at 213–14.

47. *See, e.g.,* Paul Florsheim et al., *The Young Parenthood Program: Preventing Intimate Partner Violence between Adolescent Mothers and Young Fathers,* 10 J. COUPLE & RELATIONSHIP THERAPY 117, 125–26 (2011).

48. Philip A. Cowan et al., *Promoting Fathers' Engagement with Children: Preventive Interventions for Low-Income Families,* 71 J. MARRIAGE & FAM. 663, 675 (2009).

49. Elizabeth S. Scott, *A World without Marriage,* 41 FAM. L.Q. 537, 548, 565 (2007).

50. *Id.* at 548.

51. *Id.* at 564.

52. Perry v. Schwarzenegger, 704 F. Supp. 2d 921, 933 (N.D. Cal. 2010) (quoting the trial transcript), *aff'd sub nom.* Perry v. Brown, 671 F.3d 1053 (9th Cir. 2012), *vacated and remanded sub nom.* Hollingsworth v. Perry, 133 S. Ct. 2652 (2013).

53. A child living with two *married* parents in the United States is more likely to experience a family breakup than a child living with two *unmarried* parents in Sweden. ANDREW J. CHERLIN, THE MARRIAGE-GO-ROUND: THE STATE OF MARRIAGE AND THE FAMILY IN AMERICA TODAY 3 (2009).

54. NAT'L MARRIAGE PROJECT, THE STATES OF OUR UNIONS: THE SOCIAL HEALTH OF MARRIAGE IN AMERICA 9 (2005), *available at* http://stateofourunions.org/pdfs/SOOU2005.pdf.

55. *Id.*

56. *Id.*

57. Robin A. Lenhardt, Race and the Place of Marriage, at 8 (manuscript on file with author).

58. Erez Aloni, *Registering Relationships*, 87 Tul. L. Rev. 573, 577 (2013).

59. *Id.* at 636–37.

60. *Id.* at 637.

61. *Id.* at 633.

62. *See* Definition of Spouse Amendment Act, S.B.C. 1999, c. 4 (Can.), *available at* http://www.leg.bc.ca/36th4th/3rd_read/gov21-3.htm.

63. *See* Katherine M. Franke, *Becoming a Citizen: Reconstruction Era Regulation of African American Marriages*, 11 Yale J.L. & Human. 251, 256–57 (1999).

64. Barbara A. McCann & Reid Ewing, Smart Growth Am., Measuring the Health Effects of Urban Sprawl: A National Analysis of Physical Activity, Obesity, and Chronic Disease 13–15 (2003), *available at* http://www.smartgrowthamerica.org/documents/HealthSprawl8.03-1.pdf; *Sprawl Costs*, NewUrbanism.org, *available at* http://www.newurbanism.org/sprawlcosts.html.

65. *Community: Beauty by Design*, StapletonDenver.com, *available at* http://www.stapletondenver.com/community/better-plan/beauty-design.

66. Forest City Enters., Stapleton Sustainability Master Plan 14 (2004), *available at* http://www.stapletondenver.com/sites/default/files/resources/Stapleton_Sustainability_Plan.pdf; Michael Leccese, *Denver's Stapleton: Green Urban Infill for the Masses?*, 17 Terrain.org: J. Built & Nat. Env't, Fall/Winter 2005, *available at* http://www.terrain.org/articles/17/leccese.htm; *Community: Connectivity*, StapletonDenver.com, *available at* http://www.stapletondenver.com/community/better-plan/connectivity; Stapleton Affordable Housing Plan (Jan. 29, 2001), *available at* http://www.stapletondenver.com/sites/default/files/resources/Stapleton_Affordable_Housing_Plan.pdf.

67. Leccese, *supra* note 66 (quoting Hank Baker, senior vice president of Forest City Stapleton, Inc.).

68. *Stapleton Business Ready: Who's Here*, *available at* http://www.stapletondenver.com/business-ready/whos-here.

69. *Principles of Urbanism*, NewUrbansim.org, *available at* http://www.newurbanism.org/newurbanism/principles.html.

70. *Id.*

71. *Components of Transit-Oriented Design*, TransitOrientedDevelopment.org, *available at* http://www.transitorienteddevelopment.org/.

72. John Schwartz, *Young Americans Lead Trend to Less Driving*, N.Y. Times, May 13, 2013 (quoting David Howard, a city council member who explained that Charlotte is trying to fill in urban areas and encourage development along its flourishing new rail line, as saying, "It didn't happen by mistake"), *available at* http://www.nytimes.com/2013/05/14/us/report-finds-americans-are-driving-less-led-by-youth.html?ref=todayspaper&_r=0.

73. David Baker & Partners, *available at* http://www.dbarchitect.com/ ("Our work combines social concern with a signature design character, resulting in distinctive, high-quality buildings that foster a strong sense of community").

74. Michael Kimmelman, *Design as Balm for a Community's Soul*, N.Y. Times, at C1 (Oct. 11, 2012), *available at* http://www.nytimes.com/2012/10/11/arts/design/

tassafaronga-village-and-richardson-apartments-in-bay-area.html?_r=0&adxnnl=1&page
wanted=all&adxnnlx=1374270410-kPV4pf86vrOWG5HIAOjDiA; *Tassafaronga Village*,
David Baker & Partners, *available at* http://www.dbarchitect.com/project_detail/2/
Tassafaronga%20Village.html.

75. Kimmelman, *supra* note 74.

76. Shari Roan, *Not Leaving Home*, L.A. Times, Mar. 3, 2008, *available at* http://articles.
latimes.com/print/2008/mar/03/health/he-aging3.

77. *Aging in Place: Key Ingredients*, Aging in Place, *available at* http://aginginplace.com/
mini-2/key-ingredients/.

78. Susan Enguidanos et al., *Integrating Community Experiences within A NORC: The Park
La Brea Experience*, 12 Cityscape: J. Pol'y Dev. & Res. 29, 30 (2010).

79. *Id.* at 30–31.

80. *Id.* at 30, 36; Roan, *supra* note 76.

81. Roan, *supra* note 76.

82. *Id.*

83. *Stapleton*, Denver Urban Renewal Authority, *available at* http://www.renewden-
ver.org/redevelopment/dura-redevelopment-projects/denver-county/stapleton.html.

84. *Id.*

85. Leccese, *supra* note 66.

86. *Id.*

87. *Id.*

88. *Id.*

89. *Id.*

90. Terry Pristin, *New Urbanism in Denver*, N.Y. Times, June 1, 2005, *available at* http://
travel.nytimes.com/2005/06/01/business/01staple.html?pagewanted=all.

91. *Id.*

92. *Id.*

93. *Id.*

94. Penelope Green, *Under One Roof, Building for Extended Families*, N.Y. Times, Nov.
30, 2012, at A1, *available at* http://www.nytimes.com/2012/11/30/us/building-homes-for-mod-
ern-multigenerational-families.html.

95. 42 U.S.C.§ 4321 et seq. (2012).

96. For an accessible overview of this law, *see* Exec. Office of the President, A Citizen's
Guide to the NEPA: Having Your Voice Heard (2007), *available at* http://ceq.hss.doe.
gov/nepa/Citizens_Guide_Dec07.pdf.

97. Isabel Sawhill, Adam Thomas & Emily Monea, *An Ounce of Prevention: Policy Prescriptions
to Reduce the Prevalence of Fragile Families*, 20 Future Child. 133, 139 (2010).

98. *Id.* at 140–42.

99. *Id.* at 142–46.

100. *Id.* at 146.

101. General information about the program can be found on the website for the Wyman
Center, a nonprofit organization that started TOP. *See Wyman's Teen Outreach Program (TOP)*,
Wyman, *available at* http://www.wymancenter.org/wyman_top.php.

102. Joseph P. Allen et al., *Preventing Teen Pregnancy and Academic Failure: Experimental
Evaluation of a Developmentally Based Approach*, 68 Child Dev. 729, 734–35 (1997) (finding

that participating students had only 41 percent of the risk of becoming pregnant as compared with those in the control group).

103. *Id.*

104. *See* Andrea Kane & Isabel V. Sawhill, *Preventing Early Childbearing, in* ONE PERCENT FOR THE KIDS: NEW POLICIES, BRIGHTER FUTURES FOR AMERICA'S CHILDREN 63 (Isabel V. Sawhill ed., 2003).

105. Jeffrey F. Peipert et al., *Preventing Unintended Pregnancies by Providing No-Cost Contraception*, 120 OBSTETRICS AND GYNECOLOGY 1291, 1291–92 (2012).

106. *Id.* Oral contraceptives can be highly effective, but they must be taken regularly.

107. *Id.* at 1293.

108. *Id.* at 1294.

109. *Id.* at 1295.

110. KATHRYN KOST, STANLEY HENSHAW & LIZ CARLIN, GUTTMACHER INST., U.S. TEENAGE PREGNANCIES, BIRTHS, AND ABORTIONS: NATIONAL AND STATE TRENDS AND TRENDS BY RACE AND ETHNICITY 2 (rev. 2012), *available at* http://www.guttmacher.org/ pubs/USTPtrends.pdf. The overall pregnancy rate for this age group (not just the subset of sexu- ally active teens) is 71.5 per 1,000, but that rate is skewed downward because it includes girls and young women who are not sexually active. *Id.* The higher teen birth rate of 41.9 teen births per 1,000 women was for 2006. As the text describes, the rate has since decreased to 34.3.

111. *Id.* (32 percent of the teen pregnancies in 2006 ended in an abortion).

112. KATHRYN EDIN & TIMOTHY J. NELSON, DOING THE BEST I CAN: FATHERHOOD AND THE INNER CITY 204–07 (2013)

113. NURSE-FAMILY PARTNERSHIP, ABOUT, *available at* http://www.nursefamilypartner- ship.org/about.

114. NURSE-FAMILY PARTNERSHIP, NURSES AND MOTHERS, *available at* http://www. nursefamilypartnership.org/assets/PDF/Fact-sheets/NFP_Nurses_Mothers.aspx.

115. *See* JUDITH GLAZNER ET AL., FINAL REPORT TO THE ADMINISTRATION FOR CHILDREN AND FAMILIES: EFFECT OF THE NURSE FAMILY PARTNERSHIP ON GOVERNMENT EXPENDITURES FOR VULNERABLE FIRST-TIME MOTHERS AND THEIR CHILDREN IN ELMIRA, NEW YORK, MEMPHIS, TENNESSEE, AND DENVER, COLORADO 1 (2004), *available at* http://www.acf.hhs.gov/sites/default/files/opre/effect_nursefam.pdf.

116. *See* NORTHWEST COLO. VISITING NURSE ASS'N, NURSE FAMILY PARTNERSHIP— HELPING FIRST-TIME PARENTS SUCCEED, *available at* http://www.nwcovna.org/nfp.php ("Irene's Story" video).

117. *See* Khiara M. Bridges, *Towards a Theory of State Visibility: Race, Poverty, and Equal Protection*, 19 COLUM. J. GENDER & L. 965, 971–78 (2010).

118. TAMARA DUMANOVSKY & HIMA MUTTANA, N.Y.C. DEP'T HEALTH & MENTAL HYGIENE, NURSE FAMILY PARTNERSHIP—BENEFIT/COST ANALYSIS 3 (2004), *available at* http://www.nursefamilypartnership.org/assets/PDF/Journals-and-Reports/NFP-NY-Cost- Analysis ("Outcome studies indicate a 50 percent reduction in state-verified reports of child abuse and neglect through the child's second birthday among low-income, unmarried teen mothers participating in NFP").

119. David L. Olds et al., *Improving the Life-Course Development of Socially Disadvantaged Mothers: A Randomized Trial of Nurse Home Visitation*, 78 AM. J. PUB. HEALTH 1436, 1440 (1988) ("During the first four years after delivery of their first child, nurse-visited women who

had not completed their high school education at the time they registered in the study returned to school more rapidly than their comparison-group counterparts; and nurse-visited women who were poor and unmarried were employed 82 per cent more of the time, had 43 per cent fewer subsequent pregnancies, and delayed the birth of their second child an average of 12 months longer").

120. David L. Olds et al., *Effects of Nurse Home-Visiting on Maternal Life Course and Child Development: Age 6 Follow-Up Results of a Randomized Trial*, 114 PEDIATRICS 1550, 1553 (2004) ("Between children's 54th and 72nd months of life, nurse-visited women had fewer months of using welfare and food stamps"); David L. Olds et al., *Long-Term Effects of Home Visitation on Maternal Life Course and Child Abuse and Neglect: Fifteen-Year Follow-Up of a Randomized Trial*, 278 J. AM. MED. ASS'N 637, 640 (1997) (nurse-visited unmarried women from low-SES households "reported using AFDC and food stamps fewer months than did unmarried, low-SES women in the comparison group").

121. Olds et al., *Long-Term Effects, supra* note 120, at 640 ("Table 4 shows that nurse-visited, low-SES, unmarried women reported being impaired in fewer domains by alcohol or other drug use, having been arrested fewer times, having been convicted fewer times, and having spent fewer days in jail…since the birth of their first child than did low-SES unmarried women in the comparison group").

122. Harriet Kitzman et al., *Enduring Effects of Nurse Home Visitation on Maternal Life Course: A 3-Year Follow-Up of a Randomized Trial*, 283 J. AM. MED. ASS'N 1983, 1987–88 (2000) (finding that 19 percent of women who received home visits by nurses lived with the fathers of their children three years after the program ended, compared with 13 percent of women who did not receive home visits; in the study, women were placed at random into visitation and nonvisitation groups, and the findings control for maternal race, maternal age, gestational age at enrollment, employment status of head of household, and geographic region of residence).

123. Olds et al., *Effects of Nurse Home-Visiting, supra* note 120, at 1554–56 (nurse-visited children "had higher scores on tests of intellectual functioning and receptive language…and were reported by their mothers to have fewer problems in the borderline or clinical range of the CBCL Total Problems scale.…Nurse-visited children born to mothers with low psychologic resources had higher arithmetic achievement test scores…and, in their responses to story stems, expressed less dysregulated aggression…and told fewer incoherent stories"; nurse-visited children "demonstrated higher IQs and language scores and fewer behavioral problems in the borderline or clinical range. Moreover, nurse-visited children born to mothers with low psychologic resources revealed less dysregulated aggression and story incoherence in their narrative responses to the story stems").

124. Olds et al., *Long-Term Effects, supra* note 120, at 1241 ("Table 3 shows that adolescents born to nurse-visited women…reported more frequent stops by police…but fewer arrests and convictions and violations of probation…; the arrest and convictions and probation violation effects were concentrated among children born to women who were unmarried and from low-SES families.…Nurse-visited children whose mothers were unmarried and from low-SES families were reported by their parents to have been arrested less frequently than were their counterparts in the comparison group").

125. LYNN A KAROLY, M. REBECCA KILBURN & JILL S. CANNON, EARLY CHILDHOOD INTERVENTIONS: PROVEN RESULTS, FUTURE PROMISE xxvi, xxviii (2005). These savings are for high-risk populations. For lower-risk populations in the program, every dollar invested results in $1.26 in savings.

126. John Eckenrode et al., *Preventing Child Abuse and Neglect with a Program of Nurse Home Visitation: The Limiting Effects of Domestic Violence*, 284 J. Am. Med. Ass'n, 1385, 1388–90 (2000).

127. John Eckenrode et al., *Long-term Effects of Prenatal and Infancy Nurse Home Visitation on the Life Course of Youths: 19-year Follow-up of a Randomized Trial*, 164 Archives Pediatric Adolescent Med. 1, 9, 12 (2010).

128. Edin & Nelson, *supra* note 112, at 85–86.

129. *Id.*

130. *Id.* at 157, 169, 208.

131. *Id.* at 169.

132. *Id.* at 220–27

133. *Id.* at 169.

134. McLanahan & Beck, *supra* note 29, at 27.

135. Edin & Nelson, *supra* note 112, at 215.

136. Robert Lerman & Elaine Sorensen, *Father Involvement with Their Nonmarital Children: Patterns, Determinants, and Effects on Their Earnings*, 29 Marriage & Fam. Rev. 137, 145 (2000) (finding that 49 percent of fathers with children born outside of marriage lived with at least one nonmarital child, and another 21 percent visited at least one nonmarital child once a week or more).

137. Edin & Nelson, *supra* note 112, at 213–16.

138. *Id.* at 215.

139. For an excellent discussion of the multiple barriers to father involvement, along with an analysis of child-support laws, *see* Laurie S. Kohn, *Engaging Men as Fathers: The Courts, the Law, and Father-Absence in Low-Income Families*, 35 Cardozo L. Rev. 102 (2013).

140. Solangel Maldonado, *Deadbeat or Deadbroke: Redefining Child Support for Poor Fathers*, 39 U.C. Davis L. Rev. 991, 1013 (2006).

141. *Id.* at 1017.

142. *Id.* at 1018–19.

143. *Id.* at 1018.

144. *Id.* at 1019.

145. *Id.* ("Paternal engagement not only benefits children but may also give mothers a break from parenting if only for a few hours. Parents who share parenting responsibilities are better parents").

146. *Id.* at 1016.

147. Arthur J. Reynolds & Dylan L. Robertson, *School-Based Early Intervention and Later Child Maltreatment in the Chicago Longitudinal Study*, 74 Child Dev. 3, 8 (2003).

148. *See* Arthur J. Reynolds, Judy A. Temple & Suh-Ruu Ou, *School-Based Early Intervention and Child Well-Being in the Chicago Longitudinal Study*, 82 Child Welfare 633, 643 (2003); Reynolds & Robertson, *supra* note 147, at 13–14.

149. Reynolds & Robertson, *supra* note 147, at 14.

150. *See* Reynolds, Temple & Ou, *supra* note 148, at 645.

151. *See* Michael Puma et al., U.S. Dep't Health & Hum. Servs., Admin. for Children & Families, Head Start Impact Study Final Report xxii (2010), *available at* http://www.acf.hhs.gov/sites/default/files/opre/executive_summary_final.pdf.

152. *See id.*

153. 42 U.S.C. § 9858 (1994). For an extended discussion of the Child Care and Development Block Grant, *see* Clare Huntington, *Welfare Reform and Child Care: A Proposal for State Legislation*, 6 Cornell J.L. & Pub. Pol'y 95, 97 (1997).

154. *Julie's Story about EITC*, Half in Ten, Mar. 9, 2012, *available at* http://halfinten.org/stories/julies-story-about-eitc/.

155. Internal Revenue Service, Preview of 2013 EITC Income Limits, Maximum Credit Amounts and Tax Law Updates, *available at* http://www.irs.gov/Individuals/Preview-of-2012-EITC-Income-Limits,-Maximum-Credit--Amounts-and-Tax-Law-Updates.

156. Ctr. on Budget & Pol'y Priorities, Policy Basics: State Earned Income Tax Credits 1 (2012), *available at* http://www.cbpp.org/files/policybasics-seitc.pdf (tax credits modeled on the federal EITC are available in twenty-four states and the District of Columbia); Internal Revenue Service, State and Local Government EITC Programs, *available at* http://www.eitc.irs.gov/central/press/overview/stateeitc/ (local tax credits are available in New York City, San Francisco, and Montgomery County, Maryland).

157. Corp. for Supportive Housing, Keeping Families Together 5–6, *available at* http://www.csh.org/wp-content/uploads/2011/12/Tool_KeepingFamiliesTogetherBrochure.pdf; Corp. for Supportive Housing, Keeping Families Together Matters: An Introduction to Creating Supportive Housing for Child Welfare-Involved Families 10 (2012), *available at* http://www.csh.org/wp-content/uploads/2012/07/KFT-Guidebook-120711.pdf (hereinafter Keeping Families Together Matters); Rebecca Swann-Jackson, Donna Tapper & Allison Fields, Metis Assocs., Keeping Families Together: An Evaluation of the Implementation and Outcomes of a Pilot Supportive Housing Model for Families Involved in the Child Welfare System iv (2010), *available at* http://www.csh.org/wp-content/uploads/2011/12/Report_KFTFindingsreport.pdf.

158. Keeping Families Together Matters, *supra* note 157, at 10; Swann-Jackson, Tapper & Fields, *supra* note 157, at iv, 25, 29–46.

159. Corp. for Supportive Housing, Is Supportive Housing a Cost-Effective Means of Preserving Families and Increasing Child Safety? Cost Analysis of CSH's Keeping Families Together Pilot 3, *available at* http://www.csh.org/wp-content/uploads/2011/12/Report_KFTCostAnalysisWriteUp.pdf.

160. Paul Tough, Whatever It Takes: Geoffrey Canada's Quest to Change Harlem and America 194–96 (2009).

161. Kitty Barnes, Harlem Children's Zone, A Look Inside: The Baby College 2 (2002).

162. *Id.*

163. *See, e.g.*, Paul Tough, *The Harlem Project*, N.Y. Times, June 20, 2004, *available at* http://www.nytimes.com/2004/06/20/magazine/the-harlem-project.html?pagewanted=all&src=pm.

164. Barnes, *supra* note 161, at 2.

165. Harlem Children's Zone, Early Childhood, *available at* http://www.hcz.org/programs/early-childhood.

166. *See, e.g.*, David Kirp, *Audacity in Harlem*, Am. Prospect, Sept. 19, 2008, *available at* http://prospect.org/article/audacity-harlem.

167. Harlem Children's Zone, *supra* note 165.

168. *Id.; see, e.g.*, Tough, *supra* note 163.

169. HARLEM CHILDREN'S ZONE, *supra* note 165.

170. *See, e.g.*, Tough, *supra* note 163.

171. *See* HARLEM CHILDREN'S ZONE, PROMISE ACADEMY CHARTER SCHOOLS, *available at* http://www.hcz.org/programs/promise-academy-charter-schools.

172. *See id.*

173. *See id.*

174. Will Dobbie & Roland G. Fryer, Jr., *Are High-Quality Schools Enough to Increase Achievement among the Poor? Evidence from the Harlem Children's Zone*, 3 AM. ECON. J. 158, 162 (2011); *see* HARLEM CHILDREN'S ZONE, *supra* note 171.

175. Stephen W. Nicholas et al., *Addressing the Childhood Asthma Crisis in Harlem: The Harlem Children's Zone Asthma Initiative*, 95 AM. J. PUB. HEALTH, 245, 247–48 (2005) ("28.5% have been told by a doctor or nurse that they have asthma, and 30.3% are currently experiencing asthma or asthma symptoms").

176. KITTY BARNES, HARLEM CHILDREN'S ZONE REPORT, A LOOK INSIDE: THE ASTHMA INITIATIVE 4–5 (2005).

177. HARLEM CHILDREN'S ZONE, THE HCZ PROJECT, *available at* http://www.hcz.org/about-us/the-hcz-project.

178. TOUGH, *supra* note 160, at 162; HARLEM CHILDREN'S ZONE, GROWTH PLAN FY 2001–FY 2009, at 1–2 (2003), *available at* http://hcz.org/images/stories/pdfs/business_plan.pdf.

179. HARLEM CHILDREN'S ZONE, *supra* note 177.

180. HARLEM CHILDREN'S ZONE, HISTORY, *available at* http://www.hcz.org/about-us/history; HARLEM CHILDREN'S ZONE, OUR RESULTS, *available at* http://www.hcz.org/our-results.

181. HARLEM CHILDREN'S ZONE, OUR RESULTS, *supra* note 180.

182. UNIV. OF THE STATE OF N.Y., STATE EDUC. DEP'T, CHARTER SCHOOL ANNUAL REPORT: 2009–2010, HARLEM CHILDREN'S ZONE PROMISE ACADEMY II CHARTER SCHOOL 11 (2010), *available at* http://schools.nyc.gov/NR/rdonlyres/408306E5-336A-43E4-B75C-564BCCB8B7E0/0/AnnualReportpacket84M341.pdf (nearly 63 percent of Promise Academy students who had been enrolled in the school for at least two years earned a three or a four [out of four] on the New York State Math Exam, compared with only 29 percent of students in regular schools in central Harlem; on the New York State Reading Exam, nearly 83 percent of Promise Academy students enrolled for at least two years earned a three or a four [out of four], compared with only 38 percent of the students in the same neighborhood). The results for the high school students are also excellent. The school is in the ninety-ninth percentile of all New York City public high schools. *See* NEW YORK CITY DEP'T EDUC., PROGRESS REPORT 2011–12: HARLEM CHILDREN'S ZONE/PROMISE ACADEMY CHARTER SCHOOL, *available at* http://schools.nyc.gov/OA/SchoolReports/2011-12/Progress_Report_2012_HS_M284.pdf.

183. HARLEM CHILDREN'S ZONE, OUR RESULTS, *supra* note 180.

184. Stephen W. Nicholas et al., *Reducing Childhood Asthma through Community-Based Service Delivery—New York City, 2001–2004*, 54 MORBIDITY & MORTALITY WKLY. REP. 11–12 (2005); HARLEM CHILDREN'S ZONE, OUR RESULTS, *supra* note 180 ("at pretest, 29.7% of children had missed school due to asthma in the previous 14 days. Forty-two months later, only 6.8% had missed school due to asthma in the previous 14 days").

185. HARLEM CHILDREN'S ZONE, OUR RESULTS, *supra* note 180.

186. DANIELLE HANSON, CTR. FOR POLICY INNOVATION, HERITAGE FOUND., ASSESSING THE HARLEM CHILDREN'S ZONE 5–10 (2013), *available at* http://s3.amazonaws.com/thf_media/2013/pdf/CPI_DP_08.pdf.

187. Dobbie & Fryer, *supra* note 174, at 162.

188. *Id.* at 162. Research into the elementary-school students showed even better gains for the Promise Academy students, with the students erasing the black-white achievement gap for both math and English language arts.

189. *Id.* at 179.

190. HANSON, *supra* note 186, at 5–10.

191. GOODMAN, *supra* note 2, at 8.

192. 4-5 § Föräldraledighetslag (SFS 1995:584) (Swed.), English translation *available at* http://www.government.se/content/1/c6/10/49/85/f16b785a.pdf; *Gender Equality: the Swedish Approach to Fairness*, SWEDISH INST., *available at* http://www.sweden.se/eng/Home/Society/Equality/Facts/Gender-equality-in-Sweden/; Darren Rosenblum, *Unsex Mothering: Toward a New Culture of Parenting*, 35 HARV. J.L. & GENDER 57, 109 (2012); *see also* James Savage, *How Does Swedish Parental Leave Work?*, THE LOCAL: SWEDEN'S NEWS IN ENGLISH (Aug. 8, 2008), *available at* http://www.thelocal.se/14022/20080829/.

193. Andrea Doucet, *Institute "Daddy Leave,"* N.Y. TIMES, June 14, 2011, *available at* http://www.nytimes.com/roomfordebate/2011/07/05/how-can-we-get-men-to-do-more-at-home/for-gender-equality-take-fathers-into-account; Katrin Bennhold, *In Sweden, Men Can Have It All*, N.Y. TIMES (June 9, 2010), *available at* http://www.nytimes.com/2010/06/10/world/europe/10iht-sweden.html?%20scp=1&sq=sweden%20fathers&st=cse; *see also* Rosenblum, *supra* note 192, at 111.

194. Michael B. Wells & Anna Sarkadi, *Do Father-Friendly Policies Promote Father-Friendly Child-Rearing Practices? A Review of Swedish Parental Leave and Child Health Centers*, 21 J. CHILD FAM. STUD. 25, 26 (2012).

195. Chris Gottlieb, *Reflections on Judging Mothering*, 39 U. BALT. L. REV. 371, 377–87 (2010).

196. *See* Joan Williams, *The Daddy Dilemma: Why Men Face a "Flexibility Stigma" at Work*, WASHINGTONPOST.COM (Feb. 11, 2013), *available at* http://www.washingtonpost.com/national/on-leadership/the-daddy-dilemma-why-men-face-a-flexibility-stigma-at-work/2013/02/11/58350f4e-7462-11e2-aa12-e6cf1d31106b_story.html; Joan Williams, Mary Blair-Loy & Jennifer Berdahl, *The Flexibility Stigma: Work Devotion vs. Family Devotion*, ROTMAN MAG., (Winter 2013), at 34, 36, 39. And when men do try to restructure their work commitments to facilitate caregiving, they face a "flexibility stigma," much in the same way as women on the "mommy track." *See* Scott Coltrane et al., *Fathers and the Flexibility Stigma*, 69 J. SOC. ISSUES 279, 282, 288–95 (2013).

197. Lenna Nepomnyaschy & Jane Waldfogel, *Paternity Leave and Fathers' Involvement with Their Young Children: Evidence from the American Ecls-B*, 10 COMMUNITY WORK & FAM. 427, 437 (2007).

198. Rudy R. Seward, Dale E. Yeatts & Lisa K. Zottarelli, *Parental Leave and Father Involvement in Child Care: Sweden and the United States*, 33 J. COMP. FAM. STUD. 387, 396 (2002).

199. Bennhold, *supra* note 193.

200. *Id.*

CHAPTER 9

1. Michael M. Grynbaum, *New York Plans to Ban Sale of Big Sizes of Sugary Drinks*, N.Y. TIMES, May 31, 2012, at A1. The regulation had numerous exceptions and did not apply, for example, to diet drinks, fruit juices, dairy-based drinks, alcoholic beverages, and grocery- and convenience-store

sales. *See* NYC Health Code § 81.53. As this book is going to press, the regulation had been struck down by both a trial and appellate court. *See* New York Statewide Coal. of Hispanic Chambers of Commerce v. New York City Dep't of Health & Mental Hygiene, 10508, 2013 WL 3880139 (N.Y. App. Div. July 30, 2013).

2. Press Release, New York City Mayor's Office, Mayor Bloomberg, Public Advocate de Blasio, Manhattan Borough President Stringer, Montefiore Hospital CEO Safyer, Deputy Mayor Gibbs and Health Commissioner Farley Highlight Health Impact of Obesity (June 5, 2012), *available at* http://www.nyc.gov/html/om/html/2012a/pr200-12.html.

3. Ben Forer & Olivia Katrandjian, *Soft Drink Industry Fights Back, Depicting Bloomberg as Nanny,* ABC News, June 2, 2012, *available at* http://abcnews.go.com/blogs/health/2012/06/02/soft-drink-industry-fights-back-depicting-bloomberg-as-nanny/.

4. *The Daily Show with Jon Stewart* (Comedy Central broadcast May 31, 2012), *available at* http://www.thedailyshow.com/watch/thu-may-31-2012/drink-different.

5. For an excellent discussion of the history of conceiving of poverty as private matter, *see* Angela Onwuachi-Willig, *The Return of the Ring: Welfare Reform's Marriage Cure as the Revival of Post-Bellum Control,* 93 Cal. L. Rev. 1647, 1653–63 (2005). I am not arguing that families bear the responsibility for poverty but rather that families are an essential locus for the fight against poverty and that helping parents and children develop strong, stable, positive relationships is a critical step in addressing poverty.

6. Naomi Cahn & June Carbone, Red Families v. Blue Families: Legal Polarization and the Creation of Culture 206 (2010) (citing Maggie Gallagher, *Re: Marriage Proposal,* National Review Online, *available at* http://www.nationalreview.com/corner/178528/re-marriage-proposal/maggie-gallagher).

7. *Id.* at 206–07.

8. *Id.* at 207.

9. *Id.* at 19.

10. *Id.* at 1.

11. *Id.* at 21–24, 28, 133–35.

12. *Id.* at 22, 28. As longtime family-law scholars, Cahn and Carbone are too familiar with their subject to attribute a causal relationship to family structure and family-law regimes. Instead, they carefully note that levels of income and age at marriage are the best indicators of divorce. For example, because men and women in Idaho marry at the second-lowest median age, it is no surprise that their divorce rate is among the highest in the country. *Id.* at 25, 28. By contrast, Connecticut has the second-highest median age of marriage and has a divorce rate among the lowest in the country. *Id.* at 25–28.

13. Sexual activity outside of marriage is widespread, regardless of ideological orientation. *Id.* at 85 ("By the age of 44, 95% of the entire population will have had sex outside of marriage, and they will overwhelmingly have done so with someone other than a person they will eventually marry").

14. Cahn and Carbone present convincing evidence that this is true, at least for young women in red states. *Id.* at 89–91, 104–05.

15. *Id.* at 44–46.

16. *Id.* at 46.

17. *See Election 2004 U.S. President National Exit Poll,* CNN, *available at* http://www.cnn.com/ELECTION/2004/pages/results/states/US/P/00/epolls.0.html.

18. *See Election 2008 U.S. President National Exit Poll,* CNN, *available at* http://www.cnn. com/ELECTION/2008/results/polls/#USP00p1. Breaking this down by state shows that college-educated individuals in red states, such as Arkansas and Idaho, followed their state's pattern, with 61 and 55 percent of college-educated voters reporting in exit polls that they voted for McCain, respectively. *See Election 2008 U.S. President Arkansas Exit Poll,* CNN, *available at* http://www.cnn.com/ELECTION/2008/results/polls/#ARP00p1; *Election 2008 U.S. President Idaho Exit Poll,* CNN, *available at* http://www.cnn.com/ELECTION/2008/results/ polls/#val=IDP00p1.

19. *Election 2012 U.S. President National Exit Poll,* CNN, *available at* http://www.cnn.com/ election/2012/results/race/president#exit-polls.

20. Cahn and Carbone acknowledge this, stating that family structure "strongly reflect[s] wealth." CAHN & CARBONE, *supra* note 6, at 29. But, as Cahn and Carbone also explain, there are plenty of college-educated individuals who still have red families, at least in terms of family formation. *Id.* at 73.

21. In 2008 exit polls, 95 percent of African Americans interviewed reported that they voted for Obama, *see Election 2008 U.S. President National Exit Poll, supra* note 18, and in 2004 exit polls, 88 percent reported voting for Kerry, *see Election 2004 U.S. President National Exit Poll, supra* note 17.

22. As chapter 2 explained, nearly 72 percent of all African American births are nonmarital.

23. Jonathan Haidt, *What Makes People Vote Republican?*, EDGE.ORG, *available at* http:// www.edge.org/3rd_culture/haidt08/haidt08_index.html.

24. *Id.*

25. *Id.*

26. *Id.*

27. *Cf. id.*

28. *See* GEORGE LAKOFF, MORAL POLITICS: HOW LIBERALS AND CONSERVATIVES THINK 65–66 (2d ed. 2002).

29. *See id.* at 66.

30. *See id.* at 65–69.

31. *See id.* at 67–76.

32. *See id.* at 108–11.

33. *See id.* at 112–13.

34. *See id.* at 108–40.

35. *See id.* at 143–76.

36. *See id.* at 163–65.

37. *See id.* at 165–69.

38. *See id.* at 168.

39. *See, e.g.,* DOROTHY ROBERTS, KILLING THE BLACK BODY: RACE, REPRODUCTION, AND THE MEANING OF LIBERTY 202–45 (1997).

40. *See* JOEL F. HANDLER & YEHESKEL HASENFELD, BLAME WELFARE, IGNORE POVERTY AND INEQUALITY 7 (2007) ("Instead of addressing poverty and inequality, we have demonized welfare, the program for poor single mothers and their families, and we continue our incredibly long history of blaming the victim").

41. *See, e.g.,* CHARLES MURRAY, LOSING GROUND: AMERICAN SOCIAL POLICY, 1950–1980, at 154–66 (1984).

42. *See, e.g.*, Barbara Vobejda & Judith Havemann, *2 HHS Officials Quit over Welfare Changes*, Wash. Post, Sept. 12, 1996, at A1 (describing the resignation of Peter Edelman and Mary Jo Bane over the 1996 welfare reform, a "rare" public protest in the federal government).

43. *But see* Katherine M. Franke, *Taking Care*, 76 Chi.-Kent L. Rev. 1541, 1544 (2001) ("The granting of rights and the recognition of public responsibility for depend[e]ncy is unlikely to usher in a domain of unrestrained autonomy that some liberal projects promise. Rather, to shift responsibility for dependency outside the family is to exchange one practice of rule—the private family—for another set of regulatory governance practices, those imbued in the state and the market").

44. *See* The Cultural Cognition Project at Yale Law School, http://www.culturalcognition.net. Like Haidt and Lakoff, the Cutural Cognition Project also uses a schema for categorizing people into different belief groups.

45. *See* Dan Kahan, David A. Hoffman & Donald Braman, *Whose Eyes Are You Going to Believe? Scott v. Harris and Cognitive Illiberalism*, 122 Harv. L. Rev. 837, 841–42, 866–79 (2009) (using the Cultural Cognition tools to discuss divergent reactions to a high-speed police chase).

46. *See* Cahn & Carbone, *supra* note 6, at 69–71.

47. *See* Cass R. Sunstein, *Deliberative Trouble? Why Groups Go to Extremes*, 110 Yale L.J. 71, 74–75 (2000).

48. This bumper sticker, http://www.cafepress.com/designedforyou.21312867, is an obvious play on the name of the conservative organization, Focus on the Family. Focus on the Family, *available at* http://www.focusonthefamily.com.

49. Alemayehu Bishaw, U.S. Census Bureau, *Poverty: 2010 and 2011*, at 3 tbl.1 (2012), *available at* http://www.census.gov/prod/2012pubs/acsbr11-01.pdf (listing the percentage of people living in poverty in each state in 2011; Alabama had 19 percent of its population living in poverty).

50. *See* Children's Defense Fund, Children in Alabama 2 (2013), *available at* http://www.childrensdefense.org/child-research-data-publications/data/state-data-repository/cits/2013/2013-alabama-children-in-the-states.pdf (noting that Alabama enrolls only 11.1 percent of eligible three-year-olds and 24.4 percent of eligible four-year-olds in Head Start–type programs).

51. Bishaw, *supra* note 49, at 3 tbl.1 (listing the percentage of people living in poverty in each state in 2011; Massachusetts had 11.6 percent of its population living in poverty).

52. David A. Fahrenthold, *Mass. Bill Requires Health Coverage*, WashingtonPost.com (Apr. 5, 2006), *available at* http://www.washingtonpost.com/wp-dyn/content/article/2006/04/04/AR2006040401937.html.

53. Nurse-Family Partnership, *available at* http://www.nursefamilypartnership.org/about.

54. Harlem Children's Zone, *available at* http://www.hcz.org/about-us/the-hcz-project.

55. *Planned Parenthood of Se. Pa. v. Casey*, 505 U.S. 833, 895 (1992) (noting that the spousal notification requirement "will operate as a substantial obstacle to a woman's choice to undergo an abortion. It is an undue burden, and therefore invalid").

56. *Id.* at 975 (Rehnquist, C.J., dissenting) (quoting 18 Pa. Cons. Stat. § 3209[a] [1990]; internal quotations marks omitted).

57. *Id.*

58. This typology comes from Eleanor Maccoby and John Martin, who reviewed the parenting literature and determined that there are two main axes of parenting: "demandingness"

(or strictness) and "responsiveness" (or warmth and support). Authoritative parents are both demanding and responsive. Authoritarian parents are demanding but not particularly responsive. Permissive parents are not demanding but are highly responsive. And uninvolved parents are neither demanding nor responsive. *See* Eleanor E. Maccoby and John A. Martin, *Socialization in the Context of the Family: Parent-Child Interaction*, in Handbook of child psychology: Socialization, personality, and social development, 1–101 (P. H. Mussen & E. M. Hetherington eds., 1983).

59. *See* Margaret Brinig, *Religion, Race, and Motherhood* 3 (Notre Dame Law School, Working Paper No. 10-06, 2010), *available at* http://papers.ssrn.com/sol3/papers.cfm?abstract_id=1565030.

60. *See id.* at 18–19.

61. *See, e.g.,* Lynn A. Karoly, M. Rebecca Kilburn & Jill S. Cannon, Early Childhood Interventions: Proven Results, Future Promise 55–78, 128–29 (2005) (looking at the results for twenty early-childhood intervention programs, including many preschool programs, and finding that for "cognition and academic achievement, behavioral and emotional competencies, educational progression and attainment, child maltreatment, health, delinquency and crime…and labor market success…[there were] statistically significant benefits…in at least two out of every three programs…that measured outcomes in that domain"); Michael Puma et al., U.S. Dep't Health & Hum. Servs., Admin. for Children and Families, Head Start Impact Study Final Report: Executive Summary iv–v, xxv (2010) (finding that Head Start programs positively affect a child's vocabulary, letter-word identification, preacademic skills, letter naming, parent-reported emergent literacy, applied problems, and social issues such as hyperactive behavior, health status, parent reading to child, and family cultural-enrichment activities; Head Start also has positive effects on cognitive, social-emotional, health, and parenting outcomes; "On nearly every measure of quality traditionally used in early childhood research, the Head Start group had more positive experiences than those in the control group"); Economic Opportunity Inst., The Link between Early Childhood Education and Crime and Violence Reduction, *available at* http://www.eoionline.org/early_learning/fact_sheets/ELCLinkCrimeReduction-Jul02.pdf. For a study of one specific program, *see* Frances A. Campbell et al., *Early Childhood Education: Young Adult Outcomes from the Abecedarian Project*, 6 Applied Developmental Sci. 42, 47–52 (2002).

62. James J. Heckman, *Catch 'Em Young*, Wall St. J., Jan. 10, 2006, at A14, *available at* http://jenni.uchicago.edu/papers/WSJ_Heckman_01102006_Catch_Em_Young.pdf; *see also* James J. Heckman, *Skill Formation and the Economics of Investing in Disadvantaged Children*, 312 Science 1900, 1901 (2006).

63. Heckman, *Catch 'Em Young, supra* note 62; *see also* Heckman, *Skill Formation, supra* note 62.

64. Lynn A Karoly, M. Rebecca Kilburn & Jill S. Cannon, Early Childhood Interventions: Proven Results, Future Promise xxvi, xxviii (2005). As this source explains, these savings are for high-risk populations. For lower-risk populations in the program, every dollar invested results in $1.26 in savings. For an extended cost-benefit analysis of numerous early-childhood investment programs that concludes that nearly all programs are cost-effective, *see id.* at 87–121.

65. *See* A. J. Reynolds, Judy A. Temple & Suh-Ruu Ou, *School-Based Early Intervention and Child Well-Being in the Chicago Longitudinal Study*, 82 Child Welfare 633, 645 (2003).

66. SARA EDELSTEIN ET AL., THE URBAN INSTITUTE, HOW DO PUBLIC INVESTMENTS IN CHILDREN VARY WITH AGE? A KIDS' SHARE ANALYSIS OF EXPENDITURES IN 2008 AND 2011 BY AGE GROUP 9 (2012), *available at* http://www.urban.org/UploadedPDF/412676-How-Do-Public-Investments-in-Children-Vary-with-Age.pdf. Spending at all three levels of government was $13,663 for each child age twelve to eighteen. *Id.*

67. *Id.*

68. *Id.*

69. BUREAU OF JUST. STAT., JUSTICE EXPENDITURE AND EMPLOYMENT EXTRACTS, 2010—PRELIMINARY, at tbl.1. (July 1, 2013), *available at* http://www.bjs.gov/index.cfm?ty=pbdetail&iid=4679 (showing that total justice expenditures for all types of government is $260 billion, which is broken down into $124 billion for police protection, $56 billion for the judicial and legal system, and $80 billion for corrections).

70. It is difficult to estimate the cost of special education, but one older study found that the federal government, the fifty states, and the District of Columbia spent approximately $50 billion on special education in the 1999–2000 academic year. Jay Chambers et al., *What Are We Spending on Special Education Services in the United States, 1999–2000?* (updated 2004), *available at* http://csef.air.org/publications/seep/national/advrpt1.pdf. That estimate, however, included only $3.7 billion in federal funds under the Individuals with Disabilities Education Act (IDEA), and more recent federal appropriations have been approximately $12 billion.

71. *See* Michael P. Johnson, *Conflict and Control: Gender Symmetry and Asymmetry in Domestic Violence*, 12 VIOLENCE AGAINST WOMEN 1003, 1003 (2006).

72. *See id.* at 1005–06.

73. Johnson has described this taxonomy in numerous publications, but for a particularly accessible source that includes references to longer works, *see* Theodora Ooms, Center for Law & Social Policy, *A Sociologist's Perspective on Domestic Violence: A Conversation with Michael Johnson, Ph.D.*, Interview at the Building Bridges: Marriage, Fatherhood, and Domestic Violence Conference, at 3 (May 2006), *available at* http://www.clasp.org/admin/site/publications_states/files/0314.pdf. In cases of intimate terrorism studied by Johnson, 97 percent of reported cases involved men as the batterers; in the cases involving situational couple violence, both men and women used violence, although not in exactly equal numbers. Johnson, *supra* note 71, at 1010 (tbl. 1 showing that 56 percent men and 44 percent women engage in situational couple violence).

74. Nancy Ver Steegh & Clare Dalton, *Report from the Wingspread Conference on Domestic Violence and Family Courts*, at 10–11, *available at* http://seconddistrictcourt.nmcourts.gov/Report%20from%20the%20Wingspread%20Conference%20on%20Domestic%20Violence%20and%20Family%20Courts.pdf. For additional criticism of Johnson's typology, *see* Victoria Frye et al., *The Distribution of and Factors Associated with Intimate Terrorism and Situational Couple Violence among a Population-Based Sample of Urban Women in the United States*, 21 J. INTERPERSONAL VIOLENCE 1286, 1290–93, 1303–10 (2006) (criticizing Johnson's reliance on the number of controlling behaviors used by one partner as opposed to examining the frequency of control and the "success" of the control and further contending that the two categories may not exist but instead represent different points on a time line—that situational couple violence will become intimate terrorism over time); Kristin L. Anderson, *Is Partner Violence Worse in the Context of Control?*, 70 J. MARRIAGE & FAM. 1157, 1158–59, 1166 (2008) (arguing that Johnson fails to account for the ill effects of controlling relationships that are not violent).

75. *See* Johnson, *supra* note 71, at 1015.

76. Joan Meier, *Differentiating Domestic Violence Types: Profound Paradigm Shift or New Wine in Old Bottles?* in 2 DOMESTIC VIOLENCE, ABUSE, AND CHILD CUSTODY (Mo Hannah & Barry Goldstein eds.) (in press, forthcoming 2014).

77. *See* chapter 4 for a discussion of the different severity of cases in the child-welfare system.

78. *See* Patricia Schene, *The Emergence of Differential Response*, 20 PROTECTING CHILDREN 4, 4–6 (2005) (describing the collaborative "differential response" approach to child welfare); *see also* Robert E. Emery & Lisa Laumann-Billings, *An Overview of the Nature, Causes, and Consequences of Abusive Family Relationships: Toward Differentiating Maltreatment and Violence*, 53 AM. PSYCHOLOGIST 121, 121–22 (1998).

79. DeSilva v. DeSilva, No. 350818/05, 2006 N.Y. Misc. LEXIS 2489, at *7–*10 (N.Y. Sup. Ct. Aug. 15, 2006).

80. *See* Margaret F. Brinig, *Does Mediation Systematically Disadvantage Women?*, 2 WM. & MARY J. WOMEN & L. 1, 33 (1995) (exploring the effect of risk aversion and altruism on marital-exit mediation and suggesting that because men's investments in marriage are transferable, they may have less to lose at dissolution, creating an inequality of decision-making power); Penelope E. Bryan, *Killing Us Softly: Divorce Mediation and the Politics of Power*, 40 BUFF. L. REV. 441, 454–56 (1992) ("Research on marital negotiations shows that the greater income and education and the higher occupational level of husbands, compared to wives, confers upon husbands greater power over routine decisions.... [U]nless the mediator intervenes, the husband's greater tangible resources will grant him the lion's share of power in divorce negotiations, particularly over critical financial issues"); Martha Fineman, *Dominant Discourse, Professional Language, and Legal Change in Child Custody Decisionmaking*, 101 HARV. L. REV. 727, 761–65 (1988) (noting costs, particularly to women, of moving away from deciding custody in legal settings); Trina Grillo, *The Mediation Alternative: Process Dangers for Women*, 100 YALE L.J. 1545, 1576, 1600–07 (1991); Amy Sinden, *"Why Won't Mom Cooperate?": A Critique of Informality in Child Welfare Proceedings*, 11 YALE J.L. & FEMINISM. 339, 373–87 (1999) (arguing that informal proceedings disadvantage respondent parents, who are typically "female, poor, uneducated, and nonwhite," because the informality exacerbates the power imbalance between the parent and the state, and asserting that formal proceedings lead to better accuracy in fact-finding and more just results than informal proceedings).

81. *See, e.g.*, Grillo, *supra* note 80, at 1555–57.

82. *See* Clare Huntington, *Rights Myopia in Child Welfare*, 53 UCLA L. REV. 637, 655–72, 688–95 (2006) (describing the disadvantages parents experience in the adversarial system governing the child-welfare system and describing the benefits of an alternative, problem-solving approach).

83. Suzanne Reynolds, Catherine T. Harris & Ralph A. Peeples, *Back to the Future: An Empirical Study of Child Custody Outcomes*, 85 N.C. L. REV. 1629, 1631–35, 1658–75 (2007) (reporting findings of an empirical study in a judicial district with mandatory mediation and concluding that, contrary to the concern that mandatory mediation would lead to increased joint custody, women were more likely to receive primary physical custody in mediation than in either settlements or litigation, but sounding the cautionary note that most women were represented by counsel); *see* Robert E. Emery, David Sbarra & Tara Grover, *Divorce Mediation: Research and Reflections*, 43 FAM. CT. REV. 22, 29–30 (2005) (citing a finding from their own study that women were satisfied with outcomes in mediation).

84. Nancy Ver Steegh, *Yes, No, and Maybe: Informed Decision Making about Divorce Mediation in the Presence of Domestic Violence*, 9 WM. & MARY J. WOMEN & L. 145, 180–90 (2003) (describing these concerns and suggesting ways to address them).

85. *Id.* at 181–82.

86. *Id.* at 182.

87. John Braithwaite, *Restorative Justice and Social Justice*, 63 SASKATCHEWAN L. REV. 185, 189 (2000); *accord* Donna Coker, *Enhancing Autonomy for Battered Women: Lessons from Navajo Peacemaking*, 47 UCLA L. REV. 1, 38–73 (1999) (describing benefits of Navajo Peacemaking for victims of domestic violence). *But see* Ruth Busch, *Domestic Violence and Restorative Justice Initiatives: Who Pays If We Get It Wrong?*, *in* RESTORATIVE JUSTICE AND FAMILY VIOLENCE 223–24, 228 (Heather Strang & John Braithwaite eds., 2002) (arguing that safety should be the primary goal and that "[t]here are grave risks in assuming that all relationship conflicts can be patched by consensus. Since the consensual resolution of conflict requires an attitude of 'give a little, take a little' to reach an agreement, there are risks in translating these principles unthinkingly into relationships affected by violence").

88. *See* David Bornstein, *Mobilizing the Playground Movement*, N.Y. TIMES OPINIONATOR (June 13, 2011, 10:15PM), *available at* http://opinionator.blogs.nytimes.com/2011/06/13/mobilizing-the-playground-movement/; *see also* DARELL HAMMOND, KaBOOM! HOW ONE MAN BUILT A MOVEMENT TO SAVE PLAY xv (2011).

89. *See* Bornstein, *supra* note 88.

90. *See id.*

91. *See id.; see also* HAMMOND, *supra* note 88, at xiv.

92. *See* Bornstein, *supra* note 88; *see also* HAMMOND, *supra* note 88, at xiv.

93. Miranda Perry Fleischer, *Theorizing the Charitable Tax Subsidies: The Role of Distributive Justice*, 87 WASH. U. L. REV. 505, 524 n. 101 (2010).

Abortion, 66–67, 187
    spousal-notice requirements, 214
Abstinence-only education, 185–186, 204–205
Abuse. *See* Child abuse and neglect; Child sexual
    abuse; Violence in home
Adoption
    focus on future and repair, xiv, 118
    intense emotions of, 84–85
    legal rule definition of, 59
    second-parent adoptions, 167–168
    stepparent adoption, 87
    substantive rules, new vision for, 129–130
    types of, 225n1
Adverse Childhood Experiences (ACE)
    Study, 11–12
African Americans. *See also* Race and ethnicity
    "culture of poverty" thesis, 162
    disproportionate child maltreatment, reasons
        for, 250n67
    drug arrests, 47, 254nn206–207
    educational statistics, 46
    family form and, xv–xvi, 28–31, 37
    foster care statistics, 45
    historical poverty statistics, 53
    incarceration rates, 47, 175, 254n206, 293n41
    involvement of father, 42

    marriage rates and, 178
    nonresidential father involvement, 190–191
    slavery, families during, 73–74
    substance abuse statistics, 45
    teen pregnancy statistics, 47
    test score disparities, 149
    voting and family form, 207
Aging in place, 183
Aid to Dependent Children/Aid to Families
    with Dependent Children, 74, 273n105
Ainsworth, Mary, 16
Alexman, Susan, 183
Alimony, 50, 87, 126–127, 128, 178, 279nn16–17
Allocation of Custodial Responsibility rule, 126
Altering physical context of family life, 157–158,
    180–185
    direct efforts, 180–184
    family consideration in other legal areas, 184–185
Alternatives to litigation, 131–137. *See also*
    Mediation
    gender bias in, 219, 307n80
Amato, Paul, 33
American Bar Association
    collaborative law, ethics of, 107–108
    survey on violent threats against family-law
        attorneys, 91–92

American Law Institute (ALI)
  child custody rule, 125–126
  spousal support proposal, 127
Americans with Disabilities Act, 65
Anna Karenina (Tolstoy), 22
Antidiscrimination laws, 201
Antigone, 21
Aristotle, 24–25
Arkansas
  abortion regulation, 66
  divorce and teen birth rates, 205
Arrests. *See* Crime and criminal justice system;
  Incarceration
Asher, Charles, 137–138
Asian Americans, family form and, 28–31
Assisted reproduction, 59–60. *See also* Sperm
  donors; Surrogacy
  donor-conceived families, 31
Attachment theory, 16–20, 66
Attorneys. *See* Lawyers
Australia, litigation alternatives in, 131, 191

Baker, David, 182
Bartholet, Elizabeth, 250n167
Bennett Woodhouse, Barbara, 116
Best interests of child, 88–89, 170, 268n32,
  278n8, 281n44
Birth control, 176, 185–187, 204–205
Bloomberg, Michael
  after-school voucher program elimination,
    154–155
  soda ban proposal, 203
Blue families, 205–207
Bowlby, John, 16–17, 18–19
Braithwaite, John, 283n59
Braman, Donald, 51
Brazelton, T. Berry, 196
Breastfeeding norms, 65–66
Bridges, Khiara, 189
Bronfenbrenner, Uri, 166
Brookings Institute, 185
Brown, Jerry, 171
Burton, Susan, 123, 124, 137

Cahn, Naomi, 205–206
California
  divorce trials vs. settlements, 268n33
  East Oakland neighborhood redesign,
    182–183

family group conferencing, use in, 135
Park La Brea, Los Angeles, approach to aging
  in place, 183
recognition of more than two legal parents,
  170–171
same-sex couples and marriage equality case,
  103, 177
welfare cap, 257n2
Calories, effect on child growth, 5–6
Canada, Geoffrey, 196, 197, 202
Capabilities approach, 148–149
Carbone, June, 205–206
Cash assistance programs, 273n105
Causation of better child outcomes, 35–44
  income of parents, 38–40
  involvement of father, 42
  mental health of parents, 40
  multipartner fertility, 43–44
  parental time, 40
  quality of parenting, 40–41
  relationship between parents, 41
  stability of family unit, 43, 248n143–144
Census Bureau, 31, 102
Center for Consumer Freedom, 203
Centers for Disease Control (CDC), 15, 160
Changing economy disadvantaging middle
  class, 46–47
Cherlin, Andrew, 30
Chicago School District's Child-Parent
  Center (CPC)
  cost-effectiveness of, 193, 215–216
  early-childhood education program, 192–193
Child abuse and neglect. *See also* Child sexual
  abuse; Child-welfare system
  Chicago School District's Child-Parent
    Center (CPC) reducing, 193
  children under age one and, 159
  "child-saving" movement, 75
  continuing family relationships and, 114–115
  differentiation in treatment of cases of, 117, 218
  family courts and, 139
  family decision making at times of, 136
  internal healing as focus, 218–219
  Maori families, 132
  number of victims, 44–45
  Nurse-Family Partnership reducing, 139, 166,
    189, 296n118
  reframing programs for, 212
  school reporting, 71

targeting interventions for maximum
effectiveness, 224
termination of parental rights due to, 59. *See
also* Termination of parental rights
unmarried families with increased risk of, 32,
249n150
Child care
comparative spending on, 97
structural family law, 95–98
Child Care and Development Block Grant, 96,
100, 194
Child custody. *See also* Joint custody
Allocation of Custodial Responsibility
rule, 126
dispute resolution system shortcomings
for, 88–91
joint custody, trend toward, 106
litigation alternatives, 219
new terminology for, 120
sample dispute, 113–114
substantive rules, new vision for, 125–126
Child development, 7–10
childhood trauma's impact on, 13, 139
family law to enable family to focus on, xiv–xv,
110–111, 147, 153, 164, 185. *See also* Supporting
parents in child-development work
genetics and, 227n10
high-conflict divorces' impact on, 34, 83–84
maternal attunement to infant, 83
Nurse-Family Partnership and, 167. *See also*
Nurse-Family Partnership
parental depression's impact on, 11, 40
parenting styles and, 39
parent sexual orientation's impact on, 34
politics and, 204
preschool programs and, 192, 213. *See also*
Preschool opportunities
research on, courts using, 139
Child labor, 75
Child-Parent Center (CPC). *See* Chicago
School District's Child-Parent Center
Children of color. *See* Race and ethnicity
Child-saving movement, 75–76
Child sexual abuse
family group conferencing and, 136
historical underreporting of, 53
incidence of, 45, 251n170
perpetrators of, 45, 251n172
Van Derbur family and, 121, 277–278n33

Child support
ALI proposal, 127
laws, 104
never-married vs. divorced parents, 42, 248n140
psychological parenthood and, 291n18
reform proposals, 191–192
rule of two and, 170
stepparents and, 87
Child-welfare system
child-saving movement, 75–76
courtroom focus of, 88
differentiation of abuse levels in, 218
family group conferencing alternative, 132–137
focus on future and repair, 118–119
intense emotions of, 84
litigation alternatives, 139–141, 219
state regulation of, 61–62
structural family law, 93–95
substantive rules, new vision for, 129
Choice architecture, 64, 200
Civil Rights Act of 1964, xviii
Clark, Cheryl Ann, 168–169
Coan, James, 18
Cohabitation
adoption law, lack of protection under, 87
causation of worse outcomes, 35–36
cohabiting parents, 31–32, 242n63
division of labor, 256n244
education levels and, 28–29
encouraging long-term commitment between
parents, 155–157, 173–180
international comparisons, 177–178
marriage, legal definition of, 60
race and, 28–29
statistics, 241n59
underinstitutionalized nature of, 177
welfare program's disincentives, 105
Coleman Report, 287n16
Collaborative law, 107–108, 141–143
estate planning, 285n100
Collins, Kristin, 273n105
Colorado
collaborative law, ethics on, 107–108
parental responsibilities law, 130
parenting classes for divorcing
couples, 284n72
psychological parenthood doctrine, 168
Colorado, suburban sprawl and, 180–182
Commuting times, 48, 64

Compensatory spousal payments, 127
Connecticut
  economic support to low-income families, 174
  median age of marriage and divorce rates, 302n12
Constitutional law
  after-school voucher programs, 154–155
  foreign language teaching, 70
  legal parents' rights and, 61
  negative liberty focus of, 100–101
  parochial school bans, 70–71
Contraception, 176, 185–187, 204–205
Contraceptive CHOICE Project, 186–187
Coontz, Stephanie, 52–53
Co-parents. See also Child custody; Divorce; Fathers, involvement of; Long-term commitment between parents
  cooperative co-parenting, 106–107
  legal designation of, 130
Coping mechanisms, 12
Corporal punishment of children, 66
Corrective experiences, 151
Court-based reforms, 137–141
Crime and criminal justice system. See also Incarceration
  children from CPC program and, 193
  children from Nurse-Family Partnership program and, 189, 297n124
  early-childhood intervention programs and, 290n55, 305n61
  in East Oakland, California, 182
  in inner city Chicago, 23
  neighborhood watch's effectiveness, 14
  removal of fathers from children's life, xii
  restorative justice and, 280n42
  violent crime, 44. See also Child abuse and neglect; Violence in home
Crisis, families in, 44–52
  changing economy disadvantaging middle class, 46–47
  effect of, 50–52
  incarceration, 47
  poverty and unemployment, 45–46
  social isolation, 48–49
  substance abuse, 45
  teen pregnancy, 47–48
  unequal division of family labor, 49–50, 255–256n234
  violence in home, 44–45

Crittenden, Ann, 49
Csikszentmihalyi, Mihaly, 7
Cultural Cognition Project, 209–210
"Culture of life," 67
"Culture of poverty," 162
Culture wars, 204–207
Custody. See Child custody

Decision-making authority
  collaborative, 64, 214
  gender inequality of, 307n80
  new custody terminology of, 130
  state vs. family, 56–58
  team, 281n49
Default rules. See Choice architecture
Deficit Reduction Act of 2005, 292n32
Definition of Spouse Amendment Act (British Columbia), 179
Department of ___. See name of specific department
Developmental time, 40
Diener, Ed, 7, 10
Direct state regulation, 59–62
Disabled persons, 65
Discrimination laws, xviii, xix, 201
Dispute-resolution family law, xi, xiv, 83–92
  adversarial focus of, 82
  child custody, 88–91
  consequences, 91–92
  hallmarks of cases, 84–86. See also Hallmarks of family cases
  mismatch with family disputes, 86–88
  negatives of, 84
  new vision for, 113–122. See also New vision for dispute resolution
  overview, 83–84
Divorce, 32–34
  avoiding adversarial nature of, 123–124
  child custody. See Child custody
  cognitive biases regarding, 128
  collaborative divorce, 142–143
  court-based reforms, 137–138
  economic consequences of, 126–129
  father's involvement after, 244n82. See also Fathers, involvement of
  filing party and caption of pleadings, 284n74
  focus on future and repair, 116–118
  mediation alternative, 88, 106–107

no-fault, 59, 87, 106–107
property division rules, 64
Domestic chastisement, 120
Domestic partnerships, 103
Domestic violence. *See* Violence in home
Donor-conceived families, 31
Drug arrests and African Americans, 47,
254nn206–207
Dyckman Houses, 23

Early-childhood education, 161–162, 192–193.
See also Head Start
Earned Income Tax Credit (EITC), 105,
194–195, 212
Economic stressors, 162–163, 193–195
Edin, Kathryn, 41, 44, 174–176, 187, 190–191
Education and schools
abstinence-only education, 185–186, 204–205
after-school voucher programs, 154–155
attainment predictors, 145
cohabitation and performance, 32–34
Coleman Report, 287n16
disabled students and, 65
early-childhood programs, 161–162, 192–193.
See also Head Start
family effect on attainment, 149–152
529 college-savings plans, 63
funding, 64, 71, 216
Harlem Children's Zone, 196–199
Keeping Families Together program and, 195
neighborhood schools, advantages
of, 57–58
parochial school bans, 70–71
quality, 38–39, 63
racial test score disparities, 149
reporting child abuse and neglect, 71
special education, cost of, 95, 306n70. *See also*
Special education
EITC (Earned Income Tax Credit), 105,
194–195, 212
Emens, Elizabeth, 65
Emery, Robert, 107, 117
Emotional security theory, 33–34
Ethics, legal
collaborative law, 107–108, 141–143
unethical adversarialness, 88, 91–92
Eudaimonia, 24
Eugenics, 74–75
Executive functions, 150

Families, recognizing broader range of, xv,
153–155, 167–173
altering physical context of family life,
157–158, 180–185
broadening access to marriage, 171–173
broadening definition of legal parent, 167–171
Family and Medical Leave Act, 92, 100, 147,
201–202
Family autonomy nonresponsibility ideology,
100–102
Family form, xv–xvi, 28–31
Family group conferencing, 132–137, 140, 143
as family-engagement strategy, 281n49
needs of participants, attention to, 219
success factors, 281n48
Family Law Education Reform (FLER) Project,
141–142
Family Relationship Centres, 131, 191
Family Research Council, 103
Family reunification, 62, 82, 93, 94, 95, 122,
281n49, 282n51
Family-state relations, 147–153
family need for state, 147–148
mutual dependency, 152–153
state need for family, 148–152
Family-systems theory, 22
Family violence. *See* Violence in home
Farm subsidies, 78–79
Fathers
child sexual abuse, stepfathers as perpetrators
of, 251n172
common-law right to earnings of minor
children, 277n18
common-law tradition of no obligation to
child born outside of marriage, 277n15
earnings and paid work of, 245n98,
255–256n234
government programs promoting
fatherhood, 292n32
involvement of, xvi, 34, 42, 161, 177, 190–192,
242n63, 244n82, 248n138, 275n127,
298n136
paternity leave, 200–202
Supporting Father Involvement Program, 177
in unmarried families, 248n139
Federal Housing Administration, 65
Fineman, Martha, 79
529 college-savings plans, 63
Florida, Richard, 47

Focus on the Family, 103
Food, Energy, and Conservation Act of 2008, 79
Food insecurity, 45
Food stamps, 105, 212
    marriage penalty, 174
Foreign language teaching, 69–70
Foster care
    avoiding, 62
    family ties and, 85
    Keeping Families Together project and, 195
    limitations, 95
    placements with, 81–82
    PTSD and, 94
    statistics, 45, 52
    subsidy of kinship guardianships, 129
Fostering Connections to Success and
        Increasing Adoptions Act of 2008,
        129, 281n49
Fragile Families and Child Well-Being
        Study, 37
    childbearing without reliable partners, 160
    child support statistics, 104
    involvement of father, 42
    multipartner fertility, 43
    nonresidential father involvement, 190–191
    regression analysis of data, 175
    romantic involvement of unwed parents
        statistics, 173
    stability of family unit, 43
France, *pacte civil de solidarité* (PACS), 178
Franke, Katherine, 73, 79
Freedom to Farm Act of 1996, 78–79
Freud, Anna, 106
Front porches, 23–24

Garfinkel, Irwin, 37, 43, 156
Genetics, child development and, 227n10
Georgia, unwed mother welfare denial
        in, 263n95
German Socio-Economic Panel, 11
Get Ready for Pre-K program (New York), 196
Gilson, Ronald, 142
Goldstein, Joseph, 106
Goodmark, Leigh, 120–121
Gottlieb, Chris, 200
Government support programs, 72, 74. *See also*
        Welfare programs
Guardians ad litem, 133, 136, 281n44
Guilt, role in divorce, 117

Haidt, Jonathan, 207–209, 213
Hall, Charles, 70
Hallmarks of family cases, 84–86
    intense emotions, 84–85
    need to repair relationships, 85
    ongoing relationships, 85
Hammond, Darell, 220–221
Happiness, life satisfaction vs., 229n39
Harlem Children's Zone, 196–199
    Asthma Initiative, 197
    Baby College program (New York City),
        196, 197
    building conservative support for, 212–213
    geographic specificity of, 202
    Harlem Gems prekindergarten, 196, 197
    Promise Academy, 196–199
Harlow, Harry, 15–16
Hawaii, infant study in, 12
Head Start
    availability of, 56
    benefits of, 193, 290n55, 305n61
    enrollment, effects of, 63, 193
    as nonjudgmental relationship with state,
        199–200
    participation statistics, 96
    state enrollment variations, 211
Health and Human Services Department, U.S., 195
Heckman, James, 215
Hedonistic psychology, 226n4
Hetherington, Mavis, 32–33
High-conflict divorces, 33
High-skill jobs, 252n186, 252n188
Hill, Vernice, 81–83, 118–119
Housing, mixed and set-asides for low-income
        families, 181–182

Idaho, median age of marriage and divorce rates
        in, 302n12
Illegitimacy stigma, 61, 67–68
Incarceration
    African Americans, 47, 175, 254n206, 293n41
    effect of family, 51
    racial/ethnic groups, 47
    women's rate of, 254n209
Incentives and subsidies, 63–64, 199–200
    farm subsidies, 78–79
    kinship guardianships, 129
Income
    achievement gap and, 149, 151

earnings potential, 126–127

Fragile Families and, 104

government supports for families at bottom end of income spectrum, 194, 211–212

housing and, 181

of parents, 38–40, 245n98, 255–256n234

relationship to marriage rates, 28, 36, 174, 292n33

relationship to single-parent homes, 29–30

tax filing and, 60

teen mothers and, 48

welfare program eligibility and, 174, 176

Indirect state regulation, 63–67

choice architecture, 64

incentives and subsidies, 63–64

seemingly unrelated law and policy, 64–65

social norms, 65–67

Individual responsibility plans, 74

Individual well-being, 6–15

adults, 10–11

child development, 7–10

healing, 12–13

health, 11–12

social capital, 13–15

Infant care norms, 66

Integrated Domestic Violence Court (IDVC, New York), 138–139, 143, 284n76

Intimacy, cycle of, 20–21, 116

Intimate terrorism, 217–219, 306n74

Jacobs, Jane, 13–14

Johnson, Michael, 217, 219, 306nn73–74

Joint custody, xvi, 34, 88, 106, 217, 218, 243n74, 268nn31–32, 274n120, 307n83

Justice Department, U.S., family violence study, 45

Juvenile delinquency, 12–13

KaBOOM! (organization), 220–221

Kauai infant study, 12

Keeping Families Safe project, 195

Keeping Families Together project, 195

Kefalas, Maria, 174–175, 187

King Lear (Shakespeare), 21

Kin networks, 31

Kinship adoptions, 225n1

Kinship guardianships, 129

Kuo, Frances, 23

Kymlicka, Will, 101

Labor Department, U.S., unemployment statistics, 45–46

Lakoff, George, 208–209

Lareau, Annette, 39

Latinos. *See also* Race and ethnicity

family form and, 28–31, 37

foster care statistics, 45

incarceration statistics, 47

involvement of father, 42

teen pregnancy statistics, 47

Lawrence v. Texas (2003), 79, 172

Lawyers

collaborative law, ethics of, 107–108, 141–143

as guardians ad litem, 281n44

unethical adversarialness of, 88, 91–92

violent threats against family-law attorneys, 91–92

Lenhardt, Robin, 178

Libertarianism, 77

Life satisfaction, 11, 229n39

Limits of flourishing family law, xvii, 203–221

application, limits of, 217–220

law, limitations of, 220–221

overview, 203–204

politics, limits of, 204–216. *See also* Politics, limits of

situational couple violence, 217–220

Litigation, alternatives to, 131–137

Long-term commitment between parents, 155–157, 173–180

countervailing forces, 173–175

nonmarriage options, 177–180

state role, 175–177

Louisiana, unwed mother welfare denial in, 263n95

Low-skill jobs, 252n188

Maccoby, Eleanor, 304n58

"Mancession," 47

Marital dissolution. *See* Divorce

Marriage

broadening definition of, 171–173

closely following birth of child, 245n97

decision-making powers within, 307n80

government programs promoting, 292n32

legal definition of, 60–61

rates, 28, 292n33, 293n34

teen, 53

Marriage benefit (psychological), 10–11

Marshall, T. H., 101

Martin, John, 304n58
Massachusetts
  median age of marriage and divorce rates, 205
  SPCC, 75
  universal health care, 211
Maternal depression, 9–10
McClain, Linda, 149
McLanahan, Sara, 31, 37, 43, 156, 173–175
McLeod, Elsey Maxwell, 168–169
Mediation
  divorce litigation alternative, xvi, 88–89,
    106–107, 131
  domestic violence and, 219–220
  Family Relationship Centres, 131, 191
  gender bias in, 219, 307n80
Medical decisions for children, 71
Mental health of parents, 40
Mettler, Suzanne, 72, 78, 148
Meyer v. Nebraska (1923), 69–70
Middle class, changing economy
  disadvantaging, 46–47
Middle-skill vs. high-skill jobs, 252n186
Minnesota
  economic support to low-income families, 174
  longitudinal study, 145, 149–150, 286n1
Mismatch between existing system and family
  disputes, 86–88
Mnookin, Robert, 142
Mortgage-interest deduction, 63, 65
Mothers
  earnings and work hours of, 245n98,
    255–256n234
  first-time. See Nurse-Family Partnership
Moynihan, Daniel Patrick, xviii
Multipartner fertility, 43–44, 156
Murray, Charles, 76–77
Mutual dependency, 152–153
Mutual violent control, 217

National Center for Health Statistics, 29
National Environmental Policy Act, 185
National Longitudinal Study of Adolescent
  Health, 242n63
National Study of the Incidence and Severity of
  Child Abuse and Neglect, 249–250n161
National Survey of Families and Households,
  106–107
Native Americans. See also Race and ethnicity
  foster care statistics, 45

same-sex coupling statistics, 31
Negative family law, 81–108
  definition, 83
  dispute resolution law, 83–92. See also
    Dispute-resolution family law
  narrow reforms, 106–108
  overview, 81–83
  structural approach, 92–102. See also
    Structural family law
Neglect. See Child abuse and neglect
Nelson, Timothy, 41, 44, 190–191
New Urbanism, 182
New vision for dispute resolution, 113–144
  focus on future and repair, 116–119
  implementation, 123–144
  overview, 113–115, 123–124
  practice, 141–143
  procedural rules, 131–141. See also Procedural
    rules, new vision for
  safety of family members, 119–122, 143–144
  substantive rules, 125–131. See also Substantive
    rules, new vision for
New vision for structuring family relationships,
  145–202
  altering physical context of family life,
    180–185. See also Altering physical context
    of family life
  choice architecture, 200
  encouraging long-term commitment between
    parents, 173–180. See also Long-term
    commitment between parents
  family-state relations, 147–153. See also
    Family-state relations
  form of regulation, 199–202
  Harlem Children's Zone case study, 196–199
  implementation of, 165–202
  nurturing positive relationships, 153–163. See
    also Nurturing positive relationships
  overview, 145–147
  recognizing broader range of families,
    167–173. See also Families, recognizing
    broader range of
  social norms and, 200–202
  subsidizing preferred behavior, 199–200
  supporting parents in child-development
    work, 185–199. See also Supporting parents
    in child-development work
New York
  after-school programs, 96

Harlem Children's Zone, 196–199. *See also*
  Harlem Children's Zone
infant mortality program, 189
Integrated Domestic Violence Court
  (IDVC), 138–139, 143, 284n76
same-sex marriages, 153
soda ban proposal, 203
SPCC, 75
New Zealand, litigation alternatives in, 132–137
No-drop policy, 62, 120–121
No-fault divorce, 59, 87, 106–107
Nonmarital children, 61, 67–68. *See also*
  Cohabitation
Nonresidential father involvement, 161, 190–192.
  See also Fathers, involvement of
Nontraditional family structures, xix, 31–34
  divorced parents, 32–34
  nonmarriage options, 177–180
  recognition of, 153–155, 167–173. *See also*
    Families, recognizing broader range of
  same-sex parents, 34. *See also* Same-sex parents
  single or cohabiting parents, 31–32. *See also*
    Cohabitation
Norman, Wayne, 101
North Carolina's sterilization program, 74–75
Nurse-Family Partnership
  building conservative support for, 212–213
  building parenting skills of first-time mothers,
    187–190, 199, 224
  compared to typical low-income mother's
    interactions with state programs, 189
  effectiveness of, 189, 297nn123–124
  goals of, 165–167
  savings realized from, 189, 215–216, 297n125
  support vs. self-determination balance of, 215
Nurturant parent state model, 209, 212
Nurturing positive relationships, 153–163
  altering physical context of family life,
    157–158. *See also* Altering physical context
    of family life
  encouraging long-term commitment between
    parents, 155–157. *See also* Long-term
    commitment between parents
  recognizing broader range of families, 153–155.
    See also Families, recognizing broader
    range of
  supporting parents in child-development
    work, 159–163. *See also* Supporting parents
    in child-development work

Nussbaum, Martha, 148–149

Olds, David, 165–166, 196, 200
Opposing worldviews, 207–211
Oregon
  joint custody awards, 268n32
  parochial schools, ban of, 70

Pacte civil de solidarité (PACS), 178
Parental leave
  for fathers, 200–202
  paid leave advocacy, 201
  U.S. policy, 92
Parental responsibilities, new custody
  terminology of, 130
Parental time, 40, 130. *See also* Child custody;
  Joint custody
Parentification, 35
Park La Brea (Los Angeles), 183
Parochial schools, ban of, 70–71
Parria potestas, 119–120
Paternalism, xviii, 91, 121
Paternity leave, 200–202
Pennsylvania, spousal notice of abortion in, 214
Perry, Bruce, 13
Pervasiveness of state in relationships, 58–68. *See
  also* State role in relationships
Pierce v. Society of Sisters (1925), 70–71
*Planned Parenthood of Southeastern Pennsylvania
  v. Casey* (1992), 214
Play deserts, 46, 220
Politics, limits of, 204–216
  concerns about state control, 214–215
  culture wars, 204–207
  funding, 215–216
  opposing worldviews, 207–211
  talking purple, xviii, 211–214
Positive psychology, 7, 227n6
Positive relationships, 5–25
  context for, 22–24
  elements of, 15–22
  importance of, 6–15
  individual well-being, effect on, 6–15. *See also*
    Individual well-being
  overview, 5–6
  positivity defined, 20–22
  societal well-being, effect on, 15
  strength and stability, 15–20. *See also* Strong
    and stable relationships

Positive stress, 8

Positivity defined, 20–22

Post-traumatic stress disorder (PTSD), 94

Poverty

  bootstrap solution to, 77–78

  child care subsidy and, 96–97

  child-welfare system, relationship with, 94, 132

  concentrated geographic area of, 99

  conveyor belt approach to fighting, 196

  effects on children, 38–40

  equation with laziness, 203–204

  during Great Depression, 53

  Head Start enrollments and, 211

  international comparisons, 97

  maternal depression correlation with, 9–10

  neglect related to, 43, 218

  race and, 162–163, 214

  sexual abuse, lack of correlation with, 121

  single parents, correlation with, 30, 35

  unemployment and, 45–46

Preschool opportunities, 161–162, 192–193. *See also* Head Start

Principles of the Law of Family Dissolution (ALI), 125–126

  spousal support proposal, 127

Problem-solving courts, 284n76

Procedural rules, new vision for, 131–141

  alternatives to litigation, 131–137

  court-based reforms, 137–141

Psyche (classical literature), 21

Psychological parenthood, 168–169, 291n18

"Purple" solutions, xviii, 207–211

Putnam, Robert, 14, 48

Quality of parenting, 40–41

Race and ethnicity

  "culture of poverty" thesis, 162

  disproportionate maltreatment, reasons for, 250n67

  educational statistics, 46

  family form and, 28–31, 37

  foster care statistics, 45

  historical poverty statistics, 53

  incarceration statistics, 47, 175

  involvement of father, 42

  marriage rates, 178

  nonresidential father involvement, 190–191

  slavery, families during, 73–74

  substance abuse statistics, 45

  teen pregnancy statistics, 47

  test score disparities, 149

RAND Corporation, 210

Red families, 205–207

Relationship between parents, 41

Removal of child, xiv, 76, 94, 132–133, 225n1, 250n167, 281n49, 283n57. *See also* Foster care

Reparative drive, 235n141

  definition of reparative, 276n5

Representative bias, 128

Resonance circuits, 18

Restorative justice, 280n42, 283n59

Reunification. *See* Family reunification

Reverse commutes, 64

Rhetoric of family autonomy, 68–76

  creation myth, 69–71

  descriptive inaccuracy of, 71–73

  uneven application of, 73–76

Roberts, Dorothy, 250n67

Rule of two, 87, 167

  efforts to circumvent, 170–171

Same-sex parents, 34. *See also* Nontraditional family structures

  broadening access to marriage for, 171–173

  California marriage equality case, 103, 177

  division of household labor, 50

  domestic partnerships, 103

  increasing recognition of relationships of, 30

  legal restrictions on, 55–56, 57, 59

  statistics, 31, 102

Sanger, Carol, 67

Scared straight programs, 12–13

Schoenbaum, Naomi, 52

Schools. *See* Education and schools

Scott, Elizabeth, 61, 125–126, 177

Second-parent adoptions, 167–168

Self-determination, xvii, 73, 111, 208, 214, 215

Seligman, Martin, 6–7, 10

Sensitive periods, 8

Sexual abuse. *See* Child sexual abuse

Sidewalks, continuous, 23–24

  family life, effect on, 65

  sprawl, effect on, 98

Siegel, Daniel, 8, 18
Silbaugh, Katherine, 64
Single-motherhood
    cultural norm of, 176
    rates of, 239n24
Single or cohabiting parents, 31–32. *See also*
    Cohabitation
Situational couple violence, 217
Slavery, 73–74, 179
Social capital, 13–15
Social isolation, 48–49
Social norms, 65–67, 200–202
    interplay with law, 260n51
Social Security Act of 1935, 74
Societal well-being, 15
Societies for the Prevention of Cruelty to
    Children (SPCCs), 75
Solnit, Albert, 106
Spanking, 66
Sparks, Ruby, 14
Special education, 95, 162, 193, 215, 216,
    223, 306n70
Sperm donors, 102, 169, 171
Spinak, Jane, 139–141
Spock, Benjamin, 66
Spousal support. *See* Alimony
Stability of family unit, 43, 248n143–144
Stack, Carol, 14
Stapleton, Colorado, 183–184
State role in relationships, xix, 55–80. *See also*
    Welfare programs
    direct regulation, 59–62
    indirect regulation, 63–67. *See also* Indirect
        state regulation
    overview, 55–58
    pervasiveness of, 58–68
    prescriptive vision, 67–68
    resistance to acknowledging, 76–80
    rhetoric of family autonomy, 68–76. *See also*
        Rhetoric of family autonomy
Steinman-Gordon, James, 153
Stepparents. *See also* Cohabitation
    child sexual abuse, stepfathers as perpetrators
        of, 251n172
    rights, 87
Sterilization, 74–75
Stewart, Jon, 203
Strict father state model, 209, 212
Stringer, Scott, 203

Strong and stable relationships, xvi, 15–20
    between adults, 18–20
    between parents and children, 15–18
Structural family law, xii, 92–105
    active undermining, 102–105
    child care, 95–98
    child-welfare system, 93–95
    family autonomy nonresponsibility ideology,
        100–102
    overview, 92
    reactive approach of, xvii
    suburban sprawl, 98–100
Structuring family relationships, new vision
    for. *See* New vision for structuring family
    relationships
"Submerged state," 72, 78
Subsidies and incentives, 63–64, 199–200
    farm subsidies, 78–79
    kinship guardianships, 129
Substance abuse, 45, 136
Substantive rules, new vision for, 125–131
    adoption, 129–130
    child custody, 125–126
    child welfare, 129
    economic consequences of divorce, 126–129
    new terminology, 130–131
Suburban sprawl, 98–100
    efforts to address, 180–184
    housing policy causation of, 64–65
Suitable home laws, 74
Sullivan, Andrew, 61
Sullivan, William, 23
Summer slide, 38
Supplemental Nutrition Assistance Program
    (SNAP), 105
    marriage penalty, 174
Supporting Father Involvement
    Program, 177
Supporting parents in child-development
    work, 159–163, 185–199. *See also* Child
    development
    addressing economic stressors, 162–163,
        193–195
    choosing to become parents, 160, 185–187
    nonresidential father involvement, 161,
        190–192
    overview, 159–160
    preschool opportunities, 161–162, 192–193
    transition to parenthood, 161, 187–190

Supreme Court, U.S.
on California's definition of marriage, 103
on criminalization of sodomy, 79
on mandatory school attendance, 70–71
on right to sexuality outside marriage, 79
on spousal notice of abortion, 214
on state welfare program child
limitations, 155
on teaching foreign languages, 70
Surrogacy, 31, 84, 87, 258n12
Sweden, single-mother households in, 97

TANF (Temporary Assistance to Needy
Families), 74, 104, 152, 212
Taxes
benefits to middle- and upper-income
families, 147
EITC (Earned Income Tax Credit), 105,
194–195, 212
marriage implications, 60
Taylor Grazing Act, 79
Teen Outreach Program, 186
Teen pregnancy, 47–48, 53, 160
Temporary Assistance to Needy Families
(TANF), 74, 104, 152, 212
Termination of parental rights, 59, 87, 116, 122
Tesler, Pauline, 275n125
Test score disparities, 149
Toxic stress, 8–9
Transition, families in, 28–44
causation of better outcomes, 35–44. See also
Causation of better outcomes
changing family form, 28–31
nontraditional structures, 31–34. See also
Nontraditional family structures
Transition and crisis, 27–54
context of challenges, 52–53
families in crisis, 44–52. See also Crisis,
families in
families in transition, 28–44. See also
Transition, families in
overview, 27–28
Transition to parenthood, 161, 187–190

Unemployment
African American poverty and, 162, 250n167
middle-skill vs. high-skill jobs, 252n186
state programs, 72
statistics, 45–46

Unequal division of family labor, 49–50,
255–256n234
United Kingdom, single-mother
households in, 97
Unmarried parents
child abuse and neglect risks, 32, 249n150
father involvement, 248n139. See also Fathers

Values of existing legal system, 267n22
Van Derbur family, 121, 277–278n33
Violence in home, 15
against children, 44–45. See also Child abuse
and neglect
historical treatment of, 120–121
mediation and, 219–220
New York Integrated Domestic Violence
Court, 138–139, 143
state regulation of, 62
typology of, 217–218, 306n73
Violent resistance, 217
Visitation. See Child custody

Waldman, Ayelet, 65–66
Wallerstein, Judith, 33
Washington, third party visitation in, 267n23
Webb, Stuart, 142–143, 275n125
Web of care, 158
Welfare programs, 74. See also Aid to Dependent
Children/Aid to Families with Dependent
Children; Temporary Assistance to Needy
Families (TANF)
assignment rules, 104
eligibility rules, 273n106
libertarianism and, 77
Widdowson, Elsie, 5–6
Widows, cash assistance to, 74, 273n105
Wilson, William Julius, xviii, 162
Winnicott, Donald, 20
Wisconsin joint custody awards, 268n31
Women
first-time mothers. See Nurse-Family
Partnership
incarceration rate of, 254n209
mediation and gender bias, 219, 307n80
teen pregnancy, 47–48, 53
Workplace discrimination laws, 201

Zoning, 64, 98–99